By His Grace
and for His Glory

By His Grace and for His Glory

A Historical, Theological, and Practical Study of the Doctrines of Grace in Baptist Life

Thomas J. Nettles

BAKER BOOK HOUSE
Grand Rapids, Michigan 49506

Copyright © 1986 by Baker Books
a division of Baker Book House Company
P.O. Box 6287, Grand Rapids, MI 49516-6287

ISBN: 0-8010-6742-1

Third printing, February 1996

Library of Congress
Catalog Card Number: 85-71180

Scripture quotations not otherwise identified are from the King James Version of the Bible.
Scripture quotations identified NIV are from the HOLY BIBLE: NEW INTERNATIONAL VERSION © 1978 by the New York International Bible Society, used by permission of Zondervan Bible Publishers.

Scripture quotations identified NASB are from the New American Standard Bible. Copyright © 1960, 1962, 1963, 1968, 1971, 1972, 1973, 1975, 1977 The Lockman Foundation.
Scripture quotations identified RSV are from the Revised Standard Version. Copyright © 1946, 1952 Division of Christian Education of the National Council of the Churches of Christ in the United States of America.

Printed in the United States of America

Contents

5

List of Photographs

Chronological Chart of Persons and Events

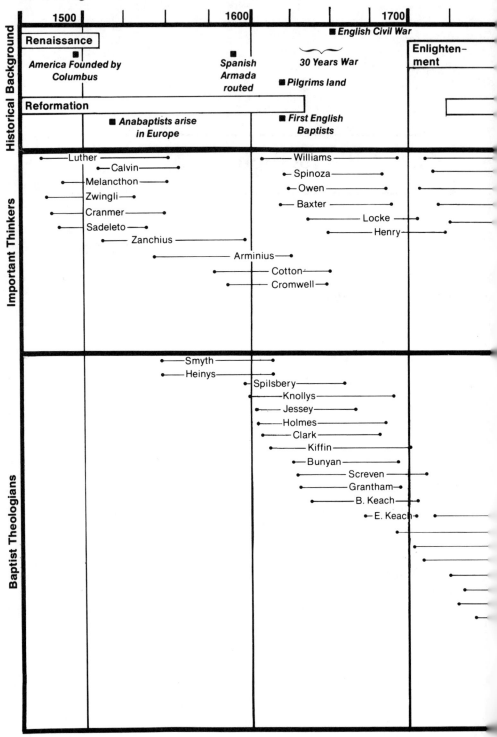

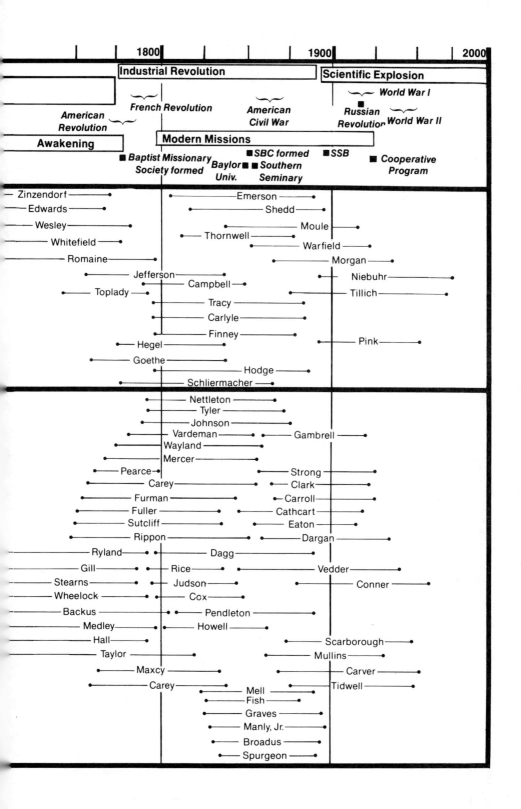

Preface

Books are written and published to meet a perceived need. Some books arise merely to anesthetize the pain over an undelivered oration of some professional academic, fearful he is about to be forgotten. Others are prompted by personal crises or victories, the literary development of which provides valuable assistance to pilgrims undergoing similar testings. Books can also leap from the interests of an issue terribly contemporary or flow slowly from the accumulated wisdom and experience of the past. Some entertain, some inform, some scold, some reflect, some ask, some answer, some edify, some depress, and some anger. Most literary efforts involve several of these purposes and motivations. But the end result of all, by the judgment of an absolute standard, should be to say in some way, "Remember now thy Creator." I pray that this volume may communicate a measure of that. It is the open intention of the author to bring to the minds of readers the claims and prerogatives of the One who is Creator, Redeemer, Sovereign, and Judge.

The perceived need for such a work came to me in the course of teaching Bible study in Southern Baptist churches in January 1980, when the topic was Ephesians. The clarity of the Doctrines of Grace in that Pauline pamphlet staggered the minds and consciences in virtually every church in which I taught. People fired earnest and honest inquiries that pressed me into the serious and heart-searching endeavor of providing an adequate answer. Originally only a short booklet on "election" was conceived. But the nature of the questions pushed me further: "Why evangelize? Why strive for holiness? How can anyone have assurance?" One of the most persistent questions asked was: "Is this Baptist?" Admittedly that should not be the primary concern,

11

for "Is this really biblical?" or "Is this Christian?" should be sufficient. But for the millions who have meshed their lives with Baptist congregations across the world, the question is certainly not irrelevant. I will say more of this in the conclusion. But for now I only mention it to say thank-you to those churches and individuals who prompted me to the type of study this volume involved.

Encouragement along the way has come from many sources. Students have stimulated and hurried me along. My family has been patient and indulged me with many hours of home study. Ernest Reisinger has read, prodded, suggested, and supported, while helping me anticipate some objections to certain ways of framing arguments. Erroll Hulse has insisted on a levelheaded and balanced approach and stirred me to accuracy as well as breadth in the English materials.

Who can write without libraries? Several have come to my aid. The personnel in the theological libraries at Southwestern Baptist Theological Seminary and Mid-America Baptist Theological Seminary have gone out of their way to find me materials that did not happen to be in the libraries at the time and to make available the plentiful resources at their command. In England, the British Museum's library and that of Dr. Williams have been of immense help in specialized areas. I give a warm and sincere thanks to all of these.

Pat Stewart and Rob Richey—Christian ministers, dear friends, and Th.D. students at Mid-America Seminary—have provided invaluable assistance in the final days. Since four thousand miles have separated me from my secretary and many of the sources used early in the composition, they have pursued the tedious task of finding proper bibliographical information on many sources quoted and have been largely responsible for the various indexes included herein. In addition, Terry Brown, assistant librarian at Mid-America, has given prompt attention to many bibliographical details.

Two secretaries have labored through this material. Jackie Madon, formerly at Southwestern Seminary and now a missionary to Brazil, aided in the initial stages of manuscript development and typing. Camille Couch, of Mid-America Seminary in Memphis, has borne the brunt of the final stages of manuscript preparation. She has been much more than a typist, working with an indefatigable sense of stewardship about the form and order of the manuscript, and investing not only time but calling in its completion. A Christian thanks to these ladies.

Finally, I thank Baker Book House for undertaking the publishing of the manuscript and Carey Publications in England for pursuing the same end in the United Kingdom. Both have made valuable suggestions that, I am convinced, have made the final product more valuable and stronger than it would have been otherwise. Weaknesses that remain are the responsibility of the author.

Introduction

It is with difficulty that men strive to define "Baptists." Some obviously find that the blast of the Baptist trumpet and the boom of the denominational drum clash incongruously with what they view as twentieth-century faith. But those who prize the name do so as one of several in their history, not all of which were fondly given or received.

The vernacular description "commonly called Anabaptists" appears at the front of the 1644 London Baptist Confession. This colloquial error reappears in history under a variety of terms. "Churches of Christ," "Christians (Baptised Upon Profession of their Faith)," "Congregations, Gathered According to the Primitive Pattern," and the more simple "Baptised Believers" have been featured as descriptions of Baptists over the past three hundred years. The gradual adoption of "Baptists" as a shortened denominational handle evidences itself by its formal use as early as 1672 in some of the English royal documents.

What particular phrase or belief can best capture the genius of the Baptist movement? Can we define a movement so dynamic and complex as the Baptist denomination in one sentence? Shall we center on liberty of conscience, uncoerced response, religious experience, a specific view of Scripture, a particular doctrine of the church, a distinctive view of missions, or some perspective of sociological or political involvement?

The particular focus of this book draws attention to soteriology in Baptist life. The writer's thesis is that Calvinism, popularly called the Doctrines of Grace, prevailed in the most influential and enduring arenas of Baptist denominational life until the end of the second decade of the twentieth century.

13

For the past seventy years, both negligence and rejection have taken their toll upon the Baptist understanding of and—even more—commitment to those truths that Baptists once held dear. Thus, the focus upon the Doctrines of Grace is intentional and unashamed. This, however, in no way implies a reductionistic approach to Baptist life.

Defining the Baptist Movement

Selecting any ideological or practical category for singular treatment may well flatten into a bland and unimpressive portrait of what is best seen as a three-dimensional figure. Baptists exist as a complex mixture of many elements, practical and ideological, essential and optional. Each factor interpenetrates the other and must be seen in relation to the whole. None by itself defines the entire Baptist movement.

In these essential categories, we recognize many points of agreement between Baptists and all other Christians, between Baptists and all other Protestants, as well as the significant divergences from both. These broad categories must receive some, if minimal, attention. The terms *orthodox, evangelical,* and *separate* give both the necessary parameters and the necessary freedom to a definition of what it means to be Baptist. The preface to *The Baptist Faith and Message* of 1963, a Southern Baptist Confession of Faith, states this very well:

> Baptists emphasize the soul's competency before God, freedom in religion, and the priesthood of the believer. However, this emphasis should not be interpreted to mean that there is an absence of certain definite doctrines that Baptists believe, cherish, and with which they have been and are now closely identified.[1]

Orthodoxy

First, Baptists are orthodox, although this term has several meanings, e.g., medieval Catholic orthodoxy, Lutheran orthodoxy, and Reformed orthodoxy. The broadest and most widely accepted meaning of the term itself refers to the trinitarian and christological affirmations of the early church. Schaff's *Encyclopedia of Religious Knowledge* (s.v. "Orthodoxy") defines orthodoxy as "a conscientious adherence to the Christian faith as taught in the Bible or rather in the ecumenical

---

1. *The Baptist Faith and Message* (Nashville: Sunday School Board of the Southern Baptist Convention, 1963), p. 6.

creed<u>s</u>." All Christians must ask, "Who is this Christ whom we worship, and what is his relationship to deity?" The first four ecumenical councils of the church sought to express an answer to this twofold question. The Creed of Nicea affirmed that Jesus was of the same essence as God the Father and in his incarnation had taken upon himself the complete human nature. This creed also affirmed his separate personality from the Father. Councils at Constantinople and Ephesus protected these affirmations against various heretical divergences until a christological definition was given final form at the council at Chalcedon. While stated in negative terms, the formula was designed to exclude certain errors related to the person of Christ. The statement said:

> We . . . teach men to confess one in the same Son, our Lord Jesus Christ, the same perfect in Godhead and also perfect in Manhood; truly God and truly man of a rational soul and body; consubstantial with the Father according to the Godhead, and consubstantial with us according to the Manhood . . . to be acknowledged in two natures, inconfusedly, unchangeably, indivisibly, inseparably; the distinction of natures being by no means taken away by the union, but rather the property of each nature being preserved, and concurring in one Person.[2]

While Baptists have not assented to this statement simply because it is a creed, but have preferred to emphasize its faithfulness to all scriptural data presented about Christ, Baptists have nevertheless used the very language of this statement in confessions and catechisms and theologies.

Christology constituted perhaps the first controversy in Baptist life. John Smyth made room for the Mennonite views of celestial flesh in his Christology; Thomas Helwys felt it was a definite compromise to make such a concession. Smyth's willingness to compromise at that point partly caused the cleavage between the two men in 1610. Thus, Helwys stated in his Confession of Faith written in 1610 and published in 1611:

> That IESVS CHRIST, the Sonne off GOD the second Person, or subsistance in the Trinity, in the Fulnes off time was manifested in the Flesh, being the seed off David, and off the Isralits, according to the Flesh. Roman. 1.3 and 8.5 the Sonne off Marie the Virgine, made of hir substance, Gal. 4.4 By the power off the HOLIE GHOST overshadowing hir, Luk. 1.35. and being thus true Man was like vnto us in all things, sin

2. Philip Schaff, *The Creeds of Christendom*, 3 vols. (Grand Rapids: Baker Book House, 1983 reprint), 2:62.

onely excepted. Heb. 4.15. being one person in two distinct natures, TRVE GOD, and TRVE MAN.[3]

The last phrase is obviously influenced by christological orthodoxy, and the phrase "made of hir substance" shows a strong aversion to docetic Christology.

The First London Confession, written by Baptists in London in 1644, also partakes of the flavor of patristic orthodoxy. Article II makes an affirmation of the Trinity in language reminiscent of the Chalcedonian and Athanasian Creeds and even includes the *filioque* clause:

> In this God-head, there is the Father, the Sonne, and the Spirit; being every one of them one and the same God; and therefore not divided, but distinguished one from another by their several properties; the Father being from himselfe, the Sonne of the Father from everlasting, the holy Spirit proceeding from the Father and the Sonne.[4]

The Second London Confession, adopted by Particular Baptists in England in 1677, followed very closely the Westminster Confession of Faith but differed significantly in ecclesiology, ordinances, and the relationship of the church to the state. Various other changes in phrases and words demonstrate that this confession is not simply an uncritical reproduction of the Westminster Confession of Faith but represents the studied and accurate opinion of the Particular Baptist churches at that time. Chapter VIII, entitled "Of Christ the Mediator," clearly aligns with an orthodox Christology:

> The Son of God, second Person in the Holy Trinity, being very and eternal God, the brightness of the Father's glory, of one substance and equal with him ... did when the fullness of time was come take upon him man's nature with all the essential properties and common infirmities thereof, yet without sin. ... So that two whole perfect and distinct natures were inseparably joined together in one Person: without conversion, composition or confusion; which person is very God, and very Man: yet one Christ, the only Mediator between God and Man.[5]

Orthodox trinitarianism is also affirmed in this confession:

> In this divine and infinite Being there are three subsistencies, the Father, the Word (or Son) and Holy Spirit, of one substance, power, and Eternity,

3. William L. Lumpkin, *Baptist Confessions of Faith* (Valley Forge: Judson Press, 1969), p. 119.

4. Ibid., pp. 156–157.

5. Ibid., pp. 260–261.

each having the whole Divine Essence, yet the Essence undivided, the Father is of none neither begotten nor proceeding, the Son is Eternally begotten of the Father, the Holy Spirit proceeding from the Father and the Son, all infinite, without beginning, therefore but one God, who is not to be divided in nature and Being; but distinguished by several peculiar, relative properties, and personal relations; which doctrine of the Trinity is the foundation of all our Communion with God, and comfortable dependence on him.[6]

Such christological and trinitarian orthoxy was not limited merely to the Particular or Calvinistic Baptists. The Arminian Baptists also joined with their Calvinistic brothers in affirming this acceptance of the decisions of the early councils of the church. In the mid-seventeenth century, confusion had arisen in General Baptist life relative to the person of Christ. In order to set straight those who were denying the accepted christological formulas of the church, the General Baptists of the Midlands produced a document entitled "The Orthodox Creed." In the preface a rather astounding statement is made by these Baptists: "We are sure that the denying of baptism is a less evil than to deny the divinity or humanity of Christ."[7]

The Orthodox Creed has a heavy emphasis upon trinitarian and christological theology. Concerning the divine nature of Christ, the confession states that the Son of God is "very and true God, of one nature and substance with the Father and God by nature—co-equal, co-essential, and co-eternal with the Father and the Holy Ghost."[8]

In addition, it affirms that the second person of the Holy Trinity took to himself a "true, real and fleshly body, and reasonable soul" and "became very and true man like unto us in all things sin only excepted."[9]

Orthodox language again makes its way into the confession when the writers say that Christ unified the nature of God and the nature of man in his own person: "The properties of each nature being preserved without change of either nature, or mixture of both." And the person thus composed is "one Christ, God-Man, or Emmanuel, God with us."[10]

Further, as if such specific language and such extended articles in these areas were not enough, Article 38 of the Orthodox Creed commends the Nicene Creed, the Creed of Athanasius, and the Apostles'

6. Ibid., p. 253.
7. Ibid., p. 295.
8. Ibid., p. 299.
9. Ibid., p. 300.
10. Ibid., pp. 300–301.

Creed to the Baptist constituency. The writers believed those creeds could be proved "by most undoubted authority of holy scripture" and were necessary to be understood by all Christians. Baptist ministers were encouraged to teach these creeds, according to the analogy of faith as recorded in the sacred Scriptures, for the edification of young and old as a means "to prevent heresy in doctrine, and practice."[11]

In the eighteenth century, General Baptists again developed internal problems related to Christology. Ministers who accepted Socinian views of the person of Christ, a view that compromised his deity, were tolerated within the general assembly. Dan Taylor determined to begin a new connection of General Baptists and formed such a group in June of 1770. Among the six articles that they wrote to show the distinguishing tenets of their organization was an article on the person and work of Christ. The first part of it states:

> We believe, that our Lord Jesus Christ is God and man, united in one person: or possessed of divine perfection united to human nature, in a way which we pretend not to explain, but think ourselves bound by the word of God firmly to believe.[12]

The 1963 *Baptist Faith and Message*, while less detailed than some of the former, nevertheless makes the same affirmation. Article II states that God "reveals himself to us as Father, Son and Holy Spirit with distinct personal attributes but without division of nature, essence, or being." God's Son has taken upon himself "the demands and necessities of human nature," and after accomplishing his work he now resides at the right hand of God, where he partakes "of the nature of God and of man."[13]

Baptist catechisms express the same orthodoxy. Keach's Catechism says that Christ the Son of God "became man by taking to himself a true body and a reasonable soul."[14] This catechism also affirms three persons in the Godhead: the Father, the Son, and the Holy Spirit; and "these three are one God, the same in essence, equal in power, and glory."[15] The catechisms of John Broadus, J. P. Boyce, Henry Fish, W. W. Everts, and others follow suit in their affirmation of orthodoxy on the trinity and the person of Christ.

Southern Baptist systematic theologies have also sought to main-

11. Ibid., p. 326.
12. Ibid., p. 343.
13. *Faith and Message*, p. 8.
14. Benjamin Keach, "Keach's Catechism" in *Baptist Catechisms*, ed. Tom J. Nettles (Memphis: Tom J. Nettles, 1983), p. 81.
15. Ibid., p. 79.

tain this adherence to orthodoxy. John L. Dagg discusses Christology under the headings of three propositions: "Jesus Christ was a man . . . Jesus Christ was God. . . . The two natures of Jesus Christ, the Divine and the human, are united in one person."[16]

J. P. Boyce, in his chapter on the Trinity, sets forth the article from the "Abstract of Principles," which he intends to expound, and states: "The peculiarity of this definition is that it is a mere statement of the Scriptural facts revealed, while, at the same time, it includes every point involved in the doctrine of the Trinity as held by orthodox Christians of all ages."[17] He also clearly expresses an orthodox Christology.[18]

Mullins affirms that the Chalcedonian definition "most fully gathers up the statements of the New Testament."[19]

W. T. Conner continues this affirmation of orthodoxy in his book *Revelation and God*. Although reticent about the philosophical basis of the ecumenical creeds and some supposed unbiblical abstractions concomitant with them, he endorses their basic purpose:

> The orthodox position, as set forth in the ecumenical creeds of the early centuries of Christian history, was to the effect that Christ possessed two whole natures, human and divine, that these natures were not to be confused, and that he was one person and the person was not to be divided. As stated above, so far as these creeds meant to affirm the religious ideas and values of the humanity of Jesus, of his deity and of his undivided personality, we cannot disagree, but rather heartily assent.[20]

Dale Moody at times appears to continue this same strong tradition, but he eventually falls short. After discussing the Nicene Creed, the Apostles' Creed, and the Athanasian Creed, he states, "Lutherans, Calvinists, Anglicans, Baptists, and most other Protestant denominations embraced all of these three Creeds." He then commends the Orthodox Creed of the General Baptists and notes that it quotes all three. Moody also affirms Chalcedon in its basic teaching about the full humanity, full deity, and indivisible personhood of Jesus. "A critical Chalcedon-

16. John L. Dagg, *Manual of Theology*, 3rd ed. (Charleston, SC: The Southern Baptist Publication Society, 1858; reprint ed., Harrisonburg, VA: Gano Books, 1982), pp. 179, 181, 201.

17. James P. Boyce, *Abstract of Systematic Theology* (Philadelphia: American Baptist Publication Society, 1887; reprint ed., North Pompano Beach, FL: Christian Gospel Foundation, n.d.), p. 125.

18. Ibid., pp. 272–291.

19. E. Y. Mullins, *The Christian Religion in its Doctrinal Expression* (Valley Forge: Judson Press, 1917), p. 178.

20. W. T. Conner, *Revelation and God* (Nashville: Broadman Press, 1936), pp. 187–189.

ian Christology, based on the Johannine Logos, is still the most adequate way to state the unity between God and Jesus Christ."[21] For Moody, however, this means an interpretation of Chalcedon according to Nestorian categories, a commitment that can hardly be distinguished from adoptionism.

In spite of Moody's departure from the historic understanding of Chalcedon, one may conclude that Baptists are defined, at least in part, by their adherence to orthodoxy. Obviously such a conclusion is not exhaustive, for it fails to distinguish Baptists from Roman Catholics, historic Presbyterians, Lutherans, and the Greek Orthodox tradition; but it nonetheless serves as an essential parameter within which Baptists have fit historically.

Evangelicalism

Second, Baptists are evangelical. From this area comes the material for the major content of this book. Although the author contends that the purest and most consistent expression of evangelicalism resides within the halls of Calvinism, he acknowledges great breadth within historic and modern evangelicalism. One need attend only one meeting of the Evangelical Theological Society (composed of Baptists, Presbyterians, Methodists, Congregationalists, Anglicans, and others) to see that disagreements in certain theological constructions are pursued with vigor, openness to truth, and love. Therefore, the careful analyst does not simplistically identify evangelicalism with hyper-fundamentalism, neo-fundamentalism, aggressive decisionistic soul-winning, or strict Calvinism.

While great openness characterizes evangelicalism, definite parameters must exist. Sometimes the nomenclature has been used to hide regrettable slides into heterodoxy and even heresy. Although this has made the word virtually useless in some contexts, historic evangelicals must make the effort to restore credibility to a word with noble heritage. Orthodoxy, as discussed earlier, is certainly a part of evangelical theology. Both this openness and exclusiveness were manifest in the 1867 formation of the Evangelical Alliance for the United States. In addition to the nine-point doctrinal statement adopted by the English branch of the Evangelical Alliance in 1846, the American group adopted the following statement:

Resolved, That in the same spirit we propose no new creed, but taking broad, historical, and Evangelical catholic ground, we solemnly reaffirm

21. Dale Moody, *The Word of Truth* (Grand Rapids: Wm. B. Eerdmans Pub. Co., 1981), pp. 8, 413–426.

and profess our faith in all the doctrines of the inspired word of God, and in the *consensus* of doctrines as held by all true Christians from the beginning. And we do more especially affirm our belief in the *divine-human person and atoning work of our Lord and Savior Jesus Christ* as the only and sufficient source of salvation, as the heart and soul of Christianity, and as the center of all true Christian union and fellowship.[22]

Orthodoxy, in the spirit of Athanasius, is discerned as a safeguard of evangelical soteriology. Bruce Shelley concurs in his description of evangelicalism as a "spirit, a concern for sinners, a way of life. Its master motif is the salvation of souls, its guiding image the redemptive Gospel of Jesus Christ. All other considerations are subordinate to this standard."[23]

The evangelical message asserts the uniqueness of Jesus Christ as the personal revelation of God, the completeness of his work in humiliation and exaltation for the redemption of sinners, the effectual working of the Holy Spirit through the preaching of the gospel, and the necessity of an uncoerced response of repentance and faith. The heart of evangelicalism throbs with the redeeming gospel of grace, expressed in a missionary passion that outreaches in evangelism. This forms the basic divide determining who is "Christian" and who is not. Those who are perishing refuse this gospel, and those being saved embrace it.

In short, the doctrine of justification by faith is the *raison d'être* of evangelicalism. Forgiveness of sins and imputed righteousness completely undercut as well as contradict the sacerdotal sacramentalism of Catholicism. All evangelicals—Wesleyan, Arminian, Lutheran, Calvinist—affirm this reality. The conflict between evangelicals centers on the discussion of how faith comes and why it comes. That it comes, the object of its coming, and the basic result of its coming admit no debate among evangelicals.

It is well attested in the documents of Baptist history that Baptists have affirmed this understanding of the gospel in line with others who could be considered evangelical. The Confession of 1644 clearly teaches that "the Gospel which is to be preached to all men as the ground of faith, is that Jesus is the Christ, the Sonne of the everblessed God, filled with the perfection of all heavenly and spiritual excellencies, and that salvation is onely and alone to be had through the beleeving in his Name."[24]

22. *The New Schaff-Herzog Encyclopaedia of Religious Knowledge*, s.v. Evangelical Alliance.

23. Bruce Shelley, *Evangelicalism in America* (Grand Rapids: Wm. B. Eerdmans, 1967), p. 17.

24. Lumpkin, *Baptist Confessions*, p. 162.

More explicitly concerning the elements of justification, Keach's (or the Baptist) Catechism defines justification as "an act of God's free grace, wherein he pardoneth all our sins, and accepteth us as righteous in his sight, only for the righteousness of Christ imputed to us, and received by faith alone." This definition is identical to that of the Westminster Shorter Catechism and demonstrates broad unanimity in evangelical truth between different Protestant denominations.

Likewise, the Second London Confession (1677) demonstrates Baptist unity with other orthodox, evangelical groups. Highlighting not only their points of uniqueness but their large areas of agreement, these Baptists expressed their indebtedness to Christians of other denominations in the preface of this confession:

> And there we did conclude it necessary to express ourselves the more fully and distinctly, and also to fix on such a method as might be most comprehensive of those things which we designed to explain our sense and belief of; and finding no defect in this regard in that fixed on by the Assembly, and after them by those of the Congregational way, we did readily conclude it best to retain the same order in our present Confession. And also when we observed that those last mentioned did, in the Confession (for reasons which seemed of weight both to themselves and others), choose not only to express their mind in words concurrent with the former in sense, concerning all those articles where they were agreed, but also for the most part without any variation of the terms, we did in like manner conclude it best to follow their example, in making use of the very same words with them both, in those articles *(which are very many) wherein our faith and doctrine is the same with theirs.* And this we did, the more abundantly to manifest our consent with both, in all the fundamental articles of the Christian religion, as also with many others whose orthodox confessions have been published to the World, on the behalf of the protestants in diverse nations and cities [author's italics].[25]

From the Westminster Confession and Savoy Declaration, a large segment of contemporary evangelicalism draws its theological nurture. Baptists in America were molded in that same tradition, largely through the incalculable influence of the Philadelphia Confession of Faith, virtually identical to the Second London Confession.

C. H. Spurgeon, still acclaimed by many as the most influential Baptist preacher of history, helped found the British branch of the Evangelical Alliance. He withdrew from some Baptist associations when he felt evangelical views were compromised and sought other Baptist fellowship where these views would be supported. Although

25. Ibid., p. 245.

Spurgeon held tenaciously to Calvinistic theology, he clearly affirmed orthodox evangelicalism as the most basic foundation for Christian fellowship. In April of 1887 he wrote:

> In our fellowship with Methodists of all grades we have found them firmly adhering to those great evangelical doctrines for which we contend. . . . We care far more for the central evangelical truths than we do for Calvinism as a system; but we believe that Calvinism has in it a conservative force which helps to hold men to the vital truth, and therefore we are sorry to see any quitting it who have once accepted it.[26]

Spurgeon expresses exactly the sentiments of this present work. The gospel-mindedness of Southern Baptists cannot be divorced from evangelical roots. The 1845 formation of the Southern Baptist Convention arose partly from the Southerners' evangelical dissatisfaction with Northern-minded home-missions policies that refused the appointment of evangelists for the growing West and South. The Southern churches were so frustrated by gospel needs unmet that they organized to meet them. Exclusion in principle from the recently initiated foreign-mission enterprise was another major reason for the division.

Historians trace the basic dynamics for the evangelism and missions so characteristic of Southern Baptists to the 1775 settlement of Separate Baptists at Sandy Creek, North Carolina. These arose directly from the "great awakening" in New England Congregationalism, which was the American expression of the English evangelical revival. Before the awakening, only forty-seven Baptist churches existed in America—only seven of these below the Mason-Dixon line. Daniel Marshall and Shubal Stearns led the Sandy Creek Baptists in establishing forty-two churches and ordaining a hundred and twenty-five preachers in only seventeen years. Both Marshall and Stearns, as well as other leaders of the awakening in America, had been influenced significantly by the preaching of George Whitefield, a leader of the English awakening. The evangelical revival in England, arising largely from the zeal of the Wesleys, influenced William Carey, a Baptist, and heralded the birth of worldwide modern missions. The Wesleys were Methodists; Whitefield an Independent. All were evangelicals.

A more recent phenomenon demonstrates the open evangelical consciousness of twentieth-century Baptists. The evangelical revival in England, arising from the new-birth preaching of the Arminian Wesleys and the Calvinist Whitefield, not only contributed to the simul-

26. Charles H. Spurgeon, *Sword and Trowel*, 1887, p. 195.

taneous awakening in America through Whitefield but received prolonged life from the New World by way of the writings of Jonathan Edwards. These writings greatly affected the Baptists Sutcliff, Fuller, and Carey, thus aiding in the birth of worldwide modern missions. What they would not accept from Wesley and seemed suspicious of in Whitefield came crashing upon them from Edwards, largely through his treatise *Freedom of the Will,* and then because they considered it "fully consistent with the strictest Calvinism."[27] The influence and benefits of this evangelical network are obvious.

"Evangelical" is a sound, biblically based word arising from the Greek term εὐαγγελίζομαι, used most often in Scripture to describe the open publication of the gospel. Baptists received their name from unsympathetic observers, who saw in the immersion of believers a strange rite yet were unaware that their protest was designed to undergird the essential nature of the church as a gathered community of regenerate believers. Baptists have little difficulty in keeping their commitment evangelical when their distinctive ordinance fittingly focuses on the gospel as the heart of all they are and do.

Separate Elements

In addition to the essentials of orthodoxy and evangelicalism, Baptists have yet another stream of influence that flows into their final form. This ingredient distinguishes Baptists from other evangelicals, such as Presbyterians, Congregationalists, and so on. It can be denominated by the term *separate.* This factor grows out of early associations with the Separatist movement of England and the Anabaptist movement on the Continent. Baptists fall heir to the separatistic tradition, first enunciated by Independents and Congregationalists but confused by them through their practice of infant baptism. Baptists persist in the question "How can the church be a gathered community of believers when the reality of a spiritual rebirth is confused by practicing baptism solely on the basis of a natural birth?"

The most revolutionary change occurring in the Separatist congregation, which moved to Amsterdam under the leadership of John Smyth in 1608 and returned to England under the leadership of Thomas Helwys in 1612, was the shift from infant baptism to believer's baptism. This was part of a larger change, in which magisterial methods of reform were revoked and replaced by free-church principles. The state-

27. John Ryland, *Life and Death of the Rev. Andrew Fuller* (London: Button & Son, 1816), pp. 9, 10.

ment of doctrines entitled "A True Confession" represents the Separatist theology of the church in its early days. On baptism it stated:

> ... such as bee of the seed, or vnder the government of anie of the Church, bee euen jn their infancie receiued to Baptisme, ond made pertakers of the signe of Gods Couenant made with the faithfull and their seed throughout all Generations.[28]

When they returned to England, their view of baptism had changed. The Confession of Thomas Helwys, printed in 1611 in Amsterdam, stated "that everie Church is to receive in all their members by Baptisme vpon the Confession off their faith and sinnes wrought by the preaching off the Gospel." Helwys added, "that Baptisme or washing with Water is the outward manifestation off dieing vnto sinn and walkeing in newness of life and therefore in no wise apperteyneth to infants."[29]

In 1644 the Baptists "commonly though falsely called Anabaptists" composed a Confession of Faith in which baptism by immersion was espoused for the first time in a "modern" confession. Having been charged with "doing acts unseemly in the dispensing the ordinance of baptism not to be named amongst Christians" (that is, baptizing women naked), the confession specifically repudiated this by affirming that baptism meant to dip under the water "so as with convenient garments both upon the administrator and subject with all modesty." They also affirmed that this ordinance was to be "dispensed onely upon persons professing faith or that are Disciples, or taught, who upon a profession of faith, ought to be baptized."[30]

Baptist conviction has remained virtually the same even to the time of the 1963 *Baptist Faith and Message*. Believer's baptism by immersion has enjoyed rather vigorous defense by the best minds produced in Baptist life—such as John Gill, Adoniram Judson, John Dagg, B. H. Carroll, and others too numerous to name.

The true Separatist position, endorsed by believer's baptism, affirms that the local and visible church exists only as a community of gathered believers and opposes the idea that the church exists as those born into the state or is associated with true believers as part of their families without personal regeneration. Thus, the regenerate nature of the church foundations the Baptist commitment to believer's baptism, the priesthood of every believer, the autonomy of the local congregation, and associated doctrines.

28. *Baptist Confessions*, p. 93.
29. Ibid., p. 120.
30. Ibid., p. 167.

Others *claim* this distinctive, but Baptists apply it with their rigorous demand for a public profession of faith, in what they view as a scriptural manner, before local fellowship is confirmed.

John L. Dagg, in his monumental *Manual of Theology* (the second part, entitled *A Treatise on Church Order*), includes a forty-page section discussing the implications of infant membership in churches. One by one, he tackles the arguments for infant membership and dismantles them with a plethora of biblical and theological argumentation. His final argument against infant membership reduces all the arguments for it to one analogy, i.e., the Gentiles have been grafted into the olive tree and so the "blessing of Abraham comes on the Gentiles; and the covenant which secures the blessing, embraces their children with them."[31] After pages of very clear, concise, and convincing reasoning, Dagg closes with these words:

> Infant membership is argued from the identity of the olive-tree; but, unfortunately for the argument, the changes which the apostle has described, infringe on the identity of the tree, exactly in the wrong place. All these changes respect the branches, and are made on one principle— the substitution of faith for natural descent; as the bond of connection between the branches and the root. Infant membership depends on natural descent; and the one principle on which all the changes are made, by taking away natural descent, leaves infant membership to hang on nothing.[32]

Another baptistic element contributing to the formation of contemporary Baptists is a three-pronged building block, including the corollaries of liberty of conscience, freedom of religion, and separation of church and state. Although these three are not to be identified simplistically with each other, they nevertheless imply one another. Liberty of conscience, for which Baptists have bled since the time of Thomas Helwys, means that no man or human doctrine is lord over the conscience. No other creature has the right to bind a man's conscience by human doctrines. Thomas Helwys said:

> ... men's religion to God is betwixt God and themselves; the king shall not answer for it, neither may the king be judge between God and man. Let them be heretics, Turks, Jews or whatsoever it appertains not to the earthly power to punish them in the least measure.[33]

31. John L. Dagg, *A Treatise on Church Order* (Charleston, SC: Southern Baptist Publication Society, 1858), p. 165.
32. Ibid., p. 183.
33. Thomas Helwys, *A Short Declaration of the Mistery of Iniquity*, (n.p., 1612), p. 69.

Obviously Helwys would not claim "heretics, Turks, Jews or whatsoever" as Baptists. The espousal of liberty of conscience relates solely to the functioning of men in civil society and does not define what a Baptist is. It is a condition Baptists seek for all men so that they may be free to hear and openly submit to the evangelical message of Christ.

Both John Murton and Leonard Busher, who followed Helwys as pastor of a small General Baptist church, wrote major works on liberty of conscience. General Baptists and Particular Baptists alike joined in the struggle for liberty of conscience until it was finally attained under the reign of William and Mary by the issuing of the Act of Toleration. Although England did attain liberty of conscience and freedom of religion, its people were never able to gain disestablishment of the Anglican Church.

However, the Baptists in America, helped by the existence of a great plurality of denominations plus the impetus of Jeffersonian libertarianism, gained separation of church and state as well as the other two freedoms. The struggle was carried on in America mainly by such Baptists as Roger Williams, John Clarke, Isaac Backus, and John Leland until it was granted in writing by the Bill of Rights of the Constitution adopted in 1789.

While the affirmation of these three freedoms is a cardinal tenet of Baptist life, Baptists may very well exist where none of these freedoms has been achieved. In fact, Baptists in the past have thrived and continue to thrive in areas where they have neither liberty of conscience nor freedom of religion nor separation of church and state. However, a Baptist church cannot exist where there is no regenerate church membership and no affirmation of believer's baptism. These are the ecclesiological *sine qua non*'s.

In summary, to be Baptist means to be *orthodox* in one's view of the Trinity and the person of Christ. To be Baptist also means to be *evangelical* in one's soteriology. Finally, to be Baptist means to be consistently *separate* in ecclesiology and to seek to encourage conditions in which all may hear the gospel.

This work details Baptist evangelicalism and claims, along with Spurgeon, that the purest biblical presentation of the gospel glides upon the waters of the Doctrines of Grace. Indeed, any rejection of these doctrines carries within it seeds that sprout into nonevangelical positions. In the words of Spurgeon, their full acceptance fits a man for battle against all the enemies of God:

> You cannot vanquish a Calvinist. You may think you can, but you cannot. The stones of the great doctrines so fit into each other, that the more pressure there is applied to remove them the more strenuously do they

adhere. And you may mark, that you cannot receive one of these doctrines without believing all. Hold for instance that man is utterly depraved, and you draw the inference then that certainly if God has such
a creature to deal with salvation must come from God alone, and if from
him, the offended one, to an offending creature, then he has a right to
give or withhold his mercy as he wills; you are thus forced upon election,
and when you have gotten that you have all: the others must follow.
Some by putting the strain upon their judgments may manage to hold
two or three points and not the rest, but sound logic I take it requires
a man to hold the whole or reject the whole; the doctrines stand like
soldiers in a square, presenting on every side a line of defence which it
is hazardous to attack, but easy to maintain. And mark you, in these
times when error is so rife and neology strives to be so rampant, it is no
little thing to put into the hands of a young man a weapon which can
slay his foe, which he can easily learn to handle, which he may grasp
tenaciously, wield readily, and carry without fatigue; a weapon, I may
add, which no rust can corrode and no blows can break, trenchant, and
well annealed, a true Jerusalem blade of a temper fit for deeds of renown.[34]

A survey of how this formidable weapon was deftly wielded, then sadly
forsaken continues and concludes this introduction.

Overview: A Map of the Baptist Journey

A survey is a sort of map. Before a trip begins in detail, travelers
need to see a map of the entire territory, including some lands that lie
outside the particular route taken. The overall fortunes of Calvinism
among Baptists (that juxtaposition of words is not proper but will do
for now) in England and America constitute the guide along the way.
Slightly more space will be devoted to England in this overview, since
subsequent text treatment of it ends in the early nineteenth century.
Some readers may feel that massive apologies are due for not including a chapter on Spurgeon. His sermons and other works, however,
are available in such abundant proportions, and he is quoted so often
in other sections of this book, that his inclusion seemed unnecessary.
Also, Ian Murray's book *The Forgotten Spurgeon*, in which a notable
discussion of Spurgeon's Calvinism forms a major contribution, is
readily available. On with the overview. . . .

Baptists and Calvinism in England

Chapter one will outline the differences between the General Baptists and the Particular Baptists. This work purposefully focuses on

34. C. H. Spurgeon, "Exposition of the Doctrines of Grace," in *The Metropolitan
Tabernacle Pulpit* 63 vols. (Pilgrim Publications: Pasadena, Texas, 1969), 7:304.

the Calvinistic section of Baptist life. The Arminian section was plagued with lamentable apostasy in the seventeenth, eighteenth, and nineteenth centuries, Socinianism playing the role of destroyer in the first two lapses and liberalism in the last. Particular Baptists remained faithful through all those years until debilitated by various currents in the last half of the nineteenth century, when the Calvinistic banner was carried forth by the Strict Baptists in a severely truncated form. Human responsibility then suffered a smashing blow from the hammer of God's sovereignty by the hand of misguided logical extension.

SEVENTEENTH-CENTURY ORTHODOXY

Hanserd Knollys (1599–1691), William Kiffin (1616–1701), Benjamin Keach (1640–1704), John Spilsbery (1593–1668), Henry Jessey (1601–1663), and John Bunyan (1628–1688), among others, stand as representative of the firm conviction, fervent piety, powerful preaching, and theological orthodoxy of seventeenth-century Particular Baptists. Although some differences on communion and church membership existed in those days of emerging from Separatism, there was unity in soteriology. The two London Confessions actually represent the theological commitments of Particular Baptists nationwide during this period, the 1689 Confession having been signed by representatives from more than 107 churches all over England and Wales.[35] Some churches in the West that followed the theological shifting of Thomas Collier gradually moved from this strong Calvinism into a reactionary position, Collier himself eventually becoming a Universalist. But if some in the West declined, others vigorously resisted this apostasy. Instead, they increased in zeal and, from Bristol, sought to promote fellowship and meaningful association between the churches in the area and even boxed the ears of the London churches for slackness in pursuing such interchurch encouragement.

EIGHTEENTH-CENTURY DECLINE

The eighteenth century has been characterized as one of decline by most historians. Deism, Socinianism, and Latitudinarian theology did severe damage to Presbyterian, Anglican, Congregational, and General Baptist churches. Particular Baptists, on the other hand, did not fall into theological error. Instead, John C. Ryland could say in 1777, "There is no apparent apostasy in our ministers and people from the glorious principles we profess." Although the middle of the century saw a decline in the number of Particular Baptist churches, by 1798 they num-

---

35. Joseph Ivimey, *A History of the English Baptists*, 4 vols. (London: Printed for the author and sold by Burditt, Buxton, Hamilton, Baynes, etc., 1811–1830), 1:503–511.

bered 361 in England, of which 320 had pastors. An additional 84 were in Wales. Much growth had come in the last fifteen years of the century.

What did cause consternation in the fellowship came in the form of the "modern question." Far-reaching consequences hung on the answer to the question: whether the unregenerate could be called upon to exercise saving repentance and faith. John Brine (1703–1765) was the leader of those writing negatively to the question. But John Gill (1697–1771), friend of Brine and acknowledged leader of Baptists for fifty years of the century, never wrote on the question. This in itself is a strange phenomenon, since Gill is characterized as the definitive hyper-Calvinist, but it is no less strange than the fact that Gill rejects Brine's main argument against the question. For this reason, one full chapter is given to Gill and a reinvestigation of the charges adhering to his reputation.

Although a major part of the century was blanketed by a sorrowful recession of growth for the Particular Baptists, too censorious a judgment upon the age would fail to recognize the outstanding contributions made by such men as Joseph Stennett (1692–1758), John Collett Ryland (1723–1792), Benjamin Beddome (1718–1795), Samuel Medley (1738–1799), and John Hirst (1736–1815). Some seem to feel that too-close adherence to Calvinism was the dominant factor of the decline, but they make the deadly error of failing to distinguish between Calvinism and hyper-Calvinism. Thus they fail to appreciate the gospel zeal inherent in the former. A broad view of the entire religious scene might lead to a contrary opinion and see Calvinism as the factor that conserved the strength of the Particular Baptists and made possible the worldwide propagation of the gospel in the next century. This seems to be the view of Joseph Ivimey as he draws conclusions from an anecdote he related about the elder Joseph Stennett (d. 1713):

> Had our ministers in general manifested this strict adherence to the *Calvinistic* doctrines which Mr. Stennett did, instead of that spurious candour and moderation expressed by some others; there is no doubt but many churches would have been preserved from the whirlpool of Socinianism, which has swallowed up some Particular Baptist Societies, and nearly all of those which at the end of the seventeenth century belonged to the General Baptists.[36]

Help to Zion's Travelers, by Robert Hall (1728–1791), was published in 1781 by request of the Northamptonshire Association. It was the book form of what had been delivered orally as a sermon on Isaiah

36. Ibid., 2:503–511.

57:14. The content vindicated Calvinism from the objections of many detractors, including Arminians, Socinians, and Antinomians. In addition, it gave a strong affirmation to the necessity of calling all men to repentance before God and faith in our Lord Jesus Christ. This book figured largely in the movements of William Carey toward the position he expresses in *An Enquiry into the Obligations of Christians to Use Means for the Conversion of the Heathen* (1791). That influence was also present in Andrew Fuller's *The Gospel Worthy of All Acceptation* (1785). A full chapter of the present work (chapter three) concentrates on Fuller's theology to demonstrate that a strong affirmative answer to the "modern question" did not involve any declension from historic Calvinism. Nor did the rise of modern missions come as a result of shaking off the fetters of Calvinism, but instead issued as the necessary expression of it. This cannot be too strongly affirmed or stressed in the contemporary scene, where it is commonly believed that the Doctrines of Grace are the enemy of evangelism. Indeed, they are the enemy of systems and methods that thrive on reductionistic perversions of the gospel—but true evangelism has no dearer friend than these doctrines.

Nineteenth- and Twentieth-Century Trends

The story of English Baptist Calvinism in the nineteenth and twentieth centuries can be given in survey form by a simple method, involving three steps. First, a survey of the theological tendency of the Baptist Union will give a fairly accurate picture of whether churches connected with that group regarded Calvinism as strategic or absolute in one's comprehension of the gospel. Second, the rise and history of the Strict Baptists show the fortunes of Calvinism from another perspective. Third, a statement on the contemporary status of the Reformation doctrines closes the overview of the English scene.

The Baptist Union: Under the picture of John Gill, in the vestry of John Rippon at the Baptist Church in Carter Lane in Southwark, near the southern end of the old London Bridge, close to sixty Baptist ministers met in 1812 to found the first Baptist Union. Among the attenders of the meeting were Andrew Fuller, John Sutcliff, John Ryland, Jr., John Rippon, and Joseph Ivimey. The latter, the main force behind the meeting, had issued a call for it in 1811 in *The Baptist Magazine* in an article entitled "Union Essential to Prosperity." Ivimey conceived of it as an opportunity for the various societies and agencies having separate organizations—yet supported largely by the same churches, associations, and individuals—to give reports of their respective progress so as to encourage and renew the zeal of the churches. Andrew Fuller was doubtful about the prospect, thinking that it would only "show the poverty of the denomination," but he could not have been less than pleased when a collection taken for the Baptist Missionary Society totaled £ 320. Among the resolutions adopted at this consultative meeting was one that called for the objectives of union to be "the promotion of the cause of Christ in general; and the interests of the denomination in particular." In addition, the first official meeting of the Union was set for June 25–26, 1813.

It is noteworthy that at this 1813 meeting a Confession of Faith headed the items that were discussed and approved. Paragraph one of this original constitution is worded in terms in which "the Calvinism of Particular Baptist churches was customarily defined."

> That this society of ministers and churches be designated "The General Union of Baptist ministers and churches" maintaining the important doctrines of "three equal persons in the Godhead; eternal and personal election; original sin; particular redemption; free justification by the imputed righteousness of Christ; efficacious grace in regeneration; the final perseverance of real believers; the resurrection of the dead; the future judgment; the eternal happiness of the righteous, and the eternal misery of such as die in impenitence, with the congregational order of churches inviolably."[37]

The doctrinal basis was strong and uncompromising. The years from 1817 to 1831, however, saw very little advance in the concept of union among the English Baptists. The burgeoning success of the Baptist Missionary Society and the origin and rapidly increasing popularity of the Baptist Irish Society absorbed the energies of the churches. Little time or creativity was left for engendering viability for the separate functioning of the Baptist Union. Baptists also saw the painful separation of the Serampore Mission from the Baptist Missionary Society. Controversy over strict communion arose during these years, pitting Joseph Ivimey on the side of strict communion against Robert Hall and F. A. Cox on the side of open communion. In addition, the high profile of Calvinism among the Particular Baptists began to take on more rounded and plainer contours, so that similarity rather than distinction began to characterize the comparison between General and Particular Baptists. Meetings of the union continued during these years, at the instigation of Joseph Ivimey, but they were so small and ineffective that Ivimey was forced to write in 1830 that the design "was never fully realized."[38]

In 1832 a reorganization occurred, which opened the door for the

37. E. A. Payne, *The Baptist Union* (London: The Carey Kingsgate Press Limited, 1959), p. 26.
38. Ivimey, *English Baptists*, 4:382.

eventual expansion of the Union, but only by means of chipping off the piercing doctrinal edges. Article one, containing the distinctive doctrines of Calvinism, gave way to an extraordinarily short doctrinal statement susceptible to the most extreme abuse: "1st. To extend brotherly love and union among the Baptist ministers and churches who agree in the sentiments usually denominated evangelical."[39]

This wording indicated a growing alienation from the Calvinism of former days. Although many pastors still held the distinguishing tenets of Calvinism, their contentment with the nebulosity of the mere affirmation of "evangelical sentiments" shows a diminishing attachment to their essentiality. History fails to reveal what positive advantage denominations actually gain by uniting around a crucifixion of truth. Any projects sponsored under such auspices are fragmented from the beginning, for, in reality, foundations and goals are always identical. The true Christian character of any enterprise can neither be guaranteed at the beginning nor measured at the end, for the pursuers of the project will confess to nothing more than the most puerile understanding of the Christian faith. Only a heroic and defiant individualism can salvage good in such a case, and that in spite of—rather than because of—its character.

"Evangelical," when precisely defined, can be a marvelously useful word. But when left without definition and combined with the amazingly insipid theological term *sentiments*, its tendency to dereliction is absolute. Ivimey saw this clearly and lamented it. Whereas two decades earlier he had criticized Gill, not for Calvinism but for what he considered as false practices built upon it, he now saw the danger from another direction. Almost the last sentence he wrote for the press was intended as a warning against flirting with Arminianism:

> Nor can I disguise the fact, that, in my opinion, the dignified tone, and denominational zeal, manifested by Booth, Fuller and others are greatly lowered; and that a general spirit of laxity is introduced among us, as to the "DOCTRINES" of grace, as well as to the "DISCIPLINE" of the New Testament.[40]

Thirty years later, John Howard Hinton (1791–1873)—who had been secretary of the Baptist Union for over twenty years and had sought to maintain commitment to the main pillars of Calvinistic orthodoxy, though modified at points—gave a surprisingly bitter evaluation of

39. Payne, *Baptist Union*, p. 61.
40. *Memoir of the Life and Writings of the Reverend Joseph Ivimey*, ed. George Pritchard (London: George Wightman, 1835), p. 311.

the doctrinal basis of the 1832 reconstitution of the Union. "What a poverty-stricken resolution it is that defines these objects, was as strongly felt then as it has often been felt since; but it was absolutely all that the assembled brethren would bear."[41]

Other events show increased determination toward vaporization of doctrine. In 1842 John Gregory Pike, the leader of the New Connection General Baptists, was invited to preside at the Baptist Union meeting. In 1857 the meeting was held in Nottingham, so that it could be nearer the largest number of General Baptist churches and thereby encourage their attendance.

Further abolition of doctrinal distinctives was evident by 1864, when the chairman of the meeting urged those attending that one immediate aim of the churches should be "the supercession, on practicable, sound and safe principles of the distinction between General and Particular Baptists."[42] Although these sentiments were present, no official action was forthcoming. In 1872, therefore, Thomas Thomas reminded the churches that such action needed to be taken, since the doctrinal differences were by then almost imperceptible:

> Our communion is becoming closer and more frequent. Not only are members of churches freely transferred from one section to the other, but brethren, if eligible for office in other respects, are irrespective of sentiment, elected to be deacons in the churches to which they are transferred. Further still, General Baptist Churches are quite accustomed to choose Particular Baptist pastors; and a proportionate, but not an equal, number of General Baptist pastors are settled over Particular Baptist Churches.[43]

No one really needs to ask whose doctrine was changing so radically as to make this interchange possible. Not only was Calvinism dying confessionally in Particular Baptist life (the nomenclature even has a hollow ring by now), but fewer and fewer held the Doctrines of Grace personally, and even fewer than that dared to preach them as essential to an understanding of the gospel. When organic union was being discussed seriously in 1874, John Clifford, editor of the *General Baptist Magazine*, could say candidly, "We were never further from Calvinism than we are today."[44] He had no fear that he would adversely affect the chance of eventual union by such forthrightness. Particular Bap-

41. Payne, *Baptist Union*, p. 61.

42. Payne, *Baptist Union*, p. 98.

43. Ibid., see footnote.

44. John Clifford, in A. C. Underwood, *A History of the English Baptists* (London: Kingsgate Press, 1947), p. 215.

tists would never think of being aroused against contemplating union
with Clifford and his kind, for in 1873 even the meager "sentiments
... evangelical" had been dropped and replaced with a lone doctrinal
statement, "The immersion of believers is the only Christian Baptism."

When, in 1877, Dr. Samuel Cox published *Salvatore Mundi*, denying
the doctrine of eternal punishment, it became evident that the issue
had degenerated from Calvinism/Arminianism to whether or not it
matters that one is a Christian at all. It should come as no surprise,
then, that by the time the official union between General and Particular Baptists occurred in 1891, the Baptist who actually had the greatest right to remain, Charles Haddon Spurgeon, had seceded from the
Baptist Union.

Spurgeon blazed in Baptist life as a somewhat solitary figure during
all his ministry. In the mid-1850s in London, his pronounced Calvinism caused such consternation that he was accused of preaching "doctrines of the most rampant exclusiveness." Spurgeon's stance for
Calvinism and against Arminianism has been documented well in *The
Forgotten Spurgeon* by Ian Murray.[45] He adhered to strict Calvinism
throughout his ministry and was never without a ready word to defend
that theology against what he felt were the destructive tendencies of
Arminianism. The situation in the Baptist Union, however, had become so desperate that by 1887 evangelical Wesleyanism held more
in common with Spurgeon than the doctrinal nothingness of the Baptist Union. Those years of controversy (ca. 1887–1892) have proved
perplexing, painful, and sometimes embarrassing to Baptist Union
historians. What does one say when the greatest Baptist preacher of
the denomination's history, a man of large and generous heart and no
small penetration, finds it impossible to maintain the facade of fellowship? The situation has been handled largely by treating Spurgeon
with paternalistic condescension as a good but sick man, unable to
cope with the evolving and developing intellect of Baptist theology.[46]
The truth appears to be undeniable, however, that his concerns about
the inerrancy of Scripture, the deity of Christ, the reality of eternal
punishment, and other fundamental tenets of the faith were well
founded. The writings of John Clifford after the death of Spurgeon
show clearly his heterodoxy—and the truth of Spurgeon's claims—on
each of these points.

Although the distinguishing doctrines of Calvinism were not the
issue in the "downgrade controversy," Spurgeon's adherence to them

---

45. Ian Murray, *The Forgotton Spurgeon* (Banner of Truth Trust, 1966) see especially
pp. 45–114.
46. Payne, *Baptist Union*, pp. 127–143; Underwood, *English Baptists*, pp. 229–233.

so shaped his views of God and truth and so committed him to the importance of principles in theology that he saw more clearly than anyone the nature of the issues at stake. Those who had no capability of understanding Spurgeon's position railed at him with very little reserve, a melancholy fact that prompted Spurgeon to remark: "Those who are so exceedingly liberal, large-hearted, and broad might be so good as to allow us to forego the charms of their society without coming under the full violence of their wrath."[47] One contemporary historian who understands in detail the theological movements of the last part of the nineteenth century regarded Spurgeon's move as "the grandest gesture yet against the debilitating forces at work within English Nonconformity."[48]

As recently as 1971 this theological malformity expressed itself vividly from the platform of the annual assembly of the Baptist Union, when Michael Taylor used the occasion to express his denial of the deity of Christ:

> I believe God was active in Jesus, but it will not do to say quite categorically: Jesus is God. Jesus is unique, but his uniqueness does not make him different in kind from us. . . . The difference is in what God did in and through this man and the degree to which this man responded and co-operated with God.[49]

Several churches and ministers seceded from the Union when no official reprimand of Taylor came from its council, but many just as surely defended Taylor's right to declare such heresy in the ranks of accredited ministers.

This should surprise no one familiar with the development of theological thought in Baptist Union circles. H. Wheeler Robinson (1872–1945), principal of Regents Park College from 1920–1942 and leading English Baptist theologian in the twentieth century, had advanced a theological method quite incapable of correcting Taylor. Robinson himself rejected the historicity of Adam and his connection with man's sinfulness.[50] In fact, he called the Old Testament narration of the fall "a minor and negligible element in the literature and religion of Israel"[51] and finally concluded that "modern views of the Bible

47. Spurgeon, *Sword and Trowel* (1888), p. 620.

48. Ian Sellers, *Nineteenth-Century Nonconformity* (n.p., Edward Arnold, 1977), p. 28.

49. Speech by Michael Taylor, Annual Assembly of the Baptist Union, in *Reformation Today*, No. 10, Summer 1972, p. 36.

50. H. Wheeler Robinson, *Redemption and Revelation in the Actuality of History* (London: Nisbet & Co., Ltd., 1942), p. 65.

51. H. Wheeler Robinson, *The Christian Doctrine of Man*, 3rd edition (Edinburgh: T. & T. Clark, 1926; reprint ed., 1934), p. 163.

and of the origin of the race remove Adam's transgressions from the data of the problem" of human sin.[52]

Robinson dismissed out of hand the doctrine of eternal punishment in favor of annihilationism or "a revised form of conditional immortality."[53] Postmortem opportunities for salvation will probably be presented to men, for "we have no sufficient ground for asserting that the final decision is always made at the present stage of our development; indeed, we all realize that many men on earth have never had a fair opportunity of making it."[54] The whole idea of hell was rather disgusting to Robinson, and he insisted "there is something unhealthy in being over-much concerned with hell."[55] Baptists in the centuries before him would have concluded the reverse.

More devastating than these (because foundational to them) are Robinson's views of revelation and the method of discerning error. Revelation comes in the interplay between Christian experience and the providential movement of history. Scripture cannot be taken in any verbal or propositional sense but must be seen as a record of divine encounters upon individual consciousness. The Bible is the "sufficiently accurate record of a religious experience which is normative and authoritative."[56] We have no right, therefore, Robinson claims, "to assume that the ethics of Amos or even of Jesus are directly applicable, as they stand, to every generation."[57]

In like manner, it would seem, one could conclude that we have no right to make the propositional beliefs of the apostles as normative for today. In his approach to the "ministry of error," Robinson makes room for that position by saying, "Obviously any dogmatic assertion of what is truth and what is error in contemporary religion would be especially out of place in such a subject."[58] When such little platform is given for establishing truth and resisting error, it is no wonder that a denial of the deity of Christ should meet with a defense of the rights of the speaker.

The years from Clifford to Robinson and beyond appear to have acclimatized the members of the Baptist Union so thoroughly that no shock at all is produced by the cold winds of infidelity. But such continued exposure to disease and death can also have the effect of lowering immunities to the point that the slightest infection can kill.

52. Ibid., p. 269.
53. Robinson, *Redemption and Revelation*, p. 310.
54. Ibid., p. 309.
55. Ibid.
56. Ibid., p. 179.
57. Ibid., p. 171.
58. Ibid., p. 22.

Christians over the world must pray that the denomination that produced Keach, Gill, Booth, Fuller, Carey, and Spurgeon may once again uncover the foundation on which they stood. It would be tragic if Calvinism is joined by other truths viewed merely as theological archaisms in the Baptist Union; for then, not only will evangelical purity be compromised, but the Christian faith itself will be lost.

The Strict Baptists: Calvinistic theology had not completely vanished from Baptist life in England, however. Theological discussion in the 1820s centered not only upon the issue of communion but upon the subtle encroachment of Arminianism into Particular Baptist life.[59] The arguments of Robert Hall (1764–1831) for open communion contemplated the possibility that eventually no "Baptist" churches as such would exist, but only "Baptist" individuals. Atheological romantic fervor for the promotion of missions alarmed and alerted some to the dangers of some styles of evangelism. These two issues characterized the concerns of Strict Baptists at their inception as a separate, recognizable entity.

By the 1830s, statements against "Fullerism" and open communion began to become common in certain areas. Not only were the terms of communion characteristic in definitions made by Strict Baptist groups, but "the doctrine which asserts that saving faith is the duty of all men" was repeatedly rejected. Definite form was given to the movement by the appearance of several publications, the most influential of which was called *The Gospel Standard*, begun in 1835 and continuing to this day. Its adherents are known as "Standard Men," and the churches endorsing its Confession of Faith are properly denominated "Gospel Standard Baptists." *The Gospel Herald*, begun in 1833, held the same basic doctrine. It merged in 1887 with *The Earthen Vessel*, a magazine started in 1845 in Southwark, the area of London eventually to be invaded by Charles Haddon Spurgeon. The *Vessel* criticized Spurgeon severely because of his obvious adherence to "duty-faith"—he constantly insisted that all men everywhere turn from sin and rebellion and bow at the feet of Jesus. The magazine did manage a word of commendation and support for him in his struggle with the "downgrade."

In 1896 another publication appeared, entitled *The Christian's Pathway*. The rejection of duty-faith and open communion characterized its content also, in addition to a positive stance on the "eternal sonship of Christ," prompted by a controversy within the pages of *The Earthen Vessel*, 1859–1860. Its position was clearly summarized in a letter to

59. *Annual Report and Bulletin of the Strict Baptist Historical Society*, No. 13 (1976), pp. 5–7.

Introduction   39

a deacon of a church wishing to be included in its list of acceptable churches:

> 1. Does your Church and Pastor endorse the doctrine stated at the head of the Directory, viz.: The Eternal Sonship of our Lord and Saviour Jesus Christ?
> 2. Does your Church and Pastor endorse all the points of Doctrine under the head "Particular," and reject Duty-Faith, or as some term it "Spurgeonism?"
> 3. Does your Church and Pastor endorse all that is implied in the word "Strict," i.e., that none but baptized believers of Churches of the same Faith and Order can commune together at the Lord's Supper?

The most pronounced affirmation of this theological tenet came in 1878 in *The Gospel Standard*, when a confession appeared, expanding the Strict Baptist antipathy to universal calls to repentance and faith. (This issue is discussed briefly in chapter sixteen.)

Developments since World War II have seen all the Strict Baptists except those holding the *Gospel Standard* confession drop their rejection of duty-faith. *Grace* magazine has replaced the *Gospel Herald-Earthen Vessel* publication, and *Reformation Today* has replaced *The Christian's Pathway*.[60] True Calvinism has been recaptured in these magazines and the doctrines of the 1689 Confession heartily espoused. The positions of Fuller, Carey, and Spurgeon are celebrated and hyper-Calvinism in every form rejected. While a period of some years in the twentieth century found the Metropolitan Tabernacle lose its distinctive evangelical Calvinistic witness, in recent years it has been rediscovered under the ministry of Peter Masters. Although maintaining and arguing for a strictly separatistic posture, the ministry there has been instrumental in leading many back to the Doctrines of Grace.

Contemporary Status of Reformation Doctrine: With the commencement of *Reformation Today* (1970), the Carey Conference for Ministers began. Meeting annually, it draws Baptist ministers from independent Baptist churches as well as Baptist Union churches. As its name indicates, experimental and practical application of great doctrinal truths forms the core of the conference's purpose. The 1985 conference was devoted to the theme of missions, while the 1986 conference is dedicated to the reexploration of the parameters of the 1689 Confession and what, in a comprehensive sense, is the Reformed faith.

Happily, the historic Calvinism of the old English Baptists has been snatched from the jaws of death, has all the marks of health, and

60. *Reformation Today*, No. 1, Spring 1970.

shows promise of multiplication. Whether it can withstand the on-slaughts of theological and ecclesiastical trendiness and maintain—like Fuller, Carey, Ivimey, Booth, and Spurgeon—a tender heart and a steel backbone does not depend upon the strength and comprehensiveness of the system itself. Certainly no other view of God, man, the world, and all things visible and invisible can approach the strength of Calvinism. Rather, under God, the tenacity of the present Reformation will depend upon the degree to which the hearts of those involved have been captured for truth and whether their affection radiates toward the temporal or the eternal.

Baptists and Calvinism in the United States

SEVENTEENTH-CENTURY ROOTS

When Roger Williams came to the New World in 1631, he brought with him not only an irrepressible conscience, which eventually brought banishment from Massachusetts Bay upon him, but the unvarnished Calvinism of his separatistic Puritanism. The Baptist Church founded under his influence in Providence, Rhode Island, in 1639 embraced this same theology. John Clarke, another Englishman who found the church-state relation of Massachusetts Bay unpalatable, also made his way to Rhode Island and, with the help of Williams, purchased land from the Indians. Under the probable influence of Williams, Clarke became a Baptist sometime between 1640 and 1644. The church he founded at Newport, the second Baptist church in America, "maintained the doctrine of efficacious grace," and at least until the time of Thomas Armitage remained Calvinistic.[61] The Confessions of Faith of both Clarke and Obadiah Holmes, who succeeded Clarke as pastor, demonstrate this truth beyond doubt. Clarke left his confession in writing, and a portion was inserted in the records of the church. Isaac Backus, in his notable *A History of New England*, published the main portion of it:

> The special decree of God concerning angels and men is called predestination Romans viii. 30 . . . of the latter more is revealed not unprofitable to be known. It may be defined the wise, free, just, eternal and unchangeable sentence or decree of God, determining to create and govern man for his special glory. . . . Election is the decree of God, of his free love, grace and mercy, choosing some men to faith, holiness and eternal life, for the praise of his glorious mercy. . . . The cause which

61. Thomas Armitage, *A History of the Baptists* (New York: Bryan, Taylor & Co., 1887), pp. 671, 673.

moved the Lord to elect them who are chosen, was none other but his mere good will and pleasure. . . . A man in this life may be sure of his election . . . but not of his eternal reprobation; for he that is now pro- phane may be called hereafter.[62]

Obadiah Holmes's Confession and Testimony are preserved in the same volume.[63] The spirit of evangelical Calvinism penetrates the en- tirety: God "knows who are his; and the elect shall obtain it," for in the covenant of grace "God hath laid the iniquity of all his elect and called ones upon him [the Son]" so that they "shall never fall away nor perish." God bestows his salvation by effecting faith through a preaching ministry sent into the world "to publish repentance to the sinner, and salvation, and that by Jesus Christ." Yes, these ministers are to declare "the grace of God through Jesus Christ, even to those that are yet in the power of satan: yea to bring glad tidings by and from the Lord Jesus Christ."[64]

The First Baptist Church of Boston arose under the downpour of ecclesiastical intimidation as Thomas Gould sought answers about the baptism of children, especially his own child, born in 1655. After ten years of confusing browbeating from the established church in Boston, Gould—along with several others who had recently come from Eng- land, including a Mr. Goodall from William Kiffin's church—entered into a church relationship. This church was also Calvinistic.[65]

One cannot take seriously the contention that these men simply adopted their soteriology from their theological milieu without critical examination. At least two factors should dissuade any from accepting such an argument. First, their radical departure from the ecclesiology of their contemporaries and neighbors, plus their willingness to suffer for this separation, shows that they were not void of personal initiative in doctrinal construction. Their openness to argue their case before men of intimidating educational credentials marks them not as arro- gant (for they were meek men), but as confident of conclusions drawn from honest and independent inquiry. Second, their insistence that all belief and practice must have a plain and clear scriptural warrant speaks highly of their retention of Calvinism while altering their view of baptism. Other soteriological options were available and known to them. We must conclude, therefore, that they conscientiously and

---

62. John Clarke, "Confession of Faith," in Isaac Backus, *A History of New England, with Particular Reference to the Denomination of Christians Called Baptists*, 2 vols. (Bos- ton: Edward Draper, 1777), 1:255, 256.
63. Ibid., pp. 208–212, 256–260.
64. Ibid., pp. 256, 258, 259.
65. Ibid., pp. 355–415.

knowledgeably adhered to Calvinism as biblical in its soteriological connections.

INTO THE EIGHTEENTH AND NINETEENTH CENTURIES

The Middle Colonies, especially Pennsylvania, benefited from the influence of the Keach family almost as much as had the English Baptists of the seventeenth century. Benjamin Keach's son, Elias, came to the New World an unconverted man. For a brief period he found great fun duping the dissenting Christians of Pennsylvania by preaching to them some of his father's sermons. Great crowds came to hear the young London divine, and his jocular experiment appeared to be faring well. In the midst of his preaching on one occasion, he was seized with terror and for a while could not continue speaking. In the mercy of God, the young Keach was converted under his own preaching and was instrumental in founding the first Baptist church in Pennsylvania—at Pennepack, now within the city of Philadelphia.

Keach, along with Thomas Killingsworth, founded other churches. Another moved intact from Wales. In 1707 these churches, now five in number, organized to form the first Baptist association in America, the Philadelphia Baptist Association. This association regularly used the Second London Confession in its doctrinal discussions and in 1742 officially adopted it with two additions as its own Confession of Faith. By far the most influential association in Baptist life in America, its power was felt greatly in the First Great Awakening, and its Calvinistic theology was formative and dominant in Baptist life in both the North and South. So strong was the Calvinism of this association that in 1752 it passed a resolution affirming that such as rejected the doctrine of unconditional election could not be members of the churches:

> Upon which fundamental doctrines of Christianity, next to the belief of an eternal God, our faith must rest; and we adopt, and would that all the churches belonging to the Baptist Association be well grounded in accordance to our Confession of faith and catechism, and cannot allow that any are true members of our churches who deny the said principles, be their conversation outward what it will.[66]

In 1774 the association adopted the practice of giving "observations and improvements of some particular article of faith, contained in our Confession."[67] These yearly "circular letters" form quite delightful ex-

66. *Minutes of the Philadephia Baptist Association from 1707 to 1807* (Philadelphia: American Baptist Publication Society, 1851), p. 69.
67. Ibid., p. 136.

positions of evangelical Calvinism. Correspondence carried on with William Carey and enthusiastic reports on the progress of missions abroad and among the Indians and in unchurched areas of America show that the members of this group maintained a healthy alliance between doctrine and practice.

In the South, the first Baptist church was also Calvinistic. The First Baptist Church of Charleston, South Carolina (actually founded in 1682 in Kittery, Maine), adopted the Second London Confession as a valid summary of its biblical faith. William Screven, upon his retirement as first pastor in 1708, urged the church to secure as pastor a man who held to the doctrines set forth in that confession. In 1751, when the Charleston Association came into being, its doctrinal understanding found accurate expression in that same document. One of the most notable pastors of the state (and indeed in the South) during the decades straddling the turn of the nineteenth century was Richard Furman. From 1787 to 1825 he served as pastor of First Baptist Church of Charleston, South Carolina. In addition, he served as first president of the General Missionary Convention of the Baptist Denomination of the United States for Foreign Missions, known also as the Triennial Convention, established in 1814. He was a staunch Calvinist.

As Baptists moved into other parts of the South, some General Baptists appeared among them. These, however, were largely swallowed up by an aggressive and warm Calvinism in the First Great Awakening during the middle of the eighteenth century. Additionally, Baptist membership grew by leaps and bounds due to the invasion of Separate Baptists. This group, whose early leaders were Shubal Stearns and Daniel Marshall, held a strong conversion theology, manifest admirable responsibility for evangelistic organization, and fervently expected powerful movements of the Holy Spirit when they preached. They had arisen initially out of New England Congregationalism. The New Lights were opposed by the Old Lights, who insisted on identifying adherence to the confession of faith and external morality with true Christian faith. Jonathan Edwards defended the New Light insistence on conversion. When many of the New Lights began to adopt Baptist ecclesiology because of its harmony with the ideal of a regenerate church, they were naturally hesitant about the use of any confession of faith. Their theology, however, was Calvinistic and when, often haltingly, they did produce confessions, their Calvinism was obvious. The Confession of Faith of the Kehukee Association, a Regular Baptist Association, paved the way for the union with several Separate Baptist churches. Two of the seventeen articles deal with the sovereignty of God in salvation:

7. We believe that in God's appointed time and way (by means which He has ordained) the elect shall be called, justified, pardoned and sanctified, and that it is impossible they can utterly refuse the call, but shall be made willing by divine grace to receive the offers of mercy. . . .

9. We believe, in like manner, that God's elect shall not only be called, and justified, but that they shall be converted, born again, and changed by the effectual workings of God's holy Spirit.[68]

Likewise, the Sandy Creek Association, the most influential Separate Baptist grouping of the eighteenth century, adopted a confession in 1816. Articles III and IV (out of ten articles) indicate the soteriological commitments of Sandy Creek and the multiplicity of Separate Baptist churches and associations that arose from its influence:

III. That Adam fell from his original state of purity, and that his sin is imputed to his posterity; that human nature is corrupt, and that man, of his own free will and ability, is impotent to regain the state in which he was primarily placed.

IV. We believe in election from eternity, effectual calling by the Holy Spirit of God, and justification in his sight only by the imputation of Christ's righteousness. And we believe that they who are thus elected, effectually called, and justified, will persevere through grace to the end, that none of them be lost.[69]

When Separate Baptists and Regular Baptists united in Virginia, the Philadelphia Confession of Faith formed the doctrinal basis. Therefore, by the time that union was complete, Baptist life in the South was characterized by strong doctrinal commitments to evangelical Calvinism, a sense of dependence upon the working of the Holy Spirit to bring about conversion (often in a dramatic fashion), and a conviction of stewardship about evangelistic organization.

The rising of Free Will Baptists, under the leadership of Benjamin Randall in the 1780s in New Hampshire, prompted New England Baptists to work through a restatement of their faith, with some special attention given to areas highlighted by the Free Will movement. In 1833 the New Hampshire Confession of Faith was completed and recommended for adoption to the churches of New Hampshire. Its influence was greatly widened in 1853, when J. Newton Brown, editorial secretary to the American Baptist Publication Society, published it in *The Baptist Church Manual*. Other church manuals, including that of

68. William L. Lumpkin, *Baptist Confessions of Faith*, 1st. ed. (Philadelphia: The Judson Press, 1959), pp. 355, 356.

69. Ibid., p. 358.

J. M. Pendleton, also published it, making it the most widely disseminated creedal declaration of American Baptists.

Many have interpreted the contents of the New Hampshire Confession of Faith as an attempt to modify the strong Calvinism of earlier days into something more palatable to the tastes of eighteenth-century churches. It is true that it is not as detailed or as lengthy as the Philadelphia Confession, but it is also true that the substance of its doctrine remains unchanged. One of its concerns is succinctness. But its framers additionally desired to show that the issues raised by the presence of the Free Will Baptists were certainly not foreign to the knowledge or concerns of historic Calvinism. One emphasis recurring in the Free Will framework of theology was the culpability of man. Culpability extends only as far as the freeness of man's will and/or the provisions of God's grace. The "power of free choice is the exact measure of man's responsibility," said Benjamin Randall.[70] And if the fall has affected the will negatively, redemption by the Triune God has placed all men on equal footing: none are excluded, but neither is salvation actually procured for anyone:

> They are all dependent for salvation upon the redemption effected through the blood of Christ, and upon being created anew unto obedience through the operation of the Spirit; both of which are freely provided for every descendant of Adam.[71]

The same teaching constituted the essence of their concept of the gospel call. The call of the gospel "is co-extensive with the atonement to all men," as are the "strivings of the Spirit." Salvation, therefore, is "rendered possible to all." If anyone fails to be saved, "the fault is wholly his own."[72]

The framers of the New Hampshire Confession were justifiably eager for people to understand and see it fully and unequivocally stated that Calvinism was not a mechanically fatalistic system but rather took full cognizance of the moral nature of man, the duties incumbent upon him as a result of that moral nature, and the relationship of the gospel to these duties. The article on the fall of man sets the theological stage for this progression:

> We believe that man was created in a state of holiness under the law of his Maker; but by voluntary transgression fell from that holy and happy state; in consequence of which all mankind are now sinners, not by

70. Ibid., p. 370.
71. Ibid., p. 371.
72. Ibid., p. 373.

constraint but choice, being by nature utterly void of that holiness required by the law of God, wholly given to the gratification of the world, of Satan, and of their own sinful passions, therefore, under just condemnation to eternal ruin, without defense or excuse.[73]

Sin is willful, condemnation is just, and all men (with or without the provision of salvation) are without defense or excuse. Man's full duty to God is in no sense abrogated by the appearance of grace.

Article VI, "Of the Freeness of Salvation," outlines the way in which man's depravity relates to the free and open preaching of the gospel:

We believe that the blessings of salvation are made free to all by the Gospel; that it is the immediate duty of all to accept them by a cordial, penitent, and obedient faith; and that nothing prevents the salvation of the greatest sinner on earth except his own inherent depravity and voluntary refusal to submit to the Lord Jesus Christ, which refusal will subject him to an aggravated condemnation.[74]

Calvinism in no way eliminates man's responsibility for believing all that God says; its affirmation of depravity and the necessity for divine initiative are not made at the cost of man's full duty to God. The harmony between the law and the gospel demonstrates this truth, for the law "is holy, just, and good; and . . . the inability which the Scriptures ascribe to fallen men to fulfill its precepts, arises entirely from their love of sin."[75] In regeneration, the Holy Spirit works in such a way as to "secure our voluntary obedience to the Gospel."[76] In addition, "repentance and faith are sacred duties"; but the fact that they are duties in no way diminishes the reality that they are "also inseparable graces, wrought in our souls by the regenerating Spirit of God."[77] The fact that inability flows from sin doesn't eliminate the reality of the inability. Sovereign grace must reign if any of these desperate sinners are to be saved. This balance is clearly expressed in the article "Of God's Purpose of Grace."

We believe that Election is the gracious purpose of God, according to which he graciously regenerates, sanctifies, and saves sinners; that being perfectly consistent with the free agency of man, it comprehends all the means in connection with the end; that it is a most glorious display of God's sovereign goodness, being infinitely free, wise, holy, and

73. Ibid., p. 362.
74. Ibid., p. 363.
75. Ibid., p. 365.
76. Ibid., p. 364.
77. Ibid.

unchangeable; that it utterly excludes boasting, and promotes humility, love, prayer, praise, trust in God, and active imitation of his free mercy; that it encourages the use of means in the highest degree; that it is ascertained by its effects in all who truly believe the gospel; that it is the foundation of Christian assurance; and that to ascertain it with regard to ourselves, demands and deserves our utmost diligence.[78]

This same concern for the proper relation between the divine and the human aspects of salvation informs the article "Of the Perseverance of Saints." The Free Will Baptists warned believers to "watch and pray lest they make shipwreck of their faith and be lost."[79] Although grace will help them, the believers' infirmities and temptations may be so strong that "their future obedience and final salvation are neither determined nor certain."[80] The Calvinistic Baptists were no less solicitous of watchfulness, but they were determined to attribute the watchfulness and perseverance to the faithfulness of God to his people. If indeed one has experienced God's sovereign goodness in regeneration, it will certainly be evidenced in a new affection directed toward the things of God. Its source and continuance are not dependent on the strength of the human will but rather on the power of God:

> We believe that such only are real believers as endure to the end; that their persevering attachment to Christ is the grand mark which distinguishes them from mere professors; that a special Providence watches over their welfare; and that they are kept by the power of God through faith unto salvation.[81]

Rather than interpreting the New Hampshire Confession as a gradual retreat from the Calvinism of former days, it is better to see it as an affirmation of the Calvinist position on the particular issues raised by the presence and growth of Free Will Baptists in New England. The Calvinists did not jettison their distinguishing tenets but rather were saying, "We have a defensible and biblical understanding of the relation of man's will and duty to the doctrines of God's sovereignty." The activities and leaders of American Baptists of the North harmonize well with the leading features of this confession. Chapter four enfleshes these concepts in the ministries of Isaac Backus, John Leland, Luther Rice, Adoniram Judson, Francis Wayland, and David Benedict. Bap-

78. Ibid.
79. Ibid., p. 374.
80. Ibid.
81. Ibid., p. 365.

tists in the South still preferred the Philadelphia Confession of Faith but felt no theological division from their Northern brethren.

The last half of the nineteenth century saw an almost imperceptible and very gradual alienation from thoroughgoing Calvinism on the part of Baptists in the North who separated in 1845 from their Southern counterparts. David Benedict (chapter four) feared that such would happen if trends he noticed in 1860 continued. By the time of A. H. Strong (chapter eight), the forces of biblical criticism and evolution (both biological and ideological) were so pervasive and compelling that schools and theologians in the North found no way to combat them. Strong's attempt to incorporate them into a defense of orthodoxy, though brilliant at times and valiant always, failed to convince his contemporaries and surrendered too much ground in the process. Both of these changes—the loss of Calvinism and the intrusion of liberalism—expressed themselves in the unions and divisions that were to characterize Northern Baptist life in the twentieth century.

TWENTIETH-CENTURY TRENDS

By the first decade of the twentieth century, the Free Will Baptists—from whom Northern Baptists had remained distinct confessionally and organizationally during the nineteenth century—saw very little difference between themselves and their Northern contemporaries. Northern Baptists had adopted a convention structure for their various societies in 1907 and became officially denominated the Northern Baptist Convention. In 1911 the Free Will Baptists merged with the larger body of Baptists in the North, giving visual and organizational demonstration of the demise of the once-strong Calvinism of that denomination. No such merger was possible with the Free Will Baptists in the South, since the Calvinism of Southern Baptists was still vigorous.

The intrusion of liberalism caused several schisms from the Northern body. The temporary appearance of the Fundamental Fellowship in 1921 eventually produced the Conservative Baptist Association in 1947. The General Association of Regular Baptists was formed from conservative churches that withdrew from the Northern Baptist Convention in 1933. They adopted the New Hampshire Confession of Faith, with a premillennial interpretation of the last article. In 1923 the Baptist Bible Union of America, led by T. T. Shields, was formed. It reached its height in 1928 and eventually disintegrated. This group's confession was very similar to the New Hampshire Confession, with phrases added to speak directly to the doctrines affected by the liberalism of the day. Other groups registered protests against the liberalism of the Northern Baptist Convention.

It is significant that none of these groups was formed to protect doctrines strictly Calvinistic, although the New Hampshire Confession had a large influence upon all of them. The main sources of division concerned the inerrancy of Scripture, the deity of Christ, the virgin birth, the eternality of the punishment of the unbeliever, and to some extent, the nature of the second coming of Christ. Individual Calvinists and Calvinistic churches have arisen in these groups. Some churches influenced by T. T. Shields hold these tenets. Liberty Baptist Seminary, the present hub of Baptist fundamentalism, has been criticized by the *Sword of the Lord* for allowing Calvinists a place of influence on the faculty. None were self-consciously Calvinistic in their origins, however, but were more concerned for separatistic purity and fundamental conservatism. Nevertheless, their forebears were strictly and joyfully Calvinistic, since their origin rested in Northern Baptist life, and at certain points along the way they have received some numbers and support from fundamentalists separating from Southern Baptists.

When the complex sectional factors of the mid-nineteenth century prompted the formation of the Southern Baptist Convention in 1845, the desire for unfettered involvement in worldwide missions was at the heart of the separation. Calvinistic theology formed the basis for the mission program. Books and sermons defending the doctrines of total depravity, unconditional election, certain and effectual atonement, effectual calling, and perseverance of the saints abound from these early leaders. Chapters five and six demonstrate this by discussing the contributions of W. B. Johnson, R. B. C. Howell, Richard Fuller, Jesse Mercer, John L. Dagg, P. H. Mell, Basil Manly, Sr., Basil Manly, Jr., J. P. Boyce, and John A. Broadus. Within that list of names we find the presidents of the Southern Baptist Convention for the first approximately fifty years of its existence, the first educators in both college and seminary circles, and the first theological writers of Southern Baptist life. These doctrinal formulations not only represented the commitment of the elite but were strongly felt in churches and associations. For example, the founding documents of the Mississippi Baptist Association, consisting of the greatest portions of the present states of Mississippi and Louisiana, included a Confession of Faith in which the Doctrines of Grace are quite prominent and painfully clear:

3. We believe in the fall of Adam and impartation of his head (sin) to all his posterity; in the total depravity of the human nature and man's inability to restore himself to the favor of God.

4. We believe in the everlasting love of God to His people and the eternal unconditional election of a definite number of the human family to grace and glory.

5. We believe that sinners are only justified in the sight of God by the imputed righteousness of Jesus Christ, which is unto all and upon all them that believe.

6. We believe all those who were chosen in Christ before the foundation of the world are in time effectually called, regenerated, converted, and sanctified and are kept by the power of God through faith unto salvation.

7. We believe there is one mediator between God and man, the man Christ Jesus; who by the satisfaction which he made to the law and justice "in becoming an offering for sin" hath, by His most precious blood, redeemed the elect from under the curse of the law: that they might be holy and without blame before Him in love.[82]

This consensus in the Doctrines of Grace was perpetuated in Southern Baptist life through the second decade of the present century. Chapters eight and nine seek to establish this by examining the thought of F. H. Kerfoot, E. C. Dargan, J. B. Gambrell, J. B. Tidwell, and B. H. Carroll. These men were leaders as heads of agencies in the Southern Baptist community, editors of denominational papers, educators, and writers. In 1905 F. H. Kerfoot could still say, "Nearly all Baptists believe what are usually termed the 'doctrines of grace.' "

This virtually unanimous belief disintegrated along the way. Among several contributing factors, most prominent from a content standpoint, were the theological methodology of E. Y. Mullins and the evangelistic methodology of L. R. Scarborough, presidents of Southern Seminary and Southwestern Seminary respectively. (This phenomenon is discussed in chapter nine.) Vestiges of the old doctrines still remained in places, as in the teaching and writing of W. T. Conner, of Southwestern Seminary (especially on the doctrine of election) and in the faithful ministry of J. B. Tidwell at Baylor University (chapter seven). With ever-increasing rapidity, however, concerns focused more and more on denominational programs that minimized and streamlined doctrinal materials. The doctrines were first ignored till they passed from the scene—and finally were either opposed openly as destructive of true piety and mission zeal or discussed as some idiosyncrasy of the past, to be recoiled from with great horror.

Crises related to biblical authority, the necessity of the atonement, and the uniqueness of Christianity as the way to God have come to Southern Baptists only because the doctrines of God's sovereignty were first jettisoned from their proper place as the fountainhead from which all other doctrines receive their coherence. Some of these issues

82. *Amite County, Mississippi, 1699–1865*, 2 vols., Albert E. Casey, comp. (n.p., 1950), pp. 128, 129.

are touched upon in the theological chapters (ten through thirteen). Southern Baptists can only expect further theological fragmentation unless God in his mercy grants a Reformation comparable to that which occurred in sixteenth-century Europe.

It is the prayer of this author that this denomination, which has all the trappings of greatness, may escape the solemn reality graphically pictured in our Lord's description of some in his day: whitewashed sepulchers, clean and bright on the outside—but inside full of dead men's bones.

Historical Evidence

1

The Longest Journey Begins

Arminians in the Vicinity

Baptist life began in England with a division between the Arminian and Calvinistic Baptists. The General Baptists, so-called because of their affirmation of general atonement, had their origin in the life and thought of John Smyth and his loyal but self-motivated church member, Thomas Helwys. While they began within the stream of Calvinistic Puritanism and Separatism, under the influence of the Mennonites in Holland they came to reject some of the more prominent features of Calvinism and affirmed the anti-Augustinianism of the Anabaptists.

Smyth himself went to the point of considering the peculiar Christology of the Mennonites a matter of indifference. He also affirmed their view of justification, a view similar to that of medieval Roman Catholicism, excepting sacraments.

In his "Short Confession of Faith in XX Articles," Smyth confesses that Jesus was conceived "in the womb of the Virgin Mary" but does not exclude the possibility of Mary's being a receptacle for a new kind of flesh created from heaven. By contrast, Helwys affirms that Jesus received his flesh "of hir substance." In addition, Smyth forsook the doctrine of justification by faith as understood by the Reformers and replaced it with the Roman Catholic synthesis between justification and sanctification:

> That the justification of man before the Divine tribunal (which is both the throne of justice and of mercy), consists partly of the imputation of the righteousness of Christ apprehended by faith, and partly of inherent

55

Benjamin Keach

John Bunyan

righteousness, in the holy themselves, by the operation of the Holy Spirit, which is called regeneration or sanctification: since any one is righteous, who doeth righteousness.[1]

This construction of justification lays to waste all the gains of the Reformation. Sanctification in Reformation thought, though essential and inevitable in the justified person, is not to be construed as a part of justification. Rather, justification is to be seen solely in terms of the imputed righteousness of Christ, as Paul affirms in Philippians 3, and as Helwys sought to protect in his Confession of Faith when he said, "Man is justified onely by the righteousness off CHRIST, apprehended by faith."[2]

In addition to his attempt to maintain justification by faith, Helwys believed total depravity to be a biblical doctrine. Men are "by nature the Children off wrath," are born in "iniquitie and in sin conceived." Other features of his former Calvinism simply appeared too harsh. Falling by the wayside were particular atonement, irresistible grace, unconditional election, and even perseverance of the saints. In Article 7 of his Confession, Helwys openly asserts that "men may fall away from the grace off God . . . and from the truth, which they have received & acknowledged." In light of this, Helwys warns, "Let no man presume to thinke that because he hath or had once grace, therefore he shall alwaies have grace."[3]

General Baptist life had severe problems with a form of Unitarianism in the late seventeenth century, leading to the publication of a confession entitled "The Orthodox Creed." The next century also saw a massive falling away into Unitarianism, leading to the formation of the New Connection of General Baptists under the leadership of Dan Taylor. Eventually the New Connection was the only strain of General Baptists who survived until the formation of the Baptist Union in 1891.

Exsurge Calvinistice

Particular Baptists arose out of the context of a Separatist congregation named after its three pastors: Jacob, Lathrop, and Jessey. Having adopted believer's baptism in 1638, they affirmed baptism by immersion in 1641 and by 1644 produced a Confession of Faith. In

1. William L. Lumpkin, *Baptist Confessions of Faith* (Valley Forge: Judson Press, 1969), p. 101.
2. Ibid., p. 118.
3. Ibid., pp. 118, 119.

large part this statement, the First London Confession, was based upon a Separatist confession written by Henry Ainsworth, a member of the Separatist congregation of Francis Johnson. It was decidedly and clearly Calvinistic. For example, touching election, the confession states in Article III:

> . . . and touching his creature man God had in Christ before the foundation of the world according to the good pleasure of his will foreordained some men to eternal life through Jesus Christ to the praise and glory of his grace leaving the rest in their sin to their just condemnation to the praise of his justice.[4]

The confession confirms with equal clarity that fallen man is so depraved that he would never turn and convert himself without the irresistible movement of the Spirit of God. Article XXIV states:

> . . . faith is ordinarily begot by the preaching of the gospel or word of Christ without respect to any power or capactiy in the creature but it is wholly passive being dead in sins and trespasses, doth believe, and is converted by no less power, than that which raised Christ from the dead.[5]

This served as reaffirmation of Article XXII, which said that faith is the *gift* of God *wrought* in the hearts of the elect *by* the Spirit of God, whereby they come to see, know and believe the truth of the Scriptures, and so on.

Nor was the doctrine of particular atonement veiled in any cloak of mystery, for Article XVII states, ". . . touching his priesthood Christ being consecrated hath appeared once to put away sin by the offering and sacrifice of himself and to this end hath fully performed and suffered all those things by which God through the blood of that his cross in an acceptable sacrifice might reconcile his elect only." Likewise, Article XXI says that "Christ Jesus by his death did bring forth salvation and reconciliation only for the elect which were those which God the Father gave him."

Article XXIII is one of the most beautiful and noble statements of the preservation of the saints that appears in any confession:

> Those that have this precious faith wrought in them by the Spirit, can never finally nor totally fall away; and though many storms and floods do arise and beat against them, yet they shall never be able to take them

4. Ibid., p. 157.
5. Ibid., p. 163.

off that foundation and rock which by faith they are fastened upon, but shall be kept by the power of God to salvation, where they shall enjoy their purchased possession, they being formerly engraven upon the palms of God's hands.[6]

It should be noted, however, that this is only half of the true doctrine of perseverance.

Other articles in this confession appear equally strong in affirming the providence of God and his sovereignty over every activity of all of his creatures.

Almost incredibly, William Lumpkin characterizes the theology of the confession as a "moderate type" of Calvinism. One wonders what "moderate" must mean in such a context, for every major and peculiar tenet of Calvinistic soteriology finds unmistakable expression in the confession. Lumpkin further states that "there is no teaching of reprobation."[7] Article XIX, however, stands in stark contrast to such an affirmation:

> Touching his Kingdome, Christ being risen from the dead, . . . doth spiritually govern his Church, exercising his power over all Angels and Men, good and bad, to the preservation and salvation of the elect, to the overruling and destruction of his enemies, which are Reprobates. . . . And . . . ruling in the world over his enemies, Satan, and all the vessels of wrath, limiting, using, restraining them by his mighty power, as seems good in his divine wisdome & justice to the execution of his determinate counsell, delivering them up to a reprobate mind, to be kept through their own deserts, in darkness and sensuality unto judgement.[8]

That Confession of Faith, written during the Puritan revolution, was satisfactory to introduce Baptists to their contemporaries. It had a marvelous effect in repressing scurrilous rumors about the Baptists. Many times and in numerous writings, Baptists had been identified with the extreme radical revolutionaries on the Continent. This confession did much to alleviate the suspicions under which they toiled.

The next forty years brought unparalleled changes in the political situation in England. A king's army was defeated by his own subjects, and the king, Charles I, was beheaded; Oliver Cromwell, a commoner, was raised to the position of Protector of England; and the fifth monarchy movement wooed many Baptists into vigorous and revolution-

6. Ibid.
7. Ibid., p. 146.
8. Ibid., pp. 161, 162.

ary political activity, even against Cromwell. After the death of Cromwell, the profligate Stuart line was restored to the throne. The Clarendon Code, a series of four repressive acts, came into effect in the years 1661–1665, bringing Baptists and other Protestant dissenters under great persecution.

In light of these changes, Baptists felt the need to identify themselves with a large body of non-Anglican Protestants. In 1646 the Westminster Assembly adopted the Westminster Confession of Faith. In 1655 the Congregationalists, with a few changes, virtually duplicated this in a confession they called "The Savoy Declaration." Following suit, Baptists in London adopted a second statement, appropriately called "The Second London Confession." In the introduction to this document, the Baptists restated the reasons for having written the 1644 Confession, affirmed their pleasure at its results, and then stated:

> . . . and for as much as that Confession is not now commonly to be had; and also that many others have since embraced the same truth which is owned therein; it was judged necessary by us to join together in giving a testimony to the world; of our firm adhering to those wholesome Principles by the publication of this which is now in your hand.[9]

They went on to affirm that though the method and manner of expressing their thoughts varied, "the substance of the matter is the same." They felt constrained to explain the reason for this procedure. In their effort to show their great agreement with the other Protestant bodies, they decided to "make use of the very same words with them both in those articles which are very many wherein our faith and doctrine is the same with theirs." In a humble spirit they stated that "we have no itch to clog religion with new words, but to readily acquiesce [sic] in that form of sound words which hath been, in consent with the holy scriptures, used by others before us."[10]

Although none could doubt the very clear soteriological Calvinism of this confession, it would be too presumptuous not to quote at least one or two articles. In chapter three, concerning God's decree, paragraphs three and four state:

> By the decree of God, for the manifestation of his glory some men and Angels are predestinated, or fore-ordained to Eternal Life, through Jesus Christ, to the praise of his glorious grace; others being left to act in their sin to their just condemnation, to the praise of his glorious justice.

9. Ibid., p. 244.
10. Ibid., p. 245.

These Angels and Men thus predestinated, and fore-ordained are particularly and unchangeably designed, and their number so certain, and definite, that it cannot be either increased, or diminished.[11]

This chapter also contains an admonition to great care in the use of the high doctrine of predestination by stating that it is "to be handled with special prudence and care," so that the doctrine will not detract from the glory of God but rather will "afford matter of praise, reverence and admiration of God and of humility, diligence, and abundant consolation to all that sincerely obey the gospel."

In addition, the confession asserts that man's fall has made him "utterly indisposed, disabled, and made opposite to all good" so that he has lost all "ability of Will, to any spiritual good accompanying salvation." Such a man is unable to convert himself; he is saved only when by effectual calling he is enabled to "embrace the grace offered" by no less power than that which raised Christ from the dead. Only those predestinated unto life are effectually called and, therefore, "freely justified." The possibility of such a salvation was purchased by Christ, the Mediator. By his perfect obedience and sacrifice, he has fully satisfied the justice of God and has obtained reconciliation and purchased an everlasting inheritance "for all those whom the Father hath given unto him." Those thus elected, redeemed, called, justified, and sanctified by the Spirit "can neither totally nor finally fall from the state of grace; but shall certainly persevere therein to the end and be eternally saved."

This perseverance of the Saints depends not upon their own free will; but upon the immutability of the decree of Election, flowing from the free and unchangeable love of God the Father; upon the efficacy of the merit and intercession of Jesus Christ and Union with him, the oath of God, the abiding of his spirit & the seed of God within them, and the nature of the Covenant of Grace from all which ariseth also the certainty and infallibility thereof.[12]

Seeing that the doctrine of perseverance rests upon such a foundation, a ripping asunder of the foundation will ultimately cause the collapse of the superstructure. Those who seek to maintain "once-saved-always-saved," without the supporting doctrines of at least unconditional election and effectual calling, may be hard-pressed to make their case.

11. Ibid., p. 254.
12. Ibid., p. 273.

Benjamin Keach

One of the Baptists most instrumental in the adoption of this confession of faith was the pastor at Horse-lie-down—Benjamin Keach. Cathcart records about Keach that "at first he was an Arminian about the extent of the atonement and free will, but the reading of the Scriptures and the conversation of those who knew the will of God more perfectly relieved him from both errors."[13] In the production of expositional, sermonic, and theological material, Keach is rivaled in Baptist life by only John Gill. Having published forty-three separate works before his death, he was spoken of as the "famous Mr. Keach." Nor was his an ivory-tower experience, for under the Clarendon Code he suffered physical persecution and great humiliation before his peers as a result of maintaining the Baptist faith.

In one of his most popular and widely read works, *Exposition of the Parables*, Keach affirms the Doctrines of Grace in unmistakable terms. From the parable of the householder in Matthew 20, Keach draws the following conclusion about backsliders:

> Because some imitate the true Christian, or counterfeit Christians come to nothing, doth it follow a true Christian may come to nothing also? Or because an artificial motion may fail, must a natural motion fail likewise? The sole of your shoe wears out, but the sole of your foot grows thicker and harder, and wears not out by going barefooted; because there is not life in the one, but there is life in the other. Hypocrites fall, but the upright in heart remain unmoveable.[14]

In treating verses 14 through 16 of Matthew 20, Keach deals at length with the doctrine of election and predestination. He states that "election is an act of God's sovereignty or the good pleasure of his will; for which he passed by the fallen angels, and only sets his heart upon, and chooses some of the lost sons of Adam. Election necessarily presupposeth some chosen, and the rest passed by."[15]

Again, after contending for a sublapsarian view of reprobation (men reprobated when considered as fallen), he says that "election to everlasting life is an absolute act of God's sovereign grace without any respect had to our foreseen faith, of holiness, or obedience, because election is the cause of our faith and holiness, and not faith and holiness that cause election." He then quotes Acts 13:48 and Ephesians

---

13. *Cathcart's Baptist Encyclopaedia* (1881), s. v. Benjamin Keach.
14. Benjamin Keach, *Exposition of the Parables* (Grand Rapids: Kregel Publications, 1974), p. 528.
15. Ibid., p. 537.

1:4. Keach, able to rise to rhetorical heights even with pen and ink, destroys the notion of the possibility of free will contributing to salvation with the following display of words:

> If election and salvation was not alone of God's sovereign grace, it would be uncertain, depending wholly upon the inconsistent and wavering principles of the creature. My brethren, had it stood upon Adam's will and obedience, it had been more firm than to stand upon our depraved wills, power, and obedience, distinct from Almighty, sovereign, and irresistible grace in Christ, to secure our standing. For Adam had free will to do good in the state of innocency, but O how soon did he fall, though he had no depraved nature, and but a young devil to encounter withal!
>
> Election is wholly bottomed upon God's sovereign grace, because whatsoever is supposed (by our opponents) to be the condition of it, lies under God's decree to give unto us, as well as the election of our persons unto eternal life. God decreed to give his Spirit to his elect, to renew them, to sanctify them, and his grace, particularly faith to believe, and strength to persevere. "You have not chosen me, but I have chosen you, and ordained you, that you should go and bring forth fruit, and that your fruit should remain," John XV. 16. Is it the fruit of repentance? is it faith? is it obedience? or is it holiness? we are ordained to bear all this fruit, and that our fruit shall remain also, and never fail. "They shall not cease bearing fruit," Jer. XVII. 8.[16]

Keach continues to assert the sovereignty of God as the sole foundation for all salvific blessings. He affirms that "repentance is God's free and sovereign gift," and his mercy is bestowed solely by the "arbitrariness of his will and inclinations." His sovereignty in creation and in providence demonstrates that he does all "at his will and pleasure"; his blessings in salvation have come as a result of his choice, for "in these things God only acts in a way of sovereignty [and] it is his own will and pleasure so to do."[17]

In commenting on Matthew 5:25, 26—"Agree with thine adversary quickly [etc.]"—Keach talks about the peace that Jesus has wrought for the elect with God:

> 2. That our peace and reconciliation with God, is alone of his free grace. It is free to us, though Christ paid dear for it: sinners could not make their own peace with God, neither do anything to reconcile God to them, or them to God; no, God alone is the Author of it, and it flows from him as an act of infinite love, grace, and favor. He found out the great Peace-maker, he sent him into the world, he accepted him as our

16. Ibid., pp. 537–538.
17. Ibid., pp. 538, 539.

Surety in our stead; he anointed him, upheld him, and raised him up
from the dead; he, by the power of his Spirit, changes our hearts, bows
our wills, draws our affections, and makes us yield to receive the Lord
Jesus Christ, and to accept of that peace he made by his blood. . . .

4. That it is a certain, a sure, and an abiding peace; "The covenant
of my peace shall not be removed, saith the Lord who hath mercy on
thee." This peace is according to God's eternal counsel: it is founded
upon his unalterable decree and purpose in Jesus Christ, and it is confirmed by the blood of his Son, and the oath of God, Heb. vi. 17–19.
Shall any of them miss of peace and reconciliation with God, for whom
Christ died, and to whom this peace is applied? No, no, that is impossible. "Let God be true, and every man a liar."[18]

Keach's strong theology of sovereignty in no way diminished his
affirmation of man's responsibility to flee to Christ, repent of sin, and
strive to enter in at the straight gate. All must bow before God's sovereignty, for God may grant repentance; sinners must be exhorted to
come to Christ, for he is offered to sinners, as sick (or sensible) sinners.
Since only God grants repentance, and only his sovereign will determines how his grace is disposed, all should be reproved who "ascribe
the power of converting grace to the will of man, as if the will of man
determineth the whole success of preaching the gospel"[19] and thus
render the grace of God ineffectual. Neither should the doctrine of
election discourage anyone from coming to Christ. When a man is sick
he does not need to know God's decree for his life before he asks for
a physician. Nor can one determine his election before he sees the
fruits of effectual calling. Keach even pleads with the sinner: "Come
and be persuaded to put in for a share of God's sovereign favour! What
though but a few are chosen, nay but twenty in this great city . . . yet
how knowest thou but thou mayest be one of the twenty?"[20]

Why does God act in an absolutely sovereign way?

1. None would be saved if he did not.

2. In this way he manifests the eternality of his distinguishing love
and decrees.

3. A seed was given to Christ of whom he was sure before he laid
down his life, else his blood be shed in vain:

. . . and to the end his death might not be in vain, God singled out some
whom he gave to his Son, and for whom Christ in a special manner died,
and not for their good only, but in their stead also, so that them, he says,
he must bring, and none of them he must lose, John x. 16.[21]

18. Ibid., pp. 70–71.
19. Ibid., p. 542.
20. Ibid.
21. Ibid.

4. God magnifies his love and mercy to some, and his wrath and divine justice upon others; he has glory "in them that perish, as well as in them that are saved."

5. Believers may have strong consolation and "ascribe for ever the glory of their salvation to God's rich and distinguishing grace alone."

John Bunyan

Probably the most famous Baptist contemporary of Benjamin Keach was the inimitable John Bunyan, the famous author of *The Pilgrim's Progress, The Holy War, The Life and Death of Mr. Badman,* and other classics. Although finding himself in conflict with many seventeenth-century Baptists on the subject of church membership and communion with those unbaptized, Bunyan nevertheless is recognized as a Baptist in his personal theology. He did identify himself as among those who call themselves Anabaptists, although he disliked all such titles. In his polemical work entitled *Peaceful Principles and True,* he said: "And as for those fractious titles of Anabaptist, Independent, Presbyterians, or the like, I conclude, that they came neither from Jerusalem, nor Antioch, but rather from Hell and Babylon. . . ."[22] Although this controversy often waxed hot during his days, Bunyan's concordance with the Baptists in other areas of theology was quite evident.

In his Confession of Faith,[23] Bunyan confirms the basic christological orthodoxy accepted by all Christians in the seventeenth century. He then presented his understanding of the Bible's teaching on "how Christ is made ours." Central to the discussion is justification by faith, outlined in bright Protestant colors. Imputed righteousness infiltrates every corner of Bunyan's picture. Only faith, not works of the law, can possess this righteousness. However, this faith "is not to be found with any but those, in whom the Spirit of God by mighty power doth work it." Indeed Bunyan states, "I believe that this faith is effectually wrought in none, but those which before the world were appointed unto glory" [Acts 13:48; Rom. 9:23; 1 Thess. 1:2–4; John 10:26]. Clearly, Bunyan rests effectual calling upon the foundation of unconditional election. Bunyan states, "I believe that election is free and permanent, being founded in grace, in the unchangeable will of God." The time of this

22. John Bunyan, *The Whole Works of John Bunyan,* 3 vols., *Peaceful Principles and True* (Paternoster Row, London: Blackie & Sons, 1875; reprint ed., Grand Rapids: Baker Book House, 1977), 2:649.

23. Ibid., *A Confession of My Faith,* 2:594–601.

election, according to Bunyan, is before the foundation of the world and "so before the elect themselves, had being in themselves."

Election, since it is unconditional, looks to neither foreseen faith nor foreseen works as a stimulus. Rather, election "containeth in the bowels, not only the persons, but the graces that accompany their salvation. And hence it is, that it is said; we are predestinated 'to be conformed to the image of his Son' [Rom. 8:29]; not because we are, but 'that we should be holy and without blame before him in love' " (Eph. 1:4). In addition, election always has in view Christ Jesus, for he is the one "in whom the elect were always considered, and without Him there is neither election, grace, nor salvation."

Bunyan, quoting the chain of events in Romans 8:30–35, admits no impediment to God's accomplishing his intended purpose: "I believe that there is not any impediment attending the election of God, that can hinder their conversion, and eternal salvation." This leads Bunyan to explain that election *per se* is beyond the realm of observation and can only be known by subsequent events: a person's being called of God and his perseverance in the means made available for the Christian life. In this light Bunyan states:

> I believe therefore, election doth not forestall or prevent the means which are of God appointed to bring us to Christ, to grace and glory; but rather putteth a necessity upon the use and effect thereof; because they are chosen to be brought to heaven that way: that is, by the faith of Jesus Christ, which is the end of effectual calling.[24]

The same emphases found their way into Bunyan's discussion of effectual calling. This doctrine is election incarnate as it relates to its historical manifestation in the life of the elect person: "I believe, that to effectual calling, the Holy Ghost must accompany the word of the Gospel, and that with mighty power; I mean that calling, which of God is made to be the fruit of electing love."[25]

Bunyan sees the call of Lazarus from the grave as a paradigm of effectual calling, "a word attended with an arm that was omnipotent." And even though he recognizes the uniqueness of the calling of Paul, "As to the matter, and truth of the work, it was no other than all the chosen have: The God of our fathers hath chosen thee, that thou shouldest know his will, and see that Just One, and shouldest hear the voice of his mouth" (Acts 22:14).

Effectual calling produces the attitudes of faith, hope, and repen-

24. Ibid., p. 599.
25. Ibid.

tance in the hearts of the elect. Whosoever "misseth of effectual calling, misseth of eternal life." God justifies only those "whom he calleth; and glorifies none but those whom he justifies." Therefore if one would know whether he is elect he must "make your calling, and (so) your election sure: 'make it sure,' that is, prove your calling right, by the word of God."

In addition to his direct affirmation of unconditional election and effectual calling, Bunyan engages in a strong polemic defending the doctrine of reprobation. The work, *Reprobation Asserted: or, the Doctrine of Eternal Election and Reprobation Promiscuously Handled, in Eleven Chapters*, covers some twenty-two double-columned pages in volume two of *The Whole Works of John Bunyan*.[26] In short, Bunyan asserts that reprobation exists because election exists. Romans 11:7, only one of numerous Scriptures cited by Bunyan, states that "the election hath obtained it, and the rest were blinded." After arguing his point from this passage, he concludes: "By 'rest' here, must needs be understood those not elect, because set one in opposition unto the other; if not elect, what then but reprobate?"

Bunyan also argues that this decree of reprobation, identified with non-election, was made before the foundation of the world while people were considered upright in Adam as an unfallen creature.

This is pure supralapsarian Calvinism. Neither Keach nor Gill (to be discussed in chapter two) maintained this view. Keach rejected it, and Gill sought to combine it with sublapsarian doctrine. That supralapsarian Calvinism was defended so strongly by Bunyan should put to rest the mistake that some make of identifying supralapsarianism with hyper-Calvinism. No Baptist was ever more warmly evangelistic than Bunyan, and none ever held to supralapsarianism more intently and purely.

Election, according to Bunyan, arises solely from the grace of God and is not prompted by any condition in the creature; likewise reprobation does not come with respect to sin but solely out of the free choice of God.

Bunyan ties reprobation to the very nature of God; in his infinite power and wisdom he brings all things into being and decrees every thing and action within creation for a purpose. Reprobation must subserve the sovereign purpose of God, because for his pleasure all things were and are created. Reprobation also highlights the distinction between distinguishing love and universal or general love. Not only does

---

26. Ibid., *Reprobation Asserted*, 2:336–358.

it highlight love, but reprobation gives an impressive picture of God's willingness to show his wrath and make his power known.[27]

According to Bunyan, eternal reprobation, just like eternal election, is unchangeable:

> This decree is made sure by the number, measure, bounds for election; for election and reprobation do inclose all reasonable creatures; that is either the one or the other; election, those that set apart for glory; and reprobation, those left out of this choice.[28]

Bunyan distinguishes between reprobation and foreordination unto eternal condemnation. Reprobation arises out of God's sovereignty; condemnation arises out of his justice. Reprobation simply leaves the creature out of the bounds of God's election; condemnation binds him to everlasting punishment. God's sovereignty operates in reprobation, for its only cause is the will of God; God's justice operates in condemnation, for its cause is the sin of man. Bunyan goes to great pains to seek to maintain this distinction, so as to remove from God the charge of actually making man a sinner that he might condemn him. In short, Bunyan asserts that sin entered the world by God's direct permission. God knew beforehand that all men would sin in Adam, the elect as well as the reprobate. Therefore, he covenanted with the Son for the salvation of the elect and prepared condemnation for reprobates, who would remain in their sin even though they were considered upright when reprobated.

Bunyan insisted that reprobation is not in itself a hindrance to any man's seeking the salvation of his soul. All men are encouraged to seek the Lord. In fact, "divers of the reprobate" have great encouragements, externally respond to the gospel, and at times even participate in the ministry of the Holy Spirit. But in the end all reprobates refuse to persevere in their seeking of the Lord.

In addition, Bunyan asserts that the gospel, with the grace thereof, "should be tendered to those that yet he hath bound up under eternal reprobation." We are commanded to preach to every creature. We see from New Testament examples that preaching of the gospel was done to all men indiscriminately. The gospel is not offered to men as elect or reprobate but is offered to men as sinners. The elect need the grace of Christ by the gospel only because they are sinners; nor are the reprobate caused to refuse it except by their sinfulness. Christ, through the words of the gospel, is to be proffered to both, without considering them either elect or reprobate but only that they are sinners.

27. Ibid., pp. 339–341.
28. Ibid., p. 341.

Nevertheless, Bunyan reiterates that it is not possible that the non-elect will receive the gospel and be saved. The reprobate will not receive the effectual working of the Spirit, without which even the elect would perish. Man in his fallen condition is dead in trespasses and sins; the natural man does not receive the things of the Spirit of God, for they are foolishness to him:

> Now I say, if the natural man at best (for the elect before conversion are no more, if quite so much) cannot do this, how shall they attain their due being now not only corrupted and infected, but depraved, bewitched and dead, swallowed up of unbelief, ignorance, confusion, hardness of heart, hatred of God, and the like?[29]

Thus, it is not simply because they are reprobated but because they are sinners that men refuse the gospel.

If there be those who are reprobate, why should the gospel even be preached to them? Bunyan gives four weighty reasons for this:

1. The preaching of the gospel to them shows that it is not reprobation that makes a man incapable of salvation but man's sinfulness.

2. The preaching of the gospel shows that God is willing to save all who will meet the demands of the gospel, although he is not resolved to save the reprobate but only resolved to save the elect:

> Wherefore you must consider that there is a distinction to be put between God's denying of grace on reasonable terms, and denying it absolutely; and also that there is a difference between his withholding further grace, and of hindering man from closing with the grace at present offered; also that God may withhold much, when he taketh away nothing; yea, take away much, when once abused, yet be just and righteous still. Further, God may deny to do this or that absolutely, when yet he hath promised to do, not only that, but more, conditionally. Which things considered, you may with ease, conclude, that he may be willing to save those not elect, upon reasonable terms, though not without them.[30]

3. The tender of the gospel to all men shows all spectators what an enemy is sin, being once embraced, to the salvation of man. By the gospel, sin appears exceedingly sinful.

4. God demands that the gospel be preached to all men so that sufficient means might be provided for the elect "both to beget them to faith and to maintain it in them to the end."[31]

A summary of the argument is quite well expressed by Bunyan in

29. Ibid., p. 350.
30. Ibid., p. 353.
31. Ibid., pp. 352, 354.

a doxology given to the grace and mercy of God. None have a claim upon God's electing love even as creatures, much less as sinners. This leads Bunyan to his paean of praise:

> Further, that all this should be the effect of unthought of, undeserved, undesired love! [Mal. 1:2; Deut. 7:7–8]. That the Lord should think on this before he made the world [Jer. 31:3] and sufficiently ordained means before he laid the foundation of the hills! For this he is worthy to be praised [1 Cor. 2:9]; yea, let everything that hath breath praise the Lord. Praise ye the Lord.[32]

Bunyan's concept of the universal offer of the gospel and its relation to God's sovereignty is expanded in his sermon "Come and Welcome to Jesus Christ," based upon John 6:37: "All that the Father giveth me shall come to me; and him that cometh to me I will in no wise cast out." This sermon consists of the two elements contained in the verse: God's absolute purpose to save his elect and the assurance by the mercy of God that none will be refused who come to Jesus Christ.

Bunyan strikes down objection after objection that men raise as to why they might not come to Christ; he appeals to them to flee to Christ for salvation. While doing so, along the way he affirms that only a particular few has the Father given to the Son; these and only these will come—and they will come absolutely.

In speaking of the word *all* Bunyan says that "wherefore that we may the better understand the mind of Christ in the use of it here we must consider that it is limited and restrained only to those that shall be saved; to wit, to those that shall come to Christ; even to those that he will in no wise cast out." Later he explains that these that come to Christ are only the particular ones given to him for the purpose of salvation. He states, "Those, therefore, intended as the gift in the text, they are those that are given by covenant to the Son, those that in other places are called the elect, the chosen, the sheep, and the children of the promise."[33]

As Bunyan closes his message, after having given the sinner every encouragement that can arise from the character of God and the freeness of salvation, he indulges his literary art to produce a matchless blending of God's sovereignty with urgent exhortation:

> Fourthly, I will add yet another Encouragement, for the Man that is coming to Jesus Christ. Art thou coming? Art thou coming, indeed? Why?

32. Ibid., p. 355.
33. John Bunyan, *The Miscellaneous Works of John Bunyan*, Vol. VIII, gen. ed., Roger Sharroch, *Come, and Welcome, to Jesus Christ*, ed. Richard L. Greaves (Oxford: At the Clarendon Press, 1979), p. 254.

1. Then this thy Coming, Is by Vertue of God's Call. Thou art Called; Calling goes before Coming: Coming is not of Works, but of him that Calleth. He went up into a Mountain, and called to him whom he would, and They came to him, Mark. 3.13.

Secondly, Art thou coming? This is also by the Vertue of Illumination. God has made thee see; and therefore, thou art coming. So long as thou wast Darkness, thou lovedst Darkness; and couldst not abide to come, because thy Deeds were Evil: But, being now Illuminated, and made to see, what, and where thou art; and also, what, and where thy Saviour is: Now thou art coming to Jesus Christ. Blessed art thou Simon Bar-Jona! for Flesh and Blood hath not Revealed it unto thee (said Christ) but my Father which is in Heaven; Matth. 16. 15, 16, 17.

Thirdly, Art thou coming, this is because God has Inclined thine heart to come; God hath called thee, illiminated thee, and inclined thy heart to come, and therefore thou comest to Jesus Christ. It is God that worketh in thee to Will, and to come to Jesus Christ. Coming sinner, bless God, for that he hath given thee a Will, to come to Jesus Christ. It is a Sign that thou belongest to Jesus Christ, because God has made thee willing to come to him (Psal. 110. 3.). Bless God for slaying the enmity of thy mind; had he not done it, thou wouldest, as yet, have hated thine own Salvation.

Fourthly, Art thou coming to Jesus Christ, it is God that giveth thee Power: power to pursue thy Will in the matters of thy Salvation, is the gift of God. 'Tis God that worketh in you both to Will and to Do, Phil. 2. 13. not that God worketh Will to come, where he gives no power; but thou shouldest take notice, that power is an additional Mercy. The Church saw that will and power were two things, when She cried, Draw me, we will run after thee (Song. 1. 4.): and so did David too, when he said, I will run the ways of thy Commandments, when thou shalt enlarge my Heart. Will to come, and power to pursue thy will, is a double Mercy, coming Sinner.

Fifth, All thy strange, passionate, sudden rushings forward after Jesus Christ (coming Sinners know what I mean), they also are thy helps from God. Perhaps thou feelest at sometimes, more than others, strong stirrings up of heart, to fly to Jesus Christ; now thou hast at this time a sweet, and stiff gale of the Spirit of God filling thy sails with the fresh gales of his good Spirit; and thou ridest at those times, as upon the wings of the wind, being carried out beyond thy self, beyond the most of thy prayers, and also above all thy fears and temptation.

Sixthly, coming Sinner, hast thou not, now and then, a kiss of the sweet lips of Jesus Christ? I mean, some blessed word droping like an Honey-Comb upon thy Soul to revive thee, when thou art in the midst of thy dumps.

Seventhly, Does not Jesus Christ sometimes give thee a glimps of himself, though perhaps, thou seest him not so long a time as while one may tell twenty?

Eighthly, Hast thou not sometimes as it were the very warmth of his wings over-shadowing the face of thy Soul, that gives thee as it were a gload upon thy Spirit, as the bright beams of the Sun do upon thy body, when it suddenly breaks out in the midst of a cloud, though presently all is gone again?

Well, all these things are the good hand of thy God upon thee, and they are upon thee to constrain to provoke and to make thee willing, and able to come (coming Sinner) that thou mightest in the end be Saved.[34]

Such was the theology and the passion of seventeenth-century English Particular Baptists.

34. Ibid., pp. 391–392.

2

Bridge over Troubled Waters

The eighteenth century brought much despair and little hope for orthodox Christianity in England. The onslaught of Deism and Socinianism brought ruin in its wake for Anglicans and dissenters alike. By the time the "great awakening" began in the fourth decade of the century, theological infidelity had so battered the churches that the awakening had to be carried on largely on the basis of the formation of new societies.

English General Baptists succumbed so thoroughly to Socinianism that the entire denomination had become Unitarian by 1770. Only a small remnant survived the apostasy and preserved any evangelical integrity at all by the formation of a New Connection of General Baptists under the leadership of Dan Taylor. Congregationalists and Presbyterians also suffered decline, not only in numbers and churches but in maintenance of orthodox Christianity. Only the English Particular Baptists remained unscathed by the theological apostasy. While growth in numbers halted and even declined, in 1777 John C. Ryland could say, "At present, blessed be God, we believe there is no apparent apostasy in our ministers and people from the glorious principles we profess."[1] Much of the credit for this unswerving allegiance to the doctrines of Scripture, under God, must be attributed to John Gill, known affectionately as "Dr. Voluminous."

John Gill was born at Kettering, in Northamptonshire, on November 23, 1697. By twelve years of age he had mastered the principal Latin classics and obtained admirable proficiency in Greek. As he had no opportunity for formal education beyond that age, Gill was thrown

1. John C. Ryland, "The Beauty of Social Religion: or, the Nature and Glory of a Gospel Church," in Northamptonshire Baptist Association, (Circular Letter, 1777), p. 7.

John Gill

on his own resources and energy to complete his education during moments when he was not assisting his father in weaving. Logic, rhetoric, philosophy, and Hebrew bowed to his efforts.

In November 1716, Gill related to the church an experience of saving grace and was baptized on November 4. On the same evening, by the request of some of the church members, Gill gave an exposition of Isaiah 53 in a private house. The next Sunday evening, again by request, he preached his first sermon; his text was 1 Corinthians 2:2. By 1719 he had received a request to supply the pulpit at Goat Street, Horsleydown, in London. In March 1720, he was solemnly ordained as pastor of a group of people who had separated from that church to call Gill as pastor. This group met for worship in a schoolroom belonging to Thomas Crosby, the Baptist historian, until the other portion of the church vacated the premises for a new meeting house in Unicorn-yard.

Doubtless, Gill began with only a small number in the church, and one should bear this in mind when reading criticisms and negative evaluations of Gill's effectiveness based on the contrast between building size and congregational numbers. Curt Daniel evidently uses that criterion when he says, "Gill pastored a congregation of above a thousand at the beginning of his ministry."[2] He gives no source for his statement. In addition, in 1753, his congregation was the largest of any Baptist church in England and Wales. Ivimey recognized that in spite of the leanness of the times, Gill's church "was indeed preserved a respectable community" and, writing in 1823, observed: "It still continues one of our most respectable churches."[3] "This "respectable" church, thirty-one years later (1854), called young C. H. Spurgeon as its pastor.

Gill remained as pastor of this same church for over fifty-one years. When he died (October 14, 1771), he was greatly mourned on both sides of the Atlantic, for his loss was felt keenly by the whole denomination of Baptists, a group still small and despised and struggling. His outstanding scholarship, zeal for truth, and pious polemics had greatly encouraged Baptists, who saw under vicious attack not only their peculiar tenets but those cardinal truths of evangelical Christianity at large. One elegy well caught the spirit of those who considered Gill, if not with love, at least with great admiration.

> What doleful tidings strike my list'ning ear,
>   or wound the tender feelings of my heart?
> Must the bright star for ever disappear?
>   Must the great Man, the learned Gill depart?
> Zion may mourn, for grief becomes her well,
>   To lose the man whose Heav'n instructed pen
> Taught knowledge clearly, while before him fell
>   Gigantic errors of deluded men.

Seeking to convince people familiar with Baptist history that Gill fits within the frame of Calvinistic theology would be like trying to convince a veterinarian that cows give milk. "Gill is a Calvinist" is a virtual redundancy. His massive and powerful influence on mid–eighteenth-century Particular Baptists approaches the certainty of a paradigm. Edward Trivett, a notable and successful pastor himself, used this general admission as grounds in 1770 for vindicating Baptists from "Some groundless and False charges." Gill had been called the "Pope" of the Baptists by an anonymous author. Trivett said, "If it is supposed that Dr. Gill is a pope to the Baptists; then it is also supposed and granted that the Baptists and he are of the same sentiments in religion." After mentioning John Brine, whom he calls

2. Curt Daniel, "Hyper-Calvinism and John Gill" (Unpublished Ph.D. dissertation, University of Edinburgh, 1983), p. 14.

3. Joseph Ivimey, *History of the English Baptists*, 4 vols. (London: printed for B. J. Holdworth, 1811–1830), 3:452.

"Braine," Trivett adds, "and I know the far greater part of Baptists in this kingdom are of the same sentiments with these two witnesses in the fundamentals of religion."[4]

However, a candid investigation of his influence, his reputation, and his personal persuasions uncovers some unfortunate misrepresentations marring the visage of Gill. Suffering calumny and disparagement from Baptist brethren who should be grateful for his effective apologetic in their behalf, perhaps no one has had more unchallenged criticism leveled against him in his absence than the learned Dr. Gill. For this reason, this chapter will engage in a threefold process: first, a brief discussion of Gill's understanding of the grace of God; second, a brief look at the function and nature of the misrepresentations of Gill; and third, an attempt to demonstrate the injustice of the caricatures that historians and others have perpetrated about Gill in the past.

Gill and Grace

When discussing John Gill's understanding of the Doctrines of Grace, no loftier evaluation could be given than that of the Anglican clergyman, Augustus Toplady: "Perhaps no man, since the days of St. Austin, has written so largely in defence of the system of grace; and certainly, no man has treated this momentous subject, in all its branches, more closely, judiciously, and successfully."[5]

Gill's first extended defense of these doctrines came in a book entitled *The Cause of God and Truth*. Divided into four parts, the first two parts evolved from a series of Wednesday-evening lectures to an interdenominational group. Located at Great Eastcheap, these lectures were begun by Gill in 1729 and continued by him for almost twenty-seven years; they were followed with admiration by dissenters and Anglicans of Calvinistic principles. A 1733 reprinting of Dr. Whitby's discourse on the Five Points, in which the Calvinistic doctrine was reputed to have been overthrown, prompted many people to ask Gill to produce a written answer to Whitby; this he felt inclined to do, and *The Cause of God and Truth* was the result.

Part I contains exposition of sixty-seven passages of Scripture purported to support the universal or anti-Calvinistic scheme of salvation. Part II presents a scriptural exposition of the doctrines of special and

4. Edward Trivett, *The Baptists Vindicated from Some Groundless and False Charges Brought Against Them by the Author of an Anonymous Pamphlet* (Norwich: 1770), pp. 4, 7.

5. Ivimey, *English Baptists*, 3:446.

distinguishing grace. Part III consists of rational arguments against the Arminians and in favor of the Calvinists. Part IV attempts to demonstrate that as the Calvinist doctrine pleads "not guilty" to the charge of novelty, even so the Arminian doctrine must relinquish the claim to have the support of antiquity. On the contrary, Gill claims, the Calvinistic scheme finds its roots in the earliest days of the church.

Prompted by Whitby's 1733 attempt to dismantle and destroy Calvinism, Gill, urged by friends, published *The Cause of God and Truth* in 1735. The doctrines he set forth at that writing he maintained throughout his life, reiterating them without change in his *Body of Divinity* in 1769. The years between these two publications brought to light Gill's exposition of the entire Bible. This detailed investigation of the Word of God uncovered nothing to diminish, but much to strengthen, his original position on the Doctrines of Grace.

The Love of God

The love of God, according to Gill, foundations all theology. God's principal object of love is himself. This is right and good, for he contains all excellence and perfection and worth. Second, God loves all that he has made, declares it very good, and rejoices in his works. Because rational creatures are the particular objects of his care, love, and delight, God supports, preserves, and bestows the bounty of his providence upon all of his creatures.

To the elect, however, the Triune God bears a special love. Gill identifies this with the "great love" spoken of in Ephesians 2:4. The love of the Father is demonstrated toward the elect by his devising and effecting a plan whereby they might be reconciled to him through Christ. The Father chose the elect in Christ from the beginning and, in him, has bestowed upon them all other blessings. The Son's love for the elect appears in his becoming a surety for their salvation by actually giving himself as a sacrifice for them, laying down his life on their account, and shedding his blood for the remission of their sins. The special love the Spirit exhibits toward the elect appears in his convincing them of sin and righteousness, shedding abroad the love of God in their hearts, and implanting every grace in them.[6]

Election

Gill's discussion of the love of God leads naturally to a consideration of God's election of particular individuals to salvation. Under the head

6. John Gill, *Body of Divinity*, 2 vols. (n.p., Tegg & Co., 1839; reprint ed., Grand Rapids: Baker Book House, 1978), 1:112–115.

of "special decrees of God," Gill expounds Ephesians 1:4. Although the passage renders "a strong truth of the doctrine of an eternal, personal, and unconditional election of men to grace and glory," the strength of the doctrine of election by no means rests entirely upon that one passage. In discussing the meaning of "before the foundation of the world," Gill flies a flag for the eternity of election and calls upon 2 Timothy 1:9 and 2 Thessalonians 2:13 to lend support to the interpretation. In addition, this eternal election culminates on individual, particular persons, not corporate bodies, thus bringing them to salvation. In short, the text proves that

> ... this eternal election of particular persons to salvation is absolute, unconditional, and irrespective of faith, holiness, good works, and perseverance as the moving causes or conditions of it; all which are the fruits and effects of electing grace, but not causes or conditions of it; since these are said to be chosen, not because they were holy, but that they should be so.[7]

In his *Body of Divinity*, after discussing the election of angels and men, the necessity of preaching the doctrine, and several inadequate definitions of election, Gill establishes the true definition:

> This is to be understood of the choice of certain persons by God, from all eternity, to grace and glory; it is an act by which men are chosen of God's good will and pleasure, before the world was, to holiness and happiness, to salvation by Christ, to partake of his glory, and to enjoy eternal life, as the free gift of God through him, Ephesians i.4, 2 Thessalonians ii. 13, Acts xiii. 48; and this is the first and foundation-blessing, according to which all spiritual blessings are dispensed; and is, by the apostle, set at the front of them all; and is the first link in the golden chain of man's salvation, Ephesians i. 3, 4, Rom. viii. 30.[8]

As the "first and foundation-blessing" from which proceeds all spiritual blessing, election is not to be confused with that which proceeds from it. Calling proceeds from it as a fruit does from the tree and derives its distinctiveness and particularity from the decree of election. The redemptive activity of Christ, which procures forgiveness, redemption, justification, and so on, comes about because of election. Christ laid down his life for the sheep, or the elect (terms Gill considers

---

7. John Gill, D.D., *The Cause of God and Truth* (London: W. H. Collingridge, 1855; reprint ed., Grand Rapids: Baker Book House, 1980), p. 85.

8. Gill, *Body*, 1:258, Article 5.

interchangeable). Nor is election dependent upon man's persevering in faith and holiness unto the end; but election procures perseverance.

Should one grant that election depends upon faith and gains its effectuality from the saints' perseverance, election as a word would be void of meaning. Who would have need of election if it only grants that which one has already attained? Gill insists that election stands at the beginning of the entire process; and this election terminates on individual persons out of every nation, bringing them to salvation for the glory of God.

Atonement

In harmony with the elective purpose of God, Christ redeems to himself the people already elected by the Father. Gill sets forth very clearly that none is ransomed by Christ but the spiritual Israel of God.[9] Election and redemption are of equal extent: "No more are redeemed by Christ, than are chosen in him; these are a special people: what is said of the objects of the one, is true of the objects of the other."[10]

The elect, therefore, are loved with an everlasting and special love. They are elected by God the Father before the foundation of the world, and they are redeemed by God the Son because he has become a surety for those and for no others. Gill's argument that Christ has become a surety of the covenant of grace for his people was later followed very closely by Andrew Fuller.

Effectual Calling

Just as surely as Christ has died as a propitiation and a sacrifice to become a surety for the chosen of God, even so the Holy Spirit calls the same effectually by his grace. Gill clearly distinguishes effectual call from the general call that comes to all that hear the gospel. All men should repent and believe, for they are called upon to bow before their Creator and Sovereign. None, however, will do this apart from the effectual grace of God; but God is under no obligation to give it to any person. Grace, therefore, is truly unmerited. If God is under obligation to give it to all men, then grace is not free and unmerited, but of duty. If it is unmerited, no man can plead unjust treatment if this effectual grace does not come to him.

Gill does not pretend that grace is something that is offered to all men. This belief, in particular, labels him in the eyes of Curt Daniel

9. Ibid., 2:3.
10. Ibid., p. 12.

as a hyper-Calvinist. Whether that item should be the strategic element of the definition of hyper-Calvinism can well be called into question. This becomes especially debatable when we observe that Gill did
not reject the reality of duty-faith and duty-repentance. Rather, all
men are called upon and have an obligation to repent and believe.
Grace, however, by its very character as the undeserved bestowment
of salvific gifts, comes only to some and effectually on them. Grace
itself is not offered. In *The Cause of God and Truth* Gill states:

> I reply . . . I do not think that any man will be punished for not accepting
> offered grace . . . because I do not believe that grace was ever offered to
> them; but then they will be punished for their willful contempt in neglect
> of the gospel preached unto them: and for their manifold transgressions
> of the law of God, made known unto them.[11]

Later, the relation between "offers" and obligation will be investigated
more thoroughly.

Gill likens effectual calling to the first creation, in which God commanded light to shine out of darkness. In the same way, through effectual calling he irradiates the minds of his called ones with the
divine light. By this illumination they comprehend the exceeding sinfulness of sin, see themselves lost and undone and ready to perish,
recognize their incapacity to save themselves, and mourn at the
wretchedness of their own righteousness. Then they are pointed to the
glory, fullness, and grace of Christ, his completeness and suitableness
as a Savior, the promises of the gospel, and its great doctrine. These
they embrace with the heart, rejoice in them, and become believers of
the glad tidings of good things. The effectual call of God results in
release from bondage to sin, the ways of the world, and Satan. When
effectually called, the elect are taken out of Satan's hands, are turned
from his power unto God, are delivered from the dominion of darkness,
and are translated into the kingdom of God's dear Son, where they are
Christ's free men.[12]

Total Depravity

This manner of dealing with man is necessitated by the corruption
of human nature. Although created in a state of innocence, with the
law written in his heart and the covenant of life made with him in his

11. Ibid., p. 181.
12. Ibid., p. 126.

state of innocence, Adam fell, bringing a change in man's nature and a verdict of condemnation on all his posterity.

Gill considers Adam as the federal head of the race, thus including all men in his sin and constituting them sinners. But he also acknowledges Adam as the natural head of the race, thus passing to all its members a corrupt nature. His theory of natural headship, however, does not involve traducianism. When Gill affirms that the corrupt nature flows from Adam, he does not mean that the soul comes by way of generation. Gill has already defined his view of man's nature in terms of creationism—that is, each living person has a soul created especially for it; and, at the proper time, this soul is united to the body. Thus he can say that corruption of nature is not "to be accounted for by the traduction of the soul from immediate parents, or by the generation of it together with the body from them." In fact, the contagion of sin does not take place on the body apart or the soul apart, but upon both when united together and not before.

Gill contends that God creates a soul, not sinful, but without original righteousness and with an impotence to good. In the same way that Adam was created first as material being and then had the breath of life breathed into him, "when matter generated is prepared for the reception of the soul, as soon as that preparation is finished, that very instant a soul is created, and ready at hand to be united to it, and it is."[13] Therefore when the soul, impotent to any good and devoid of original righteousness, unites with the body, which is from corruptible seed and has an aptitude and disposition that is sinful, these two together become corrupted. Gill closes his section on original corruption with a theodicy:

> . . . in this light, indeed, we are to consider the corruption of nature; a moral death, which is no other than a deprivation of the image of God, a loss of original righteousness, and an incapacity to attain it, was threatened to Adam, inflicted on him as a punishment. And since all his posterity sinned in him, why should not the same pass upon them? And indeed it is by the just ordination of God that things are as they be, in consequence of Adam's sin, who cannot do an unjust thing; there is no unrighteousness in him; he is righteous in all his ways, and holy in all his works; and so in this. And here we should rest the matter; in this we should acquiesce, and humble ourselves unto the mighty hand of God.[14]

Perseverance of Saints

Gill also unhesitatingly and clearly affirms the doctrine of perseverance of saints:

13. Ibid., 1:479.
14. Ibid., p. 480.

Those who are truly regenerated, effectually called, and really converted, and internally sanctified by the Spirit and grace of God, shall persevere in grace to the end, and shall be everlastingly saved; or shall never finally and totally fall, so as to perish everlastingly.[15]

He first defends the doctrine biblically. Gill quotes and exegetes several passages of Scripture, using both the Old and New Testament. Such texts as Job 17:9; Psalm 94:14; Jeremiah 32:40; Psalm 125:1, 2, and others give Old Testament foundation to the doctrine of perseverance. Likewise, in the New Testament, John 10:28; John 17:12; 1 Corinthians 1:8, 9; 1 Peter 1:5, plus many others, are cited in support of the doctrine.

Gill's second line of defense arises from a consideration of the perfections of God. Both negative and positive approaches must be considered. Anything that would bring dishonor to the perfections of God must be rejected, and that which is agreeable to the perfections of God is to be accepted. The apostasy of real saints, so as to perish everlastingly, is directly contrary to the perfections of God and reflects dishonor on them; therefore, it must be false. The final perseverance of true believers is in direct accord with all of the perfections of God. Gill lists (1) the immutability of God; (2) the wisdom of God; (3) the power of God; (4) the goodness, grace, and mercy of God; (5) the justice of God; and (6) the faithfulness of God as facets of his perfection. An example of Gill's reasoning may be seen in the following passage, which discusses the wisdom of God:

The end which God has in view, and has fixed, with respect to his people, is the salvation of them; and it can never be consistent with his wisdom to appoint insufficient means, or not make those means effectual, which it is in his power to do; which must be the case, if any of those he has appointed to salvation should perish. Now as he has fixed the end, salvation, he has provided his Son to be the author of it, by his obedience, sufferings, and death; and has appointed as means to the enjoyment of this salvation, the sanctification of the Spirit, and the belief of the truth; for which purpose he sends his Spirit to sanctify them, and work faith in them, whereby these means become effectual, and the end is answered: and so the wisdom of God is highly displayed and glorified. But where would be his wisdom to appoint men to salvation, and not save them at last? to send his Son to redeem them, and they be never the better for it? and to send his Spirit into them, to begin a good work of grace, and not finish it? But this is not the case, he has put the work of redemption into the hands of his Son, who has completed it; and as-

15. Ibid., 2:151.

signed the work of sanctification, in its beginning, progress, and issue, to the divine Spirit, who is equal to it, and will perform it; and throughout the whole, God abounds towards his people in all wisdom and prudence.[16]

Anyone who loves the doctrine of perseverance really must engage himself to read this particular section in Gill's *Body of Divinity*. It contains a most exalted, though short, defense of the perseverance of the saints, and it magnifies the glory and honor of God in the process. Not only do the perfections of God guarantee perseverance, but his purposes and decrees do also. The elect are appointed to obtain the glory of Christ, and God's will in this is "infrustrable."

The third defense enlists the promises of God as an argument for the final perseverance of the saints. God will never leave nor forsake those who have been true recipients of his grace.

Fourth, the gracious acts of God that flow from his everlasting and unchangeable love make secure the saints' final perseverance. Adoption, justification, and pardon of sin are all acts of divine grace, and these flow from unmerited and distinguishing love. These declarations of God cannot be withdrawn. Shall a child of God perish everlastingly? Shall one to whom has been imputed the righteousness of Christ suffer eternally? Shall one whose sin has been taken from him and who is made everlastingly free from the taint of iniquity be destroyed or perish everlastingly?

The fifth point arguing for perseverance arises from the love of Christ for the saints. Christ having loved his own, who were in the world, loves them to the end and determines to bestow on them everlasting salvation.

The sixth divine truth that foundations perseverance is the nature of grace and the Spirit's authorship of it. Grace is an incorruptible seed that never dies. Thus, those who receive it shall not sin unto death so as to die eternally. It is a well of living water that springs up to eternal life. Grace and glory are inseparably connected. To whomever God gives the one, he assuredly gives the other.

Gill's handling of arguments raised against the doctrine of perseverance of the saints is quite notable. The objections are specious, and Gill easily exposes their weaknesses through demonstrating the practical tendencies of the doctrine:

First, instead of creating a carnal security and indifference to salvation within persons, the doctrine of perseverance encourages the sinner to pursue salvation through perseverance. When people are assured of victory they will not shrink from the battle.

16. Ibid., p. 159.

Second, instead of encouragement to indulge in sin, the doctrine of perseverance teaches that sin is to be avoided. Such sins as committed by Lot, David, and others "without repentance toward God and faith in the blood and sacrifice of Christ, those who are guilty of them shall not inherit the kingdom of God."[17] The examples of saints who sinned and received forgiveness are not recorded to encourage sin, but rather to show that true believers have repentant attitudes toward all sins.

Third, though some pretend that the doctrine weakens the force of prohibitions against sin and exhortations to avoid it, Gill claims that such prohibitions are used as means by the Spirit of God to assure perseverance. "It would be absurd and irrational to judge otherwise; for can a man believe he shall persevere to the end and yet indulge himself in sin, as if he was resolved not to persevere?"[18]

Fourth, is the doctrine of perseverance comfortable to carnal minds and, therefore, opposed to the doctrine of godliness? "No," Gill answers. On the contrary, the doctrine of falling from grace is more uncomfortable to true saints. Since the Scriptures were written for our comfort, those who truly believe should find within the true doctrine of Scripture such things as give them comfort rather than such things as unsettle, disturb, and make them insecure.

Testimonies Against Gill

Although Gill's theology differs little from that of Keach and Bunyan (and at points is even less radical), he has doubtless been judged more harshly and even maliciously than any man of comparable repute in Baptist history. Nineteenth- and twentieth-century liberals such as Clarke, Matthews, and Fosdick have received greater expressions of appreciation and sympathy from Baptist historians than has Dr. Gill. Although J. M. Cramp devotes six full pages in *Baptist History* to discussing the life and contributions of John Gill and is mainly positive in his assessment of Gill's character, learning, and influence, he states in an earlier section that John Gill was a supralapsarian "holding that God's election was irrespective of the fall of men."[19] Cramp believes that undue prominence was given in Gill's discourses to the "teachings of Scripture respecting the divine purposes."[20] Gill

17. Ibid., p. 178.
18. Ibid.
19. J. M. Cramp, *Baptist History* (Philadelphia: American Baptist Publication Society), p. 499.
20. Ibid.

and men like him, in Cramp's opinion, could not "engage in efforts for the conversion of souls. They were so afraid of intruding on God's work that they neglected to do what he had commanded them."[21]

H. C. Vedder, in *A Short History of the Baptists,* places on John Gill the blame for the extremes of hyper-Calvinism of the Particular Baptist churches and states that he "cannot be absolved from responsibility for much of this false doctrine."[22] Vedder calls Gill's *Body of Divinity* "a great treatise of the rigid supralapsarian type of Calvinism," which can "with difficulty be distinguished from fatalism and antinomianism."[23] After describing the worst features of hyper-Calvinism and ascribing them to Gill, Vedder exclaims, "What wonder that a spiritual dry-rot spread among the English churches where such doctrines obtained!"[24]

Whitley, in his *History of British Baptists,* though he does mention hyper-Calvinism and antinomianism as problems in eighteenth-century Particular Baptist life, hardly finds time to mention John Gill. In *Calvinism and Evangelism in England and Especially Among Baptists,* Whitley quotes Cramp's statements and points out that Gill, in 1753, was preaching to only 150 hearers: "In the very years when Gill shut himself in his study to expound the New Testament, George Whitefield was preaching several times daily to thousands of people."[25] It is certainly a melancholy fact that Baptists benefited from the awakening so tardily, but one could hardly argue from God's blessings on Whitefield that Gill should not have sought seclusion to write a commentary on Holy Scripture. A. C. Underwood, in his *A History of the English Baptists,* merely mentions that John Gill "never addressed the ungodly."[26]

The phrase "non-invitation, non-application scheme" was first introduced by Joseph Ivimey in his four-volume work, *A History of the English Baptists.* He traces the beginning of this scheme to a Baptist preacher named John Skepp. In addition, Ivimey discusses the ministry of John Brine and concludes that he preached upon the same "non-application, non-invitation scheme." John Gill, though admit-

21. Ibid., pp. 499–500.
22. Henry C. Vedder, *A Short History of the Baptists* (Valley Forge: Judson Press, 1907), p. 240.
23. Ibid., p. 240.
24. Ibid., p. 241.
25. W. T. Whitley, *Calvinism and Evangelism in England and Especially Among Baptists* (London: The Kingsgate Press, 1933), p. 28.
26. A. C. Underwood, *A History of the English Baptists* (London: The Baptist Union of Great Britain & Ireland, 1970), p. 135.

tedly not so strongly into the "false Calvinistic scheme"[27] as the others, nevertheless drank water from their well and could not bring himself to make application of the truths of evangelical repentance and saving faith. Ivimey says, ". . . it appears, that neither the doctor, nor his brethren, Messrs. Skepp or Brine, had so learned Christ as Paul and Peter had understood him."[28] Ivimey infers many things from silence rather than from direct statements in Gill's writings. Gill becomes guilty by association and silence rather than from direct violation of principles.

According to Ivimey, among Gill's errors were his "very high opinion of Mr. Skepp" and his "strong personal affection for Mr. John Brine."[29] In addition, Gill defended Tobias Crisp from the charge of antinomianism. Although Ivimey admits that Crisp did not hold distinctive principles of antinomianism (which is all Gill sought to prove)—that is, "that the moral law of God is not a rule of life to a believer"[30]—he so distinctly disliked Crisp's doctrine of eternal justification that Gill must somehow also be unsound.

Crisp's doctrine teaches that since believers were elect in Christ before the foundation of the world, their sin must have been imputed to him and his righteousness to them by the same decree. Ivimey complains that many people whose hearts were carnal, and who were still at enmity with God, might draw the conclusion that the Christian need not maintain good works. Gill, therefore, must be blamed for the perversion that carnal hearts place on Crisp's doctrine. It hardly seems fair, however, to criticize a theological position on the basis of what unregenerate people at enmity with God might do with it. Ivimey called this a "poisonous drug" and regrets that Dr. Gill ever sweetened it by explaining and recommending the works of Dr. Crisp. Whether Ivimey would have passed similar judgment on Spurgeon's evaluation of Crisp must remain a matter of conjecture. Spurgeon said, "Never was there a sounder divine than Crisp, and never one who preached the gospel more fully to all under heaven."[31] Although Gill did not believe in eternal justification, this is a point in which he was followed by only a few of his Baptist brethren. He was never contentious about the issue but held in high esteem and warm affection many who did not receive the doctrine.

27. Ivimey, *English Baptists*, 3:272.
28. Ibid., p. 273.
29. Ibid., p. 272.
30. Ibid., p. 449.
31. *The Reverend C. H. Spurgeon's Anecdotes and Stories*, ed. Oliver Creyton (London: n.d.), p. 104.

In the thirty-page discussion that Ivimey devotes to Gill[32] (plus the frequent references he makes to him at other points), he includes many positive and affirmative evaluations of Gill's life and ministry, calling him the humble and holy John Gill.[33] Yet he takes it upon himself to criticize Gill at every possible point. Even after admitting the evangelical nature of a funeral oration delivered by Gill on the true nature of repentance toward God and faith toward our Lord Jesus Christ, Ivimey expostulates with Gill for not saying more: "Now this is certainly a correct statement of evangelical repentance and saving faith: but then there is no application of these sentiments so as to convince guilty sinners that except they repent they must perish; and that they cannot escape wrath if they continue to neglect so great a salvation."[34]

Admittedly, Gill does not match the exhortative talents of Andrew Fuller and Charles Spurgeon, but he was not ideologically opposed to persuasion and exhortation, as I hope to demonstrate later. It is unfortunate that such an onus of suspicion has arisen around a man of such sound gospel knowledge, simply because his application of the material does not fit a certain emotive framework. Ivimey quite often includes extensive footnotes that contain valuable and interesting historical material, but his second-guessing the statements and activities of Gill at various points is misleadingly mixed with the purely historical. He implies a criticism of Gill for receiving an honorary doctorate (certainly not the only Baptist ever to be so honored), for answering the rudeness of one particular church member in a certain way, and for not desiring to have a co-pastor during the aged years of his ministry. All of this might simply indicate detailed historiography on Ivimey's part, for every factor must be considered in the final evaluation of a man's work. Additionally, Ivimey gives Gill not only a more detailed, but often more sympathetic, treatment than many other historians. It appears, nevertheless, that Ivimey's close personal friendship with Andrew Fuller, joined with the hyper-Calvinist criticism of Fuller (which had greatly increased by the beginning of the nineteenth century), made Ivimey pause lengthily before he would let Gill go unscathed—championed as he was by the anti-Fullerites. As a result, Gill has been judged on the basis of the circumstantial rather than on the basis of that which was substantial.

Robert Hall's comment to Christmas Evans characterizes the attitude of many people toward John Gill. Evans's excited estimation of the greatness of Gill and his desire to see Gill's works in the Welsh

---

32. Ivimey, *English Baptists*, 3:431–461.
33. Ibid., p. 439.
34. Ibid., p. 375.

language occupied his thought when he said to Hall, "How I wish, Mr. Hall, that Dr. Gill's works had been written in Welsh." "I wish they had, sir, I wish they had with all my heart, for then I should never have read them. They are a continent of mud, sir."[35] Quoted by both Cramp and Underwood and perhaps others, this anecdote has been used to criticize unfairly Gill's communicative skills. Perhaps it should be used as a judgment upon the flexibility of Robert Hall rather than upon the style of Gill. Although Gill's sentences are long, he is really quite concise and clear in his style and is always fair in his presentation of his opponent's position.

Thomas Armitage, the noble Baptist historian of the nineteenth century, adds his touch of ill feeling to the reputation of Gill. After quoting a flattering estimation of Gill by Toplady, Armitage states, ". . . and yet with all his ability he was so high a supralapsarian that it is hard to distinguish him from an antinomian."[36] He also blames Gill for defending the doctrines of Tobias Crisp.

A more recent Baptist historian, Leon McBeth, endorses all these accusations and adds his own literary flare to them. In a commendable enterprise of emphasizing the dangers of hyper-Calvinism, McBeth mistakenly presents Gill as teaching that "the elect will be saved without our preaching; the non-elect will not be saved no matter what we do."[37] Gill says that such talk is "a captious and idle way of talking, to say, that if a man is elected to salvation, he shall be saved, whether he is sanctified or no, or whether he believes or no; and if he is not elected, he shall not be saved, let him be never so much concerned for faith and holiness."[38] McBeth also refers to predestination as "fate," an identification specifically treated and corrected by Gill in *The Cause of God and Truth*.[39]

Curt Daniel's mammoth dissertation is based on the assumption that Gill is hyper-Calvinist. Calling Gill the "definitive Hyper-Calvinist," Daniel studied Gill's theology for the purpose of reaching a "workable definition of Hyper-Calvinism itself."[40] Such a procedure severely prejudices both the definition and the proper ascription of nomenclature to Gill. Peter Toon's very helpful and well-researched book pro-

35. Robert Hall, *The Works of Robert Hall*, 6 vols. (London: Holdsworth & Ball, 1833), 6:155–156.

36. Thomas Armitage, *A History of the Baptists* (New York: Bryan, Taylor & Co., 1887), p. 561.

37. Leon McBeth, "Believer's Security Almost Wrecked Denomination," *Baptist Message*, Vol. 98, No. 9, p. 4.

38. Gill, *Cause*, p. 193.

39. McBeth, "Believer's Security," p. 4.

40. Daniel, "Hyper-Calvinism," p. 11.

ceeds in the same wa   istinguish some
important distinctions   lists as hyper-
Calvinists.[41]

Such have been the accusations. What can be Gill's defense?

To the Defense of Gill

Cathcart's Baptist Encyclopaedia (1881) rendered a positive judgment on the influence of Gill. The writer called Gill's commentary on
the Old and New Testament the most valuable exposition ever published. In addition, he said that Gill's major work on the Hebrew language included such masterly and profound research that had Dr. Gill
never published another word, he would still have been known as a
"prodigy of reading and literature." In addition, the writer considered
him "one of the purest men that ever lived." The following summarizes
the high estimation of Gill presented in the encyclopedia:

> His "Body of Divinity," published in 1769, is a work without which no
> theological library is complete. His grand old doctrines of grace, taken
> unadulterated from the Divine fountain, presented in the phraseology
> and with the illustrations of an intellectual giant, and commended by
> a wealth of sanctified biblical learning only once in several ages per-
> mitted to mortals, sweep all opposition before them, and leave no place
> for the blighted harvests, the seed of which was planted by James Ar-
> minius in modern times. In this work eternal and personal election to
> a holy life, particular redemption from all guilt, resistless grace in re-
> generation, final preservation from sin and the Wicked one, till the be-
> liever enters paradise, and the other doctrines of the Christian system,
> are expounded and defended by one of the greatest teachers in Israel
> ever called to the work of instruction by the Spirit of Jehovah.[42]

This section will proceed to examine Gill on supralapsarianism,
antinomianism, the concept of duty-faith, and a Christian minister's
obligation to evangelism.

Supralapsarianism

Gill comes down solidly on neither the supralapsarian nor the sublapsarian side when discussing the decrees of God. He sees strengths

41. Peter Toon, *The Emergence of Hyper-Calvinism in English Non-Conformity* (London: The Olive Tree, 1967), pp. 93, 96–100.
42. *Cathcart's Baptist Encyclopaedia*, 2 vols., 1:453–454.

in both positions and believes that both positions have been misrepresented by various opponents of God's decretal sovereignty. Especially has the doctrine of reprobation come under attack. John Wesley made this the main pillar to topple in his *Predestination Calmly Considered* and charged Calvinists with deceit in not setting forth clearly the horrible consequences of the doctrine of election. Gill responded:

> We judge it most proper and prudent, not so much to insist on this in our discourses and writings; not from any consciousness of want of evidence, but because of the awfulness of the subject. This our opponents are aware of; and therefore press us upon this head, in order to bring the doctrine of election into contempt with weak or carnal men; and make their first attacks upon this branch of predestination, which is beginning wrong; since reprobation is no other than non-election, or what is opposed to election: let the doctrine of election be demolished, and the other will fall on course; but that will cost too much pain; and they find a better account with weak minds in taking the other method.[43]

Gill divides reprobation in the supralapsarian scheme into two elements, positive and negative. Negative reprobation is simply non-election, or the passing by of some. Positive reprobation is the determination to punish men, but for their sins. The sublapsarian Calvinist considers the decree of reprobation to occur after men are considered in their state of sinfulness. This does not mean, however, that God decided after the actual historical fall to condemn sinners. Sublapsarian and supralapsarian Calvinism both consider the decrees of God to have occurred before anything was created. The only difference in the two is consideration of the order of decrees. Endorsing certain strengths of both of these, Gill concludes: "Let the objects of the decree of reprobation be considered either in the pure, or in the corrupt mass; that decree puts nothing in them, it leaves them as it finds them, and therefore does them no injustice."[44]

In his *Body of Divinity*, Gill discusses both sublapsarianism and supralapsarianism, gives the strengths of both, and seeks to explain and clarify the real intent of both. All concepts of decrees have been accused of gross injustice to man in that they consider God to have created man simply to damn him. Gill calls this understanding of decrees into question when he says that "according to their real sentiments [both supra- and sublapsarians] God decreed to make man

---

43. John Gill, *The Doctrine of Predestination Stated and Set in Scripture-Light in Opposition to Mr. Wesley's Predestination Calmly Considered* (London: n.p., 1753).

44. Gill, *Cause*, p. 157.

and made man, neither to damn him nor to save him, but for his own glory; which end is answered in them, some way or another."[45] Gill points out that the Calvinists at the Synod of Dort were divided on this particular question, as were Calvin and Beza; yet they were able to serve together to the glory of God. Gill believes certain elements of both views may be accepted, since both see the glory of God as the ultimate end of the decree. He would compose the case this way:

> Men might be considered in the divine mind as creable, not yet created and fallen; and that in the decree of the means which, among other things, takes in the mediation of Christ, redemption by him, and the sanctification of the Spirit; they might be considered as created, fallen, and sinful, which these things imply; nor does this suppose separate acts and decrees in God, and any priority and posteriority in them; which in God are but one and together; but our finite minds are obliged to consider them one after another, not being able to take them in together and at once.[46]

Categorizing Gill, in light of such evidence, as rigidly supralapsarian arises from ignoring Gill's own statements, though he evidently preferred that view. Furthermore, the candid theologian must reject the suspicion that supralapsarianism in itself is evil, or that those who embrace it must be stigmatized. The intent of the doctrine is to affirm that God is wise and will not create any being without determining that it shall exist for a purpose. The supralapsarians see the end of all things as the glory of God and believe that God considers all created beings in their original created condition with their end already in mind. Such wisdom, purpose, and power should be praised, not ridiculed.

Antinomianism

Dr. Gill has been called antinomian by many authors. Even if not labeled antinomian, it has been said that his system leads irretrievably to the error. One of his contemporaries, Dr. Taylor, accused Gill of antinomianism, which he deduced from Gill's teachings concerning eternal justification. Gill denied the charge and rejected any real connection with true antinomianism. He did, however, continue to affirm that good works were not necessary as the causes of salvation and were not necessary as a means of procuring or of applying salvation;

45. Gill, *Body*, 1:262.
46. Ibid., p. 265.

but because God had commanded them for the evidence of the genuineness of faith, for the certainty of election and calling, and for the magnifying of grace to our neighbors, good works must be maintained. Rather than trim his doctrine to affirm any more than the absolute vacuity of merit in human work, Gill would rather suffer misunderstanding. He states in his rebuttal to Dr. Taylor:

> ... but I have chosen to suffer reproach, the loss of good name and reputation,—to forego popularity, wealth, and friends—yea, to be traduced as an Antinomian, rather than to drop or conceal any one branch of truth respecting Christ and his grace.[47]

Gill discusses works and, with certain qualifications, is willing to use the adjective *good* to describe them.

For a work to be considered "good" in the ultimate sense, it must be done according to the command of God without any lack of conformity to it. It must spring from love to God, must be done in faith, and must be done to the glory of God. Since such motivations never appear at the same time or to the necessary degree in any work done by man, Gill would conclude that "the best of works, which are done by the best of men, and in the best manner, are but imperfect; there is sin in them all; there are none found perfect in the sight of God, however they may appear before men."[48]

Indwelling sin figures largely in hindering man from doing the good that he would do. Thus, because our "good works" are not really "good," we can never say they merit any favor from the hand of God. Further condemnation is the only just desert for such works. The noblest human works do not procure salvation in whole or in part. They make neither peace with God nor atonement for sin; only the active and passive obedience of Christ procure these.

Nevertheless, inability to perform works truly good does not even slightly diminish the requirement on the saints to seek to do good works. They have been made good trees by the grace of God that they might bear good fruit; they have been purified and sanctified by the life and blood of Christ; they have the spirit of Christ; and they have faith in God—and the command of the apostle is to "let ours also learn to maintain good works" (Titus 3:14). Such people are under the greatest obligations to perform good works, for God has ordained that his people should walk in them. By good works, God's grace is glorified, the believer's profession in the doctrine of God our Savior is adorned,

47. Ivimey, *English Baptists*, 3:450.
48. Gill, *Body*, 2:752.

and faith is demonstrated to others, so that one's calling and election ring genuine to outsiders. Good works constitute the only evidence believers are capable of giving to the world. Thus, good works may serve as a means of either winning the lost to Christ or stopping the mouths of those who would oppose the faith.[49]

Further evidence of the erroneous nature of any charge of antinomianism against Gill rests in his exposition of the Ten Commandments.[50] A succinct statement concerning the evangelical use of the law concludes his treatment:

> From this view of the law, in all its precepts, it appears how large and extensive it is; that David might well say, Thy commandment is exceeding broad! Psalm cxix. 96. So that it cannot be perfectly fulfilled by man in this his sinful and fallen state; and therefore he cannot be justified before God by the deeds of it, since it requires a perfect righteousness: and happy for man it is that there is such a righteousness revealed in the gospel, manifested without the law, though witnessed to by law and prophets, even the righteousness of Christ, consisting of his active and passive obedience; who is the end, the fulfilling end, of the law for righteousness, to every one that believes.[51]

This evangelical use of the law found earlier expansion under the heading of effectual calling. In describing the nature of God's salvific call, Gill reminds the reader, in accordance with 2 Timothy 1:9, that it is "a holy calling." God is a holy God, and the means through which sinners are called are holy. The lost may be awakened to their sin by the reading of the Holy Scriptures, or they may be awakened "to a serious concern about divine things" by the law. "That commandment is holy, just, and good."[52]

Gill's sermon on Romans 3:31, "The Law Established by the Gospel," is a clear and convincing exposition of the relation of the various aspects of the law to the completed work of Christ. Gill shows clearly the fulfilment of the ceremonial law in Christ, so that even it was not "abolished and made void until it was fulfilled in and by Christ." Indeed, every figure and type, shadow and sacrifice, and office and ordinance "had their entire accomplishment in him."[53] Both the evangelical and sanctifying uses of the law are established by both the doctrine and grace of faith; and the holiness and perpetuity of the law

---

49. Ibid., pp. 753–754.
50. Ibid., pp. 754–759.
51. Ibid., p. 759.
52. Ibid., p. 130.
53. John Gill, *The Law Established by the Gospel* (London: A. Ward, 1739), p. 15.

find their most eloquent statement in the gospel itself. Although no one quote could summarize the nuances and complexities of the issue entirely adequately, the following will serve to give the general thrust:

> But now, though the law is made void as a covenant of works, it still continues a rule of action, walk and conversation; though it is done away as to the form of the administration of it by Moses, the matter, the sum and substance of it remains firm, unalterable, and unchangeable in the hands of Christ; though it is destroy'd as a yoke of bondage, it is in being as a perfect law of liberty; and though believers are delivered from the curse and condemnation of it, they are not exempted from obedience to it; and though they are not to seek for justification by it, they are under the greatest obligations, by the strongest ties of love, to have a regard to all its commands.[54]

These statements, concerning both the evangelical use of the law and the use of the law as a guide to the Christian life, were not cold speculations to Gill; they governed his view of the church. Gill's discipline of some members who evidently were wanting in their desire for godly living demonstrates his adherence to the pursuit of holiness. Ivimey quotes Gill:

> Agreed, that to deny the internal sanctification of the Spirit, as a principle of grace and holiness which, though but a begun work, and as yet incomplete, is an abiding work of grace, and will abide, not withstanding all corruptions, temptations, and snares, be performed by the Author of it until the day of Christ when it will be the saints meetness for eternal glory; is a grievous error, highly reflects dishonor on the blessed Spirit and his operations of grace on the heart, is subversive of true religion and powerful godliness, and renders persons unfit for church-communion.[55]

Those members of Gill's church who held the described error were dismissed. In short, Gill strongly rejected the error of antinomianism, lived a pure life, and sought to maintain a disciplined church. He should not be accused of the errors of some who did not hold his doctrine but liked to use his name.

Duty-Faith and Duty-Repentance

John Gill affirmed that it was the duty of all men to repent of sin and the duty of all who heard the gospel to believe it. Some of his

54. Ibid., pp. 32, 33.
55. Ivimey, *English Baptists*, 3:442–443.

statements, if isolated, appear to reject duty-faith. For example, in his *Cause of God and Truth* he states:

> God does not require all men to believe in Christ and where he does it is according to the revelation he makes of him. He does not require the heathen, who are without an external revelation of Christ, to believe in him at all; and those who only have the outward ministry of the word, unattended with the special illuminations of Spirit of God, are obliged to believe no further than that external revelation they enjoy, reaches.[56]

Careful attention to context indicates that Gill's purpose is to highlight man's responsibility for that which is available to him. None is condemned specifically for not believing in Christ who never heard of Christ. Rather, men are condemned justly for their sins. If one has never heard the gospel, he stands condemned—but not for rejection of Christ. Nor does any die eternally for not believing that Christ died for him, "but [he perishes] for the transgressions of the law of God." In another place Gill states that "such who have no revelation of him, as the heathens, are not bound to believe in him in any sense."[57] He goes on to affirm, however, that these who have not enjoyed a revelation of Christ are not condemned for final unbelief but will be condemned "for their sins against the law in the light of nature."[58]

Indeed, some might ask, is it the duty of all men to love the Lord? Absolutely! Because they are the creatures of his making, enjoy the care of his providence, and are supplied by him with the blessings of life; therefore all men must joyfully love the Lord.[59] But even beyond creation and providence, Gill affirms that those who hear the gospel "are obliged to love the Lord on account of redemption by Christ; since all who see their need of it, and are desirous of interest in it, have no reason to conclude otherwise, than that Christ died for them, and has redeemed them by his blood."[60]

Gill even affirms that it is the duty of all men who hear the Word to obey it, notwithstanding their moral inability to do so.

> It is man's duty to believe the word of the Lord, and obey his will, though he has not a power, yea, even though God has decreed to withhold that grace without which he cannot believe and obey. So it was Pharaoh's duty to believe and obey the Lord, and let Israel go; though God had

56. Gill, *Cause*, p. 166.
57. Ibid., p. 164.
58. Ibid.
59. Ibid., p. 170.
60. Ibid.

determined to harden his heart, that he should not let them go. However
there are many things which may be believed and done by reprobates,
and therefore they may be justly required to believe and obey; it is true,
they are not able to believe in Christ to the saving of their souls, or to
perform spiritual and evangelical obedience, but then it will be difficult
to prove that God requires these things of them, and should that appear,
yet the impossibility of doing them, arises from the corruption of their
hearts, being destitute of the grace of God, and not from the decree of
reprobation, which though it denies them that grace and strength, without which they cannot believe and obey in this sense, yet it takes none
from them, and therefore does them no injustice.[61]

In this passage Gill carefully distinguishes between what is actually
required in the reprobate and what is not. He is condemned for no
more than that which is required of him; but even if it could be shown
that God requires the reprobate to believe savingly, Gill would happily
agree. Furthermore, Gill argues that the reprobate's unbelief arises
only from the corruption of his own nature.

Man's inability does not exempt him from any duty, though the
grace of God alone can cure man of his impenitence and unbelief. The
lack of grace causes neither. Unbelief arises from "the vitiosity and
corruption of their hearts."[62] When we see that God is pleased to withhold his grace from some men, he does not condemn them for a lack
of grace, but he condemns them for their impenitence and unbelief.
Even though they cannot repent and believe without efficacious grace,
God is under no obligation to bestow it. To conclude otherwise would
lead to an absurdity, i.e., because man is so corrupt he cannot be
subject to the law without the aid of omnipotent power, it can be no
sin in him to remain unsubjected to it.[63]

Again, Gill is careful to distinguish between what can be performed
by man in his impotent state and what must be the work of God. He
does not think that men are responsible for regenerating themselves
or for giving themselves evangelical repentance and evangelical faith.
He does believe, however, that they are responsible for believing and
doing all within their natural power to believe, obey, and accept the
revelation God has given of himself. And again, that condemnation
lies not in their inability to regenerate themselves or to give themselves evangelical faith and repentance, but in their refusal to do even
what they can.[64]

61. Ibid., p. 158.
62. Ibid., p. 165.
63. Ibid., pp. 165–166.
64. Ibid., p. 167.

Gill even shows himself willing to affirm that "men are required to believe in Christ, to love the Lord with all their heart, to make themselves a new heart and a new spirit."[65] But it does not follow that men may do these things of themselves, and the exhortation to such only shows their desperate need of them and that they ought to apply to God for them.

Several phrases and concepts in the quotes above make Gill's exposition of the duties of the unregenerate quite complex. Those who have only the "outward ministry of the word," unaccompanied by the special work of the Spirit, are "obliged to believe no further than the external revelation they enjoy, reaches." Also, Gill says it will be difficult to prove that God requires "spiritual and evangelical obedience." If these statements stood by themselves, untempered by any other considerations, they would put Gill undeniably in the hyper-Calvinist camp on this issue, and here hangs the whole framework of hyper-Calvinism. Gill, however, is ready to allow that the unsaved have the duty to believe savingly and that ministers must exhort them to this (about which more will be said). He even affirms that man must make himself a new heart and a new spirit. Nevertheless, one is not condemned because he is unconverted but because he has sinned against God's law. He also believes that refusal to believe savingly aggravates guilt, a belief possible only on a platform of duty-faith.

Help in this dilemma comes from plunging to the foundations of the question. Wayman, Hussey, and Brine—all without equivocation—rejected duty-faith. Their basis for doing so extends back to the spiritual powers of Adam in the unfallen state and the relation of those powers to the law. This will be treated in a later chapter. For now, a brief observation must suffice simply as a backdrop for Gill's understanding of man's duties and the law of God. Adam had no need to exercise saving faith and was invested with no capacity for it. None of his posterity has greater powers than Adam in the unfallen state; therefore, no powers for saving faith are or ever were a part of man's powers and never were nor now are part of his duty. He cannot be told he must repent and believe, and condemnation is not aggravated by impenitence and unbelief. A radical disjunction exists between the duty to love God and the duty to exhibit saving faith.

Gill does not attempt to make distinctions between pre-fall duties, and he holds that the duties required by the law are fulfilled by the gospel. All that the law required of man in his unfallen state is accomplished and fulfilled by Christ; fallen man may only participate in that

---

65. Ibid., p. 33.

fulfillment by coming to Christ in saving faith. His inability to achieve such faith does not argue for excluding him from the duty of it.

In *The Law Established by the Gospel* Gill argues strongly that the moral law "was written in Adam's heart in innocence."[66] This law "points out to us our duty, both to God and man . . . it directs us to love the Lord our God with all our heart, soul, and strength: and our neighbor as ourselves." None of these requirements has been diminished to the least extent.

Faith, both as a doctrine and as a grace, magnifies and establishes the law in its proper place. It is abolished in several ways—its perpetuity is maintained, its spirituality is asserted and secured, its perfect righteousness is established, obedience to it is set on the best of motives and under the best of influences, and it is put in the hands of Christ as the surest foundation. In addition, the law still functions: it informs us of the mind and will of God, convinces us of sin, serves as a mirror that we might see our continued sinfulness, makes the righteousness of Christ more dear and valuable, and serves as a rule of life. The gospel is not simply a new law or an addendum to it to show how one may circumvent the law's demands. The gospel comes as good news to lawbreakers, showing that all of the law's demands are fully met in one person. Those who are saved do not receive their salvation in spite of the law, or in contradiction to it, but in accordance with it:

> The perfect righteousness of the law is established by faith, and the doctrine of it. Whatever the law requires, according to this doctrine, is given in it. Does it require pure and spotless holiness of nature? There is in Christ an entire conformity to it in this respect; who is *holy, harmless, and undefiled*; and as such, is an high priest that becomes us, is suitable to us, as being our sanctification and our righteousness. Does the law require sinless and perfect obedience to all its commands? Christ has always done the things that pleased his Father, and has done all the things that are pleasing to him; he has perfectly obeyed the whole preceptive part of the law. Does the law require of, and threaten transgressors with the penalty of death? Christ being made sin, was made a curse for his people, and became obedient to death, even the death of the cross. So that the law, in all respects, is magnified, and made honourable by him, according to the doctrine of faith. We bring to the law in Christ our head, or rather he in our room and stead, a righteousness which answers all the demands of it, and casts a lustre and glory upon it: and, indeed, all the obedience of angels and men put together, does not, and cannot give the law such glory and honour as the obedience and righteousness

66. Ibid., p. 15.

of Christ does. Whence 'tis clear, that the law is so far from being made void, that it is thoroughly established by it.[67]

For Gill, therefore, faith is not disjoined from man's obligations to the law. Faith fulfills these obligations. Gill's conviction kept him from rejecting duty-faith and duty-repentance and inspired in him a commitment to the necessity of evangelism.

Obligation to Evangelism

While Gill believed in a decree of predestination of a fixed number of men to everlasting salvation, he nevertheless believed in the use of means for the conversion of the elect. The propagation of the gospel beyond the circle of his church claimed the attention of one article in the Confession of Faith written for his church:

> . . . we think ourselves obliged to sympathize with each other in all conditions both inward and outward . . . and particularly to pray for one another, and that the gospel and the ordinances thereof might be blessed to the edification and comfort of each other's souls, and for the gathering in of others to Christ, besides those who are already gathered—all which duties we desire to be found in the performance of through the gracious assistance of the Holy Spirit.[68]

Indeed, Gill was even capable of some remorse at the lack of zealous ministers. Around 1750 Gill said:

> . . . the harvest is great and the faithful and painful ministers are few. There are scarcely any that naturally care for the estate and souls of men, and who are heartily concerned for their spiritual welfare: all comparatively seek their own things, their honor and applause from men, their ease, reputation, and riches; and none or few the things that are Jesus Christ's, or which relate to his honor, glory, kingdom, and interest in the world.[69]

Gill called for such ardent laborers in that he knew that no person could pinpoint the location of the elect. Although no minister has the authority to offer salvation to any, since that is not strictly his commission, "yet they may preach the gospel of salvation to all men, and

67. Gill, *Law Established*, pp. 34, 35.
68. John Rippon, *A Brief Memoir of the Life and Writings of the Late Rev. John Gill, D.D.* (London: John Bennett, 1938), p. 19.
69. Ivimey, *English Baptists*, 3:277.

declare, that whosoever believes shall be saved: for this they are com-
missioned to do."[70]

The relation between an "offer of grace" and the proclamation of
the gospel is another important aspect of understanding Gill. As seen,
Gill rejected the idea that grace, Christ, or salvation could be offered.
In his rebuttal to Wesley's harangue on predestination, Gill distances
himself from any attempt to defend the sincerity of an "offer" of grace
when grace is sovereignly withheld.

> And that there are universal offers of grace and salvation made to all
> men, I utterly deny; nay, I deny they are made to any; no, not to God's
> elect; grace and salvation are provided for them in the everlasting cove-
> nant, procured for them by Christ, published and revealed in the gospel
> and applied by the Spirit; much less are they made to others; wherefore,
> this doctrine is not chargeable with insincerity on that account. Let the
> patrons of universal offers defend themselves from this objection, I have
> nothing to do with it.[71]

The same view appears in Gill's preface to a 1748 volume of hymns
by Richard Davis. The manner in which Gill discusses it on this occasion holds the key for understanding Gill on this issue. Having heartily approved the life and ministry of Davis, Gill observed that within
the hymns the phrase of "offering Christ and Grace" sometimes appears. Davis used this phrase partly through custom, says Gill, and
"partly thro' his affectionate concern and zeal for gaining upon souls,
and encouraging them to come to Christ." Gill assures the readers that
Davis changed before his death and "disused the phrase, as being
improper." Gill has no objections to encouraging sinners to come to
Christ, but considers the phrase "offer Christ and Grace" as strictly
without theological foundation. Grace strictly refers to the sovereign
bestowment of unmerited salvific blessings and cannot, therefore, be
offered, not even to the elect. On the other hand, sinners can most
urgently and sincerely be urged to come to Christ and find in him
relief for a sin-burdened conscience. Verses like the following were not
strictly correct in all their parts, according to Gill, though he took it
not upon himself to rewrite any of them.

> Sinners, this Grace is tendered to
>   the vilest of you all:
> Come Sinners, come, accept this Grace,
>   the Gospel gives a call.

70. Gill, *Cause*, p. 164.
71. Gill, *Doctrine of Predestination*, pp. 28, 29.

> Stand not for to dispute, and die;
>   free offered Grace receive;
> Such Love embrace, accept such Grace;
>   O do this Grace believe!

The following verses, however, have no phrase to which Gill appears to object:

> Sinners you must repent or die;
>   and would you then repent?
> O come to Jesus, he will give
>   your godly sorrow vent.
>
> O come to him, and do not stay
>   for mourning first, or ease,
> For change of life, or broken heart,
>   for he will give you these.

This last verse is especially remarkable for its urgent solicitations for an immediate closing with Christ. Gill's dissatisfaction with the "offers" vocabulary must not be construed as a refusal to urge sinners to come to Christ. On the contrary, Gill considers it a mark of a true minister earnestly to urge others to come to Christ. Whereas Joseph Hussey interprets the word *come* in John 5:40 and Matthew 11:28 as a "naturally-reasonable faith" and as "coming on their feet to Christ when he preach'd and wrought Miracles on Earth,"[72] Gill says John 5:40 refers to saving faith. The Jews did not believe because of the "perverseness and stubbornness" of their wills. Additionally, their not coming to Christ "for life" is "criminal and blameworthy," an affirmation completely at odds with a rejection of duty-faith.[73] When commenting on Matthew 11:28, Gill absolutely rejects Hussey's treatment of the passage and, though not calling him by name, appears to have in mind giving a final and incontrovertible refutation of Hussey's line of reasoning. "Come unto me," in Gill's treatment, bears the following meaning:

> ... by which is meant, not a local coming, or a coming to hear him preach; ... nor is it a bare coming under the ordinances of Christ ... but it is to be understood of believing in Christ, the going out of the soul to him, in the exercise of grace on him, of desire after him, love to him, faith and hope in him: believing in Christ, and coming to him, are terms

72. Joseph Hussey, *God's Operations of Grace: But No Offers of His Grace* (London: 1707), pp. 355, 366.
73. Gill, *Cause*, p. 33.

synonymous John vi.35. Those who come to Christ aright, come as sinners, to a full, suitable, able, and willing Saviour; venture their souls upon him, and trust in him for righteousness, life, and salvation, which they are encouraged to do, by this kind of invitation; which shews his willingness to save, and his readiness to give relief to distressed minds.[74]

Such an invitation is for those who are burdened; but such sinners may be required and encouraged to come to Jesus and promised that in coming they will find life. An "offer of grace" is in a different category entirely and must not be substituted for the proclamation of what God requires alongside what God graciously and sovereignly bestows. As far as Gill is concerned, this view should greatly encourage ministers of the gospel in the duties of evangelism. The means that God appoints he also makes powerful and effectual to the ends and purposes for which he appoints them. God does not leave these means to the uncertain, precarious, and impotent will of man; such would be equivalent to preaching to stones. Although it takes a power to convert sinners equal to that needed to convert stones, stones are not subjects capable of redemption.

By nature, unregenerate men are altogether like stocks and stones and can contribute nothing to their regeneration or new birth. Different, however, from stocks and stones, they have faculties with which, when converted, they will worship and praise God. Therefore, God has not only "signified it as his will, that the gospel should be preached to every creature," but determined that it shall be powerful to "the conversion of many souls." Consequently, this scheme displays the wisdom of God, as far as Gill is concerned, "in accompanying the word preached with a divine energy, and an unfrustrable operation; so that all his gracious designs towards his people are effectually answered, and not leaving it to the bare force of moral suasion."[75]

In his *Body of Divinity*, Gill includes a section on Christian zeal. True zeal for the cause of Christ concerns itself with the gospel, the ordinances, and the discipline of the church. One should be zealous for the gospel's display of the free grace of God in every part of salvation. The apostle Paul, an eminent example of zeal, "was so zealously concerned for it, as not to count his life dear to himself, so that he might finish his course with joy, by bearing a testimony to it." This testimony of the apostle was borne up by the great end of the gospel:

74. John Gill, *An Exposition of the New Testament*, 3 vols. (London: n.p., 1746), Matthew 11:28.
75. Ibid., pp. 180–181.

". . . it is the gospel of salvation, which publishes salvation by Christ, and declares, that whosoever believes in him shall be saved."[76]

As far as Gill is concerned, Paul's example of zeal is very instructive and permits universal application. When Paul stood before Agrippa and showed his desire for Agrippa and all those who heard him to be saved, he was only doing what everyone who has experienced the grace of God should do. Paul's prayer "shews his affection for the souls of men, and his great desire for their conversion." Paul wished that all that were present were "entirely and in the fullest sense Christians, as he was; that they knew as much of Christ, and had as much faith in him, and love to him, as he did, and were as ready to serve and obey him." But Gill is not yet through drawing conclusions from Paul's example. He wished they were "regenerated by the Spirit of God, new creatures in Christ, called by the grace of God with a holy calling, believers in Christ, lovers of him, pardoned by his blood." This desire for others is the natural outgrowth of one's own experience of the grace of God. In fact, it is an evidence of grace "when the heart is drawn out in desires after the salvation of others." This desire is multiplied by the fact that if hearing the Gospel does not result in conversion, "the condemnation of those that hear the words is thereby aggravated."[77]

The disciple Andrew demonstrated an admirable zeal, which should be imitated, in finding his brother Simon and bringing him to Jesus. After an experience of such joyful proportions, we want to bring others "to the knowledge of the same; for such is the nature of grace, 'tis very communicative, and those that have it, are very desirous that all others should be partakers of it."[78]

Several items are worthy of note. The minister should preach the gospel with a view to seeing all his hearers converted. In fact, Gill unashamedly affirms, in commenting on Acts 26:28, that "it is one part of the gospel ministry to persuade men," though human persuasion by itself is ineffectual. This is a very strange position for a man reputed to be a hyper-Calvinist, since earlier hyper-Calvinists such as Lewis Wayman and Joseph Hussey had specifically argued against such a stance. Wayman says a minister must tell his hearers "to wait at wisdom's gates, till they shall have further intimations of their master's will and pleasure concerning them." Only when the minister perceives grace to be bestowed upon any should he "exhort them with purpose of heart to cleave unto the Lord." Otherwise, there would probably be "millions in the world believing in Christ for life and

---

76. Gill, *Body*, 2:524.
77. Gill, *Exposition*, Acts 26:29.
78. Ibid., John 1:41.

salvation, to whom God hath not given eternal life in Christ, and who shall never obtain salvation by him."[79]

Hussey, in arguing against "offers," goes further and divides the gospel into two parts: one for the elect and one for the non-elect. His method of proclaiming these two parts is completely alien to the method and spirit of Gill:

> Do this then, when you do *not* Preach the Gospel of the Blood of Christ to them. For that is a blessing of the Kingdom, and to be given to none but to them to whom it is prepared. How can he be a Priest to all, if he hath not died for all as an Expiatory, or Atoning Sacrifice? So then if Many were made, only to be ruled over by Christ as a King, there's enough of the Gospel to be preached to them; namely the Gospel of the Kingdom of God.[80]

Gill believed that rejecting the gospel aggravated the guilt of men. Although some ambiguity exists in Gill's system concerning the exact relationship between the sinner's duty to natural faith and his duty to saving faith, this factor clearly demonstrates that Gill believed faith such a duty that the non-exercise of it made one more blameworthy. Lewis Wayman, however, argues strongly that it will not be an "aggravation of the guilt and punishment of those that perish, that they have not believed in Christ, any more than their not being chosen in him is."[81] Gill, though believing in the sovereign purpose of God, did not allow his understanding of the gracious designs of God in salvation to overthrow or eliminate his understanding of the real and damnable guilt of unbelief.

Gill's exposition of zeal in the gospel minister was not a distortion of his system or a simple flourish of affection without theological foundation. It fit well within his understanding of the nature of sin and the full demands of the gospel.

The dominical example compels the believer to the same conclusion. Christ's zeal for the doctrines of the gospel, as demonstrated by his "warm and constant preaching them even with power and authority," should energize his followers to the same zeal.[82]

In addition, the zeal of persons believing a false religion should stimulate the "professors of the true religion to show at least an equal zeal." Every person walks in the name of his own god, and the Phar-

---

79. Lewis Wayman, *A Further Enquiry after Truth* (London: J. & J. Marshall, 1738), p. 51.

80. Hussey, *God's Operation*, p. 98.

81. Wayman, *Further Enquiry*, p. 51.

82. Gill, *Body*, 2:526.

isees showed great zeal and took great pains going over land and sea to gain one proselyte. "Should not we Christians exert ourselves to the uttermost for the interest of the Redeemer, this must be a becoming zeal."[83]

Gill does not shrink from enjoining a preacher to engage in an aggressive ministry, and he even encourages a skillful display of the gospel, that men might believe. The faithful minister sees hope in his message, and its certain effectuality should give rise to an inspired zeal. The Word should be dispensed wisely, the ministers of it should be wise and faithful to give everyone his portion, and they should be skillful workmen, rightly dividing the word of truth. The public ministry requires that "they should have the tongue of the learned to speak a word in season to him that is weary; he that winneth souls is wise; and being crafty, the apostle says, he caught the Corinthians with guile, not with a sinful, but a laudable and commendable one."[84]

> The gospel of salvation, the word of salvation, and salvation itself; it is a publication of salvation by Christ; it is the faithful saying and worthy of all acceptation, that Christ came into the world to save the chief of sinners; it declares, that there is salvation in him, and in no other; and that whoever believes in him shall be saved: this is the gospel every faithful minister preaches, and every sensible sinner desires to hear.[85]

Some have made light of Gill's concept of "sensible" sinners. By "sensible" he only means "spiritually aware of personal sinfulness." None but such as those convicted of sin desire salvation, for they have no sense that they are in danger. He is not saying that a person must discern whether or not he is "sensible" or if he is elect; but he is saying that true candidates for salvation must be aware that they are in need of salvation.

In concluding his section on the public ministry, Gill considers the usefulness of the office and discusses it largely in terms of evangelism:

> In general; its use is for the enlargement of the interest of Christ in the world; and it is by means of the gospel being preached to all nations in all the world, that the kingdom of Christ has been spread everywhere; not only in Judea, where the gospel was first preached, but throughout the Gentile world, multitudes were converted, and churches were set up everywhere, Christianity triumphed, and heathenism everywhere abolished.

83. Ibid.
84. Ibid., p. 670.
85. Ibid., p. 668.

The ministry of the word is for the conversion of sinners; without which churches would not be increased nor supported, and must in course fail, and come to nothing; but the hand of the Lord being with his ministers, many in every age believe and turn to the Lord, and are added to the churches; by which means they are kept up and preserved: and hence it is necessary in the ministers of the word, to set forth the lost and miserable estate and condition of men by nature, the danger they are in, the necessity of regeneration and repentance, and of a better righteousness than their own, and of faith in Christ; which things are blessed for the turning of men from darkness to light, and from the power of Satan unto God.

Another use of it is, For the perfecting of the saints; for the completing of the number of the elect, in effectual vocation, even of those who are sanctified, or set apart by God the Father, by that eternal act of his, choosing them in Christ; or for the joining in of the saints, as it may be rendered; who were disjointed and scattered abroad by the fall of Adam; these are gathered in by the ministry of the word: so that none shall perish, but all come to repentance.[86]

Since all of the blessings accompany only the receiving of the gospel, attention to the public hearing of the Word devolves upon all men as a duty. From the hearing of the Word comes conviction of sin, in which man's lost and undone state is revealed. Three thousand people came under such conviction in Peter's sermon; even so unbelievers in the present day may see their corruption and condemnation. In addition, conversion comes through the public hearing of the Word, since the purpose of the preached Word is to turn men from "the darkness of sin and error to the light of grace and truth; from the power, dominion, and slavery of Satan, to serve the living God, from the ways of sin and folly to the paths of righteousness and holiness."[87]

Conclusion

One can accuse Gill of "non-invitation, non-application" only by clinging to an unbiblically narrow concept of "invitation," as if it were a call to physical activity at the end of a preaching service. If Gill were antinomian, may God grant the church a deeper holiness produced by this kind of "antinomianism." The nomenclature of hyper-Calvinist in speaking of Gill must be questioned seriously in light of his clear, perceptive zeal for the gospel, his earnestness of desire for the salvation

86. Ibid., p. 671.
87. Ibid., p. 681.

of his hearers, his statements regarding the perpetuity of the law as exhibited in the gospel, and his belief concerning the blameworthiness of rejecting the gospel message and all it contains. And perhaps, rather than imputing blame upon Gill for the leanness of the times, he should be credited with preserving gospel purity, which eventuated in the efforts to use means for the conversion of the heathen.

3

On the Road Again

The denomination to which he conscientiously attached himself, and whose property he invariably sought to promote, never had so distinguished an ornament."[1] So Joseph Ivimey judged the importance of Andrew Fuller.

Born February 6, 1754, in Cambridgeshire to a farming family, Fuller's earliest religious impressions were of the hyper-Calvinistic sort. Mr. Eve, the minister of the church he attended, was "tinged with false Calvinism," as Fuller would say, and had little or nothing to say to the unconverted. At about fourteen years of age Fuller began to experience conviction of sin. At times his impressions of his sinfulness drove him virtually to despair. As he had learned that no sinner had any warrant to trust Christ until he discerned himself as under the favor and gracious operations of God, his tumult with his sin, wretchedness, and sense of the wrath of God caused Fuller great pain. He knew correctly that "God would be perfectly just in sending me to hell, and that to hell I must go, unless I were saved of mere grace."[2] Utterly at an end of all hope of righteousness in himself, and perceiving the beauty of Christ and the way of salvation by his death, Fuller, with or without warrant as he perceived it, cast himself utterly upon the mercy of Christ. He continued for more than an hour, weeping and supplicating mercy for the Savior's sake, and "gradually and insensibly" his guilt and fears were removed.[3]

In 1770 Fuller was baptized in the church at Soham. Soon after, he

---

1. Joseph Ivimey, *A History of the English Baptists*, 4 vols. (London: Printed for the author and sold by Burditt, Buxton, Hamilton, Baynes, etc., 1811–1830), 4:532.
2. John Ryland, Jr., *Memoir of the Rev. Andrew Fuller* (London: 1816), p. 17.
3. Ibid., p. 19.

Andrew Fuller

began to preach. On May 3, 1775, he was ordained as pastor of the church, where he continued for more than seven years. In 1782 he moved to Kettering and remained as pastor there until his death in 1815. From Kettering he published his *Gospel Worthy of All Acceptation*, which ultimately led to the formation of the Baptist Missionary Society. Joseph Ivimey summarized the ministry of Fuller in a curious blend of exalted judgments, tempered with comparative moderation:

> He might have been excelled by some few of its ministers in some separate and distinct excellence; but when taken in the whole of his character, he excelled all others. As a writer on the various important subjects he discussed he holds a high, and, in regard to some of them, an unrivalled station. As a preacher, he greatly excelled in the simplicity of his compositions and in the correctness of his illustrations; but as the founder and conductor of the Baptist Missionary Society for twenty-two years, without any pecuniary remuneration, he will ever be remembered with esteem and veneration by all who feel an interest for the salvation of the heathen and the prosperity of the denomination.[4]

4. Ivimey, *English Baptists*, 4:532–535.

The distinguishing tenets of Fuller's theology gained such high profile in Baptist life that those who deemed themselves his true disciples became known as Fullerites. In fact, the larger part of the nineteenth century became somewhat of a contest in Baptist life between the "Fullerites" and the "Gillites." The differences in their theologies are largely overdrawn, but, nevertheless, the way people perceived these differences provided great material for polemical engagements.

The nineteenth-century Baptist historian David Benedict wrote a delightful book in 1860 entitled *Fifty Years Among the Baptists*. In describing the various changes that occurred within his five decades among Baptists, he included a chapter entitled "New Phases in the Doctrinal Creed of the Baptists." This chapter narrated the effects of what he called the conflict between the "Gillites" and the "Fullerites." He reports that the followers of Fuller were considered Arminians by the Gillite men. However, Benedict acknowledged that their theologies differed but little in the areas of election, perseverance, depravity, Trinity, and so on. Nevertheless, their differences on atonement are drawn very strongly. Benedict reports:

> The Fuller system, which makes it consistent for all the heralds of the gospel to call upon men everywhere to repent, was well received by one class of our ministers, but not by the staunch defenders of the old theory of a limited atonement. According to their views, all for whom Christ suffered and died would certainly be effectually called and saved. These conflicting opinions caused altercations of considerable severity for a time, among the Baptists, who had hitherto been all united on the orthodox side. The Gillites maintained that the expositions of Fuller were unsound, and would subvert the genuine gospel faith. If, said they, the atonement of Christ is general in its nature it must be so in its effects, as none of his sufferings will be in vain; and the doctrine of universal salvation will inevitably follow this dangerous creed.[5]

H. C. Vedder, writing in 1907 in *A Short History of the Baptists*, maintains less reserve in his discernment of the differences. Obviously unsympathetic with thoroughgoing Calvinism, Vedder characterizes Fuller's contribution in the following way:

> Fuller boldly accepted and advocated a doctrine of the atonement that, until his day, had always been stigmatized as rank Arminianism, viz., that the atonement of Christ, as to its worth and dignity, was sufficient

5. David Benedict, *Fifty Years Among the Baptists* (New York: Sheldon & Co., 1860), p. 141.

for the sins of the whole world, and was not an offering for the elect alone, as Calvinists of all grades had hitherto maintained. Along with this naturally went a sublapsarian interpretation of the "doctrines of grace," and this modified Calvinism gradually made its way among Baptists until it has become well-nigh the only doctrine known among them.[6]

Such statements could be misleading and make Fuller appear less Calvinistic than he was. An examination of Fuller's theology demonstrates his unswerving alignment with historic Calvinism in theology and methodology.

Total Depravity

Fuller's doctrine of total depravity gives eloquent testimony to his commitment to historic Reformed theology. From his understanding of its fundamental importance to all other doctrines, his biblical defense of it, and its implications for preaching the gospel, one can see that Fuller places the doctrine of total depravity in the position of a *sine qua non* in theology.

According to Fuller, all divergences from orthodox Protestantism have as their root some relinquishment of this doctrine. "I never knew a person verge toward the Arminian, the Arian, the Socinian, or the Antinomian schemes, without first entertaining diminutive notions of human depravity, or blameworthiness.[7] In short, this is a subject which "affects all the great doctrines of the gospel,"[8] and as a "fundamental principle in religion" it becomes the rock on which "almost all other principles are founded."[9]

Bible-Related Evidence

In his exposition of the doctrine, Fuller's transparent sincerity and earnestness stand out in the initial question he asks: "Is it true?" Based upon that question, which arises in the midst of a dialogue between Gaius and Crispus, Fuller presents five evidences, all of which arise from biblical authority.

6. Henry C. Vedder, *A Short History of the Baptists* (Valley Forge: Judson Press, 1907), p. 249.
7. Andrew Fuller, *The Complete Works of the Rev. Andrew Fuller*, revised by Joseph Belcher, 3 vols. (Philadelphia: American Baptist Publication Society, 1845), 2:662.
8. Ibid., p. 674.
9. Ibid., p. 665.

First, biblical passages expressly teach that man hopelessly pursues a course alien to God and will never turn from that course apart from the effectual and irresistible power of God. Fuller had such confidence in the clarity of Scripture that he considered this truth to be self-evident; therefore, his demonstration of this doctrine sometimes consists of several verses of Scripture together. "And God saw that the wickedness of man was great in the earth, and that every imagination of the thoughts of his heart was only evil continually" (Gen. 6:5). "God looked down upon the children of men, to see if there were any that did understand, that did seek God. Every one of them is gone back, they are altogether become filthy: there is none that doeth good, no not one" (Ps. 14:2–3). ". . . both Jews and Gentiles . . . are all under sin; As it is written, there is none righteous, no, not one. . . . Destruction and misery are in their ways: And the way of peace have they not known: There is no fear of God before their eyes" (Rom. 3:9–10, 16–18). ". . . The carnal mind is enmity against God: for it is not subject to the law of God, neither indeed can be" (Rom. 8:7). Fuller added other Scripture passages to these as irrefutable assertions of the doctrine of total depravity.

Second, another line of biblical evidence that clearly enunciates this doctrine as true rests upon those Scriptures that "declare the utter impossibility of carnal men doing any thing to please God."[10] "To be carnally minded is death . . . the carnal mind is enmity against God; for it is not subject to the law of God neither can be. So, then, they that are in the flesh cannot please God." Man in his present condition *cannot* please God. If nothing that unregenerate man does has the possibility of pleasing God, then he is sinful in his very nature; and the first motions of every action, as well as the actions themselves, partake of his sinful nature. Fuller would not even allow "amiable qualities" or efforts at the attainment of virtue to pass under any other nomenclature than that of an "unmixed course of evil."[11]

Third, that the sum of the law may be reduced to the commandments of love to God and love to neighbor precludes any measure of obedience in unregenerate man. A man away from God has not the love of God in him; and where God is not loved supremely, creatures are either disregarded or regarded for less than the best reason: "Such love, therefore, has no virtue in it, but is of the nature of sin."[12] Fuller illustrates this truth by telling a story of an ill-begun voyage:

10. Ibid., p. 665.
11. Ibid.
12. Ibid.

A ship's company rise against their officers, put them in chains, and take the command of the ship upon themselves. They agree to set the officers ashore on some uninhabited island, to sail to some distant port, dispose of the cargo, and divide the amount. After parting with their officers they find it necessary, for the sake of self-preservation, to establish some kind of laws and order.

To these they adhere with punctuality, act upon honour with respect to each other, and propose to be very impartial in the distribution of their plunder. But while they are on their voyage, one of the company relents and becomes very unhappy. They inquire the reason. He answers, "We are engaged in a wicked cause!" They plead their justice, honour, and generosity to each other. He denies that there is any virtue in it: "Nay, all our equity, while it is exercised in pursuit of a scheme which violates the great law of justice, is itself a species of iniquity!"—"You talk extravagantly; surely we might be worse than we are if we were to destroy each other as well as our officers."—"Yes, wickedness admits of degrees; but there is no virtue or goodness in all our doings; all has arisen from selfish motives. The same principles which led us to discard our officers would lead us, if it were not for our own sake, to destroy each other."—"But you speak so very *discouragingly*; you destroy all *motives* to good order in the ship; what would you have us do?"—"RE-PENT, RETURN TO OUR INJURED OFFICERS AND OWNERS, AND SUBMIT TO MERCY!"—"O, but this we *cannot* do: advise us to any thing which concerns the good order of the ship, and we will hearken to you!"—"I *cannot* bear to advise in these matters! RETURN, RETURN, AND SUBMIT TO MERCY!" Such would be the language of a true penitent in this case; and such should be the language of a Christian minister to sinners who have cast off the government of God.[13]

Fourth, another evidence of depravity gathers up the Scriptures that teach the necessity of regeneration. If a man could, in his present condition, do anything even partially in harmony with God's law or any part of his duty toward God, then a reformation, rather than regeneration, would be in order. But, men are "essentially depraved" and "the whole fabric must be taken down."[14] The Scriptures that teach that man must be born again—that old things must pass away and all things must become new—indicate that a mere "improvement of principles already inherent in man" will not suffice; for no "degree of virtue in the carnal heart . . . [nor] anything . . . pleasing to God" is present that might be "cultivated and increased."[15]

13. Ibid., p. 673.
14. Ibid., pp. 663, 665.
15. Ibid.

Fifth, Fuller distinguishes between the nature of the deeds done by a saved person and those done by one not yet born again. Promises are made to those who "love God" and "obey him," who "do good" or "do righteousness" or give a cup of cold water from the proper motivation. These Scriptures give no place to degrees of righteousness in the dispensing of rewards but make promises to every degree of it. The distinction in view relates to the nature of the righteous act. "Hence we may certainly conclude that unregenerate men have not the least degree of real goodness in them, or of any thing that is pleasing to God."[16]

Implications

Two important considerations spin off from Fuller's view of total depravity. One, depravity presupposes moral duty of an absolute sort. Two, though man is still a free agent, his will is in bondage to the inclinations of his rebellious heart.

As to the first point, if no absolute moral duty rests upon all men without exception, the concept of depravity becomes meaningless. This moral duty expresses itself in the revealed laws of God. All men are required to love God with mind, soul, heart, and strength. To require the opposite would require wickedness, meanness, and misery; to require less is to require duplicity, a divided heart, and partial enmity to God and each other; to require nothing results in "anarchy and confusion . . . and cold, and darkness, and misery"[17] and removes the possibility of God's judging the world. But the giving of an absolute law that demands complete obedience renders any deviation from that standard a sinful act by its very nature: "There can be no evil in sin, but in proportion to the goodness of that law of which it is a transgression."[18] In Fuller's system, God and his law are so united "that nonsubjection to one is enmity to the other."[19] Thus, one sees that depravity, or enmity against God by nature, can only be defined in light of an absolute moral duty, eternally binding upon the creature man, expressed in the decalogue, and summarized in the two great commandments of love to God and love to neighbor.

The second implication is that man's will is in bondage. This fact, however, does not reduce man's responsibility nor his free agency. The following dialogue between Gaius and Crispus gives expression to Fuller's philosophical defense of this legitimate distinction:

16. Ibid., p. 666.
17. Ibid., p. 659.
18. Ibid., p. 661.
19. Ibid., p. 660.

G. No one can conceive of a power of voluntarily acting against the prevailing inclination, for the thing itself is a contradiction; and a power of changing it is no less absurd. If a person go about to change his prevailing inclination, he must, in so doing, be either involuntary or voluntary. If the former, this can be no exercise of free agency; if the latter, he must have two opposite prevailing inclinations at the same time, which is a contradiction. And if it were not a contradiction, he still does no more than follow his inclination; namely, his virtuous inclination, which he is supposed to possess, to have his vicious inclination changed. If freedom from the influence of motives, or power to change one's inclination, be essential to free agency, the Divine Being himself is not free. God, as all must allow, possesses an immutable determination to do what is right, and cannot in the least degree, or for a single moment, incline to the contrary. His conduct is necessarily and invariably expressive of the infinite rectitude of his will. The same, in a degree, might be said of holy angels and the spirits of just men made perfect. So far from being free from the influence of motives, or having a power to change the prevailing inclination of their hearts, those motives which, by reason of the depravity of our natures, have but little effect upon us, have full influence upon them, and constantly determine them to the most ardent pursuit of righteousness.

C. And yet you say they are free agents?

G. If God, angels, and saints in heaven be not free agents, who are?

C. But this is moral *liberty*.

G. True; but the same reasoning will apply to moral slavery. If an unalterable bias of mind to good does not destroy free agency, neither does an unalterable bias of mind to evil. Satan is as much a free agent as Gabriel, and as much accountable to God for all he does.[20]

In his development of this distinction, Fuller is convinced that he is opposing the "Arminian notion of free-will." He argues against the Arminians without reserve, for they suppose a man may act contrary to, or even change, a prevailing inclination. By doing this, they claim a part, ". . . yea, the very turning point, of salvation." Such a view assumes that the sinner only needs helps or assistances "granted to men in common, to enable us to choose the path of life." But in reality, "our hearts being by nature wholly depraved, we need an almighty and invincible power to renew them, otherwise our free agency would only accelerate our everlasting ruin."[21]

Unconditional Election

Fuller believed that acceptance of the true doctrine of total depravity naturally implied the rest of the Calvinistic doctrines. A. C. Under-

20. Ibid., p. 657.
21. Ibid., p. 658.

wood misrepresents Fuller in his oft-quoted evaluation of Fuller's contribution: "He was the man who dealt the mortal blow to the system which held that it was impossible for any but the elect to embrace the Gospel and that it was therefore useless to invite the unconverted to put their trust in Christ."[22] The natural tendency of such a statement is toward concluding that Fuller opposed the doctrine of unconditional election. Such is absolutely not the case. James E. Tull is much nearer the truth when he admits that "Fuller remained a staunch Calvinist."[23] This judgment is true in every area of anthropology and soteriology, the two great doctrines by which Calvinism is defined most distinctly.

Fuller places one of his most succinct and compelling arguments for unconditional election in the mouth of Crispus, who—under the influence of Gaius—has been gradually convinced of the truth of the doctrine of total depravity. In a series of statements, he addresses the natural implications of such a view.

> Fourthly, if your views be just, the doctrine of free or unconditional election may be clearly demonstrated and proved to be a dictate of right reason. If men be utterly depraved, they lie entirely at the discretion of God either to save or not to save them. If any are saved, it must be by an act of free grace. If some are brought to believe in Christ, while others continue in unbelief, (which accords with continued fact,) the difference between them must be altogether of grace. But if God makes a difference in time, he must have determined to do so for eternity; for to suppose God to act without a purpose is depriving him of wisdom; and to suppose any new purpose to arise in his mind would be to accuse him of mutability. Here, therefore, we are landed upon election—sovereign, unconditional election.[24]

Although such treatment from logic compels the careful thinker to Fuller's conclusion, Fuller did not rest such an important doctrine upon mere argument, no matter how cogent and coherent. Divine revelation itself unceasingly calls us to glory in a salvation that has arisen from the mere unconditional pleasure of God.

Engaging in a written debate with Dan Taylor, leader of the New Connection of General Baptists, Fuller set out to demonstrate that universal grace was not necessary as a foundation for universal exhortations to repentance. In the documents that resulted, *Reply to Phi-*

22. A. C. Underwood, *A History of the English Baptists* (London: The Baptist Union of Great Britain & Ireland, 1970), p. 161.

23. James E. Tull, *Shapers of Baptist Thought* (Valley Forge: Judson Press, 1972), p. 88.

24. Fuller, *Works*, 2:675.

lanthropos and *The Reality and Efficacy of Divine Grace*, Fuller maintains that all men are obligated to obey God. This holds true whether the object of obedience is the decalogue or the command to repent and believe the gospel. If grace assumes no merit, obligation exists apart from it. Universal grace cannot be the foundation for universal obligation, or it ceases to be grace. A part of his total argument rested on the absolute and unconditioned nature of election. "Whoever are saved are indebted to sovereign and efficacious grace for their salvation."[25] The apostolic manner of addressing the churches compels such a conclusion:

> The apostles addressed *all* the believing Ephesians, Thessalonians, &c. as having been "chosen in Christ" before the foundation of the world, that they should be holy; as "*chosen to salvation* through sanctification of the Spirit, and belief of the truth;" as "elect according to the foreknowledge of God the Father, through sanctification of the Spirit unto obedience;" as being "saved and called with a holy calling, not according to their works, but according to God's own purpose and grace, given them in Christ before the world began." But if SOME were saved in consequence of such a purpose in their favour, and OTHERS without it, the apostles had no just ground to write as they did, concerning them all, without distinction. When we are told that "as many as were ordained to eternal life believed," this implies, as strongly as any thing can imply, that *no more* believed, and were saved, than such as were ordained to eternal life. Christ returned thanks to his Father that he had "hid these things from the wise and prudent, and revealed them unto babes. Even so Father," said he, "for so it seemed good in thy sight." And again, we are assured, by the apostle Paul, "The election hath obtained it, and the rest were blinded."[26]

According to 1 Peter 1, obedience in all its parts "is that of which election and sanctification of the Spirit are the proper causes." By election men are chosen for obedience, and by sanctification they are fitted for it. But obedience includes evangelical obedience, or faith, and therefore election must be the cause of our obedience and therefore precede it, "since the cause always precedes the effect."[27]

Another strong defense of election Fuller presents arises from its symmetry with the ideals of practical Christianity. Fuller strongly advocated the systematization of doctrine in order that the Christian might understand the "various connections in which acknowledged truths are introduced in the Scriptures, and the practical purposes to

25. Ibid., p. 544.
26. Ibid.
27. Ibid., pp. 466, 467.

which they are there actually applied." Assuming that election is a
"matter clearly revealed in the word of God," he sets out to show its
marvelous practicality.[28]

First, in one of its connections, election declares the source of "salvation to be mere grace, or undeserved favour, and to cut off all hopes
of acceptance with God by works of any kind." Such is the meaning
of Romans 11:5, 6, which speaks of the remnant according to the election of grace. The clarity of Paul's language there clearly excludes any
cause in salvation except electing grace. By this doctrine, saints learn
that only the grace of God has made them what they are; sinners cease
to rely on their own righteousness and learn that they must cast
"themselves at the feet of sovereign mercy."[29]

Second, the doctrine of election "is introduced in order to account
for the unbelief of the greater part of the Jewish nation, without ex-
cusing them in it." God, by his own sovereign design, has clearly
drawn a line between Isaac and Ishmael, Jacob and Esau, demonstrating that his saving purpose had always been individual and sovereign.
Even so, he has left great numbers of Abraham's descendants to perish
in unbelief. The objections Paul anticipates afford "irrefragable proof
that the doctrine maintained by the apostle was that of the absolute
sovereignty of God, in having mercy on whom He would, and giving
up whom He would to hardness of heart."[30]

According to Fuller, men in every age bring this same objection to
the doctrine of sovereign election. On the one hand the pseudo-Cal-
vinists, as Fuller named them, allowed sovereignty to eliminate man's
duty and responsibility, since he is unable to believe without sovereign
grace. Therefore, men should not be called upon and exhorted to repentance and faith. It is a matter of sober irony that the hyper- (or
pseudo-) Calvinists ran arm in arm with the Arminians in this; for
though the idea is expressed in different ways, both groups assume
that man has no duty apart from grace. The Arminians made universal
grace the ground for universal duty to believe, thus denying by implication the unmerited character of grace. Fuller spoke against both
of these by affirming two truths: the universal duty of all men to repent
and believe, thus rendering the universal dispersion of the gospel necessary; and the absolutely unmerited and sovereign character of grace,
thus ascribing salvation solely to the will of God.

Third, the doctrine of election shows "the certain success of Christ's
undertaking, as it were in defiance of unbelievers, who set at naught

28. Ibid., 3:808.
29. Ibid.
30. Ibid.

his gracious invitations." Far from prohibiting universal invitations, election encourages them and guarantees that they will not be universally unsuccessful. When our Lord upbraided Bethsaida and Chorazin for their unbelief, he immediately prayed, "I thank thee, O Father, Lord of heaven and earth, because thou hast hid these things from the wise and prudent, and hast revealed them unto babes: even so, Father: for so it seemed good in thy sight" (Matt. 11:25). Although the cities in which great deeds had been done remained recalcitrant in their sin, Jesus will not be devoid of followers. Although the builders reject the Rock of Ages as useless and find him to be a stumbling stone, he will infallibly be made the head of the corner. Those whom he fed through the miracle of the bread did not see his true nature and did not truly believe; in fact, many of them left him and followed him no more. Jesus, however, remained unshaken, for he was assured that "All that the Father giveth me shall come to me; and him that cometh to me I will in no wise cast out" (John 6:37).[31]

Not only does the doctrine of election serve to give coherence and clarity to other elements of divine truth, it is effective in producing proper Christian experience. This doctrine "is of a humbling and holy tendency." When the whole difference between the saved and the lost rests in sovereign grace, the pride of man is abased. In every other system, the sinner makes himself to differ and, thus, may "find whereof to glory." Some may allow themselves to be unable to repent and believe without the *aid* of the Holy Spirit, but maintain that these same aids are given to all men alike; therefore, faith, instead of being the "gift of God," issues forth as "the effect of our having improved the help afforded, while others neglected it." In this way, the turning point of our salvation is attributed to our own virtue.

Fuller continues, "But election, while it places no bar in the way of any man which would not have been there without it, resolves the salvation of the saved into *mere grace.*" This view of salvation tends to "humble us in the dust"; therefore, it is usually "the last point which a sinner yields to God."

A sinner's submission to election means relinquishing "every other claim and ground of hope from his own good endeavors, and falling into the arms of sovereign mercy." Because the sinner finds rest to his soul in this doctrine, "he will not be less, but more attentive to the means of salvation than he was before. His endeavours will be more ardent, and directed to a better end. Then he was trying to serve himself; now he will serve the Lord."[32]

31. Ibid., p. 809.
32. Ibid., 2:752.

Effectual Calling

Flowing in the stream with depravity and unconditional election, the doctrine of effectual calling, or irresistible grace, blends with them perfectly in the theology of Fuller; in fact, he hardly ever expounds one without relating it to the others. So it is in his *Reply to Philanthropos.*

Section 1 of the "reply" sets out to discuss "Whether our regeneration is prior to our coming to Christ."[33] Fuller's answer sets forth at least seven reasons that regeneration must precede faith. First, and sufficient in itself, Fuller claims: "The Scriptures not only represent salvation as being 'through faith,' but they ascribe *faith itself* to the operation of the Spirit of God." Into one paragraph, he weaves several Scriptures that he feels demonstrate this point: John 6:44, 45, 65; Galatians 5:22; Ephesians 1:19; Colossians 2:12; Ephesians 2:8; John 1:13. Thus, for regeneration to come about based upon any action of ours would not only violate the idea inherent in the concept, but would run opposite the "express testimony of Scripture."[34]

Another of Fuller's evidences, the third he lists, ties unconditional election to effectual calling. Effectual calling is necessary to bring to fruition the Father's purpose to save: "The Scriptures represent God as having a determinate design in his goings forth in a way of grace, a design which shall never be frustrated." But if God never determined the salvation of any particular soul or sent forth effectual provision to bring that soul to faith, "the Son of God might never have seen the travail of his soul; the gospel might have been a universal savour of death unto death . . . Satan might at last have come off triumphant; and the Creator, The Redeemer, and the Sanctifier of men might have been baffled in all the works of their hands!"[35]

In another argument, Fuller claims that "the character of the converted, during their carnal state, is frequently such as proves that their conversion is to be ascribed to sovereign, discriminating, and efficacious grace."[36] That most of the earliest converts were of the worst sort of men demonstrates that salvation is due only to sovereign and invincible grace. Jerusalem, where the Lord suffered and died at the hands of the people, and Corinth, a sink of sin, both had large churches in them. Paul, a blasphemer, murderer, and persecutor, was subdued. If man has even a tendency away from God, to say nothing of being

33. Ibid., p. 461.
34. Ibid., p. 463.
35. Ibid., p. 465.
36. Ibid., p. 466.

totally depraved, it would seem most reasonable that the least resistant would come to faith first. But how is it actually? The foolish, the weak, the base things, and the worst of sinners come; while the wise, the noble, and the "righteous" remain alien to the saving grace of God. "The worst of sinners, therefore, believing before others," can be explained only as we recognize that "to sovereign and omnipotent grace every mountain becomes a plain."

Effectual calling, with unconditional election, outstrips any optional view in ascribing salvation solely to God. What makes the difference between believers and unbelievers? The Arminian, in this case Philanthropos or Dan Taylor, must allow man to share God's glory with him at this point. Fuller becomes more animated and exercised in his writing on this subject than anywhere else. Great consequences rested on the outcome of this argument:

> That there is a difference between believers and unbelievers all will allow; but if the question be asked, "Who maketh thee to differ?" what must be the answer? If the scheme of P. be true, I should think it must be a person's own self, and not God. If he reply, "No, I do not maintain that man of himself can do any thing spiritually good, it is all by the grace of God." Be it so: this grace is supposed to be given indiscriminately to mankind in general. This, therefore, does not in the least alter the case. However the grace of God may be a remote cause of the good that is in me, yet it is easy to see that, upon this supposition, it is no cause whatever of the difference between me and another. My unbelieving neighbor had, or might have had, as much grace given him as I, but either he did not ask it, or did not improve the stock imparted to him, which I did. He resisted the Holy Spirit, but I was of a pliable temper, and yielded to his persuasions. I have, therefore, by a good improvement of the grace given or offered to me in common with my neighbour, to all intents and purposes, made myself to differ. But who am I personating?—Philanthropos?—No, surely! It is the language of his creed, not of him: no, no, whatever may escape from the lip or the pen, his heart must unite with ours, "NOT UNTO US, O LORD, NOT UNTO US, BUT TO THY NAME GIVE GLORY!"[37]

The Atonement

Fuller remained consistent to historic Calvinism in his view of the atonement. While disagreeing profoundly with many statements of the hyper-Calvinists, he never saw himself separating from Calvinists "in

37. Ibid., p. 467.

general" but defended their view of the atonement as his own. He adopted the basic formula of describing the atonement as "sufficient for all but efficient only for the elect." At various places in his works he approvingly quotes Calvin, Witsius, John Owen, the Synod of Dort, and others and purports to defend their view of the atonement.

Ivimey, who knew Fuller well, was aware of the charges of universal redemption placed upon Fuller's view of the atonement, and he rejected them outright.

> Mr. Fuller, too, by some of his explanations respecting the sufficiency of the atonement as a sacrifice equal in value to have effected the salvation of all mankind, was supposed to have pleaded for universal redemption; nothing, I am persuaded, was farther from his intention, as he considered the Holy Spirit's application of the atonement confined to the objects of the Father's election, and of the Son's redemption.[38]

Those actually redeemed by the Son stand exactly parallel with those elected by the Father. Later in his life, when Fuller said that he considered the atonement as a branch of the doctrine of election, it is this truth that he had in mind: those redeemed by the Son are identical with those elected by the Father.

Furthermore, he specifically criticizes the Arminian view.[39] On one occasion, in an open letter to Dan Taylor, Fuller clearly aligned Taylor's view of universal grace with the views of deists and Socinians and stated: "That deists and Socinians should write in this strain is no wonder; but how came the language of infidelity to escape your pen?"[40] Then, in an effort to show that the theology rather than the person of Taylor was under attack, Fuller concludes:

> Excuse this apostrophy. Utterly as I disapprove of his Arminian tenets, (which under the plausible pretext of extending the grace of the gospel, appear to me to enervate if not annihilate it, and to leave little or nothing of grace but the name,) I still entertain a high degree of personal respect and esteem for my opponent.[41]

Nor does this doctrine occupy only a small place in the writing of Fuller. Rather, in its various ramifications, atonement claims major portions of the second volume of Belcher's edition of *The Complete Works of Andrew Fuller.*

38. Ivimey, *English Baptists*, 4:88.
39. Fuller, *Works*, 2:489 ff., 520, and many other places.
40. Ibid., p. 543.
41. Ibid.

Fuller's most organized defense of the "limited design of the atonement" occurs in chapter four of his *Reply to Philanthropos*. This work was highly valued by the Baptist churches of Scotland and was reprinted by them in 1845 as a separate tract entitled "Universal Atonement Refuted." Their understanding and approval of Fuller were extraordinarily clear, for appended to the tract was a "Summary of Doctrine," which makes the following avowal: "These churches never taught nor allowed to be taught amongst them that Jesus died for all men, for the whole human family, for Judas as well as for Peter, that many for whom he shed his precious blood shall perish."[42]

This position and their specific understanding are especially significant in light of the wording of Article IX of the summary: "The Lord Jesus Christ, by his suffering and death, has made a full, an infinite atonement, which is able to save all that come to God by Him."[43]

A sermon preached by Fuller in 1803 contains the same meaning in similar words when he says that "with this sacrifice God is well-pleased, and can, consistently with all his perfections, pardon and accept of any sinner, whatsoever he hath done, who believeth in him."[44] As is evident from the elements of the Scottish summary, such words do not necessarily conclude universal atonement; on the contrary, they only presuppose the absolute uniformity of God's gracious provisions in atonement and efficacious calling.

In that same spirit, Fuller proposes an atonement consistent with the formula "sufficient for all but efficient only for the elect." This position does not place Fuller in a unique position or in any way isolate him as an amender of the historic Reformed understanding of limited atonement. He is in complete harmony with one way that consistent Calvinists have expounded that doctrine. While I personally prefer a different construction of limited atonement—and defend that construction later in this book—to label Fuller as out of step with the historic understanding of limited atonement, or to construe his position as intentionally more sympathetic with universal or general atonement, would totally miss Fuller's point. His position is in precise harmony with the canons of the Synod of Dort.

The strength of Fuller's commitment to the effectuality of Christ's death can be seen in the first query he proposes to Philanthropos: ". . . whether our Lord Jesus Christ had any absolute determination in his death to save any of the human race." He proceeds with confidence,

---

42. Andrew Fuller, "Summary of Doctrine," *Universal Atonement Refuted* (Baptist Churches of Scotland, 1845), p. 20.

43. Ibid., p. 17.

44. Andrew Fuller, *The Great Question Answered* (London: W. Button & Son, 1803), p. 24.

sure that he can demonstrate the affirmative, and concludes "if it be shown that Christ had such an absolute purpose in his death; the limited extent of that purpose must follow of course." The reason for such a conclusion is that an absolute purpose to save must be effectual.[45] He develops seven reasons for his position.

First, Fuller claims that God's faithfulness to promises made to the Christ of the certain efficacy of his death necessitate a "limitation to the absolute determination of Christ to save." If such a limitation does not exist, one must conclude that Christ did not properly redeem any man or render the salvation of anyone a certainty. Nor could the Father guarantee that "my righteous servant shall justify many" or that he should "see the travail of his soul and be satisfied." If these and numerous similar promises are to be kept, what can guarantee such apart from the "certain salvation of some of the human race"?

Second, the character roles under which Christ died show limited but effectual design in his death. He dies as a shepherd for his sheep. He will bring all of his sheep together "and there shall be one fold." He dies as a husband for his wife "that he might sanctify it by the washing of water by the word." He dies as a surety of a better testament. If he is truly a "surety," then the salvation of those for whom he died must be certain. Therefore, "we cannot extend the objects for whom he was a surety beyond those who are finally saved, without supposing him to fail in what He has undertaken."[46]

In conformity with this same idea, Fuller later discusses the covenantal character of the death of Christ. Written several years after the confrontation with Dan Taylor, the following quote demonstrates Fuller's view to be substantially the same in the later years:

> Yet as Christ laid not his life down but *by covenant*, as the elect were given him to be the purchase of his blood, or the fruit of the travail of his soul, he had respect, in all he did and suffered, to this recompense of reward. Their salvation was the joy that was set before him. It was for the covering of *their* transgressions that he became obedient unto death. To *them* his substitution was the same *in effect* as if their sins had by number and measure been literally imparted to him.[47]

Another character under which Christ presents himself is as a sacrifice of atonement. Even as the Jewish sacrifices atoned for the sins of those, and only those, on whose behalf each was offered, so Christ

45. Fuller, *Works*, 2:489–490.
46. Ibid., p. 491.
47. Ibid., p. 708.

set himself apart as a "victim to vengeance," that he might consecrate his people and present them faultless before his Father.

Third, another reason for seeing an absolute determination in the death of Christ points to the effects ascribed to the death of Christ. These effects do not terminate on all mankind but on only a portion. Redemption, the forgiveness of sins, the death of the old man, all result from the death of Christ. For this very cause he died "that he might redeem us from all iniquity, and purify unto himself a peculiar people, zealous of good works." Such privileges do not actually come to all men, nor are all men his peculiar people.

Fourth, Christ is said to have borne the sins of "many." Although "many," on some occasions, can be construed to mean "all," most often it is used for a limited number. Fuller contends that "there is no reason . . . why the many whose sins he bore, should be understood of any other persons than the many who by his knowledge are justified, and who, it must be allowed, are not all mankind."[48]

Fifth, the intercession of Christ, founded upon his death and included in its design, does not extend to all mankind. Christ prays for those given him of the Father, including those who should believe on him through the words of his present followers. Thus, Fuller reasons, Christ prayed for "all who should at any period of time believe, to the exclusion of those who should finally perish."[49]

Sixth, Fuller again exhibits the interrelatedness of the Doctrines of Grace. He says, "If the doctrine of eternal, personal, and unconditional election be a truth, that of a special design in the death of Christ must necessarily follow." Fuller then sets out to prove that the Bible teaches that men are saved because "God eternally purposed in himself, that they should believe and be saved." He lists at least twelve different Scripture passages supporting this view (Eph. 1:3; 2 Thess. 2:13; John 6:37; Rom. 8:29; Acts 18:10; 13:48; 1 Peter 1:2; 2 Tim. 1:9; John 15:16; Matt. 11:25; Rom. 9:15, 21; 11:5, 7). In addition, the death of Christ is given as a reason for nothing being laid to the charge of God's elect in the last day; but if Christ has died for all alike, his death does not give any security against such a charge. In such a case, the security of the elect (Rom. 8:33, 34) would not be based upon the death of Christ but upon what "they themselves had done in believing in him."[50]

Seventh, the character of the saints in the world above indicates that a definite design existed in the death of Christ. They will attribute their salvation to none but the Lamb and will join with the four-and-

48. Ibid., p. 492.
49. Ibid.
50. Ibid., p. 494.

twenty elders singing, "Thou wast slain, and hast redeemed us to God by thy blood, out of every kindred, and tongue, and people, and nation." Not all people of every nation are redeemed by the blood of the Lamb, but only these, a particular people *out of* every nation.

Fuller continues his defense of limited atonement by exposition of specific passages that easily teach the doctrine (e.g., Rom. 3:24, Gal. 3:13, 14). In addition, he answers accusations that several Scriptures directly contradict the doctrine by showing them to be much more compatible with limited atonement than with any supposed universal atonement. In particular, he gives space to 1 Timothy 2:6, 1 John 2:2, Hebrews 2:9, and 2 Peter 2:1.

Fuller believed that the true gospel was grossly perverted in the hands of three deadly enemies: hyper-Calvinism, antinomianism, and Arminianism. He maintained and sought to defend true historic Calvinism in opposition to all of these.

The error of both the hyper-Calvinists and the antinomians lay in their improper application of the doctrine of total depravity to the duty to keep the moral law. To the antinomians he called for an affirmation of the goodness of the moral law and its eternally binding nature. As it is briefly summarized in the commandments to love God with our whole being and love our neighbor as ourself, the force and obligatory nature of the law has not abated. Furthermore, the specific delineation those two broad commands received in the moral law of the Old Testament cannot be abrogated, though some specific cultural applications for Israel may or may not be relevant to the Christian today.

Fuller doubted that those who dismissed the perpetuity and goodness of the moral law really understood the gospel. Although they might speak great words about the grace of the gospel, such persons had no way to measure either the goodness of God or the sinfulness of man. They clearly aligned themselves with the basic assumptions of Socinus and Arminius. "In short," Fuller claims, "we may safely consider it as a criterion by which any doctrine may be tried; if it be unfriendly to the moral law, it is not of God, but proceedeth from the father of lies."[51]

To the hyper-Calvinists, Fuller regularly set forth Calvin and the sixteenth-century Calvinists as his model and as their judges.[52] In addition, Fuller gives substantial quotes from the Synod of Dort[53] to

---

51. Ibid., p. 661.
52. Ibid., pp. 711–712.
53. Ibid., p. 712.

express his position on the free offer of the gospel to all men. The gospel is for sinners as sinners, not for sinners as "sensible" sinners. After quoting at length both Calvin and the canons of the Synod of Dort, Fuller states, "I would not wish for words more appropriate than the above to express my sentiments."[54] In fact, his objection to the sentiments of those reputed to be hyper-Calvinists was not that they were too Calvinistic; rather, he complains that "what is now called Calvinism is not Calvinism."[55]

The third group Fuller opposed, the Arminians, he considered positively destructive to the gospel. His entire correspondence with Dan Taylor demonstrates clearly his sentiments on this subject.

Later, when he was accused of following Richard Baxter's "leading peculiarities," Fuller was forced into reading the polemical tracts of Baxter. In the process he found that they were "so circuitous, and full of artificial distinctions, and obscure terms" that he often could not discern their meaning, "nor could I have read them through without making myself ill."[56] In his reaction to what he could absorb from Baxter, he summarizes his objections to Arminianism:

> Finally, Mr. Baxter considers Calvinists and Arminians as reconcilable, making the difference between them of but small amount. I have no such idea . . . I should rather choose to go through the world alone than be connected with them [the Arminians]. Their scheme appears to me to undermine the doctrine of salvation by grace only, and to resolve the difference between one sinner and another into the will of man, which is directly opposite to all my views and experience.[57]

On another occasion when he was accused of changing his sentiments, Fuller replied:

> I might understand some passages of Scripture differently, might demur upon a few of the arguments used to establish my leading principles, and upon some few of the answers to those of Philanthropos; but *the leading principles themselves* I do still approve.
>
> That for which I then contended was, that Christ had an absolute and determinate design in his death to save some of the human race, and not others; and were I engaged in a controversy with Philanthropos now, I should contend for the same thing.[58]

54. Ibid.
55. Ibid., p. 713.
56. Ibid., p. 714.
57. Ibid., p. 715.
58. Ibid., pp. 709–710.

Some evidence exists in Fuller's unpublished correspondence that to a degree he came under the influence of the resurrected government theory of the atonement, propounded by several New England theologians. His appreciation for the insights of this view diminished in no instance Fuller's commitment to particular atonement. Instead, his commitment to the concept seemed strengthened and set within a more comprehensive framework. Fuller's use of governmental language did not involve him in the mistakes of the governmentalists; the atonement never became merely symbolic of justice, but maintained its character as an act of actual justice. In 1802 he published an article entitled "The Deity of Christ Essential to Atonement." This came some time after his contact with and investigation of the New England governmentalist position. He offered the following observation:

> Some, who have allowed sin to be an infinite evil, and deserving of endless punishment, have objected to the necessity of an infinite atonement, by alleging that the question is not what sin deserves, but what God requires in order to exalt the dignity of his government, while he displays the riches of his grace in the forgiveness of sin. But this objection implies that it would be consistent with the Divine perfections to admit, not only what is equivalent to the actual punishment of the sinner, but of what is not equivalent; and, if so, what good reason can be given why God might not have entirely dispensed with a satisfaction, and pardoned sinners without any atonement? On this principle the atonement of Christ would be resolved into mere sovereign appointment, and the necessity of it would be wholly given up. But, if so, there was nothing required in the nature of things to exalt the dignity of the Divine government, whilst he displayed the riches of his grace, and it could not with propriety be said that "it *became* Him, for whom are all things, in bringing many sons to glory, to make the Captain of their salvation perfect through sufferings."
>
> If God required less than the real demerit of sin for an atonement, then there could be no *satisfaction* made to Divine justice by such an atonement. And though it would be improper to represent the great work of redemption as a kind of commercial transaction betwixt a creditor and his debtor, yet the satisfaction of justice in all cases of offence requires that there be an expression of the displeasure of the offended against the conduct of the offender, equal to what the nature of the offence is in reality. . . . An atonement made by a substitute, in any case, requires that the same end be answered by it, as if the guilty party had actually suffered. . . . Otherwise, atonement is not made, and mercy triumphs at the expense of righteousness.[59]

59. Ibid., 3:694, 695.

Fuller always preferred to avoid language that appeared commercial in its import and, consequently, resisted quantitative categories in discussing the atonement. Although he was too jealous of maintaining his distance from commerical ideas (for guilt certainly admits of degrees and "degrees" is simply a nuance of the meaning of quantity), it is clear that Fuller never surrendered, but strengthened, his insistence on the elements of necessity, satisfaction, substitution, propitiation, and moral equivalence. In addition, as seen above, he maintained his belief that "Christ has an absolute and determinate design in his death to save some of the human race, and not others."

In short, Andrew Fuller not only championed the cause of foreign missions but strongly defended the Doctrines of Grace. The modern foreign-mission movement was founded upon thoroughgoing commitment to the absolute sovereignty of God, coupled with uncompromising insistence upon the full responsibility of man. Fuller was knowledgeably jealous of the union of these two positions. Shortly before his death, he wrote John Ryland, Jr., a letter concerning the future of the Baptist Missionary Society, particularly relating to its theological foundations. Some contemporaries had complained that "if Sutcliff and some others had preached more of Christ and less of Jonathan Edwards, they would have been more useful." Fuller considered such opinions based on ungodly prejudice against Edwards's theological position. He commented:

> If those who talked thus preached Christ half as much as Jonathan Edwards did, and were half as useful as he was, their usefulness would be double what it is. It is very singular that the mission to the East should have originated with men of these principles; and without pretending to be a prophet, I may say if ever it falls into the hands of men who talk in this strain, it will soon come to nothing.[60]

What could Fuller mean by putting such great stock in the particular position of Jonathan Edwards? In a funeral sermon preached at Kettering in June 1814, he related the following information as he traced the theological development of his beloved John Sutcliff:

> I cannot say when it was that he first became acquainted with the writings of President Edwards, and other New England divines; but, having read them, he drank deeply into them: particularly, into the harmony between the law and the gospel; between the obligations of men to love God with all their hearts, and their actual enmity against him, and between the duty of ministers to call on sinners to repent and believe in

60. Ibid., 1:101.

Christ for salvation, and the necessity of omnipotent grace to render the call effectual. The consequence was, that, while he increased in his attachment to the Calvinistic doctrines of human depravity, and of salvation by sovereign and efficacious grace, he rejected, as unscriptural, the high, or rather hyper Calvinistic notions of the gospel, which went to set aside the obligations of sinners to every thing spiritually good, and the invitations of the gospel as being addressed to them.[61]

Such well summarizes Fuller's own understanding of the gospel, which is "worthy of all acceptation."

---

61. Ivimey, *English Baptists*, 4:437.

4

A Long and Winding Road

In the United States, the nineteenth century began just as the nation's mourning the death of George Washington was ending. President John Adams was soon to be defeated soundly by Thomas Jefferson. A malignant fever, devastating Philadelphia, had forced the Baptist Association, which normally met there, to convene outside the city for some years. The United States Constitution had been ratified for some years, and the country was composed of sixteen states: the original thirteen, plus Kentucky, North Carolina, and Tennessee. Just eight years before, Eli Whitney had invented the cottin gin, Carey had sailed for India, and John Leland had moved from Virginia to Cheshire, Massachusetts. In that same state, Luther Rice was seventeen years old, and Adoniram Judson was twelve. Francis Wayland, one of the greatest supporters of the missionary movement begun by Judson and Rice, was four years old at the turn of the nineteenth century. David Benedict, the century's most remarkable Baptist historian, was yet nine years away from commencing his historical explorations, leading to his massive collection of narratives on Baptist life.

Baptist theology was undergoing slight but noticeable change as the differences that existed between John Gill and Andrew Fuller were heightened by each man's followers. Although little substantial difference existed between the respective systems, several observers remarked about the changes of the first half of the century. In 1857 Francis Wayland wrote:

> Within the last fifty years a change has gradually taken place in the views of a large portion of our brethren. At the commencement of that period Gill's Divinity was a sort of standard, and Baptists imbibing his opinions were what may be called almost hyper-Calvinistic. A change

131

Isaac Backus

John Leland

Adoniram Judson

Francis Wayland

David Benedict

commenced upon the publication of the writings of Andrew Fuller, especially his "Gospel Worthy of all Acceptation," which, in the northern and eastern States, has become almost universal. The old view still prevails, if I mistake not, in our southern and western States. This, however, does not interrupt the harmony which should subsist among brethren.[1]

David Benedict, D.D., seconds this view of the matter in a work entitled *Fifty Years Among the Baptists*, published in 1860.[2] J. B. Jeter, the first president of the Foreign Mission Board for the Southern Baptist Convention, adds his voice to that analysis when he states, "Fifty years ago, they mostly adhered to high Calvinism, as maintained by Dr. John Gill, of London. Since that time their views have been considerably changed through the writings of Andrew Fuller and others."[3]

Jesse Mercer is more correct in his view of the situation. After quoting Fuller's *Reply to Philanthropos*, Mercer makes the following observation:

> From the above it appears, that Mr. Fuller is not so opposed to Dr. Gill as many have thought. All that Fuller contends for, as to the infinite worth of the atonement, is comprehended in Gill's view of the scheme of redemption. What Gill places in the covenant transactions, and considers as past and done in the eternal mind, Fuller resolves into "the sovereign pleasure of God, with a regard to the application of the atonement; that is, with regard to THE PERSONS to whom it shall be applied." What then is the difference? A mere shade—a difference only in the modus operandi of the great plan. They are in perfect harmony in the totality of human depravity—the necessity and efficiency of divine influence—the fulness and sufficiency of the covenant provision for, and the certain application of them to the salvation of the elect only—The difference then, betwixt them is only speculative.[4]

Isaac Backus

Doubtless Isaac Backus would be one of those denominated "Gillite" by mid-nineteenth-century writers. A staunch defender of Cal-

1. Francis Wayland, *Notes on the Principles and Practices of Baptist Churches* (New York: Sheldon, Blakeman & Co. Boston: Gould & Lincoln. Chicago: S. C. Griggs & Co.), p. 18.
2. David Benedict, *Fifty Years Among the Baptists* (New York: Sheldon & Co. Boston: Gould & Lincoln, 1860), pp. 135 ff.
3. Jeremiah B. Jeter, et al., *Baptist Principles Reset* (Richmond, VA: The Religious Herald Co., 1902), p. 13.
4. C. D. Mallary, *Memoirs of Elder Jesse Mercer* (New York: John Gray, 1844), p. 294.

vinism, Backus saw the doctrines of God's sovereignty as the satisfactory condition for proper government and the only hope for the salvation of man.

In 1773 he wrote a pamphlet entitled "The Sovereign Decrees of God" to refute a pamphlet entitled "On Traditionary Zeal," written by an Anglican minister in opposition to the doctrines of Calvinism. Backus purposed to demonstrate from Scripture that the sovereignty of God's decrees in control of history in no way diminished man's accountability for all of his actions.

A rejection of either God's sovereignty or man's full responsibility results in several errors. First, Backus accused the writer of "On Traditionary Zeal" of substituting a subjective standard of truth for the objective written Word of God. Canonizing the will or emotion of man bears the fruit of rebellion against the sovereign decree of God. The issue must be decided on the basis of the Word that came from the apostles, confirmed by "divers miracles and the gifts of the Holy Ghost."

The second error made by Backus's antagonists amounted to an elevation of human free will above the will of God. Backus describes the tension in these words:

> ... whether the whole plan of God's government and the final issue of every action through the universe has not been known and fixed in his counsels from the very beginning so that nothing can be put to it nor taken from it? Eccl. iii, 14. or whether many events are not held in suspense and uncertainty in his infinite mind so they are decided by the free will power of men? We hold the first, they the last side of the question.[5]

A misconception of predestination constitutes the third error made by the opposition. Evidently the writer of "On Traditionary Zeal" taught that divine predestination rested solely on the basis of foreseen faith or virtue. Backus exclaims, "Can any imagination ever be entertained more absurd or more contrary to holy writ than these are!" He lists in support of his position several Scriptures: Matthew 11:25–28; Romans 8:29–30; Ephesians 1:4–5; 1 Peter 1:2; 1 John 4:19. God's decree toward his creatures does not depend in the least on their activities; rather, his decree determines their activity. This absolves none from responsibility, however.

Among the errors plaguing the non-Calvinist position, according to Backus, one is fatal: a denial of the doctrine of universal and total depravity in perfect confluence with absolute human responsibility.[6]

---

5. *Isaac Backus on Church, State, and Calvinism,* ed. Wm. G. McLoughlin (Cambridge, MA: The Belknap Press of Harvard University Press, 1968), p. 296.

6. Ibid., p. 297.

Depraved man voluntarily pursues his sinfulness, while God's purpose in every activity is being carried forth. "From whence it appears evident that there is no inconsistency in holding God's decrees to be immutable, and yet that men act as voluntarily as if it were not so."[7]

A fourth error of Backus's antagonist consists of the assumption that a man can act either with motive or against motive, just as the so-called "will" pleases. At this point Backus brings to his side John Locke, who demonstrated philosophically that inner motivation determines the will of man. Since man's fall, his inner motivation is always evil; therefore, his every action is an evil action. Backus becomes so energized on this point that he focuses on it as the undergirding foundation for all the detractors from God's sovereignty.

> In short, the main objections I ever heard against sovereign election and certain salvation by free grace alone appear to me to spring from this root, viz., Man who was flattered with the notion of being *as gods* still conceits that he has a power *in himself* to do as he pleases let that pleasure be to comply with or to disappoint God's designs; and therefore if they are not disposed at present to engage in his service that he must wait their leisure, and be ready, when ever they set about the work in good earnest to grant them the assistance of his grace and, if they improve it well unto the end, then to receive them to his glory.[8]

Backus, however, found no motive to worship a deity who could be mistaken or disappointed in any event and who could neither keep nor defend his devotees. Such a supposed deity is unworthy of our awe and worship and, therefore, is NO deity.

The remainder of the pamphlet sets forth biblical events in which means are employed to implement the sovereign decree of God. Backus also leaves the Gordian knot intact by arguing convincingly that man's inability does not detract from his responsibility but increases it and adds to his guilt. He states, ". . . yet this inability is so far from being any just excuse that the more unable they are to love God or to believe in Christ the greater is their condemnation, John 3:16–19."[9]

In 1789, in opposition to the encroachment of Wesleyan Arminianism, Backus wrote a pamphlet entitled "Particular Election and Final Perseverance Vindicated." Wesley's assertion of freedom of the will and general atonement and his denial of predestination and perseverance of the saints, came only a little short of enraging Backus. Questioning Wesley's view of general atonement, Backus rhetorically asks,

7. Ibid.
8. Ibid., p. 298.
9. Ibid., p. 300.

"If Christ died for the design to save all men, why are not all saved? Can the devil cheat him of a great part of his purchase? Or can men defeat his merciful designs?"[10] If one sought to flee the implications of those questions by retreating to Universalism, Backus simply reminded the potential escapee of all the Scriptures describing unregenerate people and the accompanying promises of eternal punishment for such people.

Backus's overall style is disjointed. He rambles and swashbuckles his way quickly from one subject to another, jamming all his arguments together in a somewhat incoherent style. He appears agitated by Wesley's writings and presents a pamphlet that is altogether hard to follow. However, his close adherence to orthodox Calvinism is unmistakable.

Again, as in a previous pamphlet, Backus rejects the notion that election is based on foreseen faith and contends that only the sovereign pleasure of God prompts his decree of election. After quoting Matthew 20:15–16, he concludes, "This is the true idea of election which men have an amazing quarrel against. For if it depends entirely upon the will of God whether he will save any of us or not, then we can have no encouragement to set up our wills against him."

Can a true believer fall from saving grace? According to Wesley, "one who is righteous in the judgment of God himself may fall finally from grace."[11] The quote is taken from Wesley's book *Predestination Calmly Considered*. Backus finds such an idea appalling. Those who fall away have experienced only the external working of the Spirit, engaged in external reform, and have received some enlightenment concerning individual truths of the gospel. Such a description might characterize many an unregenerate person. Those, however, who are truly born again are those whom the Father has given the Son; of those the Son says, "Of them which thou gavest me have I lost none." Later in the article Backus quotes John 10:15, 26–39; 17:1–2. He then states, "If particular election and final perseverance are not contained in these passages, I know not what can be intended therein."[12]

Wesley's entire argument proceeds upon the assumption that God is obligated to give every man grace. Should he not, he would be unjust. A man is then lost in accordance to his reaction to that grace. He may receive it, improve it and be saved, or reject it and be lost. Backus denies the presumption that grace is the just due of any man; a man is not lost because he rejects grace, but he is lost because his

10. Ibid., p. 454.
11. Ibid., p. 458.
12. Ibid., p. 461.

own corrupt nature and his own acts of rebellion separate him from God. True grace is the unmerited favor of God (and so cannot be obligatory), in which he regenerates those he has chosen in Christ. The man who does not receive grace is not treated unjustly but merely receives his just judgment.

Isaac Backus feared not the face of even a fellow Baptist when contending for these doctrines. In 1797 he wrote Jonathan Maxey, president of Rhode Island College, and called into question some public statements that appeared to align him with the Universalism of Elhanan Winchester of Philadelphia. The controversy centered on the nature of Christ's death. Backus argued that Christ's death consisted of the suffering of misery, a punishment promised to men if they should become sinners. This suffering of misery perfectly satisfied God's wrath for those whom God had chosen to salvation.

> They who are sanctified are set apart for God from eternity, are effectually called in time, and are kept by the power of God through faith unto eternal salvation. For as by one man's disobedience, many were made sinners; so by the obedience of one, shall many be made righteous, Ro. 5:19.[13]

The scheme of Universalism, according to Backus, hates the sovereignty of God in salvation, for it refuses to allow God to distinguish between one person and another or to make effectual provision for the salvation of one he does not make for the other. After quoting various Scriptures in which the teaching is clear that some will receive eternal condemnation, Backus sets forth a strong defense of the Doctrines of Grace:

> The enmity which men have discovered against the sovereignty of the grace of God, as revealed in the Holy Scriptures, hath now prevailed so far, that every art is made use of to put other senses upon the words of revelation than God intended therein. He said to Moses: "I will have mercy on whom I will have mercy, and I will have compassion, on whom I will have compassion. So then it is not of him that showeth mercy, Ro. 9:15, 16. This was the doctrine which God made use of in all the reformation that was wrought in Germany, England, and Scotland, after the year 1517; and by the same doctrine he wrought all the reformation that has been in our day, both in Europe and America. Elect according to the foreknowledge of God the Father, through sanctification of the Spirit, unto obedience and sprinkling of the blood of Jesus Christ, is the only

13. Alvah Hovey, *Memoir of the Life and Times of the Rev. Isaac Backus* (Boston: Gould and Lincoln, 1858), p. 355.

way of salvation which he hath revealed, I Pet. 1:2. And when any person is clearly convinced of sin by the power of the Spirit of God, and then has a revelation of the blood and righteousness of Christ as infinitely free and sufficient to relieve his guilty conscience, he hath a greater certainty of the truth of the Scriptures, than all the human learning on earth can give him. And though, as the raging sea dashes against the rocks, so men rage against this doctrine; yet it stands firmer than all the rocks and mountains upon earth.[14]

In 1756, when Backus had come to believe that only believers should be baptized, he separated from the Congregational Church in Middleburg, Massachusetts, and he, along with several of his followers, formed a Baptist church. Upon the founding of this church, the people adopted a Confession of Faith. The articles contained in that statement represented the views of Backus till the end of his days:

6. That God made man in his own image, in knowledge, righteousness and true holiness; and made with him a covenant of life, the condition whereof was perfect obedience. Gen. 1:26, 27, and 2:16, 17, Galat. 3:10.

7. Man, being left to himself, soon fell from that happy and glorious estate in which he was made, by eating the forbidden fruit, whereby he brought himself and all his posterity into a state of death. Gen. 3:6, Rom. 5:12, 19.

8. Man being thus, dead, his help and recovery is wholly in and from God. Hosea 13:9, Ephe. 2:8, John 6:44.

9. God the Father, of his mere good pleasure from all eternity, hath chosen a number of poor lost men, in Christ Jesus, to eternal salvation. Rom. 8:29, 30, Ephe. 1:4, 5.

10. Jesus Christ, the eternal Son of God, hath come and taken on him human nature; and in that nature hath yielded a perfect obedience to the laws that we have broken, and suffered death for our sins, and hath brought in a complete and everlasting righteousness; and hath risen and ascended to the right hand of God, and ever liveth to make intercession for us. Heb. 10:6–10; Dan. 9:24, Heb. 7:25.

11. The Holy Ghost, and he only, can and doth make a particular application of the redemption purchased by Christ, to every elect soul. John 3:5 and 16:7–15.

12. The Spirit of God applies this redemption by convincing us of our sinful, lost and miserable condition, and then discovering the glorious Saviour, as he is offered to us in the Gospel, in his suitableness and sufficiency and enabling us to embrace him with our whole souls, whereby he is made unto us wisdom, righteousness, sanctification and redemption. John 16:8 and 1:12, I Cor. 1:30.[15]

14. Ibid., pp. 356–357.
15. Ibid., p. 335.

John Leland

John Leland was born forty miles west of Boston on May 14, 1754, and was baptized in 1774 in Bellingham, Massachusetts. A year later he moved to Virginia where, in 1776, he united with the Baptist church at Mount Poney and for a time was its pastor. For sixteen years he preached all over the area and, according to R. R. Sample, was the most popular preacher who ever resided in Virginia. In addition to his preaching ministry, he fought valiantly for religious liberty in Virgina. In 1792, after winning the battle in Virginia, he moved back to Massachusetts, where he could unite his influence and experience with that of Isaac Backus to further the cause of liberty.

In the summer of 1811 a work of the Spirit of God moved upon the people of Cheshire, where Leland was engaged in ministerial labors. Very active in preaching, counseling, and baptizing, he was also problemed with a physical disorder at the time. He persisted through it for a while, but eventually the physical weakness manifested itself in deep spiritual conflict. Leland records, "Whatever the disease might be called, it shocked my whole nervous system, and assailed my head with such pain that it deprived me of a great part of my hearing and the power of speech."[16]

A five-hour spiritual conflict ensued. During this time Leland entered into personal debate over every major doctrine of the Christian faith, worked through it systematically, and exited the *quaestio* affirming the doctrine in its orthodox form. The existence of God, the attributes of God, the deity of Christ, the sufficiency of Christ to be a Savior, the inspiration of Scripture, the immortality of the soul, the resurrection of Christ, the doctrine of election, and Leland's personal interest in the saving work of Christ, all came under intense scrutiny.

In the context of this conflict, the doctrine of effectual call, or irresistible grace, became very precious to Leland. He asked the question as to "whether Christ had re-Adamed men by the atonement which he had made, and did no more for them." Had Christ redeemed men from the curse of the law only to release them to the self-determining power of their own wills? Does salvation depend on their choosing or refusing, or has Christ, "in addition to dying for them, wrought effectually in their hearts" and drawn them to himself.[17]

Leland's contemplations led him to several related observations: his heart was deceitful and desperately wicked; none will call upon

---

16. John Leland, *The Writings of John Leland*, ed. L. E. Greene (n.p., 1833; reprint ed., New York: Arno Press and The New York Times, 1969), p. 626.
17. Ibid., pp. 367–368.

God, since the carnal mind is enmity against God and not subject to his law; in his natural state, man is so blinded, hardened, and deceived by Satan that if salvation were dependent upon man's will, it stood in a precarious position and would come to no one.

With this in view, Leland continued, "the plan, therefore, of solving salvation by grace, to make it acceptable to sinners, neither met my case, nor relieved my soul. I felt the need of an almighty agent to work in me, to rectify my soul, as well as to work without me, to suffer for sin."[18]

His conclusion? Salvation is not of him that willeth, nor of him that runneth, but of God that showeth mercy. All those who are born again are born, not of the will of man, but of God. We are quickened while we are dead in trespasses and sins. Parallel passages affirming divine sovereignty in salvation bolted into his mind. This delighted Leland so much that he could say, "The Saviour now appeared all complete, not only in paying the price of man's redemption, but in new forming the apostate soul, and preparing men for the kingdom of God."[19] Thus, the Savior appeared entirely competent to save; so that Leland could exult, "Here is one Saviour for one sinner."

During this particular conflict, Leland contemplated redemption from several alternative standpoints: First, absolute Universalism, in which Christ not only died for all men but eventually will redeem them all and bring them to heaven, is a rational possibility. Second, Christ's atonement is sufficient for all, so that all could come if they would, but his effectual call is limited to the elect only. Third, Christ died for all, and in this death he removed the penalty for original sin. He now strives with all; and those who turn to the Lord, repent of sins, and believe in the Savior are elected. Fourth, election is personal and eternal, and Christ died for the elect only; these he will restore by grace and bring to glory.

During his 1811 conflict, Leland claimed that all of these could not be right, but they might all be wrong. "I dare not trust any of them. But the blessed Jesus, and not systems or creeds, is the foundation which the prophets and the apostles laid and built upon, and I will do likewise. Here is one Saviour, for one sinner."[20]

In reality, however, Leland held tenaciously to the fourth option. Writing twenty-one years later, in 1832, to Elder James Whitsitt, Leland set forth many questions that had arisen in his mind during the years and for which he had framed some answers satisfactory to him.

18. Ibid., p. 368.
19. Ibid., p. 368.
20. Ibid., p. 369.

Several teachings that he considered an established doctrinal position for fifty-seven years appear in the letter as a Confession of Faith. The first six of these articles relate to the Doctrines of Grace.

> 1. That all men were guilty sinners, and that God would be just and clear, if he damned them all.
> 2. That Christ did, before the foundation of the world, predestinate a certain number of the human family for his bride, to bring to grace and glory.
> 3. That Jesus died for sinners, and for his elect sheep only.
> 4. That those for whom he did not die, had no cause to complain, as the law under which they were placed was altogether reasonable.
> 5. That Christ would always call his elect to him while on earth, before they died.
> 6. That those whom he predestinated, redeemed and called, he would keep by his power, and bring them safe to glory.[21]

Leland felt no inclination to reject those articles. Although he began his ministerial career in 1774 with them—not understanding "how many and weighty the consequences of these premises were"—he determined that after fifty-seven years and after going over the ground a thousand times, he "dare not pull up stakes and make a new start."[22]

He also surveys one of the options on redemption considered above: the principle of "universal atonement and limited grace, which is now very popular." Leland concludes that such a system gives "no relief to but one hitch of the mind." To push God's distinguishing grace from the historical event of the atonement to the eternal decree of God in election ultimately solves no problem. The theological subterfuge robs the atonement of its effectual power and makes it merely an excuse for an aggravated curse toward the majority of mankind.

As Leland looks over the entire system, he affirms the sovereignty of God in the total of salvation and lifts his voice in unison with the apostle Paul in Romans 8, 9, 10, 11. In empathy with Paul's emotions in the final verses of chapter 11, Leland says, "When he undertook to wade into the goodness and equity of Jehovah, he found the water swell from the ankles to the knees—to the loins—to the heart; and, rising to the chin, before his mouth was stopped, he cried out, 'Oh! the depths of the riches, both of the wisdom and knowledge of God! How unsearchable are his judgments, and his ways past finding out.' And there he has left me to grovel still."[23]

21. Ibid., p. 625.
22. Ibid.
23. Ibid., p. 623.

Leland's submission to the sovereign grace of God also found expression within his poetic endeavors. In a poem written about the death of the Reverend John Waller, Leland highlighted the power of sovereign grace in converting a riotous and profane swearer from a child of wrath to a bearer of glad tidings. Mercy calls upon divine wrath to forbear:

> Waller is not ordain'd to wrath,
> But to employ his vital breath
> In the Redeemer's praise;
> His sins, thro' Christ, shall be forgv'n,
> And he shall ever reign in heav'n
> Thro' free and sov'reign grace.[24]

A later stanza describes Leland's observation of Waller's preaching:

> How oft I've seen the envoy stand,
> Imploring mercy for the land,
> With eyes uplift to heav'n;
> "Father, forgive the stubborn race—
> Subdue their hearts to sov'reign grace,
> That they may be forgiv'n.[25]

Thus, one can readily see that Leland's Calvinism in no way opposed true evangelism, but rather intensified the impetus to evangelize. The Doctrines of Grace were the only hope for a sinner. The creature, vile and sinful, will always reject God, always rebel against him and flee from him until, by sovereign grace, the sinner is captured and brought into the fold. Leland catches this vibrant view of grace in another poem, "The Christian's Consolation." The fifth verse states:

> Sinful nature, vile and base,
> Cannot stop the run of grace,
> While there is a God to give,
> Or a sinner to receive.

Leland never wearied of the theme of the cross. He saw within it the motive and hope of evangelism and holy living, and he displayed it as the only picture to woo and win the sinner's heart under the sovereign grace of the Spirit. The theme of the effectual call of God

24. Ibid., p. 413.
25. Ibid., p. 414.

found its way into a poem Leland wrote upon the death of Miss Laura
Whitmarsh in 1833.

> But ah! I preach what every one *should* do,
> But sad experience proves what they pursue.
> There's none that doeth good—all leave the way—
> Soon as they're born, like beasts they go astray;
> Guilty, polluted, both without and in,
> Haters of holiness, in love with sin.
>
> Here then the work increases—more to do—
> To tell what Jesus does for men below;
> He finds them in the wilderness of death,
> Or in the open field, exposed to wrath;
> No eye to pity—none to take them in,
> Nor do they wish to be redeemed from sin,
> But by his quick'ning grace, he makes them see
> The dangers they are in except they flee;
> He works in them to will, and gives them strength to do,
> Then they repent of sin, and after Jesus go;
> He draws them with the cords of love and grace,
> They run to see their dear Redeemer's face;
> He bids them go their way with sins forgiv'n;
> They follow him, and go the way to heaven.
> He leads them in a way they never knew,
> Makes darkness light, and every object new.
> They see that God is just, and wonder why
> Mercy should spare them, when they ought to die;
> The holy law is lovely in their sight,
> Although to keep it they are void of might.
> They trust in Christ's redeeming blood alone,
> And cry, "grace, grace," unto the living stone.[26]

In 1832 John Leland reviewed his life and summarized his preaching. Two words incorporate the thrust of his message: ruin and recovery. He had traveled distances that would circle the globe four times,
had suffered various privations, and had "never received anything
from a missionary fund."[27] Leland relied only on the promise of God
and the benevolence of the people. He baptized 1,525 people by immersion, upon profession of their faith in Christ. In the eve of life he
still said that with a faltering tongue he must cry, "God be merciful
to me a sinner! Save, Lord, or I must perish!"

In spite of, if not because of, his zeal for the gospel, he could not

26. Ibid., pp. 645–646.
27. Ibid., p. 668.

draw himself to support either manipulative devices from the pulpit or modern missionary agencies. Concerning some of the modern preaching designed to manipulate people into fearful decisions, he stated that "it is not the voice of my beloved, it sounds like the voice of a stranger, and I dare not follow it."[28]

John Leland believed missionary establishments were top-heavy with presidents, treasurers, corresponding secretaries, agents, printers, builders, teachers, runners, collectors, and other useless employees: "The cloud of these witnesses is so great, that a sober man who doubts the divinity of the measure, is naturally led to think of the locust in Egypt that darkened the heavens and ate up every green thing on earth." His judgment on the organizations was so candid that he could honestly say that "the machine is propelled by steam and 'does not sail by the wind of heaven.' "[29] For Leland, the only "wind from heaven" was the gospel of sovereign grace.

Luther Rice

Although Leland's contemporary, Luther Rice, shared Leland's doctrine, he did not share his view of the missionary societies. Born in Northborough, Massachusetts, on March 25, 1783, and reared within the Congregational church, Luther Rice was very early taught the Scripture and regularly memorized portions from the Westminster Catechism. For some months prior to his officially uniting with the Congregational church in 1802, Luther Rice fell under an extreme sense of guilt before God and deserving of his wrath. Much time was spent in "weeping and wailing." Finally, moved to put himself absolutely at God's disposal, he saw himself no longer "at variance in the quarrel with my maker." The theological background of his conversion enjoys clear expression in his memoir:

> After finding myself thus happy in the Lord, I began to reflect in a day or two, whether touching this reconciliation with God, there was any thing of Christ in it or not! It then opened very clearly and sweetly to my view that all this blessed effect and experience arose distinctly out of the efficacy of the atonement made by Christ. That I was indebted wholly to him for it all, and indeed the whole of that luminous system of divinity drawn out in the Westminster Catechism, opened on my view

28. Ibid., p. 668.
29. Ibid., p. 669.

with light, and beauty, and power. This I had been taught to repeat, when a child. I then felt and still feel glad that I had been so taught.[30]

The story of Rice's growing interest in missions and his conversion to Baptist life is too well known to be repeated here. Early in his Christian life Rice encountered conflict with Arminian theology. According to Rice, the Arminians found fault with his zeal for the souls of perishing sinners,[31] and on one occasion he wrote to his aunt that he had a dispute against both Arminianism and Universalism. Thinking that he should quite probably have more, he asked his aunt to pray that he would defend the truth for the sake of truth, not for the sake of victory, and that he would maintain the doctrines of the Bible with "meekness, disinterestedness, and love."[32]

His adherence to doctrinal truth, specifically the Doctrines of Grace, undergirded Rice's herculean efforts for missions. He believed that the religious sentiments and doctrines that molded a person's early life unfortunately created diversities in Christian experience and doctrine. Based upon this observation, he emphasized the importance of "having correct ideas and to stamp the first impressed upon the mind."[33] Because of these early impressions made by doctrine, Baptists must be careful that the doctrines they maintain are eminently scriptural.

According to Rice, the doctrine of the depravity of the human heart must hold a place of formative importance in our understanding of the beauties of salvation by the grace of God. The biblical symmetry of soteriology depends to a large degree on one's full adherence to this doctrine. Sinners must perceive themselves to be lost before they are ready to receive the aid of the Savior. They must have a "proper sense of their own sinfulness and guilt and love Christ because he is holy before they are true candidates for salvation."[34] This guilt is such that cannot be removed by man. Only the effectual and sovereign working of the Spirit of God, and that on the basis of the substitutionary atonement of Christ, suffices for such a radical procedure. A man's being born again is God's work and not man's.

Rice found great mental and spiritual satisfaction in the doctrine of God's sovereignty. He considered it the very groundwork of his hope of immortality in glory, the only worthy basis of submission to God, and the only adequate ground for joyfulness in religious experience.

30. James B. Taylor, *Memoir of Rev. Luther Rice* (Nashville: Broadman Press, 2nd ed., 1937), p. 33.
31. Ibid., p. 34.
32. Ibid., p. 42.
33. Ibid., p. 286.
34. Ibid., p. 288.

That God has "foreordained whatsoever has come to pass" should be a fact that prompts everyone to give himself up in absolute submission to the will of God.

In fact, Rice was so convinced of this that he became a rather profound advocate of the doctrine of God's decrees. Rice conjoined the theoretical and the practical with such biblical balance that both the despisers and the abusers of decretal theology were reprimanded. He said to those who ignored God's sovereignty and dwelt only on the exhortations and admonitions of the Scriptures: "You have forgotten that Jesus Christ said, 'No man can come to me except the Father draw him.' "[35] According to Rice, these people failed to preach the whole counsel of God. If such detractors from God's sovereignty object to purposes and decrees, they object to a vital part of the gospel and ignore the admonitions of Paul to preach all the counsel of God. Do these deniers of God's sovereignty reject such purposes as are stated in Scripture?

By *decrees*, does he mean any thing different from *predestination*? If not, could he be displeased with *the preaching* of such as: "Having PRE-DESTINATED us unto the adoption of children of Jesus Christ to himself, according to the good pleasure of his will." "For whom he did foreknow, he also did PREDESTINATE to be conformed to the image of his Son." "For we are his workmanship, created in Christ Jesus unto good works, which God hath before ordained;" (is not here a blessed *decree*, and one that should be preached?) "that we should walk in them?"

Similar passages are numerous, and surely the "good minister of Jesus Christ" cannot excuse himself, or be approved in it by his master, if he shuns to declare this part of the counsel of God, while he certainly ought to press the obligation of "all men every where to repent," and to "believe the gospel"; in short, to urge "repentance towards God, and faith towards our Lord Jesus Christ," as the immediate duty of all, and earnestly to "assert the claims of Messiah upon every mortal."[36]

Such affirmation should quiet contentions that Rice believed with equivocation that God will have mercy on whom he will have mercy, and he hardeneth whom he will. Rice exclaims, "How absurd it is, therefore, to contend against the doctrines of election, or decrees, or divine sovereignty."[37] In spite of such absurdity, however, Rice never lost sight of the purpose he expressed to his aunt during earlier conflicts with the Arminians not to "become bitter against those who view

35. Ibid., p. 296.
36. Ibid., p. 298.
37. Ibid., p. 293.

this matter in a different light, not treat them in a supercilious manner"; rather, he desired to be "gentle towards all men."[38]

To those who abused the doctrine and found themselves bound up
in mere metaphysical wrangling, he gave reminders that admonitions,
exhortations, and proclamations of duty to seek God with a whole
heart, repent of sin, and believe in Christ were well suited for carrying
out the purposes and decrees of God. Rice was convinced that the
Christian lost many of the comforts of religion by negligence in duties,
by not living for heaven daily and hourly, and by failing in sincere
watchfulness, walking circumspectly, and diligence in the opportunities that lay before him:

> But in addition to a correct and enlarged view of the truth of God,
> systematically apprehended as ascertained in the sacred Scriptures, to
> the attainment of which a right state of heart is so exceedingly impor
> tant, it is also exceedingly important to our daily practical comfort, to
> be decided and prompt in the path of duty and holiness.[39]

Adoniram Judson

Rice's good friend and co-laborer in establishing missionary work
among Baptists in America was Adoniram Judson. Judson was born
August 9, 1788, into the home of a respected Congregational minister
who had high aspirations for his oldest son in that particular calling.
Manifesting unusual gifts of concentration, extended labor, and mental
alacrity, Judson seemed well suited for a prestigious position within
the religious establishment of Massachusetts. After a severe bout with
deism in college, he entered Andover Theological Seminary, unconverted, as a special student. Through a process of investigating evidence for the Christian faith and contemplating its infinite moral
excellence, he was converted in December 1808 and made his profession public in 1809. February 1810 saw him solely commit himself to
missions, and by 1812 the Congregational church had formed the
American Board of Commissioners for Foreign Missions, which sent
Judson, his wife, and another couple to India and eventually to Burma,
as missionaries. Their instructions included baptizing "credible believers and their households." Soon after arriving in India, Judson and
his wife, Ann, became Baptists. He had studied the matter intensely
on board the ship and, during the first weeks of his stay in India,

38. Ibid., pp. 293–294.
39. Ibid., p. 290.

rejected the paedobaptist arguments and became willing to be known as a "weak, despicable Baptist who has not sense enough to comprehend the connection between the Abrahamic and the Christian systems."[40] This change, along with that of Rice, prompted Baptists in America to organize on a nationwide basis for the support of foreign missions.

Judson's conversion to Baptist views in 1812 in no way necessitated his leaving behind the Calvinism of the Congregationalists. Rather, he found the soteriology of Baptists quite compatible with that which he maintained within his former denomination. This is evident in his theory of missionary motivation, the methodology he pursued, and in the remarks he quite often enters into his missionary journal. In addition, the Confession of Faith written for the Burmese in 1829 clearly indicates the doctrinal stance upon which he proceeded.

Judson's understanding of missionary motivation intertwined strongly with the example of Christ in the covenant of redemption. This stands out clearly in the only English sermon he ever preached while in Burma. Using John 10:1–18 as a text, he speaks of Christ as seeking his sheep, calling his sheep, and subordinating everything to the will of the Father.

As the Good Shepherd, Christ saw his flock on the verge of destruction, with the wild beast of hell cornering them to rend and devour them. This flock—"given him by the Father, and on which he had set his heart from all eternity"—had become involved in the fall and was thus outside the pale of paradise and exposed to imminent danger. Christ "spared nothing, shrunk from nothing which would conduce to the salvation of his people"; even so must a faithful minister give up all for the good of the people to whom he ministers.[41]

The true shepherd calls his own sheep by name; and Christ calls his people by his Word. But the minister or missionary does not know his sheep by name: "Though enclosed in the Saviour's electing love, they may still be wandering on the dark mountains of sin." Therefore, the Christian minister must lift up his voice to all, even many "who will never listen and be saved," in order that the "invitation of mercy and love which will penetrate the ears and hearts of the elect only" may be made effectual. Then those who thus listen must be taught to obey all that Christ has commanded.[42]

But even with all of this, says Judson, the preacher must remember

40. *Memoir of the Life and Labors of the Rev. Adoniram Judson, D.D.*, 2 vols. ed. Francis Wayland (Boston: Phillips, Sampson, & Co., 1835), 1:102.

41. Ibid., 2:486–487.

42. Ibid., p. 490.

that Christ's labors and sufferings for the good of his people "sprang not so much from compassion and love to them as from love to the Father, and desire to please him." All of God's activity has the purpose of displaying various aspects of the unfathomable perfections of God in all their complexity. The doctrines of denial of self and abandonment to the will of God bottom on this foundation. Still further, ". . . our compassion for souls and our zeal for their salvation must be kept in subordination to the supreme will of God." Christ came from heaven's glory, knowing beforehand that a large portion of those to whom he spoke were not given to him to save, and he foresaw their certain doom. Nevertheless, so chastened was Christ's love and so subordinate was he to the will of God that he would still say, "I thank thee, O Father, Lord of heaven and earth, that thou hast hid these things from the wise and prudent, and hast revealed them unto babes; even so, Father; for so it seemed good in thy sight" (Luke 10:21). And ministers and missionaries must be enabled to respond to this sentiment with a hearty Amen.

In 1846, after over thirty-three years of missionary work, Judson finally returned to America for a stay of less than a year and was in great demand at all sorts of meetings. Because of a severe throat ailment, he was unable to speak. Quite often others would read short written addresses Judson composed. The last of these came in Boston, Massachusetts, where Dr. Sharp read a message entitled "Obedience to Christ's Last Command a Test of Piety." One passage summarizes both Judson's message and his theology of missions.

> For what purpose did he leave the bosom of the Father, the throne of eternal glory, to come down to sojourn, and suffer and die in the fallen rebellious world? For what purpose does he now sit on the mediatorial throne, and exert the power with which he is invested? To restore the ruins of paradise—to redeem his chosen people from death and hell—to extend and establish his kingdom throughout the habitable globe. This is evident from his whole course on earth, from his promises to the church, and especially from his parting command, "Go ye into all the world, and preach the gospel to every creature."[43]

For Judson, the redemption of the elect constituted a vital and invincible portion of the broader purpose of God for the entire created order; it was the particular part in which we as human agents could be most directly involved—though, as Judson was thoroughly convinced, our activity in absolute terms was completely unnecessary.

43. Ibid., p. 519.

God often removes a man from what is considered a vital mission work. Why? Judson concluded: "It is a way God has of showing us what really worthless creatures we are, and how altogether unnecessary, as active agents, in the working out of his plans."[44]

Moreover, these broad plans of God are as certain of fulfilment as the redemption of all the elect in particular. Standing before the magnificent ruins of idol temples, Judson called upon the ancient prophets of that false religion to weep and wail over the scenes of a past greatness. But should they scorn the feeble voice of a frail and impotent missionary, Judson answers confidently, "A voice mightier than mine— a still small voice—will ere long sweep away every vestige of thy dominion."[45] And when immediate difficulties seemed to impede the present observable progress of the mission, Judson remained unintimidated and affirmed: "At the right time, the time marked out from all eternity the Lord will appear in his glory."[46] By this statement he meant a sovereign display of power in the conversion of numberless masses of the heathen, so that the chanting of the devotees of Buddha would die away before the Christian hymn of praise.

This confidence did not rest upon any undervaluation of the hardness and moral impenetrability of the heart of unregenerate men. Judson had an unobstructed view of the thoroughness of man's rebellion and his resistance to—and, yea, even hatred of—the gospel message. No romanticism encouraged his hopes about the conversion of the heathen. He knew full well that only the efficacious working of omnipotent power could bring one into saving obedience to Christ. Total depravity was a living doctrine to Judson.

Judson not only believed strongly in the doctrine of the total depravity of man, but he saw it operative every day. On one occasion, as he demonstrated to two Buddhists the inadequacy of their system of thought, he so clearly refuted their position that they themselves expressed assent to and approbation of his doctrine. However, they concluded that it was impossible for them to think of embracing a new religion. So remarkable was the incongruity between apprehension of the truth and affection of mind that Judson said, "I never saw more clearly the truth of our Saviour's words, 'Ye will not come unto me.' "[47]

As far as Judson was concerned, the only remedy for such painful incongruity is the sovereign and effectual working of the Spirit of God.

44. Ibid., p. 366.
45. *Memoir of Mrs. Ann H. Judson*, ed. James D. Knowles, 3rd ed. (Boston: Lincoln & Edmands, 1829), p. 162.
46. Ibid., p. 185.
47. *Memoir, Adoniram Judson*, 1:229.

Moung Ing was a frequent visitor to Judson's home in the year 1819. After one extended conversation, Judson exclaimed, "Today he has made me half inclined to believe that a work of grace is begun in his soul."[48] Later he speaks of another conversation that he had with Moung Ing and says, "We conversed all the evening, and his expressions have satisfied us all that he is one of God's chosen people."[49] Moung Ing was later converted and baptized.

Extended and profitable discussion with another Burman native led Judson to state: "He seemed to obtain some evangelical discoveries, and to receive the humbling truths of the gospel in a manner which encourages us to hope that the Spirit of God has begun to teach him."[50] Judson's commitment to the doctrine of irresistible grace is demonstrated further in the report of his conversations with Moung Shwa-Gnong. Having discussed the possibility, yea, the necessity, of divine revelation; and having pointed to the evidence proving the Bible to be that revelation, Judson concluded that "the way seems to be prepared in his mind for the special operation of divine grace. Come Holy Spirit Heavenly Dove!"[51] In later discussion with the same man on the subject of the atonement, Judson entertained hopes that Moung Shwa-Gnong was converted; but Judson concluded the entrance into his journal by pondering whether the advancement was made solely on the basis of the philosophical commitment of the philosopher or "from the gracious operations of the Holy Spirit." The final journalistic ejaculation remarks, "O Lord the work is thine! O Come Holy Spirit!"[52]

Judson's confrontation with Moung-Long exemplifies his hard-headed approach in evangelism, combined with his utter dependence on the Spirit of God. Moung-Long came to Judson simply for the thrill of a debate. Like many others in Burma, he was an utter skeptic who scarcely believed in his own existence. After Judson perceived this from the nature of questions asked by the man, Judson said he had the "happiness to be enabled, for about twenty minutes, to lay blow after blow upon his skeptical head, with such effect that he kept falling and falling." The skeptic made several valiant efforts to arise from his defeated position, but "he found himself, at last, prostrate on the ground, unable to stir."[53] Interviews with the man and his wife continued until one day the main question they desired to discuss was how they could obtain faith in Christ. Judson entered his answer into

48. Ibid., p. 232.
49. Ibid., p. 233.
50. Ibid., p. 233.
51. Ibid., p. 234.
52. Ibid., p. 237.
53. Ibid., p. 297.

his Journal: "May the Holy Spirit solve their difficulties, by giving them an experimental acquaintance with that saving grace!"[54]

Judson showed submission to the absolute sovereignty of God in his personal circumstances. In pondering whether a visit to the new emperor of Burma would be encouraging or disheartening, Judson resolved the query with this affirmation:

> . . . but if the Lord has other purposes, it becomes us meekly to acquiesce, and willingly to sacrifice our dearest hopes to the divine will. We rest assured, that, in either case, the perfections of God will be displayed, and desire to be thankful that we are allowed to be in any way instrumental in contributing to that display.[55]

The essence of Judson's theology was stated in concise but clear terms in the Burman liturgy he wrote for the use of the church established through his labors. The formula of worship is an eight-point statement on the character, attributes, and purposes of God. One of the statements is soteriological. Article seven states:

> The God who pitied the sinful race of man, sent his only, beloved Son into the world, to save from sin and hell; who also sends the Holy Spirit to enable those to become disciples who were chosen before the world was, and given to the Son, we worship.

"A Creed in Twelve Articles" forms the second part of the liturgy. After affirming the existence and perfections of God and the inspiration of Scripture, Judson spoke of the original righteousness of man, which was perverted by his fall. As a result of his fall, all the posterity of the first couple "contracted a depraved, sinful nature and became deserving of hell." Articles four, five, and nine of this creed affirm other elements of the Doctrines of Grace:

> IV. God, originally knowing that mankind would fall and be ruined, did, of his mercy, select some of the race, and give them to his Son, to save from sin and hell.
>
> V. The Son of God, according to his engagement to save the elect, was, in the fulness of time, conceived by the power of God, in the womb of the virgin Mary, in the country of Judea and land of Israel, and thus uniting the divine and human natures, he was born as man; and being the Saviour Messiah, (Jesus Christ) he perfectly obeyed the law of God,

54. Ibid., p. 299.
55. Ibid., p. 244.

and then laid down his life for man, in the severest agonies of crucifixion, by which he made an atonement for all who are willing to believe.

IX. Disciples, therefore, though they may not in this world be perfectly free from the old nature, do not completely fall away; but through the sustaining grace of the Spirit, they persevere until death in spiritual advancement, and in endeavors to keep the divine commands.[56]

One can clearly see that Judson operated on the basis of the doctrines of total depravity, unconditional election, effectual calling, substitutionary atonement, and perseverance of the saints. Although he does not give a specific exposition of limited atonement, his statement that the elect were given to the Son "to save from sin and hell" certainly implies it. In addition, there is his view of Christ as the Good Shepherd who spared nothing "which would conduce to the salvation of his people" which had been "given him by the Father" and on which "he had set his heart for all eternity," and who, "to redeem his chosen people from death and hell" came down "to suffer and die in a fallen rebellious world" and now sits on "the mediatorial throne." This view, I say, leaves virtually no alternative but to conclude that Judson believed in the special and selective efficacy of the death of Christ for the redemption of his chosen people.

This affirmation of the doctrines of distinguishing grace, as established in the eternal counsel of God and wrought in history by the work of the Son and power of the Spirit, was no dry and merely intellectual endeavor for Judson. Rather, he saw them as foundational to true spiritual life and proved to be genuinely apprehended only by godly living. In writing to his sister in 1829, he stated: ". . . that faith which consists merely in a correct belief of the Doctrines of Grace, and prompts no self denial . . . is no faith at all."[57]

Francis Wayland

Francis Wayland's life was touched by both Luther Rice and Adoniram Judson. Rice was preaching when Wayland was converted, and the intense dedication of Judson inspired Wayland's own faith and prompted him to set forth the memoirs of Judson for the world. Francis Wayland's acquaintance with the Doctrines of Grace doubtless came at the knee of his father. In a reminiscence of his childhood, Wayland judged that his father and the latter's associates were far better ac-

56. Ibid., 2:469.
57. Ibid., 1:480.

quainted with the Scriptures and with the doctrines of the gospel than Christians of Wayland's own time. Among those he had heard quoted in conversations among the laity were Fuller, Gill, Booth, Romaine, Hervey, Toplady, and Newton. In addition, morning and evening devotions were a regular part of the Wayland-family routine. On Sunday all the children learned a hymn before dinner and "a portion of the catechism" before tea, although Wayland does not remark what catechism it was. It was probably the Westminster Shorter Catechism or Keach's Catechism, an adaptation of the Westminster Shorter Catechism prepared especially for Baptists.

In 1816, during medical studies in Troy, New York, Wayland came under conviction of the need for regeneration. He set aside days on end when he sought nothing but the salvation of his soul, but he emerged from his secret chambers unchanged. During these times, however, he found that he loved the doctrines of the gospel, desired the salvation of souls, and felt a love for Christians. More vivid and dramatic descriptions of the new birth abounded in the literature he read, and, in harmony with those, he had outlined the course that his conversion must follow. However, upon hearing Luther Rice preach on the subject "The Glorious Gospel of the Blessed God," Wayland came to the conclusion that the sentiments of his heart were in harmony with the gospel and that he truly had found salvation through Christ. When he realized that the grace of God had converted him, the doctrine of election, a troublesome thought in previous days, now gave him great comfort:

> My mind at one time rebelled against the doctrine of election. It seemed to me like partiality. I now perceived that I had no claim whatever on God, but that if I were lost, it was altogether my own fault, and that if I were saved, it must be purely a deed of unmerited grace. I saw that this very doctrine was my only hope of salvation, for if God had not sought me, I never should have sought him.[58]

Early in his academic career, Francis Wayland was called upon to tutor languages at Union College in Schenectady, New York. During his time there, a great religious awakening occurred under the preaching ministry of Asahel Nettleton. Wayland described Nettleton as:

> . . . among the most effective preachers I have ever known. I never heard logic assume so attractive a form or produce so decisive an effect. When reasoning on any of the great doctrines in Romans, for instance, election,

58. Francis Wayland and H. L. Wayland, *A Memoir of the Life and Labors of Francis Wayland, D.D., LL.D.*, (New York: Sheldon & Co., 1867), 1:55.

the utter depravity of man, the necessity of regeneration, or the necessity of atonement, his manner was often Socratic.[59]

In 1821 Wayland was approached by First Baptist Church of Boston and called to be their pastor. After being ordained to the position that year, he preached two sermons from the words "It is required in stewards that a man be found faithful," emphasizing that the preacher must deliver without addition or retrenchment the whole gospel to the people—to those for whom it is designed and in such a manner as it is set forth. Such calling demands that one be willing to deal with truths that are difficult for the human mind to grasp—sometimes because of their intensity and sometimes because other truths seem to be in great tension with them. Among these truths were the doctrines of God's decrees and man's responsibility. Twice Wayland approached this subject in the message:

> Another will not preach the doctrine of divine sovereignty, lest men should abandon all concern for their salvation. But is he a faithful steward who thus mangles the word of God? Has infinite wisdom revealed more truth than it is prudent for man to know, and is it the business of the minister of Christ to becloud it? . . . Again, God has clearly revealed the fact of his superintending control. All things that take place happen under his direction and by his control; yet man and all God's intelligent creatures act freely and voluntarily. Who can show the connection between these truths? What mortal eye has glanced along the chain of Jehovah's operation, and fixed upon the link which connects the decrees of God with the agency of man? Such are some of the obscurities connected with the truths of God's word, and with all this obscurity must the minister of Christ preach them.[60]

Wayland treated the doctrine of perseverance of the saints in the same way. He would preach vigorously on the warnings of Scripture that those who are now considered beloved of God might at one time be found out of the love of God. All those who profess faith in Christ should be warned of such. However, what if one would ask what is to become of the doctrine of the perseverance of the saints? Can it be that Christ's sheep will cease hearing his voice and not follow him? Can it be that some force, either outside or within man, can pluck the redeemed out of God's hand? Wayland would say, absolutely not. If Scripture teaches that Christ's sheep hear his voice and always follow him and that nothing can pluck those out of the hand of God, it is

59. Ibid., p. 108.
60. Ibid., pp. 122–123.

undoubtedly true—for the teaching is found in the Word of God. But exhortations to keep within the love of God are also found. Therefore, both should be implicitly believed, because from Scripture we are called upon to believe them both.

Wayland contended that if he could preserve these tensions within Scripture, he could just as well have the same attitude toward Calvinism. In 1861, *Bibliotheca Sacra* carried an article by Dr. Withington in which three questions were addressed: (1) Why am I a Christian?; (2) Why am I a Calvinist?; (3) Why am I a moderate Calvinist? Moderate Calvinism, according to Withington, resided, not in denying any of the great doctrines, but in maintaining those doctrines in harmony with other equally important truths of Scripture. Human minds must mingle the truths as they appear in Scripture, recognizing both the magnitude of scriptural truth and the weakness of man's moral and intellectual powers. Wayland applauded this article, identifying his own position with that of Withington. He, too, liked the phrase "moderate Calvinist," desiring to hold no opinion about the sharp angles of Calvinism as a system. Theologian and preacher must allow the revelation of God to rest in its own clarity and not seek to build a system with the use of human logic. When such is done, absurdity is the result, according to Wayland. The points at which he differed from what he called the "out-and-out Calvinist, are precisely those in which they have gone beyond the revealed truth, and inferred from it, logically perhaps, conclusions where we dare not conclude."[61]

This same moderate Calvinism is set forth in Wayland's *Notes on the Principles and Practices of Baptist Churches*. In reviewing the doctrinal characteristics of the Baptist churches, Wayland contends that all Baptists agree on man's universal guilt and desert of punishment. Because men are depraved, none has any claim upon the mercy of God. Therefore, no injustice is done if it is withheld from some.

In this way, Wayland moves to justify the doctrine of unconditional election. God in infinite mercy "has elected some to everlasting life and, by the influence of the Holy Spirit, rendered the word effectual to their salvation and sanctification." Although salvation is honestly and sincerely offered to all, this offer in no way interferes "with his gracious purpose to save by his sovereign mercy such as he may choose."[62]

Wayland shied away from the idea of a particular atonement and maintained that Christ died for all men. Candidly identifying himself with a view that believers in limited atonement see as the Achilles'

61. Ibid., p. 126.
62. Ibid., p. 20.

heel of general atonement, Wayland states that the way of salvation was opened to the whole race by the death of the second Adam. Nevertheless, ". . . this alone renders the salvation of *no one certain*, for so steeped are men in sin, that they all, with one consent, begin to make excuse, and universally refuse the offer of pardon."[63]

Wayland identified himself, so he thought, with the Fullerites of the nineteenth century. However, such a statement on atonement as Wayland's would never be admitted by Andrew Fuller, for he believed that—in fulfillment of the covenant made between Father and Son—Christ actually redeemed for himself a specific people. Christ did not merely render redemption possible but actually accomplished the redemption. Not only was Wayland's grasp of Fuller inadequate, but he was guilty of perpetuating an unfortunate caricature of John Gill, as one of his anecdotes should illustrate. On one occasion Wayland wished to talk to the family of one of his church members about the necessity of trusting Christ. The man of the house plainly told Wayland he did not wish anyone to converse with his children on the subject of personal religion. If they were elected, God would convert them in his own time; if not, talking to them would only make them hypocrites. Wayland concludes, "He was, I believe, the last pillar of Gillism then remaining in the church."[64] Under this kind of misrepresentation, Gill has suffered since the first part of the nineteenth century.

David Benedict

David Benedict, always wary of hyper-Calvinism, found some comfort in the compromised Calvinism of the Francis Wayland type, but also found some cause for alarm. Writing in 1853, Benedict claimed that hyper-Calvinism had been "the bane of the denomination" for two centuries. Hyper-Calvinism, however, only represented an "abuse of the orthodox system," and its reformers were just as capable of error. Such would be their plight should they go "over to the opposite side."[65]

Benedict attributes this shift, as does Wayland and a host of others, to Andrew Fuller. Benedict realized that little actual difference existed between Fuller and Gill except in their emphasis on the atonement. He did pass on a slight misrepresentation of John Leland, probably

63. Ibid.
64. Ibid., p. 19.
65. David Benedict, *A General History of the Baptist Denomination of America* (New York: Lewis Colby & Co., 1853), p. 942.

picked up from his letter of valediction on leaving Virginia in 1791. After acknowledging Leland's Calvinism, Benedict reports that Leland believed two grains of Arminianism with three grains of Calvinism would make a tolerably good compound.[66]

Speaking of the Baptists who preached during his early years, Benedict says they were "strong Calvinists as to their doctrinal creed," who sometimes "ran Calvinism up to seed," and when they preached the gospel to the unconverted would point out the lost condition of sinners and "point out the duty of all men to repent and believe the gospel," but could not bring themselves to make rousing appeals to the consciences of the lost. Those who were of this theological persuasion and did manage to appeal to the conscience had to do so in such a delicate manner that Benedict remarked:

> I well remember with what ingenuity and dexterity this class of preachers would so manage their addresses to their unconverted hearers, as to discourse to them much in the style of reputed Arminians, and yet retain the substance of the stereo-typed phraseology of their orthodox creed."[67]

Although Benedict was convinced that "rousing appeals to their consciences on the subject of their conversion" should be given, he was not quite comfortable with other departures from the old orthodoxy that followed. He remarked that "this extreme of orthodoxy has been followed by laxity and indifference."[68] In former days, said Benedict, the content of present-day preaching would have been "considered the quintessence of Arminianism, mere milk and water, instead of the strong meat of the gospel."[69] Doctrinal ignorance in the people followed such preaching, so that at present more emphasis is placed on "the eloquence of their ministers . . . than their doctrinal expositions." The people are more interested in someone who is pleading to the young people and who can attract "large assemblies and enable them to compete with their neighbors, numbers and style."[70]

In illustration of the changes that had taken place in one generation, Benedict told the following humorous anecdote:

> "Total depravity," said a good sister to her minister, "must be as true as the Bible. So I read and so I feel. But your new-fangled way of preaching goes to undermine it, and to make people much better than they are,

66. Benedict, *Fifty Years*, p. 138.
67. Ibid., p. 141.
68. Ibid., p. 137.
69. Ibid., p. 138.
70. Ibid., p. 143.

and also to make them think they can do something for themselves. I know that I am totally depraved. I tell you, Elder _____, this kind of preaching will never do. You take away my depravity and you take away my all." "O, no, my good sister," said the elder, "I hope not; I think better of you than that; I think there would be something left still." With a hearty laugh on both sides the discussion closed.[71]

Benedict, however, was not laughing so heartily. As much as he disliked the hyper-Calvinism of some in the days gone by, he was melancholy about the prospects of the future. He felt that if the moderating of doctrine continued we would be able to say, "We have a Calvinistic creed . . . and an Arminian clergy."[72]

In the midst of the observation that Baptists were changing their stance, Benedict also recognized that a much greater influence of the Doctrines of Grace persisted in the South than in the New England states. He saw that the Philadelphia Confession of Faith was especially influential in the middle and southern states and that the doctrines of "depravity, election, divine sovereignty, final perseverance, etc., were enforced strongly further south."[73]

He was right.

71. Ibid., p. 138.
72. Ibid., p. 144.
73. Ibid., p. 137.

5

Thy Fear Forbids My Feet to Stray

The men responsible for the birthing of the Southern Baptist Convention rocked it in the cradle of evangelical, experiential Calvinism. The anti-mission-society movement that spun off into various brands of hyper-Calvinism had already excluded itself from the major thrust of Baptist life in the South and had no influence over Southern Baptists. An Arminianized anti-creedal movement, also advocating baptismal regeneration, had gained a large following in the 1830s under the influence of Alexander Campbell. Baptists were thereby warned of the dangers of any system that discounted the necessity of the effectual and sovereign power of the Holy Spirit in regeneration and, understandably, guarded against those errors. Southern Baptists were committed to a view of theology that saw God as both Righteous Judge and Sovereign Redeemer and saw man as a rebellious, culpable sinner, helplessly enmeshed in trespasses and sins and in absolute need of sovereign mercy to deliver him. This can be demonstrated by investigating the theologies of the early presidents, writers, and educators of Southern Baptist life.

Johnson, Howell, and Fuller—Preacher Theologians

W. B. Johnson

The first president and single most influential architect of the Southern Baptist Convention was W. B. Johnson, who was active in the founding of the South Carolina Baptist Convention in 1821 and the only man present at the founding of both the General Missionary

161

John L. Dagg

P. H. Mell

Convention in 1814 and the Southern Baptist Convention in 1845. For twenty-eight years he served as president of the South Carolina Baptist Convention and from 1841 to 1844 held the same office in the General Missionary Convention. In 1845 he became president of the Southern Baptist Convention, a position to which he was elected through the year 1851.

In a missionary sermon preached before the Charleston Baptist Association in 1826, Johnson discussed the plan of redemption as one part of a magnificent purpose in the mind of the Creator to display every aspect of his glorious being to the entire created order. God, in his infinite and absolute wisdom, has devised a plan, which "in its execution will infallibly secure the accomplishment of the great object he proposes to himself."[1] This plan includes every event in the history of the created order: creation, fall of both angels and men, redemption initiated and completed. Within this context, Johnson affirms that God has selected a certain portion of the fallen human race for the display of his infinite love and mercy. He chose them as his own, he sent the Son to die for them in particular (that is, "actually to redeem and introduce to glory . . . all who are his people"), sends the Holy Spirit to regenerate them (that is, "the renovation of their hearts by the Holy Spirit"), continually and progressively renews the temper of their minds until "they are ripe for the heavenly state," and then takes them to "those regions of glory in which their Saviour dwells." Finally, these chosen ones are resurrected and given a body "fashioned like to his own most glorious body," in which state they shall "exhibit his glorious praise throughout eternal ages."[2] Christians must, therefore, be willing to spend and be spent in an enterprise that has as its goal the extension of God's glory by the publishing abroad of this message, which displays God in all his glorious attributes, his sovereignty, justice, and mercy.

R.B.C. Howell

Convention president from 1851 to 1859 was R.B.C. Howell. Although he loved unity and eschewed a spirit of controversy, Howell was not afraid to argue for a position he considered right and essential for a proper understanding of the gospel and its demands. In his books, *The Covenants* and *The Way of Salvation*, his warm evangelical Calvin-

1. W. B. Johnson, "Love Characteristic of the Deity" in *Southern Baptist Sermons on Sovereignty and Responsibility*, ed. Tom J. Nettles (Harrisonburg, VA: Gano Books, Sprinkle Publications, 1984), p. 45.
2. Ibid., pp. 52–58.

ism comes to the front. The covenant of redemption, involving as it does the consideration of a sinful and rebellious race, demonstrates the sovereign prerogative of God in saving according to his own purposes. Howell states:

> The whole arrangement was, therefore, of his own sovereign grace, uninfluenced by human merit. But this conclusion is not only inferrable from the facts before you. His entire sovereignty in this whole transaction is expressly affirmed in his word:—"not by works of righteousness which we have done, but according to his mercy he saved us, by the washing (purifying) of regeneration, and the renewing of the Holy Ghost; which he shed on us abundantly through Jesus Christ our Savior, that being justified by his grace, we should be made heirs, according to the hope of eternal life."[3]

But not only is the beginning of the arrangement by sovereign grace, its continuance and culmination depends upon the same divine initiative. "Salvation," Howell remarks, "is preeminently the work of God. . . . He has redeemed, regenerated, and sanctified his people, with a view to their salvation, and the glory of all his attributes demands that the end proposed shall be accomplished." Will God choose such a glorious end and leave the issue in the hands of mutable man at any point? Never, for the means God has chosen he makes effectual for the salvation of his people. "His power is absolute, and perpetually exerted for their preservation, and protection."[4]

The nature of the saints' connection with the Lord Jesus Christ also assures their final and complete salvation. Such were chosen in him from all eternity, were redeemed by his atonement, were adopted so that they are heirs with Christ, and have been given everlasting life by their belief in him. In addition, he presently intercedes for them and will not fail of success:

> Now if in Christ Jesus you were from the beginning chosen, to salvation, and to secure it you have been actually called, and endowed with faith, and sanctification; if through him you have been pardoned and the claims of the law against you fully satisfied; if you are recognized, and proclaimed heirs with Christ of the heavenly inheritance; if you already have everlasting life; and have his glorious promise—"Because I live ye

3. R.B.C. Howell, *The Covenants* (Charleston: Southern Baptist Publication Society, 1855), pp. 37, 38.

4. R.B.C. Howell, "Perseverance of the Saints" in *Southern Baptist Sermons on Sovereignty and Responsibility*, ed. Tom J. Nettles (Harrisonburg, VA: Gano Books, Sprinkle Publications, 1984), p. 84.

shall live also;" what can we conclude but that your connection with Christ secures effectually, your final and complete salvation.[5]

If Howell did not discuss these doctrines in as detailed a manner as some other Southern Baptists, it was because (1) other controversies claimed his energies; and (2) he lamented the historical reality that Arminian Baptists had been left outside the organizational structure of Southern Baptists. He wanted to seek ways of including them, so long as doing so would not compromise Southern Baptists as being "Baptists of the old apostolic stamp, taking the Bible as our exclusive guide, loving all who love Christ and ready always to do what we can to reclaim the erring and to save the lost."[6]

Richard Fuller

The third president of the Southern Baptist Convention (1859–1863), Richard Fuller, also imbibed this same spirit of evangelical Calvinism. His sermon on predestination maintains the razor's edge of truth on sovereignty of God and responsibility of man in an amazingly acute and unrelenting fashion. For predestination he preached:

If any thing be certain, then it is that the anti-predestinarian system is wholly untenable. It is good for nothing, since it solves no difficulty and stultifies our reason, it is practical atheism and it contradicts express assertions of the Bible.[7]

At the same time, he spoke the truth that "man is a free responsible agent."[8] To deny either of these teachings would be to deny Scripture and to deny God's omniscience and/or impeccable character. Fuller contended that in this, as in other mysteries of godliness, "our speculations must cease," and we must subject all of our ideas to the "decisions of revelation."[9] And there Fuller rests them. He did not try to reconcile the two truths nor to soften the edges of either. If someone would try, Fuller would reply, "My brethren, the guide, the arbiter we seek is before us. It is God himself. He understands fully his decrees; he also comprehends man's free agency; and he declares as we have

5. Ibid., p. 85.
6. R.B.C. Howell in Joe Burton, *The Road to Augusta* (Nashville: Broadman Press, 1976), p. 163.
7. Richard Fuller, "Predestination," in *Baptist Doctrines*, ed. Rev. Charles A. Jenkens (St. Louis, 1884), p. 490.
8. Ibid., p. 503.
9. Ibid., p. 504.

seen, that all our speculations are wrong; that both these doctrines are true; and, of course, there is no discrepancy between them."[10]

Fuller's application of these doctrines is as bold and uncompromising as his exposition. First, we must learn the folly of human wisdom and forsake the "lurking infidelity," which implicitly calls into question either the justice or the veracity of the "Sacred Oracles," as if they were not a direct revelation of God to man. Second, we must learn to cultivate reverence and moral character at least as much as polemical abstractions. Third, we must acquiesce in all the mysteries of divine sovereignty while pursuing with unabated energy all the duties of the life of faith. Fourth, even as Paul in Corinth, after he was assured that God had many people in the city, we must recognize our solemn obligation to seek the salvation of men. Last, we must work out our own salvation with fear and trembling.[11] In addition, Fuller pleaded to the unconverted, after earnestly urging them to seize the moment for salvation:

> Or, if you are bent on self-destruction—if no entreaties from God, no restraints of his providence, no solicitations of the Spirit, no expostulations, no tears of your Saviour can stop you—at least do not insult Heaven by pretending that you are waiting for more effectual influences. This plea admits that you feel some strivings of the Holy Ghost; why do you not comply with these? Why resist these, and desire more powerful movements? What is this, but openly to proclaim that you will try conclusions with the Almighty? that you are resolved to strive against your Maker, to yield nothing to him willingly, to defy him as long as you can, and only to submit to a sad necessity when he shall compel you? Is there anything in revelation—do you seriously think there is anything in the secret counsels of eternity—to justify the hope that God will thus be appeased? What, my beloved friend, what can you expect from such deliberate, unrelenting opposition to the Sovereign of the Universe? What must be the issue of such an unequal, disastrous, desperate conflict?[12]

Mercer, Dagg, and Mell—Educator-Preacher Theologians

Jesse Mercer

Mercer University was founded in 1833 out of forces initiated by Silas Mercer and continued by his eldest son, Jesse. Money from the

---

10. Richard Fuller, "Predestination," in *Southern Baptist Sermons on Sovereignty and Responsiblity*, ed. Tom J. Nettles (Harrisonburg, VA: Gano Books, Sprinkle Publications, 1984), pp. 111, 112.

11. Ibid., pp. 118–121.

12. Ibid., p. 124.

Mercer estate provided the earliest land and buildings for the educational institution. The theology of its early days finds no better expression than in the writings of Jesse Mercer and two of the most esteemed professors of those days, John L. Dagg and P. H. Mell.

Elder Jesse Mercer's commitment to the Doctrines of Grace was doubted by none in the Baptist denomination. His discussion of them tended to radiate from his understanding of the atonement. Although Mercer strongly argued for the infinite worth of the atonement, he just as strongly argues: "By this atonement is secured the complete and final salvation of all the elect, or church of Christ."[13]

Mercer continued, "I cannot resist the conclusion that Christ died specially for those who shall be the heirs of eternal salvation."[14] Indeed, Mercer has no commitment to a view that would picture Christ as dying for sins in general or even for all men's sins in general, but sees an organic relationship between the death of Christ and the sins of the specific ones whom God intended to benefit thereby: "the satisfaction of justice . . . requires to be equal to what the nature of the offence is in reality—and to answer the same end as if the guilty party had actually suffered."[15]

Statements affirming the specificity of the atonement could be multiplied. This definitive effectuality of the atonement makes possible all other graces toward those unconditionally elected, or, as Mercer says, "the different departments of the great atonement form but one mighty scheme of mercy."[16]

Unconditional election terminates on this act of reconciliation. Effectual calling and final perseverance spring from it. All these graces are necessary because all men in themselves are totally depraved, without will or moral ability to turn to God and without just means of being restored, should they even desire to return. All salvific activities are "departments of atonement."—"All the measures of divine grace necessary to effect and bring about all the purposes of God in the full and final salvation of his people" reside in Christ as the Redeemer, so that he "directs and renders efficient" all of them to the end that he be all in all.[17]

It comes as no surprise, then, and certainly is not inharmonious with the intent of the great Mercer, that the university bearing his

13. *Memoirs of Elder Jesse Mercer*, C. D. Mallary, ed., (New York: printed by John Gray, 1844), p. 300.
14. Ibid., p. 301.
15. Ibid., p. 290.
16. Ibid., p. 302.
17. Ibid., p. 301.

name also enfleshed his theology in the forms of John L. Dagg and Patrick Hues Mell.

John L. Dagg

John Leadley Dagg was born in Virginia in 1794. Although he gained little formal education, his personal tenacity brought Greek, Hebrew, and Latin under his control. Converted in 1809, subsequent study brought him to a Baptist position on baptism, and he was accordingly immersed in 1812 into the Baptist Church in Ebenezer, Virginia. Because of Dagg's observable mental acuteness, a leading Virginia lawyer encouraged him to enter the legal profession. Dagg, however, rejected the obvious flattery of the overtures and, over and against the prestige and wealth of being a lawyer, "contemplated the reproach of being a Baptist minister, and the poverty to be expected." After full and honest examination, Dagg concluded, "Give me reproach and poverty, if I may serve Christ and save souls."

Dagg's life was filled with hardship and tragedy, so that in the context of his arduous ministry he lost his voice, gradually became blind, and lost the ability to walk without the use of a crutch. Nevertheless, he enjoyed an effective ministry of nine years, from 1825 to 1834, as pastor of Fifth Baptist Church in Philadelphia. From 1834 to 1836 Dagg served as president of Haddington College, near Philadelphia; from 1836 to 1844 he held the same position at Alabama Female Athenaeum, in Tuscaloosa, Alabama; from 1844 to 1854 he was president of Mercer University of Georgia and taught theology at the same time. Dagg's *Manual of Theology*, part one, appeared in 1857 when Dagg was sixty-three years old; part two appeared the next year. In 1859 his ethics text, *Elements of Moral Science*, appeared. Ten years later (1869), when Dagg was seventy-five years old, a book on apologetics, *The Evidences of Christianity*, was published. In 1879, when Dagg was eighty-five, the Southern Baptist Convention passed a resolution asking John L. Dagg to write a catechism for the instruction of children and servants. This action stands as firm testimony to the confidence Southern Baptists had in the theological position of Dagg, in that they were willing to submit the religious impressions of their children to his hands.

No small part of Dagg's theology centers upon the doctrines of God's sovereignty in the salvation of sinners. Although these themes permeate the system in all its parts, Dagg gives them specific exposition in chapter four, book "seven," entitled "Doctrine Concerning Divine Grace."[18]

Maintaining a vigorous defense of God's sovereignty as a foundation, Dagg proceeds by elucidating the nature of God's sovereignty as expressed in redemption. Three subjects arrest his, and our, attention: (1) election; (2) particular redemption; and (3) effectual calling.

Dagg states his thesis: "God bestows the blessing of his Grace, not according to the works of the recipient, but according to his own sovereign pleasure."[19] No being superior to God exists; therefore, none can call his actions into question or hinder him from executing his desires.

Is this arbitrary and capricious action, arising from raw power? "How offensive," some might think. Dagg resists that accusation, however, because God's activities are not pursued without reference to a wise and good purpose, but are always in accordance with his good pleasure. God's pleasure is always good, because it is directed to the end of manifesting his own nature:

He is sovereign in his acts, because his acts are determined by his own perfections. He has a rule for what he does; but this rule is not prescribed to him by any other being, nor does it exist independently of himself. It is found in his own nature. In his acts, his nature is unfolded and displayed.[20]

The divine revelation concerning God's attributes and the general rules to which God's nature conforms are certainly clear. Just as clear, however, are the affirmations of God's incomprehensibility. Therefore, Dagg warns against any effort to circumscribe God by our own limited understanding of his nature and purposes. Great diversity and apparent inequality dominate both the essence and fortunes of plant life, animal life, human life. Pleasure and pain are often inexplicable in terms of personal conduct. "As he is sovereign in creation and providence, so he is sovereign in the dispensations of his grace."[21] Full regard is given to justice in these dispensations, and nothing unjust is done to anyone; but grace rises above justice when God displays his sovereignty by distributing blessings to some, to which no individual can legitimately lay claim:

18. John L. Dagg, *Manual of Theology* (The Southern Baptist Publication Society, 1857; reprint ed., Harrisonburg, VA: Gano Books, 1982).

19. Ibid., p. 305.

20. Ibid.

21. Ibid., p. 307.

A Saul of Tarsus, though chief of sinners, is made a happy recipient of divine grace, while an amiable young ruler, who had kept the law from his youth up, is left to perish in his self-righteousness. Publicans and harlots enter the kingdom of heaven; while multitudes, less wicked than they, are left to the course to which natural depravity inclines them. These cases exemplify the explicit declarations of Scripture, which teach, that "we are saved and called, not according to our works."[22]

God's sovereignty in the redemption of sinners manifests itself in Scripture in the orderly arrangements of the covenant of grace. The work of the Father in election, the work of the Son in redemption, and the work of the Spirit in calling combine to constitute this covenant. Dagg's thesis on unconditional election is, "All who will finally be saved, were chosen to salvation by God the Father, before the Foundation of the World, and given to Jesus Christ in the covenant of Grace."[23]

ELECTION

Citing Romans 8:33; 1 Peter 2:9; 2 Thessalonians 2:13; 1 Peter 1:2; Ephesians 1:4, 5; and so on, Dagg affirms without equivocation that "the Scriptures clearly teach, that God has an elect or chosen people." The doctrine is undeniably taught in the Bible, according to Dagg, and one cannot reject election "without rejecting that inspired book."

We are bound by the authority of God, to receive the doctrine; and nothing remains, but that we should make an honest effort to understand it, just as it is taught in the sacred volume.[24]

In his "honest effort to understand it," Dagg makes five affirmations about the doctrine and seeks to elucidate the relation of reprobation to election:

First, God's people are chosen to *salvation*. With all due acknowledgement of the election to certain offices and to service, one could never do justice to the biblical text who omitted election to salvation, not merely the means of salvation but the actual bestowal of salvation.

Further, this gracious election extended to individuals has been established from eternity. Before the foundation of the world, some individuals were elected to salvation, and others were not. Otherwise, there would be no peculiar people. God's eternal selection marked off people out of every nation but was not purposed for the entire race of

22. Ibid., p. 308.
23. Ibid., p. 309.
24. Ibid.

man. The eternality of election probably raises objections in many minds. Any creature's objection to the will of the Creator is wrong. In his righteous final judgment, God will sentence many to eternal damnation, and others will inherit the eternal life in bliss prepared for them.

> All that will then be present to the divine mind, was before it from all eternity; and what God will then do, he purposed to do from the beginning; and the reasons for which he will do it, are the reasons for which he purposed to do it. There can be no wrong in the purpose, if it does not exist in the execution. If God can fully justify at the last day, before the assembled universe, all his dispensations toward the children of men; all these dispensations must be right, and the purpose of them from eternity must have been right: and if a division of the human race can then be righteously made, that division was righteously made in the purpose of God; and consequently God's election was made in righteousness.[25]

Third, election is of grace, not of works. The election of individuals is unconditional, not based upon any observable criteria in the individual's life. For reasons wholly unknown to mortals and lying deep within the infinitely wise counsels of God, he discriminates between one person and another. "The purpose to effect this first actual discrimination is God's election; and the ground of the discrimination when it actually takes place, is nothing different from that of the purpose to discriminate; that is, it is the ground of election." Foreseen faith or obedience play no part in election, for the Scripture is clear that individuals are chosen, not because of holiness, but that they may be holy.

Fourth, election certainly is founded on the foreknowledge of God. Foreknowledge, according to Dagg, goes far beyond a mere foresight or prescience of things to come. The objects of divine foreknowledge are the persons of the elect, not their faith or good works (Rom. 8:29; 11:1). Furthermore, foreknowledge means affection and regard for a certain people rather than information about those people: "He loved them because he would love them." It implies "a peculiar regard not founded on any superiority in the objects of it, but arising from the sovereign pleasure of God."[26]

Finally, all three persons of the Triune God participate in the effecting of election. Dagg quotes 1 Peter 1:2 in support of his discussion: "Elect according to the foreknowledge of God the Father, through sanc-

25. Ibid., pp. 310–311.
26. Ibid., p. 313.

tification of the Spirit, unto obedience and sprinkling of the blood of Jesus Christ. . . ."

All the rest, according to Dagg, are "vessels of wrath" (Rom. 9:22) and are not made subjects of the effectual grace of God. Their hearts become harder as the natural consequence of human depravity's rejection of the continual general mercies of God and thus remain under condemnation. The word *reprobate* does not refer to a class that God purposefully hardens, according to Dagg, but refers to all who are outside of Christ at any moment. Therefore, numbers of the elect may be reprobate for the present. "Reprobation, as a positive act of God, is no other than the condemnation under which all unbelievers lie."[27]

Dagg anticipates that several objections may be presented to the doctrine of unconditional election. The first objection decries the doctrine of election as offering no incentive to human effort. Such is not the case, Dagg replies. Just observe the earnest striving of Paul, enduring all things for the sake of the elect. The electing purpose of God involves his providential ordering of circumstances in such a way as to pave the way for effectual grace. Those who are finally saved attend most energetically to such means of salvation as repentance, belief, and hearing the word, as well as the sincere pursuit of holiness. Dagg concedes that election is certainly discouraging to human effort of the wrong kind. It shows that one can never gain one iota of standing from works of righteousness but must rely solely on the sovereign mercy of God. He concludes:

> The objection to the latter, if thoroughly analyzed, will be found to contain in it some lurking idea that it is safer to trust in something else than in God's absolute mercy. As such lurking trust is dangerous to the soul, the doctrine of election has a salutary tendency to deliver us from it. It tends to produce precisely that trust in God, that complete surrender of ourselves to him, to which alone the promise of eternal life is made; and if we reject the doctrine, we ought to consider whether we do not, at the same time, reject our only hope of life everlasting.[28]

A second objection raises the protest that election is unfavorable to the interests of morality. This objection fails to take into account the relation between election and holiness. Says Dagg: "None have a right to expect acceptance in the great day who do not, in the present life, serve God in sincerity and with persevering constancy."[29] God renders his elect holy and obedient.

27. Ibid., p. 314.
28. Ibid., p. 316.
29. Ibid., p. 317.

A third objector may exclaim, "But does not election represent God as partial?" Dagg answers that God's "impartiality" refers to God's activity as a just judge. No man will receive less than justice. Therefore, none can say he is treated unjustly if God bestows favors on those God claims as his own.

Yet another objection, the fourth, argues that election represents God as a respecter of persons. Such an objection can only arise if one has failed to grasp the unconditional nature of election. God's favor toward individuals is not based on their persons but on his will. No one class of individuals, except sinners, more naturally commends itself to God's favor than another—their financial condition, intelligence, race, or social standing notwithstanding. The poor, ragged, and uncircumcised are equally eligible for the sovereign call of God.

Surely the fifth objection—that election represents God as insincere—is unanswerable. Not at all, for this objection rises from a misconception of the nature of the call of repentance and faith. God requires men to believe in Christ and promises condemnation if they do not. Both his requirement and his promise are utterly sincere, and the alleged issue from either condition surely will come to pass. The sincerity of the requirement and the certainty of the punishment are not abated in the least by man's unwillingness to perform his duty or by God's knowledge of this unwillingness. The bestowment of special grace on some in no wise reduces the sincerity of the requirement for all:

> While men regard the call of the gospel as an invitation which they may receive or reject at pleasure, it accords with their state of mind to institute the inquiry, whether God is sincere in offering this invitation: but when they regard it as a solemn requirement of duty, for which God will certainly hold them accountable, they will find no occasion for calling his sincerity in question.[30]

According to yet a sixth objection, the doctrine of election confines the benevolence of God to a part of the human race. This objection is valid only if it can be shown that "the election of grace lessens the number of the saved." However, instead of diminishing the saved and increasing the obstacles to salvation, election "opens the channel in which the mercy of God can flow, to bless and save the lost."[31]

A seventh objection is that the doctrine of election represents God as an unamiable being. Dagg replies: "If men will pronounce the char-

30. Ibid., p. 319.
31. Ibid., p. 320.

acter of God unamiable, because he is just, and dooms sinful beings to hopeless misery, they prove thereby that they do not love the God whom the Scriptures reveal, and by whom they are to be judged."[32]

Some may seek to maintain a just God but remove from him the responsibility of determining who shall be saved, choosing rather to let salvation be contingent on the decision of man. However, even this would not secure the salvation of all men. If God should adopt this method based upon human contingency, "he would foreknow all its results, and precisely how many persons, and what persons, would finally be saved by it." If he should make this plan his own, knowing all of its results, it would fix as definitely the salvation of those who will be saved, as the plan of election presently does, and it would still leave the rest to eternal doom. Therefore, God's present plan cannot be considered unamiable: "As the plan is his chosen plan, so the people whom it will save are his chosen people. We must prove that our plan would be better, before we can maintain that the deity of our imagination would be more amiable than the God of the Bible."[33]

In one last gasp for credibility, an eighth objector states the cause of his resistance to the doctrine: Election is received only by those who believe themselves to be among the number of the elect. Surely, Dagg claims, no one can seriously maintain the validity of this objection. The truth or falsehood of a teaching is never determined by the number of people who are willing to accept it. A man's rejection of the gospel does not prove it untrue. Nor does a man's, or many men's, rejection of election prove it false; rather, it gives opportunity to the regenerate heart to receive the part of divine truth that is most objectionable to the carnal heart. "Hence it arises, that the doctrine of election, or, which is the same thing, of God's sovereignty in the bestowment of his grace, often becomes the point at which a sinner's submission to God is tested."[34] If a man refuses to submit to God's sovereignty in this matter of highest importance, "his submission to God is partial, and the spirit of rebellion has not departed."[35]

The doctrine of election, according to Dagg, is not subject to man's approval but stands as a reality of God's majesty to subdue sinners to him in humble submission and repentance.

If men, as interested judges, decide in favor of the doctrine, and regard it with pleasure merely because they suppose themselves to be among

32. Ibid.
33. Ibid., p. 322.
34. Ibid., p. 323.
35. Ibid., p. 323.

the favorites of heaven, their faith will be unavailing. No submission to God is implied in our approving of his supposed favoritism toward us. The gospel calls on every sinner to give himself up, through Christ, into the hands of his offended sovereign; and to do this as a guilty creature, and not as a supposed favorite of Heaven. In this complete surrender, the heart becomes fully reconciled to the doctrine of election.[36]

PARTICULAR REDEMPTION

The doctrine of particular redemption constitutes the second element of the covenant of grace. Dagg's thesis is stated thus: "The Son of God gave his life to redeem those who were given to him by the Father in the covenant of Grace."

Dagg believed that Christ in his death had the salvation of a particular people in view. A plethora of Scripture passages is presented in support of this assertion: Matthew 1:21; John 10:11; Ephesians 5:25–27; Isaiah 53:10, 11; John 6:37, 39; John 8:24; Hebrews 2:13; and Revelation 5:9. His main positions are summed up in one paragraph:

> Redemption will not be universal in its consummation; for the redeemed will be out of every kindred, tongue, nation, and people; and therefore cannot include all in any of these divisions of mankind. And redemption cannot have been universal in its purpose; otherwise the purpose will fail to be accomplished, and all, for which the work of redemption was undertaken, will not be effected.[37]

Dagg draws clear distinctions at this point between God's will of precept and his will of purpose. God's precept is that the gospel should be preached to every creature, that all should repent and believe, and that salvation comes to all those and only those who do so. The measure, however, of the benefits secured by the gospel is properly understood only in terms of individual persons who actually receive its promise. Only those who believe are actually saved. Thus, God gives grace to all the obedient, provides the grace to render them obedient, and infallibly secures the benefits of such obedience. "According to God's secret will, or will of purpose, redemption is secured by the death of Christ to all the elect; according to his revealed will, it is secured to those only who believe."[38]

Dagg even argues that the particular nature of the atonement can be viewed in terms of the extent of the suffering of Jesus—the quantitative amount he was actually punished. This idea should not be

36. Ibid.
37. Ibid., p. 324.
38. Ibid., p. 326.

dismissed lightly, according to Dagg, for it is clear that even in hell some eternal punishment will be more severe than other eternal punishment. If some sins deserve more punishment than others, it is not unreasonable to conclude that a propitiatory death involves just as much suffering as is necessary to attain proper justice for just so many sins of just a certain nature. While Christ, by his nature and in his suffering, was fully capable of redeeming all, as well as a few, his specific actions do not justify our concluding this:

> So far as we have the means of judging, the sufferings of Christ, when viewed apart from the purpose of God respecting them, were in themselves as well adapted to satisfy for the sins of Judas as of Peter. But we cannot affirm this of every act which Christ performed in his priestly office. His intercessions for Peter were particular and efficacious; and these, as a part of his priestly work, may be included with his sufferings, as constituting with them the perfect and acceptable offering which he, as the great High Priest, makes for his people. The atonement or reconciliation which results, must be as particular as the intercessions by which it is procured.[39]

This doctrine also is in full accord with the universal obligation to believe in Christ, for the call of the gospel is a call to full surrender to the sovereign lordship of Christ:

> The gospel brings every sinner prostrate at the feet of the Great Sovereign, hoping for mercy at his will, and in his way: and the gospel is perverted when any terms short of this are offered to the offender. With this universal call to absolute and unconditional surrender to God's sovereignty, the doctrine of particular redemption exactly harmonizes.[40]

EFFECTUAL CALLING

Dagg completes his trinitarian treatment of the sovereignty of grace by discussing the Holy Spirit's work in effectual calling. His thesis: "The Holy Spirit effectually calls all the elect to repent and believe."[41]

There is an external call from the Holy Spirit to all who hear the gospel. But men resist and disobey this call of the Spirit, so it is often ineffectual. There is another call that is internal and effectual. "This always produces repentance and faith, and therefore secures salvation."[42]

39. Ibid., p. 330.
40. Ibid., p. 331.
41. Ibid., p. 331.
42. Ibid., p. 322.

In effectual calling the Holy Spirit displays both his omnipotence and his sovereignty. His omnipotence is demonstrated in that he "creates" us in Christ Jesus and raises us from death to life. He is sovereign in that he shares in the sovereign choice the Triune God makes of his elect and then bestows the grace of regeneration, which produces repentance and faith.

If one objects to this doctrine of effectual call on the ground that the finally impenitent cannot be blamed since they did not receive the call, then he is guilty of an absurdity. Dagg says, "The objection virtually assumes, that men are under no obligation to serve God further than they please; or that if their unwillingness to serve him can be overcome by nothing less than omnipotent grace, it excuses their disobedience."[43]

Efficacious grace, rendering the gospel successful, is a unique activity of the gospel dispensation. The outpouring of the Spirit at Pentecost resulted in a massive number of conversions. Had the work of the Spirit been ineffectual, this would not have occurred, nor could it ever occur. "Had God bound himself, by rule, to give an equal measure of grace to every human being, and to leave the result to the unaided volitions of men, the extraordinary success which marked the first period of Christianity would not have existed."[44] Nor would any success in any age exist.

Dagg concludes his section on the sovereignty of grace by setting forth several practical advantages of these doctrines:

1. The doctrine of grace is the remedy for self-righteousness. Self-righteousness is the fatal error that condemned the Jews who "went about to establish their own righteousness."

Self-righteousness greatly offends God. The filthy rags of human righteousness only gain rejection at the wedding feast. Such an attitude underestimates the holiness and justice of God, rejects the mediation and righteousness of Christ, and sets aside the whole counsel of God in the scheme of salvation. In short, self-righteousness is destructive to the soul, for it lulls one to sleep and makes him cry "peace and safety" when there is neither. It is exceedingly difficult to arouse one from the sleep of self-righteousness so as to see the need of forgiveness for sins. Thus, the publicans and harlots entered the kingdom before the self-righteous Pharisees, and Paul counted "all things as loss" to gain righteousness from God.

The doctrine of grace remedies this. It slays the unholy but self-righteous heart and lays it helpless at the feet of sovereign mercy. No

43. Ibid., p. 334.
44. Ibid., p. 335.

amount of trust in self is possible, and no amount of worthiness or comparative merit will commend a person to God. Grace says that one must come as a vile and guilty sinner whose salvation can come only from the sovereign hand of God.

2. The doctrine of grace excludes all human boasting, for it gives clear vision to the reality that none can boast of anything before God (Rom. 3:27; 1 Cor. 1:30, 31; Eph. 2:8, 9). Only the doctrine of sovereign grace is sufficient to wipe all boasting from the mind of man.

3. The doctrine of grace presents the strongest motive toward holiness. This doctrine destroys the love of sin: "A sense of obligation for free and unmerited mercy occupies the heart, and constrains to holy obedience."[45]

4. The doctrine of grace is honorable to God. Sovereign grace exalts God alone and teaches us to glory in the cross alone. The full salvation—as it comes from the Triune God in its completeness and perfect conformity, both to our needs and God's character and glory—becomes the object of our marvel and praise and our only delight.

5. The doctrine of grace unites the people of God. None has greater merit than another. All stand before him without distinction of rank: "All melt before him into penitence and love, and their hearts become one."[46]

6. The doctrine of grace prepares us to sing the song of the redeemed in heaven. Even on this side of heaven one may learn to sing, "Not unto us but unto thy name give glory" (Ps. 115:1); for when we stand before the throne of grace the song will be "Salvation, and glory, and honor, and power unto the Lord our God."

P. H. Mell

In his time of trouble, John L. Dagg had no better friend than Patrick Hues Mell. When Dagg's resignation from the presidency of Mercer was accepted under conditions that did not sufficiently highlight Dagg's great usefulness, Mell registered a vigorous protest in the form of a petition signed by all faculty members except one, asking that Dagg not be retired for the reason of "failing strength." Eventually both Dagg and Mell resigned, but, in the months of tension, they managed to maintain untarnished characters and reputations. The uni-

45. Ibid., p. 338.
46. Ibid.

versal approval Mell enjoyed among Baptists, as well as his expertise in parliamentary procedure, is well demonstrated by table 1 of official positions he held in Baptist life.[47]

Not only were Dagg and Mell loyal friends, they were one in their concerns about the purity of the gospel. The stewardship of preaching placed upon Mell an urgency for the clear communication of divine truth. Mell's preaching style, designed to give the greatest weight and dignity to the wonder of his subject matter, fully impressed his own son. P. H. Mell, Jr., leaves the following description of his father's pulpit ministry:

> The little thirty-minute sermons that some preachers offer to an already over-fed congregation pale beside the matchless discourses he used to give the crowds at Antioch and Bairdstown. His slender, lithe figure rose in its strength; his piercing eyes glowed or melted in tender pathos as his mind grasped the glorious truths of the Gospel; he held his hearers spellbound many times a full hour, and, if the theme was unusually grand, and far-reaching in its fuller development, he stood for an hour and a half, and yet his people never thought he preached long. He started out by stating his propositions clearly and distinctly, and then proceeded to bring forward and support them with such an array of argument and of Scriptural authority, and clothed his ideas in language so plain, so simple, so strong, so beautiful, that the truth was fixed in the minds of his listeners.[48]

What themes could be so grand as to hold simple country people spellbound for more than one hour? A member of the Antioch church, Mrs. D. B. Fitzgerald, recalled Mell's initial emphases at that church. Finding it in "a sad state of confusion" and discerning that several members were "drifting off into Arminianism," Mell determined to preach the doctrine peculiar to the Baptists. Therefore, with "boldness, clearness, and vigor of speech" he preached the doctrines of "predestination, election, free grace, etc." Mell considered it his business "to preach the truth as he found it in God's Word, and leave the matter there, feeling that God would take care of the results."[49] The same convictions, undiminished and uncompromised, were observed by Samuel Boykin. In his *History of the Baptist Denomination in Georgia*, Boykin analyzed Mell's kerygmatic contribution:

47. P. H. Mell, Jr., *Life of Patrick Hues Mell* (Louisville: Baptist Book Concern, 1895), p. 151.
48. Ibid., pp. 64–65.
49. Ibid., pp. 58, 59.

TABLE 1 **Abilities as a Presiding Officer**
Table of Record

Years	Ga. Association	Ga. Baptist Con.	Southern Baptist Con.
1845/46	Clerk	Clerk	
1847	Clerk	Clerk	
1848	Clerk	Clerk	
1849	Clerk	Clerk	
1850	Clerk	Clerk	
1851	Clerk	Clerk	
1852		Clerk	
1853		Clerk	
1854		Clerk	
1855	Moderator	Clerk	
1856	Moderator		
1857	Moderator	President	
1858	Moderator	President	
1859	Moderator	President	
1860	Moderator	President	
1861	Moderator	President	
1862	Moderator	President	
1863	In the army	President	President
1864	Moderator	President	No Convention
1865	Moderator	No Convention	No Convention
1866	Moderator	President	President
1867	Moderator	President	President
1868	Moderator	President	President
1869	Moderator	President	President
1870	Moderator	President	President
1871	Absent by sickness	President	President
1872	Absent by sickness	Absent by sickness	Absent by sickness
1873	Absent by sickness	Absent by sickness	Absent by sickness
1874	Moderator	Absent by sickness	Absent by sickness
1875	Moderator	Absent by sickness	Absent by sickness
1876	Moderator	Absent by sickness	Absent by sickness
1877	Moderator	President	Absent by sickness
1878	Moderator	President	Absent by sickness
1879	Moderator	President	Absent by sickness
1880	Moderator	President	President
1881	Moderator	President	President
1882	Moderator	President	President
1883	Moderator	President	President
1884	Moderator	President	President
1885	Moderator	President	President
1886	Moderator	President	President

Dr. Mell was one of the original delegates present at Augusta when the Southern Baptist Convention was first organized. (1845.)

As a preacher Dr. Mell is strong, able, argumentative, and sound doctrinally, holding his audiences spell-bound by the clearness of his statements and the strength of his reasoning. His arguments, founded on sound premises, reach inevitable conclusions. On the grand doctrines of Christianity and especially the (so called) "five points" in theology, he is especially able. On the distinguishing doctrines of his denomination he is particularly strong and conclusive, always refuting those who put them selves in opposition to him.[50]

Mell's estimation of the importance of the doctrines of grace diminished none with the passing of years. Divine election was the focus of the last sermon he preached: ". . . God hath from the beginning chosen you to salvation through sanctification of the Spirit and belief of the truth" (2 Thess. 2:13).

Unlike Dagg, who preferred the serenity of systematics, Mell had no reticence about using polemics as part of his arsenal for defense of the truth. The tendency of some preachers in his day to preach doctrines inconsistent with the Doctrines of Grace, of others to give only a "cold and half-hearted assent," and of some few others openly to deride and denounce them led Mell to write a treatise "to counteract as far as [he] was able the tendencies to Arminianism" he observed around him. A book entitled *Predestination and the Saints' Perseverance* constituted his consummated efforts.

The occasion for this treatise arose from the attempts of Russell Reneau absolutely to exterminate Calvinism from the earth. Such arrogant vanity received no reward from Mell. Surely, if Calvinism had survived the attacks of Arminius, Whitby, Wesley, Fletcher, and Watson, its adherents may "live in hopes therefore that it may possibly survive even Mr. Reneau."[51] In fact, so ludicrous was Reneau's ambition that Mell sought to shake him to his senses by pointing out that "Calvinism has never heard of him before, and if its advocates ever think of him hereafter it will never be in a connection flattering to his vanity!"[52]

Mell did not intend merely to demonstrate that Reneau was filled with "self-satisfying confidence," made uglier by "impotent rage," but had a positive purpose of defending the Doctrines of Grace. He pursued this course with great precision. Careful definition, relevant philosophical arguments, pertinent theology, concise biblical exegesis, and clear refutations of opposing arguments characterize Mell's approach. Predestination, as far as Mell was concerned, is "not only sustained by the Bible, but is consistent with sound reason."[53]

50. Samuel Boykin, *History of the Baptist Denomination in Georgia* (Atlanta: The Christian Index, 1881), p. 382.
51. P. H. Mell, *Predestination and the Saints' Perseverance* (Charleston: Southern Baptist Publication Society, 1851), p. 8.
52. Ibid., p. 11.
53. Ibid., p. 43.

Zanchius defines predestination in a manner acceptable to and repeated by Mell:

> Predestination is that eternal, most wise and immutable decree of God, whereby he did from before all time, determine and ordain to create, dispose of, and direct to some particular end, every person and thing to which he has given, or is yet to give, being; and to make the whole creation subservient to, and declarative of, his own glory.[54]

Mell then followed with expositions of God's sovereignty as creator, upholder, and governor of the universe. The totality of God's redemptive activity flows from these relationships God sustains to his created order. Although an analytical outline of this entire book might be warranted, the interests of time and space demand a more synthetic approach to Mell's specific soteriology.

God's sovereignty in reference to men is divided into two parts: (1) as it relates to the elect; and (2) as it relates to the non-elect. The non-elect, or reprobate, are passed over and left to perish in their sins. They are vessels of wrath, fitted to destruction and left to follow the inclinations of their own hearts, with no active principle of rebellion imparted to them, and they feel no restraint on their wills. Mell calls this "preterition." Their hearts have become rebellious because of the fall of Adam and Eve, which fall God decreed to permit for the eventual manifestation of his own glory:

> Doubtless, it was for reasons the most infinitely wise that sin was permitted to enter into the world; some of which are manifest even to us. Had sin not entered, God would not have been manifested in the flesh; Christ would not have been preached as the Saviour of sinners; the attributes of God's character would not have been exhibited and harmonized before men by the cross of Christ, at which mercy and truth meet together, righteousness and peace kiss each other."[55]

The activities of sinful men do not come in spite of God's power, but rather they sin against him without his hindering them, that they may "accomplish ulterior objects he has in view."[56]

All of this does not make God the author of sin but rather is permitted so that he might give clear display of his wrath against sin. God's purpose in decreeing to permit sin arises from the most magnificent and worthy purposes, while man's activity in sin arises from

54. Ibid., pp. 22, 23.
55. Ibid., p. 39.
56. Ibid., p. 33.

the most damnable rebellion. Such rebellion then results in the second of God's activities toward the non-elect (the first being preterition), that is, condemnation.

The elect, however, experience God's grace and loving-kindness. They were chosen to holiness and eternal life and, through the covenant of redemption, have all the means for their salvation secured. Both particular atonement and effectual calling are parts of their covenant, and the natural outcome of the entire process is that true believers certainly persevere.

Election is personal, unconditional, and unto salvation. The elect are, by the influence of sovereign grace, made willing in the day of God's power. Selected as individuals before the foundation of the world, all the means designed to bring them to repentance, faith in Christ, and holiness of life are just as surely predestined by God, so that his will is secured infallibly.

In responding to Reneau's gross misunderstanding or purposeful misrepresentations of an election totally apart from any foreseen virtue, Mell summarizes his perception of the Calvinistic doctrine:

His Bible teaches the total depravity of all men. It asserts that they that are in the flesh cannot please God—that the carnal heart is enmity to God, not subject to His law, and unable to be; and, consequently, that none but those influenced by His grace will ever repent, believe and obey. He could not, therefore, elect them because of faith and good works foreseen; for He forsaw that none would believe and serve Him if left to themselves. If elected at all, therefore, they are elected not in consequence of, but in spite of their character: not because they are obedient, but that they might be obedient. And this is the apostle Peter's opinion. "Elect according to the foreknowledge of God the Father, through sanctification of the Spirit *unto obedience*" (1 Peter 1:2).[57]

Effectual calling, clearly affirmed in the preceding quotation, is sprinkled liberally but judiciously throughout Mell's various levels of refuting Reneau. Here as an element of God's decree, there as the only sufficient existential course of repentance and faith, and again as an evidence of God's graciousness toward rebellious creatures.

At times Mell compares the Arminian view with the Calvinist view, demonstrating the clear gospel purity of the latter. Arminians, Mell claims, maintain that faith and good works are the cause of election. They also believe God's grace is granted to all men in a measure sufficient to bring them to faith. Such grace can be either "improved or misimproved, received or rejected according to the will of the crea-

57. Ibid., p. 57.

ture" and God chooses those who, he sees, will "properly improve its influences."[58] Calvinists, however, believe that the work of the Spirit is bestowed subsequent to election and "with the design to make its decree effectual, and, in its influence upon the elect, is invincible."[59]

The atonement also is viewed by Mell as part of the covenant of redemption designed specifically for God's elect. Indeed, the Son was appointed "as their substitute, to suffer in their stead, and, having died, to rise again and appear as their advocate before his throne . . . ."[60] God from eternity decreed the event of the cross, and in this atonement Christ "paid the full price for the redemption of His people."[61] The sins of the elect were so imputed to Christ that he suffered their penalty; thus, forever exempting them from the necessity of suffering the punishment due to their sins, and, in addition, purifying them from these and preparing them for the enjoyment of heaven.[62]

Not all Calvinists agreed with Mell on this, and Mell candidly recognized that a difference of sentiment existed on the point. Nevertheless, all concerned felt no hesitation in calling on all men to repent and believe in a crucified Savior. It appears that Mell personally embraced the formula "sufficient for all, efficient for the elect." If the Bible "places a limit to the intention of the atonement," and Mell believed it did, the Bible also represents the atonement's "merits to be infinite, and sufficient to save a thousand times the number of the descendants of Adam, if applied to them."[63]

That true saints persevere is the natural concomitant of electing grace. The final twenty pages of Mell's book purpose to demonstrate that truth. Mell finds himself defending the Westminster Confession's exposition of perseverance. If he is reticent in any way to pursue such a basis of argument, he gives no hint of it. He intends to demonstrate, against Reneau's line of thought, that "those whom God hath accepted in his Beloved, effectually called and sanctified by his Spirit, can neither totally nor finally fall away from the state of grace; but shall certainly persevere therein to the end, and be eternally saved." This perseverance, of course, does not at all depend on the free will of man "but upon the immutability of the decree of election."

Mell actually viewed the immutability of God's decree as only one-eighth of the formulation of perseverance. In addition, Mell affirms the perfections of God, the covenant of redemption between the divine

58. Ibid., p. 66.
59. Ibid.
60. Ibid., p. 26.
61. Ibid., p. 81.
62. Ibid., pp. 83, 84.
63. Ibid., p. 68.

persons of the Trinity, the covenant of grace God made with his people, the atonement of Christ by which he paid the full price for the redemption of his people, Christ's intercession, the inhabitation of the Spirit, and the distinct and explicit declarations of Scripture as conclusive that the saints persevere.

A summary of Mell's view of God's sovereignty is capsuled well for the reader in a powerful passage representing the conclusion to a long and cogent argument in which he establishes three premises: (1) God has intimate relations with all the works of his hands; (2) in these relations, God governs himself by a determinate plan; (3) this determinate plan existed from all eternity. Thus Mell writes:

> Let these premises be granted (and we see not how they can be denied,) and Predestination comes in like a flood. . . . Is it true that the elements and all inanimate nature are controlled by Him? Then, all their conditions and mutations were foreordained by Him, before the beginning of time. Is it true that He rules, with as sovereign sway, in the moral as in the physical world?—That the hearts of all men are in His hands, and that He turns them as the rivers of water are turned?—Does he send His Spirit to a certain number, and no more and convince them of sin, of righteousness, and of judgment?—Call them, effectually, by His grace—regenerate, sanctify and save them? And does He do all this in accordance with a plan entertained from eternity? Then, it follows that they were predestined to this grace, according to the purpose of Him who worketh all things after the counsel of His own will. Has moral evil entered into His system, and do wicked men sin against Him, he not paralyzing their faculties nor changing their hearts? And, does he leave some, as vessels of wrath, to hardness of heart and blindness of mind, that they might be damned? and, does all this occur, too, in accordance with a plan entertained from eternity? Then, it follows, that, from all eternity, He decreed, for wise purposes, to permit the entrance of moral evil into His system; to permit men to use the powers He gave them in opposition to His authority; then, it follows that some were before, of old, (i.e. from eternity) ordained to condemnation (Jude 4). Finally, it follows that the world, in all its physical and moral details, is just as God designed it to be.[64]

Conclusion

If Johnson, Howell, Fuller, Mercer, Dagg, and Mell accurately personify the theological commitments of the first Southern Baptists—and I see not how this can be denied—Calvinism without compromise

64. Ibid., pp. 36–37.

was considered soteriological orthodoxy. The long journey since then has introduced the Pilgrim to By-Path Meadow, but also to many a Faithful and Hopeful. Giant Despair has held captive many a Pilgrim, and Apollyon has waylaid others. How we came to walk such a road will soon appear, but only after observing others whose fear of God kept them in the way.

6

Beware the Slough of Arminianism

The first seminary in Southern Baptist life rested on a Calvinistic foundation. In fact, Southern Baptist Theological Seminary, in the eyes of its founders, constituted a bulwark against the gradual encroachments of the Arminian fox into the Southern Baptist vineyard. The seminary's four faculty members, Boyce, Broadus, Manly, Jr., and Williams, as well as its most ardent promoter, Basil Manly, Sr., shared a common and aggressive commitment to the Doctrines of Grace.

Basil Manly, Sr.

An educator, preacher, administrator, and denominationalist, Basil Manly, Sr., played a strategic role in the development of the uniqueness of Southern Baptists. No man of his generation possessed greater contextual insights or sympathetic gifts for discerning the needs of the Baptists of the South in the mid-nineteenth century.

Born in 1798 in Chatham County, North Carolina, Manly graduated from the College of South Carolina in 1821. After approximately four years at Edgefield, South Carolina, he entered a twelve-year tenure as pastor of First Baptist Church in Charleston, South Carolina. While there, in addition to satisfying the remarkable demands of such a church field, Manly aided in the establishing of a Baptist newspaper for the South and led with others in the founding of Furman University.

From 1838 to 1855 Manly presided over the University of Alabama at Tuscaloosa. In addition to his settling the floundering institution on a solid basis during that time, he played the part of concertmaster in

Basil Manly, Sr.

Basil Manly, Jr.

J. P. Boyce

John A. Broadus

orchestrating the events that resulted in the eventual formation of the Southern Baptist Convention. In 1844, when Baptists in the South suspected they were gradually but certainly being excluded from equal participation in both the home- and foreign-mission organizations, Manly produced a strongly worded resolution from Alabama Baptists to the acting board of the Triennial (or General Missionary) Convention in Boston. This six-point resolution, according to a letter written to his son Basil, Jr., "passed standing and unanimously."

> 2. *Resolved*, That our duty at this crisis requires us to demand from the proper authorities in all those bodies to whose funds we have contributed, or with whom we have in any way been connected, the distinct, explicit, avowal that slaveholders are eligible, and entitled, equally with non-slaveholders, to all the privileges and immunities of their several unions; and especially to receive any agency, mission, or other appointment, which may run within the scope of their operation or duties.[1]

When the new convention was formed, Manly was elected as president of the Domestic Mission Board to be located in Marion, Alabama. Unable to continue long in the responsibility due to heavy obligations elsewhere, his continued desirability among Baptists in the South is seen from offers extended to him to accept the presidency of Mercer, Furman, Howard, and at least two other schools.

His commitment to education prompted Manly to expend great amounts of energy upon the establishing of Southern Baptist Theological Seminary. He presided for several years over an *ad hoc* committee convened specifically for ascertaining whether the difficulties standing in the way of establishing a seminary were insuperable. When finally established, Basil, Jr., and his former parishioner, J. P. Boyce, formed one-half of the original faculty.

Even when his administrative gifts are properly recognized and appreciated, one must still conclude that Manly's greatest love—indeed, his point of greatest power—was the proclamation of the gospel. John A. Broadus, no mediocre evaluator of preachers, describes Manly's gifts in *Memoir of James Petigru Boyce*:

> His preaching was always marked by deep thought and strong argument, expressed in a very clear style, and by an extraordinary earnestness and tender pathos, curiously combined with positiveness of opinion and a masterful nature. People were borne down by his passion, con-

1. "The Alabama Resolutions (1844)," *A Baptist Source Book*, ed. Robert A. Baker (Nashville: Broadman Press, 1906), p. 107.

vinced by his arguments, melted by his tenderness, swayed by his force of will.[2]

Manly's commitment to the Doctrines of Grace shines brightly in a sermon he preached with a view to salvaging some brethren on the verge of straying from the truth. A polemical situation had arisen between the Tuscaloosa and the North River associations in Alabama. The North River Association, under the leadership of David W. Andrews, had altered its confession on the doctrines of election and effectual calling so that the danger of susceptibility to Arminianism was very real. One church had even cast aside its entire confession, an action that prompted pointed response from an investigative council: "While the scriptures of the Old and New Testaments are the only authoritative standard of doctrine, and rule of duty, it is still deemed expedient to have summary statements or abstracts of principles, for the sake of distinctness."[3]

In an effort to reconcile both parties to the question, the council recommended adoption of the sermon preached by Basil Manly, Sr., entitled "Divine Efficiency Consistent with Human Activity." All members stated candidly that the "sentiments and doctrines . . . meet our cordial and entire approbation."

Manly purported to demonstrate conclusively from the full range of biblical and theological considerations that no final contradiction exists between divine sovereignty and human responsibility. He studiously and admirably avoided diminishing one truth for the sake of the other. "Both truths together, that men act and are acted upon, seem to be included in the general fact that all holy exercises are both commended as a duty and promised as a gift."[4]

The duality of these truths persists in the Bible's admonitions concerning faith, repentance, regeneration, quickening, conversion, love, coming to Christ, and perseverance in holiness. The Bible commands all as a duty and clearly teaches that only God can grant the will and power to perform any of these commands. When God sovereignly and efficaciously grants such will and power, men do indeed repent and believe and change and have a new heart and come to Christ and persevere.

Why do men reject the doctrine of divine efficiency? According to

2. John A. Broadus, *Memoir of James Petigru Boyce* (New York: A. C. Armstrong and Son, 1893), p. 16.

3. From *The Proceedings of a Council at Pleasant Grove Church*, Fayette Co., AL (Tuscaloosa, AL: M.D.J. Slade, 1849), p. 5.

4. Basil Manly, D.D., "Divine Efficiency Consistent with Human Activity," preached at Pleasant Grove Church, Fayette Co., AL (Tuscaloosa, AL: M.D.J. Slade, 1849), p. 8.

Manly, it is because "the doctrine of dependence on the divine being throws us constantly into the hands, and on the mercy of God. Proud man does not like it."[5] Man's performance of any gospel duty utterly depends on the prevenient and effectual grace of God's call. Manly testifies in the first person: "It is all due to God who loved me first, and gave himself for me;—who, when I was guiltily disinclined to it, brought my unyielding heart to seek him."[6]

Such an action of God in time means that he purposed it from eternity. "Whatever he does, he intended to do." Manly handles the Arminian objection, based on foreknowledge, in his own southern-philosophical way. The passage deserves quoting in full:

Now, if God knows all things, he knows who will be saved. But, could God know who will be saved, if it were not capable of being seen, as certain? But if, in order to be saved, a divine operation is necessary, and the incipient part of that operation belongs to God, could he foreknow that the man would believe, unless he had a gracious purpose to work this operation in him, so that he might believe? I have sometimes conversed with my Arminian brethren, in a private and friendly way; (for I never had a *dispute* in my life and hope I never shall;) and, when they are brought to this point, they always, in effect, deny the foreknowledge of God; that is, they say he can know all things, but he *chooses* not to know some things; and this is of the number. Now, there seems to me to be a manifest inconsistency here. How could he choose not to know some things, unless he first knew them, and then willed them out of his knowledge?—Is this Omniscience? Or again;—is it, in the nature of things, possible, to know a thing and then to will it out of knowledge? Suppose that you were to will that you would never know anything about hearing me speak to-day, and set yourselves with persevering and determined effort to will it out of your remembrance;—Could you do it? Would not this very effort fix it indelibly in your mind? And how can it be conceivable that the Creator should voluntarily contract his knowledge to be less than the bounds of things knowable; or that his knowledge should be imperfect, whether made so by his own will, or by circumstances without him? But, if it be admitted that all things *even may be* known by the Creator, this is sufficient to prove that things which may thus be known are definite and certain; else how could they be known? View the subject in whatever light you will, sound reasoning will bring you round to the same conclusion.

My brethren, however mysterious and incomprehensible it may be, that God chose a poor sinner like me—freely chose me, loved me, redeemed me, called me, justified me, and will glorify me—I will rejoice

5. Ibid., pp. 13–14.
6. Ibid., p. 15.

in the truth, and thank him for his free grace! O, where is boasting, then? Not at the feet of Jesus; not at the cross. It belongs not to that position.[7]

In the course of the message, Manly is careful to avoid—in fact, he reprimanded—several common misunderstandings.

First, he never identifies human responsibility with free will. Although he speaks of men acting freely, of sinners freely working their own destruction, of moral freedom, and so on, he always does it in light of one's nature and motivating powers. God's divine operation does not take away "the power of understanding, or the faculty of conscience, or the capacity to will, freely, in view of motives."[8]

Second, Manly does not assume that God owes grace to man if man is to have duty to God. No, he allows grace to be grace—free, unmerited, and sovereign. "The sinner's inability consists not in his dependence on God, which is no hindrance; but in his guilty disinclination to him." Therefore, men have "no right to that grace; they have no claim on God for it; they are guilty and condemned, and deserve nothing but woe at his hands."[9]

Third, Manly does not permit man's sinfulness and culpability to snatch certain events away from the sovereign control of God. The cross becomes paradigmatic in Manly's understanding of the absolute congruity between divine sovereignty and human responsibility: "This fact was foreseen—predetermined: yet will any man say that the parties concerned were not both free, and guilty, in their course."[10] Furthermore, God is never the author of any event "so as to excuse the actors, or to involve him in the guilt of them. . . ." God may well be the author of the events but not "so as to excuse" the guilt of the men involved. Men are rightly judged for the sins they commit while performing the decreed will of God.

None of these truths diminishes in the least Manly's pulsating evangelical calls to repentance and faith. All men are duty-bound to repent and believe, although they have no right to grace and no claim on God for it. Manly exhorts: "I desire that I may be enabled to present the truth of God in such a light to your minds, as to carry conviction to your consciences."[11]

Manly viewed altar calls as entirely inappropriate and inconsistent with the nature of the gospel. In spite of this—or, better, consistent with this—his love of the gospel and desire for the sound conversion

7. Ibid., pp. 15, 16.
8. Ibid., p. 16.
9. Ibid., p. 23.
10. Ibid.
11. Ibid.

of sinners thrust him into the arena of controversy to affirm the consistency of divine efficiency with human activity.

Boyce and His Colleagues

Possibly Manly's greatest work during his years as a minister is seen in his formative and pivotal influence on the life of James Petigru Boyce. Born in 1827, for the first ten years of his life J. P. Boyce benefited from the inimitable ministry of Manly. In his funeral discourse upon the death of Manly in 1868, Boyce recalled the effectiveness of Manly's ministry:

> After a lapse of more than thirty years I can yet feel the weight of his hand, resting in gentleness and love upon my head. I can recall the words of fatherly tenderness, with which he sought to guide my childish steps. I can see his beloved form in the study, in the house in King Street. I can again behold him in our own family circle. I can remember the very spot in the house, where the bands which he was accustomed to wear with his gown were laid on a certain Thanksgiving Day on which he dined with us. I can call to mind his conversations with my mother, to whose salvation had been blessed a sermon preached on the Sunday after the death of one of his children upon the text, 'If I be bereaved of my children, I am bereaved.' And once more come to me the words of sympathy which he spake while he wept with her family over her dead body, and ministered to them as it was laid in the grave.[12]

James P. Boyce focused the genius of all the energies and gifts of his maturity on the subject of theological education. In an address delivered to the trustees of Furman University in 1856, Boyce suggested what he called "Three Changes in Theological Institutions." One, education should be provided for the non–college-graduate. Two, a special course to produce scholars—teachers and authors—for Baptist life was deemed essential. Three, a precise definite abstract of doctrine must be signed by all teachers.

One of Boyce's major concerns about theological education stemmed from what he perceived as a decline in understanding and indeed a crisis in the maintenance of the "doctrines which formerly distinguished us."[13] "The distinctive principles of Arminianism have also been engrafted upon many of our churches," Boyce lamented. Worse

12. Broadus, *Memoir*, p. 176.
13. J. P. Boyce, *Three Changes in Theological Institutions* (Greenville, SC: C. J. Elford's Book and Job Press, 1856), p. 34.

yet, "Even some of our Ministry have not hesitated publicly to avow them."[14]

His alarm prompted him to definitive action, not only in theological education, but in his public preaching and his efforts at indoctrination of children. One of Boyce's sermons in full manuscript form, based on Titus 3:4–8, stressed "The Value of a Complete and Accurate Knowledge of the Doctrines of Grace to the Successful Preaching of the Gospel." His catechism, first published in 1864 by the Southern Baptist Sunday School Board, was billed as a document that "brings out the doctrines of grace and the views of Baptists." Indeed, it is so, and was endorsed by John Broadus as an "excellent little work, which has been a good deal used, and deserves to be used very widely."[15] The question-answer exchanges on "election" demonstrate the Calvinistic soteriology espoused:

1. What name is given to those whom God effectually calls to salvation?
They are called the elect or the chosen ones of God.
2. Why are they so called?
Because God, before the foundation of the world, chose them unto salvation through Christ Jesus.
3. Did God make this choice because He foresaw that these persons would be pious and good people?
He did not; for the goodness and piety of any are due to the influence of the Spirit.
4. Was it, then, because He foresaw that they would believe?
On the contrary, it is through His choice that they are led to believe.
5. What, then, was the ground of that choice?
His own sovereign will.

As a pioneer in Southern Baptist theological education, Boyce knew the power of a classroom teacher and sought to take advantage of that position. Upon Boyce's death, E. E. Polk, editor of the *Baptist Reflector,* said: "He was a great teacher. . . . And though the young men were generally rank Arminians when they came to the Seminary, few went through this course under him without being converted to his strong Calvinistic views."

David M. Ramsey, in the founders' lay address at Southern Seminary in 1924, said of Boyce:

14. Ibid., p. 33.
15. Broadus, *Memoir,* p. 304.

He resented the suggestion that the doctrine of election was a reflection
on the goodness of God. His strength was put out in defense of the doctrine of preterition, that dismal account of the destiny of the non-elect.
When he was teaching, it always seemed to me that here was a loyal son
defending the ways of his father. . . . As I think of it now I doubt very
seriously whether any man taught these intricate and inexplicable doctrines better than did my old teacher of Systematic Theology.[16]

Although one must allow for some overstatement resulting from the
adulation this student had for his teacher, Ramsey's estimation of
Boyce is not too far removed from reality. Even the celebrated Prince-
ton theologian B. B. Warfield has these words about Boyce's *Abstract
of Systematic Theology*:

> The special note of the late Dr. Boyce's Abstract of Theology is judi-
> ciousness. In the selection and ordering of the matter, in the proportion
> of its distribution, and in the method of presentation, the same fine
> judgment is displayed which has governed his theological conceptions
> themselves. Dr. Boyce stands judiciously by the old forms of conception
> and presentation; he is not taken captive by any of the bright new the-
> ories. He rejects "kenosis" and points out its central error; he rejects
> "trichotomy" he rejects the "New Theology" in all its items. The result
> is that he has given us a text-book which we are glad to place on the
> same shelf with ours Drs. A. A. Hodge, Dabney, and Smith, and with his
> Dr. Strong, as another admirable compend of the Augustinian theology.
> We find the treatment of the topics which fall under the caption of
> Theology, in the narrow sense, especially excellent. The long and inter-
> esting chapter on the "Being of God," for instance, is one of the best in
> the volume; while those on the "Decrees of God," the "Trinity," and
> "Providence" are scarcely inferior to it.[17]

Although some details may vary, Boyce expounded the Doctrines
of Grace as they had existed in Baptist life since the 1640s. His views
on election, atonement, effectual calling, depravity, and perseverance
all gave prominent attention to the absolute sovereignty of God in
giving complete salvation to particular individuals. Nor did his col-
leagues in the seminary disagree with this position. John Broadus, on
September 2, 1891, wrote a letter to the *Western Recorder* in Kentucky,
outlining some features of a trip to Europe. A stop in Geneva prompted
a strong commendation of the Calvinism upon which Boyce had sought
to establish Southern Seminary:

16. David M. Ramsey, *James Petrigu Boyce: God's Gentleman* (Nashville: Sunday
School Board of the Southern Baptist Convention, n.d.), pp. 19, 20.
17. B. B. Warfield, review of J. P. Boyce's *Abstract of Systematic Theology* in *The
Presbyterian Review*, July 1889, Vol. 10, pp. 502–504.

Several great departments of systematic theology seem to me more thoroughly discussed and luminously stated by Turretin's noble work than by any other of the great theologians. The people who sneer at what is called Calvinism might as well sneer at Mount Blanc. We are not in the least bound to defend all of Calvin's opinions or actions, but I do not see how any one who really understands the Greek of the Apostle Paul or the Latin of Calvin and Turretin can fail to see that these latter did but interpret and formulate substantially what the former teaches.[18]

Essential in Boyce's soteriological scheme is the fall of man, whereby a threefold effect flowed from the transgression of Adam. Boyce asserts that physical death, spiritual death, and eternal death all came from the fountain of the first sin, and their course remains unaltered except by the work of Christ. All men inherit these effects from Adam. Boyce defends a position which posits Adam as both the natural and federal head of the race.

Seeing that such is man's condition, nothing less than an act of Almighty God could effect a change. Basil Manly, Jr., described this change in the *Abstract of Principles*, under the head of "Regeneration."

Regeneration is a change of heart, wrought by the Holy Spirit, who quickeneth the dead in trespasses and sins, enlightening their minds spiritually and savingly to understand the Word of God, and renewing their whole nature, so that they love and practice holiness. It is a work of God's free and special grace alone.[19]

Broadus, in his "Catechism of Bible Teaching," couches his understanding of effectual call in a question-answer exchange treating the relation of regeneration to faith. "Does faith come before the new birth?" he asks. "No, it is the new heart that truly repents and believes."[20] The sanctifying power of God's Spirit as an inseparable element of the effectual call satisfies the need for a cleansing from corruption. Boyce states:

Corruption can only be removed by a cleansing of human nature sufficient to root out all taint of sin and to restore a holy disposition and habits. This is the work of the Holy Spirit in the people of Christ. All not

18. A. T. Robertson, *Life and Letters of John Albert Broadus* (Philadelphia: American Baptist Publication Society, 1909), pp. 396, 397.

19. Basil Manly, Jr., "Regeneration," *Abstract of Principles*, in James P. Boyce, *Abstract of Systematic Theology* (Philadelphia: American Baptist Publication Society, 1887; reprint ed., North Pompano Beach, FL: Christian Gospel Foundation, n.d.), Appendix B.

20. John A. Broadus, "Catechism of Bible Teaching," in *Baptist Catechisms*, ed. Tom J. Nettles (Tom J. Nettles, 1983), p. 263.

thus sanctified by him are left forever corrupt. The Scriptures show such to be man's condition that he cannot cleanse himself.[21]

Election

If God acts sovereignly in regeneration in time, he has determined to do so from eternity. Thus enters the reality of God's electing purpose. Boyce points out four views various theologians have held in explaining the terms *elect, election, foreordination, chosen, foreknow,* and *foreknowledge.* Boyce mentions briefly and then rejects the theories of "nationalism" as expounded by Locke, "election to external church privileges" as detailed by George Faber, and "perseverance to foreseen faith" as defended by the Arminians. Boyce contends that the biblical words refer to a "personal, unconditional, and eternal Election."

His full definition of election suffers from parenthetical and subparenthetical explanations but is well worth quoting in full:

> The latter theory is that God (who and not man is the one who chooses or elects), of his own purpose (in accordance with his will, and not from any obligation to man, nor because of any will of man), has from Eternity (the period of God's action, not in time in which man acts), determined to save (not has actually saved, but simply determined so to do), [and to save (not to confer gospel or church privileges upon)], a definite number of mankind (not the whole race, nor indefinitely merely some of them, nor indefinitely a certain proportionate part; but a definite number), as individuals (not the whole or a part of the race, nor of a nation, nor of a church, nor of a class, as of believers or the pious; but individuals), not for or because of any merit or work of theirs, not of any value to him of them (not for their good works, nor their holiness, nor excellence, nor their faith, nor their spiritual sanctification, although the choice is to a salvation attained through faith and sanctification; nor their value to him, though their salvation tends greatly to the manifested glory of his grace); but of his own good pleasure (simply because he was pleased so to choose).[22]

This view asserts six succinct truths related to election.

1. Election is an act of God, and not the result of the choice of the elect. Boyce briefly mentions Scriptures in support of this point: John 13:18; 15:16; Romans 8:33; 9:15; Ephesians 1:4, 11; and 2 Thessalonians 2:13.

21. James P. Boyce, *Abstract of Systematic Theology* (Philadelphia: American Baptist Publication Society, 1887, reprint ed., North Pompano Beach, FL: Christian Gospel Foundation), p. 246.
    22. Ibid., p. 347.

2. Election refers to the choice of specific individuals and not of classes. These individuals become a class of believers because they are elect; they do not become elect because they are believers. Scriptures mentioned in support are Acts 13:48; Ephesians 1:4, 5; 2 Thessalonians 2:13; Romans 8:29.

3. Election is not the result of any merit, action, or condition in the elect individual but is done irrespective of any condition in the creature.

4. Election is made through the good pleasure of God, and his sovereign will alone is the cause of election. Expository support for numbers three and four is given together, since Boyce considers these as two sides of the same coin. Some Scriptures speak of the sovereignty of God's choice: Matthew 24:40–41; Luke 17:33–36; John 3:3–8; 6:37, 39, 44, 64, 65; 15:16; 17:2; Acts 22:14; Ephesians 1:5; James 1:18. Others explicitly deny causative factors within those elected: Ezekiel 36:32; John 1:11–13; Romans 9:11–16; 11:5–6. Still others emphasize the fact that many are chosen who appear to be the most unlikely: Matthew 11:25, 26; Luke 4:25–27; Acts 26:12–23; 1 Corinthians 1:26–30; Galatians 1:15, 16; Ephesians 2:1–13.

Boyce defends his fullness on this point by reminding the reader that all has not been mentioned that could have been and that this is "the point upon which all that is important in this controversy turns." Although Boyce recognizes other matters to be equally essential to the doctrine, the whole opposition, as far as he is concerned, "arises from an unwillingness on the part of man to recognize the sovereignty of God, and to ascribe salvation entirely to grace."[23]

5. This election was according to an eternal purpose as opposed to one formed in time. This point Boyce supports with representative biblical texts: Jeremiah 1:5; Matthew 25:34; Ephesians 1:4; 2 Thessalonians 2:13; 2 Timothy 1:9; Revelation 13:8; 17:8; 21:27; 1 Corinthians 2:7; Ephesians 3:11.

6. Election is to salvation and not to mere external privileges. In addition to recording the following Scripture passages, Boyce gives a short summary statement of some of them. He mentions Jeremiah 31:31–34; 32:37–40; Ezekiel 36:24–27; John 10:16, 26, 27; Ephesians 1:4–9; 2 Thessalonians 2:13. An example of the method of Boyce's citation follows:

Rom. 8:28–30. "We know that to them that love God all things work together for good, even to them that are called according to his purpose." Paul now proceeds to tell who these are. "For whom he did foreknow, he also foreordained to be conformed to the image of his Son, that he

23. Ibid., p. 353.

might be the first-born among many brethren: and whom he foreordained, them he also called; and whom he called, them he also justified: and whom he justified, then he also glorified." This passage shows that foreknowledge, foreordination to holiness, calling, justification, and a state of glory are inseparably connected, and hence that the election, from which they proceed, is to salvation.

Reprobation

Following the chapter on election, Boyce appears to feel that one cannot avoid handling the subject of reprobation. Four points are involved in his understanding of this doctrine:

1. The decree not to elect.
2. The decree to pass by in bestowing divine grace.
3. To condemn for sins committed.
4. To harden against the truth all or some persons, already sinners, and to confirm them in sin.

Boyce treats reprobation not so much as a positive and aggressive activity of God as a negative passing over. Although he recognizes that "rejection must have accompanied Election" and the fact that some were chosen involved the "rejection of others," he contends that all that happens to the reprobate can be explained in terms of their naturally depraved condition apart from the effective hardening of God. Boyce is quite willing to accept the effectual and direct hardening of man as the means of reprobation, but he contends that the language of Scripture paints another picture.

God is represented as responsible for all events, even though they are accomplished through secondary causes. There are sufficient secondary causes apposite with man's condition, his depravity, and the captivity of Satan to effect reprobation. James 1:13, 14 uses language inconsistent with the idea that God efficiently causes sin. Hardening of the heart results from merciful action, which should have the opposite tendency. Therefore, reprobation, according to Boyce, is sufficiently explained as the purposeful passing over of some in God's intent to bestow effectually the gifts of grace to others.

The Atonement

The work of the second person of the Trinity for man's salvation, or the atonement, is also particular in nature. Boyce outlines the view that he accepts on page 317 of his *Abstract of Systematic Theology*:

7. The Calvinistic theory of the atonement is, that in the sufferings and death of Christ, he incurred the penalty of the sins of those whose substitute he was, so that he made a real satisfaction to the justice of God for the law which they had broken. On this account, God now pardons all their sins, and being fully reconciled to them, his electing love flows out freely towards them.

The doctrine as thus taught involves the following points:

I. That the sufferings and death of Christ were a real atonement.

II. That in making it Christ became the substitute of those whom he came to save.

III. That as such he bore the penalty of their transgressions.

IV. That in so doing he made ample satisfaction to the demands of the law, and to the justice of God.

V. That thus an actual reconciliation has been made between them and God.[24]

These five points are then expounded, defended, and proved through the next eighteen pages, accompanied by a plethora of Scripture quotations.

Christ's atonement does not render salvation a mere potential for all men, according to Boyce, but infallibly secures the salvation of those whom God the Father had elected. God's justice requires satisfaction and finds it in Christ's bearing the guilt of the elect and absorbing the wrath due their sin, thus removing all obstacles to God's dealing mercifully with man. The activity of the Holy Spirit is also rendered possible, for "Christ hath redeemed us from the curse of the law . . . that we might receive the promise of the Spirit through faith" (Gal. 3:13–14).

However, after so strongly affirming and defending particular atonement, Boyce introduces an element of ambiguity into his discussion. Seeking to demonstrate that his view had all the strengths of the general-atonement–particular-application view (Andrew Fuller's view, as Boyce sees it) and none of its weaknesses, he virtually adopts the view he is seeking to displace. Although Christ made an actual atonement for the elect, he rendered the salvation of all others possible, dependent upon their repentance and faith. In effect, the particularity of redemption rests not in the atonement but only in unconditional election and effectual calling, the work of the Father and Spirit respectively:

Christ, at the same time, and in the same work, wrought out a means of reconciliation for all men, which removed every legal obstacle to their

24. Ibid., p. 317.

salvation, upon their acceptance of the same conditions upon which salvation is given to the elect.[25]

One might well ask: If "every legal obstacle" has been removed from all men, in what particular does Boyce's treatment of atonement differ from a general atonement? The problems involved in Boyce's view will be discussed later.

Broadus appears to share the broad outline of Boyce's understanding of the atonement. Without equivocation, Broadus asserted the atonement as a substitutionary, propitiatory sacrifice willingly undertaken by Christ for those the Father had given him. One question in Broadus's catechism asks: "What does the New Testament reveal that corresponds to the effect of Adam's sin upon his descendants?" The answer propounds an unmitigated cause-effect relationship between the death of Christ and the salvation of those for whom he died. Broadus wrote: "The benefits of Christ's salvation for His people correspond to the effect of Adam's sin upon his descendants."

If this relationship between Adam-Man and Christ-His People is sustained, no conclusion is possible other than a definite effectual atonement limited in its purpose, though not in its sufficiency, to the redemption of "those whom he always purposed to save."

Perseverance of the Saints

Boyce defines the doctrine of final perseverance of the saints in this way:

> The doctrine of the final perseverance of the saints teaches that those who are effectually called of God to the exercise of genuine faith in Christ will certainly persevere unto final salvation. This is not taught of a class of mankind in general, as something that will usually be true of the persons composing that class, but of each individual in it,—so that not one will finally apostatize or be lost; but each will assuredly persevere and be saved.

Perseverance, according to Boyce, while a sovereign act of God, is not accomplished co-incidentally with man's passivity. Election, atonement, and effectual calling are unilateral works of the Triune God and done apart from any cooperation of man. Perseverance, how-

25. Ibid., p. 340.

ever, involves the redeemed person as a cooperative agent in the process. God leads his elect "unto salvation through their own perseverance in faith and holiness."[26]

After establishing the facticity of the doctrine biblically, Boyce fits this teaching into the whole picture theologically. It cannot be held independently from the other "doctrines of grace," for this doctrine is inseparably associated with the other doctrines of grace which we have found taught in God's Word.

> All the evidence, therefore, of the truth of the doctrines already examined, may be presented in favour of this which is a necessary inference from them. In like manner; all the independent proof of this doctrine confirms the separate doctrines, and the system of doctrine, with which it is associated.[27]

In conformity with his assertion of symmetry and consistency in the "doctrines of graces," Boyce explains perseverance as a result of the purpose of God. Not only could this be inferred from the other doctrines, it is directly asserted in Scripture (e.g., John 6:39).

Boyce points out that the final salvation of the believer is due to the *power* of God (John 10:27–29; 1 Peter 1:5, and so on). It is also due to the *grace* of God that the saints persevere. Thus, persevering power is an unmerited favor bestowed on the elect according to the purpose of God. These elements of God's activity are necessary if anyone will finally be saved, because of "the natural weakness of the Christian and his liability to fall."[28]

The many warnings to Christians illustrate the tendency of the flesh to succumb to the many traps that are set to waylay the believer. The Bible and history abound with examples of believers falling into grievous sin, and the end of all the warnings and examples is stated clearly by Boyce:

> The extent to which this weakness of man is seen to exhibit itself is evidence not only of what, but for the intervention of God, might occur in each case, but, also, that so far as man is concerned, the final apostasy of each one is not only possible but probable, nay certain. We thus have additional proof that the final salvation is due to the purpose, power and grace of God.[29]

26. Ibid., p. 426.
27. Ibid., p. 428.
28. Ibid., p. 429.
29. Ibid.

Boyce is careful to point out, however, that a person is not saved "while indulging in sin, and walking after [his] own lusts," but that he is sanctified through the work of the Holy Spirit, which enables him to persevere. This inevitably brings forth the cooperation of the believer. The believer must be holy and blameless, unreprovable in God's sight, and conformed to the image of his Son. While this is not accomplished fully in this life, one must nevertheless be in the constant process of taking advantage of the means through which holiness comes. Faith is one means enjoined upon the believer. Consecration to God is another duty of the Christian. Boyce mentions self-purification as a means of perseverance, and Scriptures mentioned in support are Romans 6:13, 2 Corinthians 7:1, Galatians 5:24, and 1 John 3:3. The constant warnings of God's Word also serve as means to prompt believers into greater efforts to pursue holiness. These warnings show how those who have had great spiritual advantages have yet fallen and cannot be recovered. The redeemed should make great efforts to avoid falling into that class and should realize that if they persevere it will only be because of the purpose, power, and grace of God.

Echoing this treatment by Boyce, Broadus maintains a historic Calvinist position on perseverance of the saints. In addition to his confidence that God will preserve a true believer in Christ to the end, Broadus unswervingly contends that "the only sure proof of being a true believer is growing in holiness and in usefulness, even to the end."[30] God's work and man's work in sanctification continue to the end, and both are essential in a true doctrine of perseverance.

Broadus preached the reality of this doctrine with great power. In a sermon entitled "He Ever Liveth to Intercede," the inevitability of growth in grace forms the burden of Broadus's art at a strategic moment:

Ah! brethren, though it might often seem to us the bitterest irony now for a man to call you and me the saints of the Lord, yet, if indeed we are in Christ, and thus we are new creatures, we have but to trust in his intercession for the sanctifying Spirit, and earnestly strive to "grow in grace," and we shall make progress; yea, sadly imperfect as is now our conformity to the Saviour's beautiful image, "we know that when he shall appear we shall be like him, for we shall see him as he is." O burdened spirit, crying, "Wretched man that I am, who shall deliver me from the body of this death?" be sure to add, "I thank God, through Jesus Christ our Lord." The Saviour will continue to intercede, the Spirit

30. Broadus, "Catechism," pp. 265–266.

will help your infirmities, and you shall at last be pure from sin, and safe from temptation to sin, a saint of the Lord forever.[31]

In a sermon on Matthew 1:21 entitled "Jesus: Saviour," Broadus reflects on what it means that Jesus died to save his people from their sins. At least a part of such a magnificent work rests in his rescue of them from the dominion of sin. Yea, his people's love for him invest them with new motives to resist their sinful tendencies. His death for them has procured the Holy Spirit as the Sanctifier. Because of this we may pray "for his gracious influences," that we may become "more and more holy." Certainly the hope of every Christian consists partially of gaining "more and more the mastery over . . . sinful dispositions, till the hour of death shall be the hour of perfect deliverance." Then comes the "eternal existence of sinlessness, of purity. That, that will be heaven."[32]

Boyce and Broadus thus avoid the modern caricatures of "once-saved-always-saved" by taking seriously the full biblical witness to the nature of salvation. Divine grace meshes with human cooperation in a perfect confluence of spiritual power, achieving the eternal infallible purpose of God, producing holiness in man and conformity to the image of Christ—that he might be the firstborn among many brethren—and bringing praise to God.

Conclusion

Boyce and Broadus, joined by the Manlys, spoke virtually with one voice during their lives and died with the same passion for perpetuity of God's truth among their Baptist brethren. At least partially this commitment lay in the mind of Broadus as, at the close of his memoir of Boyce, he penned a final apostrophe to his departed colleague:

O Brother beloved, true yokefellow through years of toil, best and dearest friend, sweet shall be thy memory till we meet again! And may the men be always ready as the years come and go, to carry on, with widening reach and heightened power, the work we sought to do, and did begin![33]

---

31. *Favorite Sermons of John A. Broadus*, Vernon Latrelle Stanfield, ed. (New Harper and Brothers Publishers, 1959), p. 35.
32. Ibid., p. 145.
33. Broadus, *Memoir*, p. 371.

7

Steps Along the Way

F. H. Kerfoot

The successor to J. P. Boyce, and the Joseph Emerson Brown Professor of Systematic Theology at Southern Seminary, was Franklin Howard Kerfoot. Born in Clark County, Virginia, Kerfoot adorned Baptist life as a minister, theological professor, and secretary of the Home Mission Board of the Southern Baptist Convention. He fought briefly in the Confederate Army, attended Columbian College in Washington D.C.; Southern Baptist Theological Seminary in Greenville, South Carolina; Crozer Seminary; and the University of Leipzig. After serving several pastorates in Kentucky, Maryland, and New York, Kerfoot entered Southern Seminary in 1886, where he was elected as Co-Professor of Systematic Theology after one semester of additional student work. In 1889 he became a full professor, succeeding James P. Boyce. Ten years later Kerfoot became corresponding secretary for the Home Mission Board in Atlanta, Georgia, where he remained until his death in 1901.

While serving as pastor of the Eutaw Place Baptist Church in Baltimore, Maryland, Kerfoot prepared a Confession of Faith to be used in the church as an expression of its doctrinal stance. The confession was adopted by several other Baptist churches and in 1905 was issued by the Sunday School Board in a volume entitled *The Doctrines of Our Faith*, written by E. C. Dargan. It made its way into print again in 1913 as part of the *New Convention Normal Manual*. Included as an appendix and entitled *What We Believe According to the Scriptures*, the confession was set forth by Kerfoot in two major sections. The first was entitled "Doctrines Which We Hold in Common With Other De-

206

nominations." The second was "Distinctive Doctrines of Baptists."
Part one is introduced by this statement: "We believe, in common with
all evangelical Christians." Such an affirmation should make one pause
long before proclaiming that Baptists have never considered themselves evangelicals. Among the doctrines cited in that section are: One
God, Maker and Ruler of Heaven and Earth revealed as Father, Son
and Holy Spirit, all who are equal in every divine perfection; the Holy
Scriptures as his infallible word; the fall of man and his condemnation
as a sinner; salvation in the name of Jesus Christ, who was the Word
made flesh, the God-man who obeyed, suffered and died for the sins
of man, is risen and exalted as Priest and King; the free offer of eternal
life in the gospel and the aggravated guilt of those who reject it; the
necessity of regeneration by the Holy Spirit; justification and adoption
through the blood and righteousness of Christ, and so on.

The second section under this first heading begins with these words:
"And, in common with a large body of evangelical Christians, nearly
all Baptists [italics mine] believe what are usually termed the 'doctrines of grace.' " The following doctrines are listed in this category:

> . . . the absolute sovereignty and foreknowledge of God; his eternal and
> unchangeable purposes or decrees; that salvation in its beginning, con-
> tinuance and completion, is God's free gift; that, in Christ, we are elected
> or chosen, personally or individually, from eternity, saved and called out
> from the world, not according to our works, but according to His own
> purpose and grace, through the sanctification of the Spirit and belief of
> the truth; that we are kept by His power from falling away, and will be
> presented faultless before the presence of His glory. Read Romans 8, 9,
> 10, 11; Acts 13:48; Eph. 1:4, 5; Eph. 2:1–10; 1 Pet. 1:2–5; Jude 24; 1 Tim.
> 1:9; Tit. 3:5.[1]

E. C. Dargan

A contemporary of Kerfoot's at Southern Seminary was Edwin
Charles Dargan, born in Darlington County, South Carolina, in 1852.
Both his father and grandfather were eminent Baptist ministers, a fact
that provided rich opportunity for young Dargan to have broad ac-
quaintances in Baptist circles. He received the M.A. from Furman
University in Greenville, South Carolina, and in 1877 graduated
from Southern Baptist Theological Seminary (also in Greenville at
that time). After serving as pastor at several churches in North Caro-

1. F. H. Kerfoot in E. C. Dargan, *The Doctrines of Our Faith* (Nashville: Sunday
School Board of the Southern Baptist Convention, 1905), pp. 230, 231.

lina, South Carolina, and Virginia, Dargan served as Professor of Hom-
iletics at Southern Baptist Theological Seminary from 1892 to 1907.
While there he produced his significant study *History of Preaching*. He
left his seminary position in 1907 to serve as pastor of First Baptist
Church in Macon, Georgia. In 1917 he became editorial secretary for
the Southern Baptist Sunday School Board, a service he rendered until
1927.

The Doctrines of Our Faith first appeared as a series of articles published by the Southern Baptist Sunday School Board for the educational programs of the churches. When published as a book, the board
recommended it for use in B.Y.P.U. Christian-culture courses, Sunday-
school normal classes, and individual study.

The book's affirmations concerning the sovereignty of God are made
in clear and unmistakable terms. Chapter six, "The Sovereignty of
God," is divided into two major sections: "What Is God's Sovereignty?" and "How Is God's Sovereignty Proved?" In the first, Dargan
defines sovereignty: "That God is sovereign means that having perfect
knowledge and perfect power he governs all things according to his
own will."[2]

According to Ephesians 1:11, Dargan asserts, God works by a plan
that he unalterably brings to pass. "If he thinks, he plans; and if he
purposes according to his knowledge, as we do, then he purposes according to perfect knowledge."[3] God's sovereignty includes all things:

> (a) Things in our view—nature, in all its boundless extent and num-
> berless details, men in all their works and ways, past, present and future;
> time, in all its unfolding and continued progress. But the sweep of God's
> rule goes even further and takes in: (b) Things beyond our view—heaven,
> the universe beyond sight and thought; the angels, and whatever other
> beings and intelligences may lie out of our range of knowing or thinking;
> eternity, the backward and forward reach of time till it is lost. What a
> wonderful thing is God's sovereign rule over all his works! Let it not
> terrify us—it is the rule of perfect wisdom and perfect love.[4]

Such a lofty doctrine should not be held if it arises only from human
speculation. According to Dargan, it is incumbent upon us to set forth
clearly the reasons why such a belief in the sovereignty of God has
been given. Initially Dargan sets forth what he calls a proof from Scripture: "If the Bible be, as we hold it to be, a true message from God,

2. E. C. Dargan, *The Doctrines of Our Faith* (Nashville: Sunday School Board of
the Southern Baptist Convention, 1905), pp. 47–48.
3. Ibid., p. 48.
4. Ibid., p. 49.

then what it teaches on this subject is God's affirmation to us concerning the nature and extent of his rule over his own work."[5] Dargan then lists several Scripture passages in support of this thesis (Gen. 50:19, 20; Exod. 9:12, 16; Ps. 33:8–15; 46:8–10; 90:2–4; 103:19; 119:89–91; Isa. 14:24; 46:9–11; Dan. 4:35; Matt. 11:25–27; 25:34; Luke 22:22; John 6:37, 39, 44, 65; Acts 2:23; 4:27, 28; 13:48; 17:26; Rom. 8:28–30; 9:14–24; 11:33–36; 1 Cor. 2:7; Eph. 1:3–12; 2:10; 3:9–11; 2 Tim. 1:9; Heb. 2:10; 1 Peter 1:2, 20; Rev. 17:17). Dargan assumes that this doctrine of the sovereignty of God pervades the general teaching of Scripture, as well as being taught in specific passages, and is the constant underlying assumption of the entire biblical record.[6]

Dargan then sets forth his proof from "reason." To offer any reason for the movement of events other than the "complete and perfect" sovereignty of a personal God issues in an indefensible position:

> If we limit in any direction the actual and complete sovereignty of God we encounter as many and as great difficulties as we think to escape. The safest and soundest position to take is to accept in all its fullness the great truth, explaining as best we can its difficulties, and waiting humbly for more light.[7]

Dargan's doctrine of providence is contained in chapter seven, "God's Care of His Creation." Dargan affirms that all things, small as well as great, fall under divine care. There are no exceptions. Providence is not to be identified merely with the rule of the law, for law does not operate as a coequal force with God, much less an overruling one. Rather, it is a part or an expression of his care and is inferior to him. Nor is God's providence to be considered fate, but is his personal dynamic working in every event of history.

In this context Dargan affirms the legitimacy of decrees. "He has decreed what has been, is, and shall be forevermore; but the decree includes his own care. He has not decreed himself out of loving and constant touch with his creation, but into it. The decree does not supersede providence, it contains it."[8] Not only is God's sovereignty operative in the flow of human history, it expresses itself most specifically in the salvation of man. The doctrine of sin—total depravity, that is—foundations this discussion and demonstrates the acute need for the sovereign power of God in the salvation of sinners.

5. Ibid., p. 50.
6. Ibid., p. 51.
7. Ibid., p. 52.
8. Ibid., p. 57.

Dargan first dismisses the error that total depravity assumes the complete and equal wickedness of all men. Instead, he affirms that

> . . . the total man, the whole sum of human life and being, is perverted; that all the faculties of man are more or less twisted out of shape by sin; that each man, from the whole, is turned from God rather than toward God; so that the whole nature of man, as it now exists, is warped and twisted by sin."[9]

In other words, as Dargan states, "Man is both in mind and heart, in purpose and in deed . . . apart from God, lost and straying."[10]

Dargan also pictures God as angry at sin and determined to punish sin, an anger he describes as the "unutterable recoil of perfect holiness from its opposite."[11] This hatred of sin is combined in Dargan's theology with the love of God toward man. Dargan does not perceive of God's love as utterly and absolutely promiscuous. Rather, God's love is controlled and always accomplishes its end; so, in its fullest manifestation the inevitable result is the salvation of the man who is its object. For example, when Dargan discusses love as an attribute of God, he demonstrates its reality in the context of election:

> In the Old Testament this is brought out more especially in the declarations of God's love toward his chosen people; as in Deut. 4:37; 7:7 and 8; and most beautifully in Jeremiah 31:3, where God says to Israel: "I have loved thee with an everlasting love."[12]

Indeed, although God's love is manifest toward all his creation in his fatherly care toward it, the fullest and most pointed expression resides in his deeds toward those who are actually redeemed. The gift of his Son as the propitiation for sins was the supreme manifestation of this love. The concept of God's love is furthered when Dargan discusses the other gracious acts that reveal it:

> In his providential care (Matt. 6:25–34); in the gift of the Holy Spirit (Luke 11:13); in his own abiding presence (John 14:23); in the supports of his grace (Rom. 5:3–5); in the protection of his sovereign choice (Rom. 8:28–39); and in the chastenings of his Fatherly hand (Heb. 12:5–13), we have great assurances of the mighty love of God.[13]

In each of these, God's love culminates on the one who is elect.

9. Ibid., p. 101.
10. Ibid., p. 116.
11. Ibid., p. 120.
12. Ibid., p. 123.
13. Ibid., p. 125.

While no individual of the race deserves to be loved of God, surely there is something in the uniqueness of this created humanity that calls forth or at least legitimates redemptive love. What within the depraved lump of humanity can "awaken and call out his wonderful love"?[14] Dargan gives three reasons: (1) Man, though fallen, bears the likeness of God; (2) Man needs the help of God because he is lost; (3) Man, though human, is capable of a heavenly destiny.[15] These facts however, in no way place God under obligation to redeem any individual, much less each and every one. Under point one, when affirming that men, though sinful, still bear the likeness of God, Dargan warns the reader not to infer too much from the passages by concluding that all men are naturally the children of God. He states:

> No, for we are distinctly told (John 3:3, 5) that man must be born again, that to those who receive Christ (John 1:12) the right to be sons of God was given, that even the Jews (John 8:42, 44) were not children of God, but of the devil, and that by nature (Eph. 2:3) men are children of wrath. We may only go so far as to say that in man, ruined as he is, the good God still recognizes traces of himself and yearns with love toward his own.[16]

Given Dargan's views on sovereignty and his view of election, yet to be discussed, the phrase "yearns with love toward his own" is highly significant: God's redeeming love is particular and effectual.

In point three, Dargan affirms that God loves the possibilities of redeemed humanity, that he sees a possible free man of God in one who is now a poor slave of sin, and that "he sees a future saint in this lost and undone sinner; therefore he loved him, and in order to bring many sons unto glory he made a perfect Savior by the discipline of human suffering (Heb. 2:10)."[17] He refers to Romans 8:29; Ephesians 4:22–24; Colossians 3:10–11 and 1 John 3:1–2 as supportive of this view.

Continuing his soteriological discussion, Dargan affirms that God's hatred toward sin and necessary judgment of it, and his love toward those he determined to redeem, demand that he send a mediator:

> For the Scriptures teach that on the one hand God's holy justice demands the punishment of sin, and that on the other his holy love demands the

14. Ibid., p. 126.
15. Ibid., pp. 126–127.
16. Ibid., p. 126.
17. Ibid., p. 127.

restoration of the sinner, and that a way is found for both of these essential parts of the divine nature to be satisfied without injury to either. . . . Justice and mercy are equally characteristic of God, and their united demand is for a mediator.[18]

This mediator, Jesus Christ, appears as perfect God and perfect man in one person. The mediator then dies a substitutionary death:

> Christ voluntarily took the nature of man and with it the place of man as a sinner before God, though without personal sin; that so in man's stead he suffered the penalty of sin in his cruel death on the cross; that being God he could by becoming man offer himself as a sufficient and suitable substitute for man; and being man his death was a real human death, a penalty for sin.[19]

Dargan then concludes the discussion that Christ is sufficient for all the race, "though actually efficient only in the case of those who by faith accept him as their substitute."[20]

But, in saving man, does God only provide historical redemption, or is there more? Dargan affirms there is more. Nothing is clearer in the Scriptures than "the gracious and positive declaration that God does actually save men from their sins."[21] In the sovereign dispensing of salvation, God "works in perfect accordance with his own nature, and also with that of man."[22] The doctrine of election, according to Dargan, ties together all the attributes of God that he has previously discussed and gives a truthful, uncompromised display of them. Since God acts *as* God in saving men, Dargan affirms that "we naturally look for rich displays of the divine sovereignty, power, wisdom, righteousness, love."[23] Since love is God's crowning attribute and since sovereignty is essential to God's perfection, both of these come together in the word that Paul uses, "grace." Dargan says this word means both sovereign love and loving sovereignty.

This grace works in two ways: election and regeneration. In election God chooses those who shall be saved. This is the choice God makes before the foundation of the world. It is made in an unconditional way, not "because he foresees that a man will repent, or on the con-

18. Ibid., p. 135.
19. Ibid., p. 139.
20. Ibid.
21. Ibid., p. 140.
22. Ibid., p. 142.
23. Ibid., p. 143.

dition of faith," but in this choice God is "sovereign, free, untrammeled, gracious, acting on his own initiative."[24]

The same sovereignty works in regeneration. The Holy Spirit works in a sovereign way to change the lives and affections of those whom God has chosen to save.[25]

What shall we say to these things? Dargan would ask and then answer in the spirit of Paul: "If he chooses some, regenerates them, and actually saves them . . . we can only answer with all reverence that this is God's affair, and he will see to it."

> We are not his guardians. He is sovereign and does what he will with his own; he is just and will always do right; he is holy and cannot do wrong; he is love and will not be cruel. For our part we can wait. God will take care of himself, and of us (See Rom. 9:19–21).[26]

Dargan continues espousing this same theology in *An Exposition of the Epistle to the Romans*. Commenting on Romans 9, Dargan says:

> The gist of the argument is that God is sovereign and can do what he will with his own. . . . In other words, God is perfectly free in the exercise of his mercy toward individuals, and consequently toward groups of men. He is not under bonds to have mercy on any. It is a matter of free choice with him. . . . both God's mercy and God's hardening are dependent upon his sovereign will. If he shows mercy to the penitent sinner, it is not because the sinner deserves it, but because in grace God so wills it. . . . As creator and sovereign over living and free men, God acts as an artisan over lifeless and plastic material.[27]

In both books Dargan has sections in which he seeks to demonstrate the congruity of human freedom with divine sovereignty. His favorite illustration pictures a man on a fast-sailing vessel, which is moving in one direction while the man himself is running on the deck of the boat in the other. One could truly say that the man is moving both east and west at the same time. This is the way Dargan views God's sovereignty. The sailing vessel is the movement of God; the running of the man on the deck is the will of man. God is going exactly where he wants to go and controls all events, and within that larger movement man acts freely but in direct accord with God's sovereignty. The apparent conflicts that exist do not involve two equal powers. To assume any real

24. Ibid.
25. Ibid., p. 144.
26. Ibid., p. 145.
27. E. C. Dargan, *An Exposition of the Epistle to the Romans* (Nashville: Sunday School Board of the Southern Baptist Convention, c. 1914), pp. 102–105.

Historical Evidence

conflict is highly incongruous, for such would assume that both parties have equal dignity, equal claim for protecting their own interests, and relatively equal power to effect their claim. The case is simply not so.

Dargan's complete view is perhaps best summarized in the statements that he makes on Romans 11:33–36. He entitles this section "God Glorified as Sovereign."

> The closing thought of the preceding section leads to this splendid outburst of praise which suitably concludes the argumentative and doctrinal portion of the Epistle. In his dealing with mankind, even in their sin and rejection of him, God has not only displayed exhaustless mercy, but fathomless wisdom. Well may the apostle exclaim over the depth of the divine richness, wisdom and knowledge shown in the great plan of redemption and its working, as these have been described and followed in the arguments preceding. God is infinite. His judgments are "unsearchable" to human wisdom, and his ways beyond "tracking out" by human investigation. God transcends the human. Man does not know God's mind, nor has he been called to give advice to the Almighty. Neither has man given of riches or wisdom or knowledge to God so that it shall be repaid in God's dealings with him. No; in all these things God remains Supreme Sovereign. All things come "of him" as their origin, they work out "through him" as the Power which makes them active, and they tend "to him" as the final goal of all their activity. God alone is supreme Lord and Sovereign of all. And so this great discussion ends with the devout words, "To whom be the glory unto the ages. Amen!"[28]

J. B. Gambrell

One of the foremost leaders of Southern Baptists during the first part of the twentieth century was J. B. Gambrell. Born in Anderson County, South Carolina, in 1841, Gambrell moved with his family to northeast Mississippi when he was four years old. He served as a scout in the Confederate Army, fought at Gettysburg, and ended his tenure in the army as a captain. He enrolled in the University of Mississippi after the Civil War and served as pastor of the Oxford Baptist Church for five years. Gambrell edited the *Baptist Record* from 1877 to 1893, when he was elected president of Mercer University. In 1896, after serving three years at Mercer, he became Superintendent of Missions in Texas, serving in that position for fourteen years, until 1910. He then edited the *Baptist Standard* for four years and served as a member of the faculty of Southwestern Baptist Theological Seminary during

28. Ibid., see remarks on Romans 11:33–36.

two of those years. In addition, Gambrell was secretary of the Southern Baptist Convention for six years and president for four. He died in 1921.

In a book entitled *Baptist Principles Reset*, published in 1902, Gambrell sets forth his confidence in the Doctrines of Grace as an effective evangelistic tool. He was not so much concerned with the pragmatic value of evangelism as he was with one's commitment to the truth. In his article entitled "Obligations of Baptists to Teach Their Principles," Gambrell expresses some sympathy with those who react negatively to the preaching of "dry doctrine." However, he was convinced the trouble did not lie in the doctrine itself but in the dry preaching of it, whereby the bread of heaven was turned into stones, and the stones were used merely to cast at theological adversaries. According to Gambrell, we can scarcely wonder that hungry souls "turn away from a ministry which preaches predestination without pathos, election without grace, baptism without its sublime spiritual meaning, communion without sensibility, and all duty without beauty."[29] The reaction to this dry preaching was no better and probably worse than the prior condition. Men have moved from doctrine into the "myths of mere sentimentalism."[30] Doctrine was being replaced by feeling. Gambrell feared that such a notion was at the bottom of "modern revivalism of the sensational order."

It abounds in clap-trap, and after a community has been swept by it, by-and-by, when the revivalist has gone, nothing substantial remains. There is no substratum of truth upon which the convert can stand. I do not undervalue evangelism. The true evangelist is a gift from Christ, and two things go with him—he preaches in the Spirit and he preaches God's revealed truth. By these signs he may be known with infallible certainty. The cure for both evils named is a return to biblical preaching, both as to Spirit and substance.[31]

Such a return, according to Gambrell, would cure the ills of Baptists. In the same way that Paul regarded himself as a trustee of the gospel, Baptists in particular must follow that succession. When few in number and despised by elite religionists, they held aloft the great principles of Scripture in the midst of the dust and smoke of mighty spiritual conflicts and suffered for the sake of the truth. Even now, Gambrell contends, must Baptists continue to hold aloft the truth

29. J. B. Gambrell in Jeremiah B. Jeter, D.D., *Baptist Principles Reset* (Richmond, VA: The Religious Herald Co., 1902), p. 245.
30. Ibid., p. 245.
31. Ibid.

and work to create "a spiritual hospitality for doctrinal teaching" in their churches.[32] Preachers who follow public opinion and form alliances with people of alien doctrinal views, create a real hindrance to "honest, thoroughgoing, New Testament teachings on doctrines."[33] Gambrell continues:

> We may invigorate our faith and renew our courage by reflecting that divine power has always attended the preaching of doctrine, when done in the true spirit of preaching. Great revivals have accompanied the heroic preaching of the doctrines of grace, predestination, election, and that whole lofty mountain range of doctrines upon which Jehovah sits enthroned, sovereign in grace as in all things else. God honors the preaching that honors him. There is entirely too much milk-sop preaching nowadays, trying to cajole sinners to enter upon a truce with their Maker, quit sinning, and join the church. The situation does not call for a truce, but for a surrender. Let us bring out the heavy artillery of heaven, and thunder away at this stuck-up age as Whitfield, Edwards, Spurgeon, and Paul did, and there will be many slain of the Lord raised up to walk in newness of life.[34]

During his tenure as editor of the *Baptist Standard*, Gambrell quite often rapped the knuckles of Hardshellism, an anti-mission expression of genuine hyper-Calvinism. Contemporary critics of Calvinism usually caricature it as Hardshellism. Gambrell, however, who considered himself a true Calvinist, saw just as many problems with Hardshellism as he did with Arminianism. Neither was a true theology. He accused the Hardshell element of Baptist life of denying the Scriptures, for they accepted only half the Scriptures on predestination.

In order to illustrate this point, Gambrell chose the analogy of well-digging. A Hardshell is a man who determines that he wants to dig a well and dig it in a certain place. That is, he predestinates who he predetermines to have it. But at that point he stops and makes no plan, buys neither pick nor shovel, and merely waits for the well to be dug.

Another man begins to dig. He knows not what he is digging—a well, a posthole. He knows not whether his digging will succeed or fail. He is simply digging. According to Gambrell, ". . . that is an Arminian, and he is as foolish as a Hardshell, but no more so."[35]

A third man, however, decides to have a well, and he chooses all

32. Ibid., p. 246.
33. Ibid.
34. Ibid., p. 247.
35. Ibid., p. 253.

the means necessary for carrying out his purpose. His decision determines both the ends and the means. Gambrell comments that this represents God's predestination:

> It is wise in all its goings, selecting and making efficient all means leading to the end. "If a man is going to be saved he will be saved anyway," is not true. He will be saved, but God's way, not anyway. And God's way is by the preaching of the gospel, which he has given command shall be preached to every creature. Through the preaching of the gospel he will take out of all nations a people for himself.[36]

Gambrell never substituted one passage for another or eliminated one truth by the other. Instead, following Richard Fuller and other historic Calvinists, he saw that both human responsibility and God's sovereignty were taught and that one type of teaching should never be used to displace the other. Rather, they should be held hand and glove. God's sovereignty prompts a man to missions, guaranteeing him success and determining the integrity of his methods. The fact that God employs responsible humans as the means to the end makes necessary planned and vigorous involvement. Speaking for himself and those like him, Gambrell said, ". . . we glory in the divine sovereignty, in predestination, and in the election of grace"—but to imply Hardshellism from those doctrines should be shunned "as we would the black plague."[37]

J. B. Tidwell

In the mid-twentieth century, perhaps the best-known Bible teacher in Texas Baptist life (if not Southern Baptist Life) was Josiah Blake Tidwell. Influenced greatly by Dargan, he perpetuated the teaching of the Doctrines of Grace with the same conviction and represented a continuance of historic Baptist soteriology well into the 1940s.

Born in 1870 and educated at Howard College in Birmingham, Alabama, and Baylor University, Tidwell taught Greek and Latin at Decatur Baptist College in Decatur, Texas, before he served that institution as president. After his 1910 election as head of the Bible department at Baylor, he served the institution in that position for thirty-six years, until his death in 1946.

For over twenty years Tidwell's expositions of the Uniform Sunday

36. Ibid.
37. Ibid., p. 256.

School lesson appeared in the Texas *Baptist Standard.* Among his more than a dozen books are *Christian Teachings, The Bible Book by Book, The Bible Period by Period, Christ in the Pentateuch,* and *John and His Five Books.*

Christian Teachings consists of fifteen chapters. Although it orders Christian doctrine in a systematic fashion, it is not intended as a formal display of systematic theology. Instead, it is in the form of a bare outline. Ideally this format would prompt students to study the outline and pursue the Scripture references provided under each point, thus developing a systematic approach to the study of Bible doctrine.

The soteriological elements of such study amounted to no less than an exposition of the main tenets of the Doctrines of Grace. Unashamed and uncompromised exposition of man's absolute sinfulness, helplessness, and utter dependence on the sovereign electing love of God forms the heart of Tidwell's understanding of the gospel. The logic of Tidwell's system assumes a foundation of human depravity, necessitating his development of that doctrine first. His later exposition of the doctrines of unconditional election, effectual calling, and perseverance found coherence on that foundation.

Although Adam was created in the image of God, possessing original innocence and enjoying dominion with the Creator, mankind was plunged into despair and wretchedness by the sin of that first forebear. Tidwell viewed Paul's explanation in Romans 5 as literal truth: the total ruin of the race arose from Adam's sin. Universal death and the universal corruption of man's nature, the source of individual sins, plague the world as each person stands separated from God and an enemy of God. This corruption of nature is passed down biologically, and the actual sins of individuals further aggravate man's helpless condition.

In short, Tidwell affirmed the doctrine of total depravity, that is, that "the whole man is perverted, warped, turned from God." This perversion of human nature came about by the historic fall accurately reported in Genesis 3, "a historical account." Adam, "in one supreme choice of self instead of God . . . became a transgressor." In this free act, Adam "revolted against God, thereby corrupting his nature and causing every manifestation of human nature to be corrupt. Rom. 5:12." Man, therefore, is a guilty, condemned culprit worthy of punishment. Man is responsible "for both his acts of sin and his state of sin . . . for which outraged divine justice demands death."[38]

How, then, does salvation come? The historical work of Christ on

38. J. B. Tidwell, *Christian Teachings* (Grand Rapids: Wm. B. Eerdmans Pub. Co., 1942), pp. 47–49.

the cross as a vicarious atonement for our sins is essential. The holiness of God demands punishment of sin, while the love of God sacrifices for the sinner. In his priestly work, Christ "suffered in man's stead; satisfied divine holiness and opened the way for God to pardon and restore the guilty."[39]

However, God goes beyond this in bestowing salvation. Christ's death, though essential in itself, is only part of what the Triune God has done in granting salvation to his people. According to Tidwell, salvation originates in the eternal counsel of God and culminates in the effectual working of the Spirit.

That God elects to salvation is given clear expression by Tidwell in his introduction to the chapter on salvation:

> Salvation is the biggest Christian word, and includes first, a plan of salvation, which is all of the Father; second, the preparation of salvation, which was wrought out of Jesus the Son; and third, the application of salvation, which is accomplished by the power of the Holy Spirit. All this involves the great divine covenant of redemption; the work of the atonement of Christ and the regenerating and sanctifying work of the Holy Spirit.[40]

In answering the question "What is election?" Tidwell says that "it is God's decree to act so that certain ones will believe and be saved."[41] Clearly, by such a decree, God has chosen "certain men to receive his unmerited grace and be made voluntary recipients of Christ's salvation."[42] Without such action on God's part, none would receive Jesus; all would reject him. For this reason, eternal election results in an efficacious call, which "infallibly leads the sinner to salvation."[43]

Tidwell poses another question: "When does he elect?" Certainly not after man chooses him, nor is it contemporaneous with man's choice. Election, according to Ephesians 1:4, took place before the foundation of the world. This is the only view that is reasonable and "makes God sovereign." What conditions aid or determine God's choice? No merit in those chosen, nor even repentance and faith, serve as conditions. In fact, election is unconditional and rests solely "in the sovereign will and wisdom of God."[44] Nor is it on the foreknowledge of our obedience, because our election precedes and brings about obe-

39. Ibid., pp. 39, 40.
40. Ibid., p. 50.
41. Ibid., p. 51.
42. Ibid., p. 52.
43. Ibid.
44. Ibid.

dience. Foreknowledge of merit or holiness falls short also, because we are chosen unto holiness or that we might be holy. Neither is it on foreknowledge of repentance and faith, because these themselves "are the gifts of God's grace and are the effect of the election rather than its cause."[45]

Several aspects of the nature of God—his foreknowledge, his wisdom, and his immutability—require election. Foreknowledge implies fixity, for something could not be known beforehand if it were uncertain. Only election by the decree of God makes events certain. Wisdom requires a plan in which "every detail and circumstance would have to be provided for." And immutability means that God has only one plan; thus, he does not have to change plans in order to "meet emergencies." These qualities of the divine character require election.

If some would raise objections to the doctrine, Tidwell is ready to answer them. To those who say election is unjust to those not elected, Tidwell responds that they "suffer justly as do all rebellious creatures." Better that God be praised for saving some than resented for not saving all. If some accuse the doctrine of making God partial, Tidwell questions the validity of the objection on the grounds that election does not rest on any preferred condition or characteristic within man but only in the good pleasure of God himself. If others would say that election makes God arbitrary, Tidwell would answer "not arbitrary but sovereign." The exercising of personality and wisdom "for good reason, known to himself, but not known to man" is a sovereign act of God. This procedure is most orderly and exactly the opposite of whimsical or arbitrary in the negative sense. "Is not human freedom violated?" some might ask. Tidwell answers that this view maintains human freedom, that only God's sovereignty sets us free. Humans act freely and sense no compulsion on their wills. Absolute responsibility accompanies all our actions.

Tidwell asserts that both freedom and election are doctrines that exist on two levels: human and divine, earthly and heavenly. Since they are parallel planes that never meet, there is no conflict between them.

Several important values find their true strength when proper regard is given to unconditional election. First, this view encourages evangelistic effort because it gives the assurance that some are certain to be saved. Second, it encourages the penitent sinner by showing him that there are some who will be saved. Hence, he has a chance. Third, it teaches the Christian worker that he is wholly dependent upon God's

45. Ibid.

power for success. Fourth, it enables Christian workers and mission-aries to endure suffering "for the elect's sake" (2 Tim. 2:10).[46]

Following upon election, God focuses two other activities upon the person of the sinner to produce a person for himself; regeneration and preservation. Regeneration is described as a begetting, a new birth, a passing from death unto life, and a re-creation. By regeneration, God reverses the inmost dispositions and principles of the sinner so that a new direction is given to the sinner's power of affection.[47] To this rad-ical change, man is at first passive and then active. Tidwell summa-rizes this discussion in the following passage:

> Third—Here are the two sides. On the one hand God acting as a caus-ative agent regenerates or changes our moral disposition, thereby turns us from sin to Christ. On the other hand we voluntarily turn and exercise the holy disposition of our souls. The first of these changes is regenera-tion—God's change of our souls; the second is conversion—Our volun-tary change—God's work and our response.[48]

God's third activity toward the sinner in salvation is termed "pres-ervation" by Tidwell. Arising from God's electing love as the only ad-equate foundation for the perpetuity of salvation in the sinner, Tidwell discusses preservation immediately before "What Man Experiences in Salvation." God's work in preservation assures and produces the saints' work of perseverance. These combine to compose the process of sanc-tification. In preservation God continues the divine life in us unto immortality and glorification. Tidwell lists Philippians 1:6 in this con-text. This preservation is accomplished in accordance with God's pur-pose (Acts 13:48; Rom. 8:29; 2 Tim. 2:19; John 6:39), God's power (John 10:29; Phil. 1:6; 2:13; 2 Thess. 1:3–11, and so on), and God's grace (Rom. 4:16; 8:4; 9:16; 1 Thess. 5:23–24).

Perseverance is the inevitable response to preservation, and it con-tinues until death, for God works in us so that we work out our own salvation. Tidwell calls perseverance the "human side of the divine process of sanctification . . . the outworking of the divine power work-ing in us to accomplish his own purposes and decrees."[49] Tidwell con-tends that God's regenerating grace produces within the Christian a striving to be faithful and "to become better." In perseverance "we consecrate ourselves to God, concern ourselves for the divine warn-ings, and try to purify ourselves from sin."[50]

46. Ibid., p. 54.
47. Ibid., p. 55.
48. Ibid., p. 56.
49. Ibid., p. 59.
50. Ibid., see also pp. 65–68.

Conclusion

The theology of the early twentieth century among Baptists re-
tained the form of sound words handed down by these fathers. Men
like Kerfoot, Dargan, Gambrell, and Tidwell gave little, if any, evidence of compromise. During the same period of time, however, some
were planting seeds whose eventual fruit would dull the ears of the
following generations—so the sounds of grace became strange indeed.[51]

51. Ibid., pp. 47–48, 51–57.

8

A House by the Side of the Road

Two denominational giants of the late-eighteenth and early-nineteenth centuries were B. H. Carroll and A. H. Strong. Both sought to retard, if not reverse, the trends of modernism they saw. Both were pastors, then theological educators and presidents of influential theological institutions. However, their perceptions of the dangers to traditional Christianity differed as significantly as the results of their efforts. While both approved the Doctrines of Grace, with some degree of fluctuation on the atonement, their respective denominations were at the edge of doom concerning those doctrines. Like a puff of smoke in a strong wind, they vanished in American Baptist life; like a fish struggling to survive out of water, they gradually died away in Southern Baptist life as they were removed from their vivifying context. Strong saw his own generation turn away from the doctrines; Carroll's efforts merely delayed their demise.

B. H. Carroll

Later to be known as the "Colossus of Baptist History," B. H. Carroll was born in Carroll County, Mississippi, in December 1843, seven years after A. H. Strong. Having served in the Confederate Army during the Civil War, he lived several years as a vigorous yet dismayed agnostic. Ironically, his agnosticism crystallized as a result of a high-pressure, decisionistic, evangelistic appeal of which he was the victim. Carroll knew his heart was unchanged, but well-meaning counselors assured him that his response had certainly been a genuine Christian

223

experience. If that were so, he comments, "religion . . . was not worth having."[1]

During the summer of 1865, Carroll was converted after engaging in an experimental test of the Christian faith that temporarily appeared to fail. He felt flashing upon his mind the Scripture "Come unto me all ye that labour and are heavy laden, and I will give you rest." At that point, in his mind's eye, he saw Jesus standing before him, rebuking him and inviting him to come. Carroll testifies, "In a moment, I went, once and forever, casting myself unreservedly and for all time at Christ's feet."[2]

Carroll served as pastor of First Baptist Church in Waco, Texas, for twenty-nine years. His ministry from the pulpit, according to L. R. Scarborough, constituted a virtual theological education in itself. *Cathcart's Baptist Encyclopaedia*, published in 1881, called Carroll "one of the first preachers of his age in the Baptist ministry of the Southern States" (s.v. Carroll, B. H.).

At the writing of those words, Carroll's most notable achievement, the founding of Southwestern Seminary, was yet at least twenty-five years away. This institution was organized first as Baylor Theological Seminary in 1905 and eventually was located at Fort Worth, Texas, its charter being granted on May 14, 1908.

While many leaders of American Baptist life were finding ways to be reconciled to the burgeoning influence of evolution in every intellectual endeavor, Carroll was seeking to establish a permanent barricade against it. While the great A. H. Strong was concluding, "Neither evolution nor the higher criticism has any terrors to one who regards them as parts of Christ's creating and educating process,"[3] Carroll was applauding a Baptist layman, G. R. Freeman, who began a permanent endowment for establishing a "permanent break-water against the invading tide of practical infidelity."[4] Carroll himself testifies: "And so to the origin of things, the philosophy of Democritus, developed by Epicurius, more developed by Lucretius, and gone to seed in the unverified hypothesis of modern evolutionists—such a godless, materialistic anti-climax of philosophy never had the slightest attraction or temptation for me."[5]

Such differences, only subtle at the beginning, led to the rapid distinctions between American Baptist and Southern Baptist life and go

1. B. H. Carroll, "My Infidelity and What Became of It" in J. B. Cranfill, *From Memory* (Nashville: Broadman Press, 1937), p. 140.
2. Ibid., p. 147.
3. A. H. Strong, *Systematic Theology* (Valley Forge: Judson Press, 1907), p. vii.
4. *Proceeding of the Baptist General Convention of Texas*, (1902), p. 35.
5. Carroll, "My Infidelity," p. 137.

B. H. Carroll

A. H. Strong

Alva Hovey

far in explaining the different paths each took to the loss of the Doctrines of Grace.

Carroll, intensely concerned that Southwestern Seminary be founded
on the "rocks of predestination," adhered clearly and strongly to traditional Baptist Calvinism. His own dynamic conversion and immediate reading of Bunyan's *The Pilgrim's Progress* no doubt predisposed
him to that stance. He writes:

> I spent the night at her bedside reading Bunyan's *Pilgrim's Progress*. I
> read it all that night, and when I came with the pilgrims to the Beulah
> Land, from which Doubting Castle could be seen no more forever, and
> which was in sight of the heavenly city and within sound of the heavenly
> music, my soul was filled with such a rapture and such an ecstasy of joy
> as I had never before experienced. I knew then as well as I know now
> that I would preach; that it would be my life-work; that I would have
> no other work.[6]

Carroll valued Romans 8 as pivotal in understanding the eternal
decrees of God, since the passage stretches out in graphic manner the
links composing the chain of salvation. Verses 29 and 30 constitute a
"chain of correlative doctrines reaching from eternity before time to
eternity after time." Foreknowledge, foreordination, calling, justification, and glorification—all are inevitable events in the life of each elect
person, because an eternal covenant of grace has been established by
the Triune God. Carroll affirms:

> Before there was any world, a covenant of grace and mercy was entered
> into between Father, Son, and Holy Spirit, the evidences of which cove-
> nant are abundant in the New Testament, and the parts to be performed
> by each person of the God-head are clearly expressed, viz.: The Father's
> grace and love in agreeing to send the Son, his covenant obligation to
> give the Son a seed, his foreknowledge of this seed, his predestination
> concerning this seed, his justification and adoption of them here in time.[7]

Carroll describes the work of the Son as promised in this covenant,
involving his incarnation and all the elements of his humiliation and
culminating in his death on the cross. His humiliation gave way to the
events of his glorification. The Spirit's covenant obligations consist of
calling, convicting, regenerating, sanctifying, and resurrecting the seed
promised to the Son. Thus, the plan of salvation is not an afterthought,
but rather, ". . . the roots of it in election and predestination are both

6. Ibid., p. 148.
7. B. H. Carroll, *An Interpretation of the English Bible*, ed. J. B. Cranfill (New York:
Revell, 1913–1917), 13 vols., Romans 8:28.

in eternity before the world was, and the fruits of it in eternity after the judgment."[8]

Carroll reaffirms this view of the eternal and unconditional nature of election in his discussion of 1 Peter 1:1, 2. Peter's doctrine of election, no less than Paul's, illustrates the work of the Trinity in the salvation of men. Election means "chosen to salvation." God the Father is the one who has elected, and he has elected according to his foreknowledge, which, in Carroll's opinion, means virtually the same thing as predestination, or determined. Always full of good stories, Carroll relates an anecdote concerning a Baptist preacher who promulgated a type of conditional election:

> When I was a young preacher, a Baptist preacher who was a good man, but Arminian in his theory, preached a sermon on election; and he said, "election is according to foreknowledge; God foreknew that certain men would repent and believe, and having before seen they would repent and believe, he elected them." When he got through I told him that the New Testament use of foreknowledge was just about equivalent to predestination, and that any Greek scholar would tell him so, and that election was not based upon any foreseen goodness in man or any foreseen repentance or faith in man, but that repentance and faith proceed from election, and not election from them. So that what Paul means by foreknowledge is just about the same as predestination; that in eternity God determined and elected according to that predestination.[9]

Carroll's comments on the two Epistles to the Thessalonians reconfirm his commitment to the doctrine of unconditional personal election to salvation. In the comments on 1 Thessalonians, Carroll reminisces about an ordaining committee upon which he served on one occasion. He had set forth the following series of questions to the candidate:

"What does election mean?"
"To choose."
"Who chooses?"
"God."
"When?"
"Before the foundation of the world."
"Unto what?"
"Salvation."
"In whom?"
"In Christ."

8. Ibid.
9. Ibid., 1 Peter 1:1, 2.

"Was this election based on foreseen repentance and faith, or did repentance and faith result from election?"

Then, after affirming that repentance and faith result from election, Carroll highlights the external evidences that demonstrate one's election. Several factors listed in the text accompanied Paul's preaching to the Thessalonians and convinced him they were elect. First, Carroll says, they listened with great seriousness, as if he were preaching to them the Word of God. Second, their affections shifted "unto God from idols." Third, their manner of life became characterized by the patience of hope. Fourth, their suffering persecution for the sake of the faith is a clear mark of election. Here Carroll cites the incident Bunyan describes in *The Pilgrim's Progress:*

> John Bunyan tells how Christian and Pliable came to the Slough of Despond, and they both fell in the mire, and Pliable began to say, "Is this the great road you are talking about to the great country you are going to? I am going back to the country I came from." As we look at him we know that he was not elect. But if this other man, though sinking in the Slough of Despond, finally pulls out, covered with dirt, yet with his face toward the heavenly city, that is a token that he is elect.[10]

Fifth, Carroll mentions that these Christians became an example to all the believers in Macedonia and in Achaia. Therefore, for all of these reasons, Paul concluded that the Thessalonians were indeed elect of God.

Carroll repudiates the idea of any special revelatory insights into the secret archives of God whereby to see one's name written in the Lamb's Book of Life; but, by discerning the activities that have resulted from the call of the gospel, one may discern whether or not he is elect.

This same emphasis, that election produces an elevated and progressively sanctified lifestyle, is the subject of a sermon Carroll preached: "Relation of Faith to Character and Morals." He intended to demonstrate that the preaching of salvation wholly of grace through faith in Jesus Christ produces the most elevated ethical and cultural society the world can conceive.

> Here is a much better argument. It is better because the ground upon which it is based is so much broader. It is better because of the vast multitude of facts aggregated. The test passes beyond any exceptional individual. My example is this: All Calvinists, Presbyterians and Baptists, or you may call them Augustinians, or Paulicians, it matters not

10. Ibid., 1 Thessalonians 1.

which, hold what is called the hard doctrines of grace; that, election, predestination, foreordination, salvation by grace through faith, and that not of ourselves, but by the gift of God. They have preached it until it has become their distinguishing characteristic. It is what they believe and what they call upon others to believe.

Now, what has been the morality of the Calvinists of the world? You will find here and there that some of them (not Baptists) have been persecutors; for instance, the putting to death of Servetus; the persecution by the Puritans in New England; the persecution by Hollanders of their Arminian brethren. Grant that.

But I want to look at the whole body, and I want to ask the dispassionate men, from the standpoint of history, to testify what has been the morality promoted by their faith. Mr. Froude would tell you; Mr. Huxley would tell you; Herbert Spencer would tell you; any disinterested infidel will tell you, that the highest form of morals this world has ever known is found among these people; that among no other people on the face of this earth has there been a higher regard for father, mother, brother, and sister, nor has there been a sterner adherence to truth and honesty and fair dealing with neighbors.

I do challenge the whole world for anything comparable to the morality of Calvinists.[11]

In regards to atonement, Carroll does not dogmatize concerning its extent. He is unbending and uncompromising when discussing whether or not it was vicarious, for he certainly affirms its substitutionary nature. Likewise is he certain concerning its penal aspects—and that God had set Christ forth in an act of divine justice by a predetermined plan admits of no debate with Carroll, for, he affirms, "It was divinely decreed, and permissively carried out by the hands of wicked men. He was put to death by the divine stroke, on the charge of sin."[12]

When discussing Isaiah 53, verses 10–12, Carroll seems to accept the absolute effectuality of Christ's ministry on the cross. He affirms that the verses given are not contingent promises, but—all conditions having been fully met—their literal and complete fulfillment must naturally follow. None can doubt that the promises of God will be absolutely fulfilled. Relating this particular idea to a discussion of the delay of the coming of Christ in 2 Peter 3, Carroll comments:

The imperiousness of the "shall see" is the ground of positiveness in the "shall come" applied to all sinners given to our Lord by the Father. And the "shall be satisfied" guarantees and necessitates the salvation of

11. B. H. Carroll, *River of Pearls* (Nashville, TN: Broadman Press, 1936), pp. 138, 139.
12. Carroll, *English Bible*, Acts 2:23.

all the elect. And though a thousand portents forbode a dissolution of the earth before his satisfaction be complete, it cannot be prematurely dissolved, for the Messianic days of salvation shall be prolonged until his purposes be fully accomplished. . . .

But the Lord, unwilling that any of his elect should perish and unsatisfied until they shall repent and live, prolongs his days. We may not propound to a weary and cowardly church the question, "Are you satisfied?" The church might consult its selfish greed and fear and stop the good work of salvation too soon. We may not carry the question to death and Hell, "Are you satisfied?" But only one may answer that question, our Lord himself. Men must be saved and saved and saved until he is satisfied—men of all grades of personal guilt, men of all nations and tribes and tongues. Poor, outcast, wandering Israel must be saved. We may be assured he will not be satisfied until the redeemed constitute a host that no man can number, a host whose hallelujah will be louder than mighty thunderings, louder than the voice of many waters. If the "great" and the "strong" of this context refer to Satan, we may be sure Christ will not be content with the present division of these spoils. Though Satan's goods be now at peace the stronger than he will bind him and despoil him. But if "strong" it is equally sure he will make their portion far greater than their present possession. Thus the context illumines the text and makes it reasonable.[13]

The sharply silhouetted outlines that mark Carroll's picture of the atonement in Isaiah 53 softens into less distinct contours in his commentary on Ephesians 1. While not retreating in any way from close adherence to the absolute effectuality of the atonement for the elect, Carroll does not want to dogmatize against the broadest possible understanding of the inclusivistic language often associated with the death of Christ. Concerning the universal sufficiency of Christ's atoning work, he quotes Dr. William C. Buck's *Philosophy of Religion* approvingly, although with some reticence. He states, "These questions are submitted for consideration in the realm of the study of systematic theology. The author does not dogmatize on them." Recognizing the necessity of effectuality in the atonement, while struggling with such words as "all" and "the world," Carroll summarizes his view in the following paragraph:

Let us do with this or any other philosophy what we will, but let us not hesitate to accept all that the Scriptures teach on this matter. When we read John 10:14–16; 11:26–29; Acts 13:48; Romans 8:28–29; Ephesians 5:25–32, let us not abate one jot of their clear teaching of Christ's death for the elect and their certain salvation. And when we read John 1:29;

13. Ibid., Isaiah 53:10–12.

3:16; 1 Timothy 4:10; Hebrews 2:9; 1 John 2:2; Ezekiel 33:11; Matthew 28:19; 1 Timothy 2:4, let us beware lest our theory, or philosophy, of the atonement constrain us to question God's sincerity, and disobey his commands. There are many true things in and out of the Bible beyond our satisfactory explanation. Let faith apprehend even where the finite mind cannot comprehend.[14]

Thus, in summary, B. H. Carroll believed in total depravity, unconditional election, effectual calling or irresistible grace, and he certainly believed in the perseverance of the saints. Theologically and exegetically, his convictions lay with the concepts of limited and effectual atonement. Pure verbal realities, however, led him to protect the mysteries of the atonement, in which he saw universal benefits beyond the closures of our systems and even our present comprehension.

Carroll's influence salvaged conservative theology for Baptists in the South for several decades. Additionally, Calvinism awaited a slow and subtle decline, more from neglect than positive opposition, more from ignorance than from learning, more from methodology than from theology, and more from denominational zeal than from denominational disaffection.

American Baptists Before Strong

Although largely in basic harmony with traditional Calvinistic theology, American Baptist life in the nineteenth century prior to the advent of A. H. Strong's influence began to show signs of fragmentation. A brief look at several pre-Strong leaders will show the general accuracy of this evaluation.

W. W. Everts (1814–90), pastor of Walnut Street Baptist Church in Louisville, Kentucky, for seven years and First Baptist Church in Chicago for twenty, represents a broad consensus of Baptists in his *Compend of Christian Doctrines Held by Baptists: In Catechism.* Everts describes God's decrees as "the prescribed plan of creation and providence, according to which all events takes place." Election is his "gracious purpose . . . according to which he regenerates, sanctifies, and saves sinners." Christ is Prophet, Priest, King, and Mediator, who has endured the "frown of his Father" to secure his people from God's wrath by satisfying divine justice. All those enabled by the Holy Spirit receive these blessings and are progressively conformed to the divine

14. Ibid., Ephesians 1:7.

law. Regeneration, justification, sanctification, and perseverance are all given Calvinistic definitions.

Henry Clay Fish, pastor of First Baptist Church in Newark, New Jersey, producer of more than twenty publications and frequent contributor to various compendiums of Baptist theology, wrote "The Baptist Scriptural Catechism" in 1850. The work filled eighty-seven pages with questions and answers of an apologetic, systematic, and evangelistic nature. Men in their depravity are "wholly destitute of love to God or true holiness . . . [and] in a state of enmity against Him."[15] Although sufficient by its nature for the salvation of all mankind, the atonement of Christ by its "saving design" embraces only the elect.[16] Election is the eternal choice God made of certain persons to grant them salvation. Their election is not based on any foreseen merit or faith in them but comes about solely from the sovereign work of the Spirit, in which a sinner's nature is renewed so that he repents and is converted and manifests faith. These spiritual graces remain throughout his life, so that the child of God, by taking advantage of the means of grace, will persevere unto the end.[17]

Alvah Hovey (1820–1903), friend and older contemporary of Strong and president of Newton Theological Institution, wrote *Manual of Christian Theology* (1900), in which he demonstrated himself to be a theologian sharply inferior to Strong. Hovey was less than precise at defining terms and less than convincing in mounting evidence for positions he espoused. Often his stance indicates a lack of sensitivity to the issues at stake in classical theological questions. His monothelite position on the person of Christ is a case in point.[18] Hovey's view of unconditional election suffers from the same imprecision. After affirming the reality of unconditional election, Hovey immediately seeks to isolate reasons for the election of God and makes this choice dependent upon his knowledge of every man's "life and character" and the necessities imposed by the intricacies of interpersonal relationships and historical situations.[19]

Hovey disposes of the question of the extent of the atonement in one page by affirming: "The Self-Sacrifice of Christ [was] made for all Men." Although acknowledging that the proposition is rejected by

15. Henry Clay Fish, "The Baptist Scriptural Catechism," in *Baptist Catechisms,* ed. Tom J. Nettles (Tom J. Nettles, 1983), p. 210.

16. Ibid., p. 211.

17. Ibid., pp. 214–226.

18. Alvah Hovey, *Manual of Christian Theology,* 2nd ed. (New York: Silver Burdett, c. 1900; reprinted by permission, Memphis, TN: Mid-American Baptist Theological Seminary Press, 1982), pp. 228–231.

19. Ibid., pp. 285–287.

many Calvinists, Hovey remarks, "They do this against the obvious meaning of Scripture."[20] He lists Matthew 23:37; John 3:16, 17; 1 John 2:2; Hebrews 2:9; and 2 Peter 2:1—accompanied by no exposition but only the judgment that "It would be easy to increase the number of such testimonies." Hovey mistakes the universal obligation of all men for the universal provision of grace, and he cites Paul's language in Romans 1 concerning the heathen as evidence for this identification. He misuses the same Scripture, combined with Romans 10:17, to bolster a tacit affirmation that some of the heathen who never hear the gospel come to possess spiritual life.[21]

Hovey's views on human responsibility in the sinful state are helpful and even compelling at times.[22] He is much less helpful, and even timid, in his discussion of total depravity and the relation of the race to the sin and guilt of Adam.[23] This same timidity is then transferred to Hovey's discussion of the place of the Holy Spirit in the beginning of Christian life. He allows that as the originator of the Christian life, the Spirit's work is necessary, and perhaps the word "effectual" could be used.[24] Hovey hesitates, however, to form too precise a doctrine. While the work of the Spirit is subconscious and "cannot be resisted by the will of man," the effects, feelings, and convictions concomitant with his work may be resisted. Indeed, in the case of Lydia, because she already worshiped God before hearing the truth from Paul, ". . . the work of the Spirit may have been sanctifying rather than regenerating."[25]

A. H. Strong

A. H. Strong (1836–1921), the younger contemporary, born in Rochester, New York, was educated at Yale and Rochester Divinity School, and spent one year of study and travel in Germany. He served two churches as pastor, including a seven-year tenure at First Baptist Church, Cleveland, Ohio, where John D. Rockefeller was a member. From 1872–1912 he was professor of theology and president at Rochester Theological Seminary.

Though Strong admired Alvah Hovey, and referred to his writings where appropriate, he recognized Hovey's erroneous tentativeness and

20. Ibid., p. 278.
21. Ibid., p. 306.
22. Ibid., pp. 144–170.
23. Ibid., pp. 171–176.
24. Ibid., pp. 300–304.
25. Ibid., p. 304.

even took the opportunity to grant it a mild corrective. He quoted Hovey's summary of Calvinistic thought:

> Calvinism, reduced to its lowest terms, may then be said to teach, that all persons who truly believe in Christ were chosen from eternity to be called by the influence and justified by the authority of God himself, not on account of any foreseen conduct of theirs, either before or in the act of conversion, which would be spiritually better than that of others influenced by the same grace, but on account of their foreseen greater usefulness in manifesting the glory of God to moral beings and of their foreseen non-commission of the sin against the Holy Spirit.[26]

But Strong then reminds the reader:

> But even here we must attribute the greater usefulness and the abstention from fatal sin, not to man's unaided powers but to the divine decree: see Eph. 2:10—"For we are his workmanship, created in Christ Jesus for good works, which God afore prepared that we should walk in them."[27]

Strong's corrective should have been more forceful, for traditional Calvinism concedes nothing in the creature as sufficient to prompt the election of one over another. That was not Strong's way, however; wherever he could, he preferred to employ a principle of continuity and redirection rather than confrontation and contradiction. While this method helps one appreciate the complexities of theological nuances, at times it forfeits the ground that should be protected. In an atmosphere of aggressively mounting liberalism for some, tentativeness toward classical orthodoxy for others, intimidating claims to credibility for higher criticism, and the adoption of evolution as an intellectual method as well as a biological truth, A. H. Strong sought to protect the essence of historic Christianity while utilizing the best of modern scholarship. Strong, nevertheless, stands as quite an enigma in the history of Baptist thought. Irwin Reist has judged that "Strong was attempting to mediate between the old orthodoxy, which was hardening into fundamentalism, and the new liberalism, which seemed to be losing the case of the Christian confession."[28]

In spite of what some, including myself, judge as Strong's failure to salvage orthodoxy for his own or succeeding generations, one cannot help but admire the brilliance and valiance of his attempt. Strong

26. Ibid., p. 287.
27. Strong, Theology, p. 785.
28. Irwin Reist, "Augustus Hopkins Strong and William Newton Clarke" in Foundations, Vol. 12, No. 1, p. 28.

admired and advocated the old doctrine of total and universal depravity and set himself against the "New School" and its tendency to diminish the seriousness of man's condition. Schleiermacher, Leibniz, Spinoza, Hegel, Goethe, Carlyle, Emerson, and so on, all are reviewed by Strong and refuted in their views of sin. Strong rejects the theories of federal headship and defends that of the natural headship of Adam, while affirming that (in case all such theories finally failed to satisfy scrutiny):

> . . . a central fact is announced in Scripture, which we feel compelled to believe upon divine testimony, even though every attempted explanation should prove unsatisfactory. That central fact, which constitutes the substance of the Scripture doctrine of original sin, is simply this: that the sin of Adam is the immediate cause and ground of inborn depravity, guilt and condemnation to the whole race.[29]

As the result of Adam's transgression, all his posterity are born into an estate of total depravity, by which Strong means "incapability of doing anything which in the sight of God is a good act." The sinner is thus "supremely determined in his whole inward and outward life, by a preference of self to God."[30] This condition is accompanied by, or perhaps productive of, both a moral inability and—because diminished morality also diminishes the power of natural faculties—a natural inability to do anything to change his anti-God bias.

Men, therefore, must be regenerated. Strong rejects the viability of the human will as an efficient cause of regeneration; nor can truth as a simple motivating factor effect the change, for truth is received only when motives and dispositions are such as will acquiesce to and even love the truth. Therefore, the immediate agency of the Holy Spirit upon the sinner's heart constitutes the efficient cause of regeneration. Strong identifies regeneration with "efficacious call."[31] Man is passive in this initial change of his ruling disposition, but soon, if not immediately, he becomes active in expressing it by a love of God's holiness and truth and a hatred of idolatry, sin, and falsehood.

Who will experience such mighty works from the Spirit of God? Strong would not be embarrassed to answer, "Only the elect of God." Strong defines election as:

> . . . that eternal act of God, by which in his sovereign pleasure and on account of no foreseen merit in them, he chooses certain out of the num-

29. Strong, *Theology*, p. 625.
30. Ibid., pp. 638, 639.
31. Ibid., p. 793.

ber of sinful men to be the recipients of the special grace of his Spirit, and so to be made voluntary partakers of Christ's salvation.[32]

Arguing for what he considered the sublapsarian position on the order of the decrees, Strong contended that supralapsarianism was identical with hyper-Calvinism. Election, in his scheme, was decreed only after (1) the decree to create, (2) the decree to permit the fall, and (3) the decree to provide a salvation in Christ sufficient for the needs of all. Although election was particular, unconditional, and salvific in Strong's view, it followed on the heels of a general atonement.

Strong gives twelve proofs of election from Scripture and four from "reason." Scripture expressly declares God's determination to save some, as well as his special love and care toward them from eternity. It also states that grace is bestowed in eternity, that the Father has given some people to the Son as a peculiar possession, that unity with Christ is due wholly to God, and that only those whose names are written in the Lamb's Book of Life will be saved. Additional proofs found in Scripture are the surety of the success of the apostles, effectual call, the character of the new birth, the nature of repentance, the nature of faith, and the origin of holiness—all necessarily implying such an election.

Reasoning from God's eternality, the nonmeritorious character of all human activity, the depravity of the human will, and the decree to create, Strong concludes that "in spite of difficulties we must accept the doctrine of election."[33]

Inherent within Strong's discussion of atonement lies an affirmation that it is general. Ironically, both election (the work of the Father) and effectual call (the work of the Spirit) terminate on individuals and infallibly produce salvation. The work of the Son, however, "has made objective provision for the salvation of all, by moving from the divine mind every obstacle to the pardon and restoration of the sinner, except their wilful opposition to God and refusal to turn to him."[34] Strong generally approves of the formula "sufficient for all; effectual for many" and quotes Matthew Henry in approval on that issue. "The atonement is unlimited," says Strong—"The whole human race might be saved through it; the application of the atonement is limited,—only those who repent and believe are actually saved by it."[35]

Strong's proposal for a general atonement has several unresolved

32. Ibid., p. 779.
33. Ibid., p. 785.
34. Ibid., p. 772.
35. Ibid., p. 773.

problems. He does not attempt to explain how the work of reconciliation while objective for all, may, nevertheless be rendered ineffectual when one who has been held safe under its shelter becomes "old enough to repudiate it."[36] Nor does he give any explanation as to why the "wilful opposition" of many who are eventually saved can be forgiven, while the continued "wilful opposition" of those who remain unregenerate is not forgiven. If he agrees that one type of opposition comes under the provisions of the atonement and another does not (which he does state), then he does little to distinguish his view of atonement from that of a definite limited atonement. In fact, Strong quotes John Owen's famous syllogism and offers no answer to it.

Those who fear that general atonement sparks Universalism see those sparks fanned into a small flame by Strong. Just as one may benefit from the law of gravitation without understanding much about its nature, Strong claims that "patriarchs and heathen have doubtless been saved through Christ's atonement, although they have never heard his name, but have only cast themselves as helpless sinners at the mercy of God." Not satisfied with only the example of "patriarchs and heathen," Strong continues that "our modern pious Jews will experience a strange surprise when they find that not only forgiveness of sin but every other blessing of life has come to them through the crucified Jesus."[37] May I reverently suggest that Jesus would be even more surprised to discover such "pious Jews" finding forgiveness if they look not on the Son of man who was lifted up.

Strong's affirmation of a general atonement does not harbor nearly as many dangers as does his insistence upon the immanence of Christ in the human race as a principle for understanding the atonement. Highly provocative and creative, this principle represents Strong's attempt to turn a major theme of liberalism to the defense of orthodoxy and at the same time explain the part of Christ in the process of evolution. Rather deftly, he wields the sword of orthodoxy, though alloyed with Christic immanentism, in disposing of the example, moral influence, and governmental views of the atonement. Strong defends his personal view with the same weapons. He denominates it the ethical theory.

Blending classical Protestant orthodoxy with late–nineteenth-century liberal emphases on the immanence of God, the ethical theory posits as its guiding motif the holiness of God.[38] Wickedness demands punishment, and the atonement of Christ is aimed primarily at ful-

36. Ibid., p. 773.
37. Ibid., p. 772.
38. Ibid., p. 751.

filling that law of holiness. Sacrifice, propitiation, substitution, and reconciliation are all prominent, and the Godward aspect of the atonement is considered primary. No benefit toward mankind could possibly accrue were God not reconciled and propitiated. Forgiveness and mercy do not usurp holiness but arise from and find strength within its fulfillment.

Despite the erudite and compelling defense of the substitutionary or ethical view of the atonement, immanentism transports major problems into it:

First, Christ's historical suffering on the cross is viewed not as a once-for-all work but as a revelation of the "age-long suffering of God." Because of Christ's organic union with humanity since creation, the suffering produced by the fall has been resident within God as well as within humanity. Strong does not discuss how this suffering can be excluded from the eternal joys of heaven, in light of Christ's continued humanity and the eternal wickedness and suffering of the condemned. Nor does the biblical picture of Christ as the one who "was once [for all] offered to bear the sins of many" (Heb. 9:28) find easy expression in Strong's scheme. In fact, the writer of Hebrews appears to contradict directly Strong's portrait of age-long suffering in God. Contrasted to the continued sacrifices of the priests, Christ has not been, nor will he be, the subject of such a continued sacrifice. Assuming that such continued suffering on the part of Christ is self-evidently absurd, the writer of Hebrews dismisses the idea by stating the absurd conclusion and responding with its corrective counterpart: "For then must he often have suffered since the foundation of the world: but now once in the end of the world hath he appeared to put away sin by the sacrifice of himself" (Heb. 9:26).

Second, Jesus' connection with humanity takes some heterodoxical (to avoid heretical) overtones in Strong. He reasons that Jesus as immanent in humanity, becomes "responsible with us for the sins of the race."[39] Since Colossians teaches that in him all things consist, even as in him all things were created, Strong concludes "it follows that he who is the life of humanity must, though personally pure, be involved in responsibility for all human sin."[40]

Concomitant with Christ's responsibility for sin is the guilt of sin—not that of personal sin or that of depravity, but that of the race as fallen in the loins of Adam. Strong contends that the justice of Christ's substitutionary atonement is derived from the fact that the guilt of

39. Ibid., p. 715.
40. Ibid., p. 758.

Adam's first sin justly devolves upon Christ as organically related to humanity:

> I cannot justly bear another's penalty, unless I can in some way share his guilt. The theory we advocate shows how such a sharing of our guilt on the part of Christ was possible. All believers in substitution hold that Christ bore our guilt: "My soul looks back to see The burdens thou didst bear When hanging on the accursed tree, And hopes her guilt was there." But we claim that, by virtue of Christ's union with humanity, that guilt was not only an imputed, but also an imparted, guilt.[41]

Strong's support for such a conclusion rises from 2 Corinthians 5:21, whereby "made sin" is interpreted as true in that "he took our guilt by taking our nature."[42] Imputation has less impact than impartation. When seeking to answer whether Christ was not simply suffering for his own sin—that is, his own share in the sin of the race—Strong can only reply that this "is not the sole reason why he suffers."

The sole reason! Certainly Strong's weakness at this point is evident to all. If Christ suffers at all for his own sin, even though only racial, it can hardly be proclaimed that he suffered "the just for the unjust" (1 Peter 3:18) as a lamb "without blemish and without spot" (1 Peter 1:19). Nor can Strong explain how imparted sin and actual guilt in Christ coincide with the biblical affirmation of Christ as one who was "holy, harmless, undefiled, separate from sinners" (Heb. 7:26).

The liberals' insistence on immanence seemed to have overwhelmed Strong at this point. While he desired to forge the raw materials of modernism into weapons for orthodoxy, he failed to remove the dross from the liberal's aversion to transcendence.

Third, another problem with Strong's adoption of immanentism in his treatment of the atonement concerns the necessity of the atonement. Traditional orthodoxy grants that if man is to be redeemed, atonement is necessary. Strong consents to this view but carries necessity a step further and insists on the natural necessity of atonement arising from Christ's union with the race. The result of that union is "obligation to suffer for men since, being one with the race, Christ had a share in the responsibility of the race to the law and justice of God."[43] In another place, Strong contends that "although Christ's nature was purified, his obligation to suffer yet remained."[44]

Strong is inconsistent in relating the necessities of Christ's suffering

41. Ibid., p. 759.
42. Ibid., p. 761.
43. Ibid., p. 755.
44. Ibid., p. 757.

to the incarnation. On the one hand Christ could have avoided suffering had he never been born of the virgin, but once born "he was bound to suffer."[45] Later, however, Strong relates the necessity of Christ's suffering, not to his incarnation but to "a prior union with the race which began when he created the race." He concludes on that basis that "he who is the life of humanity must, though personally pure, be involved in responsibility for all human sin, and it was necessary that the Christ should suffer (Acts 17:3)."[46] Indeed, Christ's sharing of man's life "justly and inevitably" subjected him to God's wrath against sin.[47] If such obligation existed by virtue of Christ's union with the race prior to incarnation, only by sundering his preincarnate relation with the race could he avoid suffering. But such a sundering would change man into a thing not man, since Christ *is* the image of God in man.

Changing the necessity involved in the atonement from its relation to the decree of God and the nature of a just redemption into a natural necessity derived from an eternal organic union of Christ with the race alters the freedom of God as related to his gracious purposes. The focal point of redemption moves from the cross to Christ's pre-fall union with created humanity. If man is to exist at all, God of necessity binds himself to redeem. Mercy becomes debt.

Further enigma attaches to Strong's puzzle when, as before pinpointed, the necessities arising from such union do not terminate on all the members of the union in particular. Christ's work becomes utterly disjointed from the work of the Father and Spirit by Strong's insistence that "Christ has made objective provision for the salvation of all."

Beyond Strong

Despite Strong's strategic position in theological education and his valiant attempt to salvage orthodoxy via modernity, he had little impact on the future of American Baptists. He sought to construct a wall of protection, but the enemy had already passed by—in fact, many of them benefited from Strong's benevolence. Strong resembles a man pushing a merry-go-round. As a handle comes speeding toward him from one side, he grabs it only long enough to sling it past him to the other side, but he is left standing in the same place.

Three facts neutralized the beneficial impact Strong might have

45. Ibid., p. 757.
46. Ibid., p. 758.
47. Ibid., p. 755.

had, rendering his creative use of modern emphases merely a skip-stone to dominant liberalism. First, his adoption of immanentism and higher criticism agreed more with what he opposed than what he espoused. Second, his protection of "free enquiry" at a denominational school (Rochester Theological Seminary) allowed it to become liberal, right under his nose. Third, his desire for a great Baptist university found fruition in William Rainey Harper's University of Chicago, rather than in New York City. In short, as Leroy Moore has concluded, "Strong's attempt to mediate failed; he was ignored."[48] Further explanation of these happenings seems appropriate in assessing Strong's influence:

As mentioned above, the doctrine of immanentism in its nineteenth-century form, which Strong sought to bring to the aid of orthodoxy, fit much more naturally into William Newton Clarke's liberalism. Immanence was used by Strong to explain both evolution as a divine method of creation and the development of the canon of Scripture in light of the so-called assured results of higher criticism. But why stop the efficiency of the immanent working of God with those processes? Why not adopt the entire modern intellectual scene as the work of God immanent in the process of modern thinking? By that manner of thinking, the modern rejection of dogma (especially orthodox dogma) could not be opposed but only applauded as the work of God, since, as Clarke contended, "whatever God makes grows" and "no forms of being are unchangeable, but all are destined to pass into higher forms for higher uses."[49] Strong's liberal contemporaries viewed his orthodoxy as a remnant of a narrow sectarian past. His modernity was seen as creative and as stimulating progress, which should naturally lead into an acceptance of the entire spirit of the age.

As to the second neutralizing factor, Strong's protection of the right of full inquiry at Rochester, though courageous and admirable, resulted in the movement of the school into thoroughgoing liberalism during his lifetime. Leroy Moore, Jr., documents Strong's benevolent attitude toward the men who gradually riveted Rochester in liberalism, and he narrates this revealing chronicle about Strong's last year and the three years immediately following his retirement:

As previously indicated, the transition to theological liberalism at Rochester was already well under way during Strong's tenure. In 1925

48. Leroy Moore, "The Rise of American Religious Liberalism at the Rochester Theological Seminary, 1872–1928" (Unpublished Ph.D. dissertation, 1966), p. 91, cited by Reist, op. cit.
49. W. N. Clarke, *Christian Union: The Denomination and the Church Universal* (New York: E. Scott Co., 1895), p. 23.

J. W. A. Stewart recalled that "change had already begun in Dr. Strong's time, and after his retirement in 1912 it went forward rapidly. It has not been a revolutionary change; it has rather been an inevitable and wholesome evolution." Change did proceed rapidly after 1912. During Stewart's three years as acting president, C. H. Mochlman was elevated to a full professorship; George Cross, Henry Burke Robins and Ernest William Parsons were added to the faculty, and Glen B. Ewell was named the school's first full-time librarian. Ewell, an alumnus of the seminary, was a staunch supporter of that liberalism he had imbibed from men whose colleague he now became. Mochlman, Cross, Robins and Parsons were devotees of the scientific method after the manner of "the Chicago school," and together with Ewell provided at Rochester for a generation a solid phalanx for advanced liberal views. Thus, by virtue of these personnel changes, the transition to religious liberalism at the seminary was in effect completed during Stewart's interim administration.[50]

Finally, the third event in which the past vaulted beyond Strong into the future was the founding of the University of Chicago. Long an advocate of a Baptist university designed to be a trend-setter, Strong was overlooked by his friend John D. Rockefeller when the latter loosened his purse strings to initiate such a venture. Strong gave way to William Rainey Harper, and New York gave way to Chicago. By 1910, Rockefeller had put thirty-five million dollars into the school to support its broad-minded scientific community of scholars. Thoroughgoing and unashamed in its modernism, Chicago reduced Christianity to the moral maxims of Jesus and identified the kingdom of God with a democratic society.

The conservative reaction in American Baptist life was by and large fundamentalistic rather than historically orthodox, and it won its way only by separation rather than permeation. Liberalism came to such quick dominance that the Doctrines of Grace were thrown out bodily by the nape of the neck as a vestige of obsolete transcendent theology—and a highly speculative department of it at that. Fundamentalists struggled to salvage special revelation, the deity of Christ, vicarious atonement (forget any discussion of its extent), sin as individual moral evil punishable by God (forget intricate discussions of the effect of depravity on the will, affections, and mind), and the necessity of personal regeneration rather than broad social redemption (forget any discussion of the *ordo salutis*).

The quickness of Calvinism's demise does not mean that personal

---

50. Leroy Moore, "Academic Freedom: A Chapter in the History of the Colgate Rochester Divinity School," in *Foundations*, Vol. 10, No. 1, (Jan.–Mar., 1967), pp. 71–72. Quote is from *Rochester Theological Seminary Bulletin*, May 1925, p. 45.

struggles with the Doctrines of Grace were nonexistent. The issues simply appeared to be more broadly catholic than strictly Reformed in nature. The heart of the gospel, therefore, was lost as nonessential.

Conclusion

Carroll appears to have perceived more clearly than Strong the dangers of modernism; for that reason he sought utterly to exclude it from the seminary curriculum. Meanwhile, Strong protected those who eventually destroyed that to which he was committed. Strong held an advantage over Carroll in systematics and consistency and more clearly perceived the necessity of demonstrating the absolute consistency between ultimate truth and scientific (yea, even poetic) truth. If it is truth, it is all of God. However, the faulty presupposition to which Strong was committed wrought havoc within his entire system.

Carroll, on the other hand, gloried in the pulpit and was perhaps unequaled in his age for impassioned and moving sermonic rhetoric. The truth of God does not need to be reconciled with anything, for it stands as the one unmovable and unchanging rock in a world of shifting sand. The preacher needs only to seek reconciliation between the enmity of men's hearts and the justly enraged wrath of God.

Broadly speaking, Strong officiated reluctantly but with great dignity over the interment of Calvinism and conservatism in American Baptist life. Carroll managed to delay that event so others could do the job more slowly and less noticeably in the Southern Baptist community.

9

"The Road Not Taken"

Any casual observer of the contemporary Southern Baptist scene can readily observe that the Doctrines of Grace no longer hold sway over the majority of Southern Baptist people, or even a significantly large minority of them. Theologians, professors of Bible, professors of history, and a variety of pastors now speak of these doctrines with such incredibly demeaning language as "diabolical," "hell-conceived," "heretical," "pagan," and "destructive." Dale Moody candidly (and joyfully) points out that Baptists "left at least four of the points behind" (*The Western Recorder*) and openly calls for abandoning the fifth, perseverance of the saints.

Why did such a radical change take place? None would say that it occurred quickly, and all would agree that the factors involved in such a phenomenon are so complex that a thoroughly accurate analysis is not possible. This elusiveness, however, should not discourage one from seeking to approximate a helpful discussion.

One factor has been the dominating aura of the Cooperative Program. The monetary support engendered by this ingenious plan has ignited such an adherence to Southern Baptist programs that doctrinal distinctives tend to be overlooked for the sake of fiscal unity. As the program crowded out identifying doctrine, the basis of Southern Baptist fellowship gradually became loyalty to a program rather than unity in the faith. In 1925, when the Cooperative Program was adopted, *The Baptist Faith and Message* was also set forth as the first Southern Baptist Confession of Faith. Orthodoxy is now described in terms of support for the program rather than as reflective of the confession.

A second factor in the change involves increasing indifference to-

244

E. Y. Mullins

L. R. Scarborough

ward doctrine in literature and Baptist papers. In fact, not only is doctrinal distinctiveness overlooked, it is actually discouraged by many contemporary Southern Baptists. When the possibility of adherence to definite doctrines is mentioned in Southern Baptist company, it becomes evident just how antipathetic the denomination has become to such distinctives. One theological professor, B. Elmo Scoggin, reacts: "Not only would I not vote for it, I would categorically refuse and I would fight to the last drop of my blood to keep the denomination from adopting a creed." Lynn May, executive director of the Southern Baptist Historical Commission, said, "A set of doctrinal statements to which [Baptists] must subscribe . . . would be totally out of keeping with the historic position of Southern Baptists."[1]

As such a climate develops, it is inevitable that the Doctrines of Grace will be ignored. It does not really matter that the above statements in themselves are a departure from Baptist heritage. They can be made without fear of contradiction because the communicative aims of Southern Baptist life have cast off the Doctrines of Grace as legitimate content for teaching.

A third factor in the decreased emphasis on doctrine is the gradual ascension of the liberal mentality, which has crept in the back door of Southern Baptist life. Actually, rather than being a cause of Calvinism's decline, the increase of liberalism is a result. The man-centeredness of changing soteriological patterns has diminished the Baptist sensitivity to the anti-supernaturalism of rationalistic-romantic liberalism. Therefore, while this surge of liberalism has stomped with all its might on the quivering body of the once-vigorous Baptist Calvinist, it is more of an effect than a cause of Calvinism's temporary decline.

Although each of the above trends deserves full treatment, this author contends that the shift began in the inimitable influence of two Baptist giants: E. Y. Mullins and L. R. Scarborough. Mullins, through his theological method, and Scarborough, through his evangelistic method, shifted Baptist theological commitment and opened the door to other specters.

E. Y. Mullins

Although the doctrine of unconditional election was accepted by E. Y. Mullins, both his theological method and his specific exposition of divine election served to compromise the earlier views of Dagg, Boyce,

1. *SBC Today*, Vol. 1, No. 9, pp. 2, 3.

Broadus, Manly, Mell and others. Emphasis on human consciousness and experience so predominate in the totality of Mullins's theology that human decision and freedom eventually overshadow and crowd out effectual divine activity. This is evident in his view of Scripture, justification, and the panorama of theology, but is especially clear in his exposition of the doctrine of election.

Mullins rejected the view of God's sovereignty that defined election in terms of his mere will or good pleasure. He concluded that predestination conforms to the character of God as righteous love. Although he agreed that "the salvation of individual men is to be traced to the initiative of God,"[2] he denied that God's eternal purpose is to save only his elect individuals. Rather, God desires the salvation of all men. Mullins paraphrases 2 Peter 3:9, 10 to say, "He willed that none should perish but that all should live."[3]

The atonement of Christ, according to Mullins, is also universal in nature: "The atonement of Christ, was for all men."[4] However, it is ineffectual in its universal aspects, for many men remain in unbelief and are not saved. Therefore, God is not able to save all men; nor does every man "share equally in the benefits of the atonement of Christ."[5]

Only in light of God's larger purpose, as Mullins calls it, can the theologian understand God's method of saving individuals. This larger purpose is toward the whole race of mankind, not toward only one nation or isolated individuals. Mullins illustrates this understanding by contending that Israel was to be a light to the nations, and Jesus came as the "Son of Man." Also, the gospel is to be preached to every creature, and the mystery of the gospel is that the middle wall of partition has been broken down between Jew and Gentile. All of this, according to Mullins, illustrated God's universal salvific intention.

Mullins sees several advantages to this universality. The "larger plan" supposedly eliminates any appearance of capriciousness in God's character. In addition, it gives reasons for the apparent delays in God's plans. The seemingly slow execution is not due to indifference but to God's awaiting the fullness of time. Further, God's continued interest in the Gentile nations is affirmed in this universal scheme. Finally, this tentative universalism avoids the errors of what Mullins called the older Calvinism. These errors characterized a system that proceeded solely by logic on the basis of the mere will of God.

2. E. Y. Mullins, *The Christian Religion in Its Doctrinal Expression* (Valley Forge: Judson Press, 1917, reprint ed., 1974), p. 339.
3. Ibid., p. 340.
4. Ibid., p. 336.
5. Ibid.

Election in the "Larger Plan"

However, even in light of these modifications, Mullins accepts the doctrine of the particular election of individuals and seeks to explain how the salvation of individuals is consistent with this larger plan for mankind. He first affirms that one individual is saved, whereas another remains lost, "because God's grace is operative in the one case beyond the degree of its action in the other."[6] Such Scripture passages as John 15:16; John 6:37; John 6:44; Acts 13:48; and Romans 8:28–30 serve as support of Mullins's understanding of efficacious election. He views God's choice of Jacob above Esau prior to their birth, as expounded in Romans, as scriptural proof of election and paraphrases Ephesians 1:4 in affirmation of the doctrine.

Election, according to Mullins, is the only method through which anyone could be saved. For "God knows that some will not accept. Indeed, he knows that all will refuse unless by special grace they are led to believe."[7] Later, in a section discussing the work of the Holy Spirit in salvation, Mullins says:

> Again, the Scriptures make it plain that responsibility for rejection is upon those who reject the gospel offer, not those who make it, much less upon God himself. Again, it is clear that God desires the salvation of all, although he does not efficaciously decree the salvation of all.[8]

To the objection that the doctrine of election cuts the nerve of Christian endeavor, Mullins counters that, on the contrary, election is the only consistently defensible basis for Christian endeavor. Without the internal conviction of a divine purpose, all effort would be fruitless and would soon die. Mullins claims that "all great reformers and evangelists have had the conviction."[9]

Mullins also contends that all systems of soteriology must eventually affirm some kind of effectual election—all systems, that is, that believe in the omniscience of God.

> A fifth question is: Would it not be fairer and more just if God left men to accept or reject when the gospel is preached to them, without any previous choice on his part? The reply is that if the final outcome is the salvation of some and the loss of others, any other system would be ultimately traceable to God's sovereignty and election. Assume that equal

6. Ibid., p. 343.
7. Ibid., p. 354.
8. Ibid., p. 366.
9. Ibid., p. 355.

grace is given to all. Some are receptive, and some hostile to it. The receptive are saved, the hostile lost. Then God's sovereignty and election operated to provide efficaciously for the receptive only. He did not give grace to overcome hostility. He elected thus the receptive and only the receptive. Assume again that with equal grace to all, some respond and believe because they are better morally, or less stubborn in will, or more believing, or for any other conceivable reason. Clearly if these are saved and the others lost, it is because God elected to offer a gospel adapted to reach one class and not adapted to reach the other class. As we remarked at the outset, the fundamental truth is that of Genesis 1:1, "In the beginning God." If it be assumed that God could save all, but refuses to do so, then any scheme whatever carries with it the idea of an election based on God's sovereignty.[10]

Additionally, Mullins discusses faith, repentance, and good works as results of God's gracious activity and not causes of it. He says: "It should be easy to multiply passages showing how the calling of sinners effectually to repentance, their regeneration and conversion, are all attributed to God's initiative and grace. (See Acts 18:9–10; John 1:13; I John 4:10; I Cor. 1:24–29; 11:29; Gal. 1:15, 16)."[11]

Even though Mullins affirms and defends the doctrine of election, his method of defending it does not maintain its most pungent characteristics. Rather, it virtually reshapes the doctrines from their historical form. The shift is ostensibly not so much theological as philological, but the gradual reshaping of vocabulary lays the groundwork for the changing of substance.

As Mullins seeks to relate election to the human will, he asserts that "the will of man is not coerced, but is left free." Indeed, "in his free act of accepting Christ and his salvation man is self-determined."[12] Although man would never make this choice if left to himself, the grace of God is not irresistible as a "physical force." The gospel appeals to moral, spiritual, and personal aspects as a persuasive power rather than a compelling force, and it is effective through the use of observable means, i.e., church ordinances, Bible, lives of Christians, the ministry. Even the work of the Spirit should not be considered as sheer power exerted upon the will of man, but a "moral conquest in the soul."

Mullins reemphasizes that "election is not to be thought of as a bare choice of so many human units by God's action independently of man's free choice and the human means employed."[13] Salvation is not "bare

10. Ibid., pp. 349–350.
11. Ibid., p. 34; see also pp. 368–392.
12. Ibid., p. 334.
13. Ibid., p. 374.

forgiveness and justification" but is "far richer" in that it involves human agents and agencies and a complex series of human relationships and influences.

According to Mullins, one must also understand election in the light of certain barriers that hinder God. Man's freedom is one barrier: "We are conscious of freedom as an ultimate fact of experience" and cannot conceive of any plan not consistent with man's freedom. "God is limited by man's freedom." He cannot take the soul by sheer omnipotence, for such a display would only crush and lay waste the moral character of man.[14]

Man's sin is a second barrier. Man's will has a bias that "inevitably leads to the rejection of the gospel except when aided by God's grace in Christ."[15] Man inevitably breaks God's law and indeed cannot be subject to the law of God. God must interpose if salvation is to come, but he must work in light of both the freedom and sinfulness of man. Therefore, he reduces his own activity "to the minimum lest he compel the will."[16]

God is also bound by the slowness of the historical process. God cannot save any more than he actually does. Some believe that although God could save all, he refuses to do so and saves only some. Mullins rejects that view. He states: "But there are many indications that God is seeking to save men as rapidly as the situation admits—in view of sin and freedom and the necessity for respecting human freedom."[17]

Had God moved more quickly in history, disaster might have befallen the gospel. "In a moral kingdom, men must be prepared before great epoch-making advances are possible."[18]

With an implicit curtsy to nineteenth-century concepts of moral and ideological evolution, Mullins draws attention to the historical events necessary to effect God's electing purposes. The call of Abraham, the giving of the land to Abraham and his descendants, the unity of the world under Rome, the spread of the Greek language and the career of the apostle Paul (including his moving the gospel westward rather than eastward) were all necessary in the ever-widening purposes of God's electing grace:

> He has been ever eager to prepare men for larger blessings than they could receive at the time. His purpose and plan have ripened as rapidly

14. Ibid., p. 348.
15. Ibid., p. 348.
16. Ibid., p. 349.
17. Ibid., p. 350.
18. Ibid.

as the moral and spiritual and personal kingdom and its appropriate forces could bring it to pass. His love has ever sought to overleap the barriers which human sin and unbelief have interposed.[19]

That the movement of history somehow thwarts the supreme desire of God is emphasized again by Mullins when he discusses the possibility of finding a guiding principle in the electing love of God. After denying human merit as a principle and affirming that election is for service, Mullins indicates that election "pursues the course which will yield the largest results in the shortest time."[20] God elects strategic men ("kingpins," using bowling analogy) so that his widening purpose might swiftly come to fruition.

One of the great strengths of Mullins's treatment of election is his sensitivity to the persuasive element of God's grace. His constant emphasis on the moral and spiritual changes that occur in the elect individual avoids the antinomian errors that at times have plagued Calvinistic theology. This emphasis bears no uniqueness in Mullins, but places his treatment in direct line with traditional Baptist understanding.

Also, he clearly sets forth election as a matter of God's mercy and grace toward some rather than his exclusion of some who otherwise would desire to be saved. He emphasizes that none would be saved without the efficacious grace of God, and those who remain under condemnation have only their own rebellion and recalcitrant sinfulness to blame: "There is absolutely no barrier to the salvation of any, save their own wills."[21]

Further, Mullins rightly explains that, in light of man's condition, election should serve as an impetus rather than a deterrent to various types of Christian endeavor. Election gives a sense of purpose to the Christian calling and assures the Christian worker of the effectuality of the Christian message.

When Mullins discusses perseverance, his understanding of the cooperation and consistency between divine initiative and human activity serves him well. He affirms the inviolability of the will of God in maintaining the salvation of those who are savingly joined to Christ[22] and avoids also libertarianism[23] and perfectionism.[24]

Mullins treats the warning passages with sensitivity and sees them

19. Ibid., p. 352.
20. Ibid.
21. Ibid., p. 354.
22. Ibid., pp. 434–435.
23. Ibid., pp. 427–429.
24. Ibid., pp. 429–432.

as a legitimate means to preserve and forward the faith of the truly saved. Apparent apostates either return to God—"or else they were cases of spurious conversion where the real spiritual life never existed."[25]

Weaknesses in Mullins's System

Mullins introduces several inconsistencies and problems into the basic doctrine. At points his methodology allows the experiential element to overshadow the biblical. Mullins argues strongly, and with good reason, that one must avoid the error of understanding faith in merely historical terms unaccompanied by experiential knowledge. In the section of his book (*The Christian Religion in Its Doctrinal Expression*) entitled "Religion and Theology,"[26] Mullins characterizes his method of dealing with the doctrines of the Christian religion as "that which gives prominence to Christian experience."[27] He did not have the intent of allowing experience to overshadow other elements. Rather, experience acts in conjunction with and informs other elements. To allow Christian experience an explicit place in theology is to adopt the very thrust of the New Testament. Experience as a methodological factory "does not render theology less biblical, or less systematic, or less historical. The Bible is the greatest of all books of religious experience."[28]

Four guiding principles governed Mullins in his work:

First, "We must recognize Jesus Christ as the historical revelation of God to men"; one's understanding of the Christian faith is bound up "indissolubly" with the facts of the historical Jesus.

Second, Scripture, especially the New Testament, is indispensable for a proper understanding of the work of the historical Jesus.

Third, sensitivity to the work of the Holy Spirit is essential.

Fourth, Christian experience must be given its proper place: "We must seek to define and understand the spiritual experiences of Christians as subject to the operation of God's Spirit revealing Christ to them. The history of doctrine will aid in this, but we must make also a direct study of experience itself."[29]

Mullins's intent, in the midst of a burgeoning liberalism in American Christianity, was to set forth such a comprehensive methodology

25. Ibid., p. 438.
26. Ibid., pp. 1–34.
27. Ibid., p. 2.
28. Ibid., p. 3.
29. Ibid., p. 4.

that all might see the inadequacy of the liberal reconstruction of Christian doctrine. All four of the above-mentioned elements were necessary to Mullins and, in his opinion, scientific study of the Christian religion cannot be done without a proper blending of them.

> In the light of these statements we see how defective are some efforts which are called scientific, to explore the meaning of Christianity. . . . But usually they are efforts to extract from the Gospel records some small remainder of what is held to be the religion of the New Testament by Christians generally, and cast away the other elements as worthless. . . . But too often efforts of this kind fail to take account of all the elements in the problem. . . . Again, Christianity cannot be construed under the guidance of some previously formed world-view or philosophy of the universe. We must begin with the facts in their totality and reckon with them. This is simply another way of saying that we must adopt the scientific method of dealing with the question.[30]

In his efforts to integrate the elements of Christian experience into the methods of theology, apologetics, and proclamation, Mullins allows the experimental principle a dominant place. Since this often overcomes other elements, it severely minimizes the value of the systematic approaches of the past.

For example, in his argument for biblical infallibility, Mullins rejects the methods of classical apologetics that sought to give biblical, rational, and demonstrable answers for objections raised by both unbelievers and true seekers. For rational and historical arguments Mullins substitutes the combination of Christian experience with biblical rationale for that experience as an objective authority:

> Christian apologists used to expend great energy and pains in answering all of these charges. Finally they came to see that the objector demanded more than faith required. We are not bound to prove in a way which compels assent that the Bible is the supreme authority for Christian faith. Such proof would not produce faith at all. It could only produce intellectual assent. The Christian's acceptance of the Bible arises in another way. It comes to him in "demonstration of the Spirit and of power." It is the life in him which answers to the life the Scriptures reveal which convinces him.[31]

The elevation of experience above systematic, historical, and rational defense of biblical authority has brought about a receptivity to existentialist modes of thought unsympathetic with historic Christian-

30. Ibid., pp. 6, 7.
31. Ibid., p. 10.

ity. Mullins's statement, "So that the Bible is not for him an authority on all subjects, but in religion it is final and authoritative" has led some to affirm that Scripture is erroneous in historic and scientific areas.

In the same way, Mullins's emphasis on experience led him to affirm human freedom in terms that greatly diminished God's sovereignty: "We are conscious of freedom as an ultimate fact of experience."[32] Although he tries to affirm God's sovereignty in words, he diminishes it in fact: "God is limited by man's freedom."[33] Thus, any historic understanding of sovereignty is abolished. Human experience unwittingly becomes a tool used to reshape the understanding of the "exceeding greatness of his power toward us who believe."

This thought leads to the discussion of a second weakness in Mullins's treatment. Historically, Baptists identified the power that converts with the omnipotence of God (e.g., Dagg). Paul seems to do the same in Ephesians 1:19–2:10. Man's deadness, captivity, and enmity to God call for an act of sovereign, gracious power.

Mullins, however, states, "God cannot take the soul by sheer omnipotence."[34] According to Mullins, this would only overpower and crush the rational and spiritual capacities of man. One weakness in this position is that it assumes that omnipotence cannot work by degrees or by means of convincing, persuading, and creating rather than destroying. This objection had already been met by John Gill in 1736. Gill discussed the nature of free will in man as it relates to the omnipotence of God and drew upon Augustine for his formulation:

> Moreover, it is free from a necessity of coaction or force; the will cannot be forced; nor is it even by the powerful, efficacious, and unfrustrable operation of God's grace in conversion; for though before, it is unwilling to submit to Christ, and his way of salvation, yet it is made willing in the day of his power, without offering the least violence to it; God working upon it, as Austin says, *cum suavi omnipotentia et omnipotenti suavitate*, with a sweet omnipotence, and an omnipotent sweetness. . . .[35]

Another problem relates to the reality of the carnal mind's enmity against God. Mullins admits that it is not subject to the law of God, "neither indeed can be." How then does human freedom comport with this, and does it not take an act of omnipotent creative power to con-

32. Ibid., p. 348.
33. Ibid.
34. Ibid.
35. John Gill, *The Cause of God and Truth* (London: W. H. Collingridge, 1855; reprint ed., Grand Rapids: Baker Book House, 1980), p. 8.

vert what cannot be subject into that which is being renewed in the spirit of its mind?

A third weakness in Mullins's system is his ambivalence between the conditionality and the unconditionality of election. The latter is supported in various places. "The gospel is efficacious with some and not efficacious with others because God's grace is operative in the one case beyond the degree of its action in the other."[36] Mullins affirms that "faith, repentance, and good works are all the gift of God."

In spite of all these realizations, Mullins does not rest salvation in the mere will of God. He declares that the approach to God's sovereignty from the standpoint of his "mere will" is an error.[37] He also paraphrases and conflates John 3:16 and 2 Peter 3:9, 10 to mean that God desires that every individual should not perish but live.[38]

Mullins summarizes this position in dealing with the disparity between God's desire for the universality of salvation and the particularity of his election:

> Again, it is objected that God does not desire the salvation of all, or else he would elect all. But the Scriptures expressly declare that "God so loved the world" that he sent his Son, and also that he wishes none to perish, but that all should come to repentance. (2 Peter 3:9.) The objection assumes falsely that there are no moral limitations of any kind in God, and that he can do anything he desires. But human freedom limits God, as does human unbelief and sin. Men cannot be made righteous by sheer omnipotence. God cannot force or compel any one to be good. The situation does not admit of the use of force. It is a situation rather in which a race of men is bent on self-destruction, or moral and spiritual suicide. God interposes by a method which respects their freedom and gradually works out a universal purpose of blessing.[39]

However, the objection has not been answered. If God "cannot force or compel any one," and men are "bent on self-destruction," how is anyone saved? Clearly it must be because God exerted enough power on those who cannot believe to cause them to believe—or because there is some condition existent in the character or pliability of some that is not existent in the character or pliability of others. Mullins admits later that this condition exists, as he continues to struggle with this inconsistency in his treatment:

36. Mullins, *Christian Religion*, p. 343.
37. Ibid., p. 338.
38. Ibid., p. 340.
39. Ibid., pp. 354–355.

How can we explain this divergence between the desire and purpose on God's part? It cannot be due to any conflict in his own nature. It must be due to conditions with which he has to deal. We have already pointed out those conditions in a previous section. Human sin and human freedom are factors in God's problem with man. His grace goes as far as the interests of his moral kingdom admit. His omnipotence does not enable him to do a moral impossibility.[40]

One can see that—though Mullins tries to avoid affirming any merit in man,[41]—he cannot escape affirming some sort of human merit, since the cause of election is not the "mere will" or "arbitrary selection" of God. Since it is "due to conditions with which he has to deal," it must be due to moral and spiritual conditions within the men actually saved or lost. Therefore, these conditions relate to the will and reason of man and assume that one man is by nature more susceptible to God's saving activity than another. Whether or not the word *merit* is used to describe this condition, the effect is the same. Mullins's view is identical to one he describes and rejects:

> Assume again that with equal grace to all, some respond and believe because they are better morally, or less stubborn in will, or more believing, or for any other conceivable reason. Clearly if these are saved and the others lost, it is because God elected to offer a gospel adapted to reach one class and not adapted to reach the other class.[42]

Someone may say, "But Mullins has previously stated that God's grace is operative in some cases beyond that in others; so it is not with 'equal grace to all' and therefore not conditioned upon something in man." *Exactly,*—but then we are back to God's "mere will" for exerting power in one person arbitrarily beyond what he exerts in another, which, according to Mullins, cannot be true.

The degree to which Mullins's personal struggle and ambiguity wrought definitive change within Southern Baptist life can be documented easily.

Interpretation by H. Hobbs

In Herschel Hobbs's rendition of Mullins's *Axioms of Religion*, particular unconditional election suffers an unmitigated rejection in favor

---

40. Ibid., p. 366.
41. Ibid., p. 350—"not at all on human merit," p. 352—"men are not chosen because of merit of any kind on their part."
42. Ibid., pp. 349–350.

of a conditional election of categories, not people. Hobbs quotes Mullins's statement: "Election is not to be thought of as a bare choice of so many human units by God's action independently of man's free choice and the human means employed."[43]

This statement then serves to bolster Hobb's own disregard for pre-Mullins Baptist theology in several particulars:

1. Free will eats up divine sovereignty: "To ignore man's free will is to see God arbitrarily electing some to salvation to the neglect of all others."[44]

2. Election concerns a category rather than persons: "So God elected that all who 'are in Christ' will be saved. All outside of Christ will be lost."[45] This position must certainly be regarded as true, as far as it goes, but it ignores the truth that persons as individuals are the objects of God's electing love. God considers *them* as in Christ rather than the category "in Christ" apart from the individuals contemplated as being in that position.

3. Belief loses its gracious character and becomes synonymous with "free will." "Man's free will is seen in 'believed' in verse 13."[46]

4. Foreknowledge is changed from predetermination to mere cognizance of events before they occur. "God's foreknowledge as to those who would or would not believe does not mean that he caused it."[47]

5. The final cause in the effecting of redemption is the will of man: "The final choice lay with man. God in his sovereignty set the condition. Man in his free will determines the result."[48]

Hobbs failed to recognize Mullins's insistence that man, left to his own will, always refuses to worship God. He also is eluded by Mullins's understanding of the efficacious purpose of God to save some. Blame, however, for such inadequacy in contemporary exposition lies not only with Hobbs but with Mullins's own inconsistency.

L. R. Scarborough

Another major figure who contributed to the shift in Southern Baptists' understanding of grace was L. R. Scarborough. Under B. H. Car-

---

43. E. Y. Mullins, *The Christian Religion in Its Doctrinal Expression* (Nashville: Baptist Sunday School Board, 1917), p. 347, cited by Herschel H. Hobbs, *The Axioms of Religion* (Nashville: Broadman Press, 1978), p. 71.
44. Ibid.
45. Ibid., p. 72.
46. Ibid.
47. Ibid.
48. Ibid.

roll's insistence and with a keen sense of the leadership of God, Scarborough went to Southwestern Baptist Theological Seminary in 1908 to fill the "Chair of Fire." The establishment of a chair of evangelism in itself signaled a unique development in theological education. The growth of Scarborough's influence in Southern Baptist life began under the patronage of B. H. Carroll and increased steadily through his classes in the seminary. He became more of a public figure when he was elected president at Southwestern in 1914. An even wider platform became his through his first book, *With Christ After the Lost* (1919). Perhaps most strategic in Scarborough's convention-wide influence was his part in the "75-Million Campaign," a five-year money-raising effort for state- and convention-supported agencies and institutions that eventuated in the establishment of the Cooperative Program of the Southern Baptist Convention. Thus granted a sizable audience, his influence was not without corresponding effect.

Scarborough, a strong conservative, recognized the sinister nature of encroaching liberalism and set himself steadfastly against it. He unequivocally affirmed the infallibility of Scripture, the deity of Christ and trinitarian nature of God, the depravity of man, the necessity of regeneration, the vicarious atonement, and special creation as opposed to evolution. His greatest energies, however, were to be spent in the "fine art of training ministers in the work of winning souls."[49]

In pursuing the "fine art of winning souls," Scarborough necessarily sought to align this art with the doctrine of God's sovereignty in election. Having no desire to enervate either election or the course Carroll set for Southwestern, he often duplicated Carroll's language in giving public addresses. For example, in 1911 Carroll had reported to the Baptist General Convention of Texas that the purpose of Southwestern Seminary was "to preserve inviolate and transmit unimpaired the old-time faith of God's elect without wavering or shadow of turning."[50] The report to the BGCT in 1913 was delivered by L. R. Scarborough and maintains great fidelity to the words of Carroll: ". . . to preserve inviolate and transmit unimpaired the old-time faith of God's elect without wavering or shadow of turning."[51]

Scarborough tried to maintain the spirit and content of Carroll's views as well as his language, for toward the end of this 1913 report Scarborough exclaimed:

49. L. R. Scarborough, *A Modern School of the Prophets* (Nashville: Broadman Press, 1939), p. 208.
50. B. H. Carroll in *Proceedings of the Baptist General Convention of Texas* (1911), p. 22.
51. L. R. Scarborough in *Proceedings of the Baptist General Convention of Texas* (1913), p. 21.

Brethren of the Convention, let's build on Seminary Hill a theological power house on the rocks of predestination, around the person of our Risen Redeemer, knowing no orders but his command, fearing nothing but his disfavor, loyal to his revealed will, carrying his gospel of redeeming love and blood around the world in the holy fires of his Divine Spirit, till Jesus comes again.[52]

Scarborough intended more than just rhetoric when he spoke of the "faith of God's elect" and the "rocks of predestination." Like Carroll, he affirmed the doctrine of election. This often appears in his writings and just as often is accompanied by little or no exposition. The affirmation of God's sovereignty in the order of salvation, combined in a consistent way with human response, characterized Scarborough's discussion of "Distinctive Baptist Doctrines" in 1918:

The last mentioned distinctive doctrine of Baptists I am pleased to call a double doctrine. On the one side is the divine will and purpose based on God's foreknowledge carrying out his fore-ordaining, electing purposes, and program in the salvation of man. On the other side is human activity, aggressiveness, purpose, progress, included in the three-fold activity of Christ's churches—evangelism, education, and benevolence. We hold that all the activities of Christ's redeemed people, as well as their eternal salvation, is part & parcel of God's fore-ordination and election.[53]

In *With Christ After the Lost*, Scarborough includes two major sections of "Scripture Passages for Workers" that outline predestination. Typically, however, these include very little personal remarks and exposition by Scarborough and consist mainly of long Scripture quotations. As a result, evaluation will at best be ambiguous, as one can only surmise Scarborough's thought from the position in which he places these doctrines.

The first section of Scriptures is in chapter five, "God's Provision for the Sinner's Redemption." The eighth provision carries the title "A Preserving Predestination." Among the seven entries that precede this section are paragraphs on the Scripture, the incarnation, the new birth, and the church. The section itself consists of two Scripture quotations, Ephesians 1:5, 11, 12 and Romans 8:29–31, 35–39. Scarborough's only comment is:

52. Ibid., p. 26.
53. L. R. Scarborough, "Distinctive Baptist Doctrines," *Baptist Courier*, (November 7, 1918), Vol. 49, No. 45, p. 1.

He here teaches us the watchful care of unchanging love and omnipotent power enabling us surely without any doubt to realize his age-long purpose for us. He guarantees a safe passage for all who believe, through life, death, resurrection, judgment and with him forever.[54]

Predestination serves to guarantee security to the believer. Whether it causes salvation initially is left untouched.

Chapter six, "The Spiritual Steps to God—The Soul's Salvation," begins with a section listing "What God Does Before Salvation." The order of divine activity is consistent with the Calvinism of the earlier Baptists. Virtually without comment Scarborough lists six steps of divine activity, including the supportive Scriptures:

1. He foreknows, predestinates, elects.
2. He calls.
3. He convinces and convicts of sin.
4. He quickens.
5. He worketh Godly sorrows.
6. He giveth repentance [in the text this step is numbered (7) but should be (6)].

In this scheme, human response clearly arises from God's effectual activity. Not only is predestination first in the series, but quickening precedes repentance, which itself is given by God. This is a thoroughly Calvinistic *ordo salutis*.

Scarborough also speaks of the "effectual atoning sacrifice of Jesus Christ."[55] Nothing he says is antithetical to a definite, effectual (limited) atonement. It appears, in fact, that he studiously avoids affirming a general atonement and prefers a straightforward placarding of the cross itself or the hope and judgment of sinful man and the vindication of God. The substitutionary and propitiatory aspects of the atonement stand foremost in Scarborough's presentations. "The two arms of the cross," an imagery in which he delighted, point to the clearest demonstration of "God's best love for man at his worst," and shows how "unspeakably bad" is the disease of sin. "Let every saved man know that it is through this blood, the blood of Christ, he was saved and let every unsaved man know that this constitutes his only hope."[56]

One succinct summary of Scarborough's theology of the cross is found in a list of what he called "agencies of triumph" in the work of saving men:

54. L. R. Scarborough, *With Christ After the Lost* (Nashville: Broadman Press, 1919), p. 316.

55. L. R. Scarborough, *Endued to Win* (Nashville: Sunday School Board of the Southern Baptist Convention, 1922), pp. 208, 215.

56. L. R. Scarborough, *Christ's Militant Kingdom* (Nashville: Sunday School Board of the Southern Baptist Convention, 1924), p. 102.

3. Christ's atoning death, bearing our sins and nailing them to the cross, standing in our shoes and under God's wrath, becoming our substitute and making atonement for us for us who are unworthy and sinful while he is altogether worthy and holy. The uplifted cross is God's ultimatum to a lost world.[57]

In spite of his positive affirmations of God's sovereignty and his apparent consistency with definite, particular atonement in his understanding of the cross, Scarborough introduces some ambiguity when he distinguishes between quickening and regeneration. After justification, forgiveness, washing and cleansing the soul, putting away sins and casting them behind his back, God "regenerates ["the believing sinner"] by a spiritual birth and gives him a new nature."[58]

In another place, Scarborough confidently sets forth as a fundamental of evangelism the conviction that "The disciples clearly believed that repentance toward God for our personal sins and a personal heartfelt faith in the Lord Jesus Christ always result in the regeneration of the soul."[59]

This ambiguity in the use of terminology plus Scarborough's sparsity of explanatory exposition allowed the seeds of anthropocentrism to sprout and grow. By 1924 Scarborough had lost the balance between God's sovereignty and human responsibility. Instead he chose to speak of man's sovereignty. This becomes a dominant factor on which Scarborough builds. Although still counting "the elective grace, unmerited by man . . . determinative and pivotal in all man's relations to God,"[60] factors that do not merely complement but flatly contradict such language are allowed their own place. Scarborough clearly subordinated divine sovereignty to human sovereignty as another of his "undergirding truths."

> The complete sovereignty of choice in man, the recognition of God's part, of his right to choose, to decide between God and darkness, sin and righteousness, that he has rights as an individual and as a free moral agent to decide the direction of his destiny and whatever he does in life or in eternity is based on the recognition by God himself of his individual freedom of soul. All God's salvation is based on persuasion and not on force. All his doom of man is based on God's force and sovereignty in the light of man's free choice. God says to man, "You may choose and

57. L. R. Scarborough, *A Search for Souls* (Nashville: Sunday School Board of the Southern Baptist Convention, 1925), p. 44.
58. Ibid., p. 326.
59. Scarborough, *Endued*, p. 136.
60. Scarborough, *Kingdom*, p. 48.

after your choice is made, then my sovereignty steps in and my power obtains thereafter."[61]

Scarborough contended that Jesus worked in accordance with this principle. In his confrontation with the rich young ruler—an interview, incidentally, in which Jesus "failed because of unbelief"—the total outcome was dependent on the will of the young man. Not that Jesus did not try—he did—but certain factors innate to the process render him unsuccessful at times. Scarborough tells it this way:

> He exercised his human and divine persuasion on this young man. Jesus never compelled anybody to be saved. He has willed that he will not force men into heaven. He puts in the human heart the whole program of redemption on the voluntary principle and hangs the destinies of men on the pivot of their own free will.[62]

Scarborough developed his evangelism method in accord with the powers of man's free will. At this point, his influence made its greatest mark on Southern Baptist life. One would know, even from the briefest scan of his life and writings, that evangelism consumed his passions. Scarborough produced more books on evangelism and personal soul-winning than any other individual in the life of the church. His book *With Christ After the Lost*, a discussion of general principles of evangelism, was the textbook for the first-year required study of evangelism at Southwestern Seminary. *Endued to Win*, an evangelistic interpretation of the Book of Acts, constituted the second year's evangelistic study. Other books appeared on the same subject: *The Tears of Jesus* (1922), *A Search for Souls* (1925), *How Jesus Won Men* (1926). Scarborough describes his passion as the natural result of his own salvation:

> Out of what Christ put in me when he saved me came a hunger and a passionate longing for the salvation of others. And now, for nearly forty years, that longing abides. I hear the call of God from heaven, from the gospel, from the Divine Spirit, from the cross of Christ, from the needs of men, to win men and to carry the gospel to them; but the most clarion call, the most pungent pressure, the most dynamic, inner compulsion driving me towards the lost comes from within my own regenerated soul. I want to see the bodies of men healed, the minds of men trained, the characters of men securely built; but my primal, preeminent passion, coming from within my own saved soul, is to see the souls of men saved.[63]

61. Ibid.
62. L. R. Scarborough, *How Jesus Won Men* (Nashville: Sunday School Board of the Southern Baptist Convention, 1926), p. 111.
63. Ibid., p. 33.

To call into question either the sincerity or the genuine Christian piety of Scarborough would be criminal, not to mention grossly erroneous. To preclude on that basis a candid analysis of his evangelistic methodology would be equally erroneous. Among the many opportunities Scarborough provides for such analysis, one is particularly illuminating. A Search for Souls contains detailed instruction on how to bring a soul to decision, or "draw the gospel net." This illustrates how easily the "sovereignty of choice in man" eats up the sovereignty of God and must produce an ever-diminishing acquaintance with the Doctrines of Grace.

> If conditions are right and you are in a private place, have the sinner kneel with you in prayer. Do not force him to his knees, but persuade him. If he seems to be under conviction, ask him to lead the prayer. If he hesitates, help him. Tell him what to say. . . . Many a stubborn will has been broken when brought to the knees.
> At the proper time offer your hand and say, "Are you a sinner?" If he answers, "Yes," say, "Do you want to be saved now?" If he answers, "Yes," say "Are you willing to give up your sins?" If he answers, "Yes," say "Do you believe Christ can save you?" If he says "Yes," you say, "Then, are you willing to give up your sins now and trust Christ to save you?" Say to him, "Leave it all to Christ and give me your hand, thus confessing Jesus as your personal Savior." If he hesitates, press your case, get close up to him, say, "There is every reason in the world why you should settle this matter now. You have sin in your life; death and peril are everywhere; your time is not your own. Christ is the only Savior for you, and you must give up to him. Do not delay. I am not asking you to join the church or to be baptised now. The thing I am asking you to do will forever be best for you, and that is to give up your sins and take Christ as your personal Savior. Do it won't you? . . . Your destiny hangs on your decision. . . . Turn him not away. Would you turn away a friend? Would you turn away your mother? Then, do not turn Christ away." . . . Press the matter on his heart and hold out your hand. Do your best persuasively to get him to take your hand. Pray all the time, let your soul silently go up to God, depending on the gospel and the work of the Holy Spirit to bring conviction, repentance, faith, which will result in regeneration.[64]

In such a presentation several cardinal areas of Calvinistic soteriology are ignored. In the first place, the method is highly manipulative. Instructions concerning leading in prayer, kneeling, taking the hand, questions which call for a "yes" answer, and the reference to the sinner's mother hardly fit the Pauline example of setting forth the

64. Scarborough, Search, pp. 122–134.

truth plainly. Although Scarborough does not deny the truth in words, of course, he rests the success of the gospel on the timing and motions of the personal interview rather than the power of the gospel's content. The taking of the hand, the kneeling, and the recitation of a prayer all appear to have sacramental power.

In addition, the whole interview proceeds as if the will of the sinner remains untarnished, and one actually saves himself by the power of his own decision. "Your destiny hangs on your decision," Scarborough says. This is "decisional regeneration" and violates the prerogatives and efficacy of God's grace, just as surely and violently as any scheme of baptismal regeneration.

Finally, repentance and faith lose their gracious character and become identified with a manageable human activity. Repentance and faith are tantamount to apologizing and praying. Scarborough says, "Give me your hand," *thus* "confessing Jesus as your personal Savior." Since when did taking someone's hand equal confessing Christ? Thereby repentance and faith are reduced to the quality of Roman Catholic penance, rather than maintaining the character of evangelical graces.

Although Scarborough's influence benefited Baptists in many areas and held off the intrusion of liberalism into Southern Baptist life, his major emphasis enervated the gospel as believed by Southern Baptists for seventy years before him.

Conclusion

The two major influences producing the gradual theological shift of Southern Baptists from a thoroughgoing Calvinism to semi-Arminianism were E. Y. Mullins and L. R. Scarborough. Both were presidents of theological seminaries, and both were aware of the theological currents that threatened to undermine the fundamentals of the Christian faith. Ironically, while they did what they could on one front to stop that erosion, they actually contributed to it by substituting human consciousness for divine grace in the process of salvation. The result of such thinking in the long term was that the gospel was lost in a just-as-devastating-but-less-observable way than if liberalism had had its way in the beginning.

PART TWO

Doctrinal
Exposition

10

Unconditional Election

The doctrine of unconditional election, perhaps more than any other biblical doctrine, inspires a marvelous awe before the almighty God and humbles his creatures. While shattering all glory that man may seek for himself, the doctrine rivets in our minds the truth that God indeed is the blessed and only potentate, the King of Kings and Lord of Lords who will bring to pass in his own time not only the appearing of our Lord Jesus Christ but all things. To him be honor and might forever!

In spite of its purpose to give sole glory to God, unconditional election is perhaps one of the most feared and ignored doctrines in contemporary evangelicalism. Many who affirm that God has given man an errorless revelation and who should delight in preaching the whole counsel of God have somehow failed to see the strategic position of this teaching in Scripture.

The doctrine of election provides a foundation for every legitimate enterprise of Christian endeavor. Biblical worship, biblical evangelism, biblical social ministry, holiness in the believer, and a Christian understanding of religious liberty all have their truest and most basic justification in this doctrine.

Definition and Biblical Basis

In short, the doctrine of election states that—before the foundation of the world—God chose certain individuals to salvation and ordained the means by which they are saved. It is hardly a matter of dispute that this is a very clear teaching of many passages in Scripture. The first chapter of Ephesians begins its great benediction (vv. 3–14) with the following assertion:

> Blessed be the God and Father of our Lord Jesus Christ, who hath blessed us with all spiritual blessings in heavenly places in Christ: According as he hath chosen us in him before the foundation of the world, that we should be holy and without blame before him in love [vv. 3–4].

Peter likewise addresses the scattered churches of Asia Minor with a reminder of their election: "Elect according to the foreknowledge of God the Father . . ." (1 Peter 1:2). In his Second Epistle he admonishes them to pursue the kinds of lives that demonstrate externally their effectual calling, and, thus, their certain election (2 Peter 1:10).

Unconditional election asserts, in line with these Scriptures, that those who are saved are saved only because God out of his mercy and grace chose to save them—not with a view to anything he foresaw in the creature, but only for his own glory, his own pleasure, and because of his own purpose determined within himself. Ephesians 1:3–14, though rich and bountiful in doctrine, also abounds in complexity. It is structurally difficult because these verses constitute one long sentence of over two hundred words. An astounding catalog of spiritual blessings illustrating "all spiritual blessings in heavenly places" finds an organizing principle in the prominence given to the three persons of the Trinity and their part in the work and plan of salvation. Granting this principle of organization, the passage may then be divided into three stanzas, each closing with the refrain, "to the praise of his glory," and dealing in turn with each person of the Godhead.

Therefore, in substance, what is affirmed about the scope and purpose of redemption as it relates to one person of the Triune God could be affirmed of all. Although the specific function and manner of effecting the work differs from one divine person to another, an interpreter should be safe in assuming a unity in purpose within the Godhead and therefore a unity in the objects of redemptive activity. Verse 3 makes election the specific work of the Father. Verses 11–13 make those elected by the Father identical with those sealed by the Spirit. Therefore, the "we" of verse 7 for whom Christ shed his blood to procure forgiveness of sins must be in harmony with the "us" of verse 4 and the "you" and "our" of verses 13 and 14.

Thus, what is at first sight a linguistically difficult passage attains such depth as to make it difficult in an even greater respect—comprehension. It contains such doctrines as election, adoption, predestination, the sovereign grace of God, the death of Christ, the eternal counsel of God, the sealing of the Spirit. The difficulty of comprehension does not arise from lack of clarity—Paul is clear—but from the overwhelming scope of the passage. Paul moves from eternity past to eternity future in the span of twelve verses, and such sweeping looks at God's eternal purpose understandably boggle the mind (Isa. 55:8–9).

The verb translated *choose* (v. 4) is ἐξελέξατο, a verb that means "to choose or select for oneself." It is in the aorist tense, indicating the fact of a definitive action of God. Point in time, though implied in the aorist, gives way to the idea of facticity and definitiveness. The noun form, ἐκλεκτός, is used twenty-four times in the New Testament, and six of these uses are found in the Pauline writings. Of the twenty-four uses the word refers to angels once, a named person once, Jesus three times, a church possibly twice. All the other references are to people denominated as the elect, as opposed to the rest of the world, and who would otherwise have no coherent factor to characterize them. The verb, ἐκλέγομαι, is used twenty-one times. The great majority of these uses do not relate to salvific intent. They do demonstrate, however, that the word is used to communicate a deliberate placing of preference upon one or several specific objects to the exclusion of others (cf. Luke 14:7; Luke 6:13; 10:42). Those passages that are salvific in nature reinforce this impression. Some people are deliberately chosen by God for his own out of his mere pleasure, not because some feature of the chosen one commends it to the attention of God (cf. 1 Cor. 1:27–28; James 2:5). Related to this point, an interesting feature of the word is that it always appears in middle voice. Thus it has a reflexive thrust— "to select for oneself." This heightens the unconditional nature of the divine activity and emphasizes its origin and end in the pleasure of God.

The object of the verb is "us," meaning that those specific persons (*us*) were the objects of the divine selection. Although election can at places be interpreted as directed toward more general groups, the point Paul emphasizes here is that the individuals in the churches that received this Epistle were elect individuals.

The sphere of our election is "in him" or "in Christ," meaning that we were elected as his own through Jesus Christ. This is not a decree that will take place apart from the work of Christ. It is accomplished only in him—that is by virtue of his work. The eternal choice is so completely bound up with the person of Christ that in light of the divine purpose the elect are described as being "in Christ" before the foundation of the world. Nor can the phrase be interpreted to mean that Christ is the elect one and all who come into him become elect. Although Christ is elect and precious (1 Peter 2:6), the objects of election here, as in the majority of New Testament passages speaking of the elect, are specific individuals. Christ and his work are the means by which this divine election becomes effectual in history. This is the specific point of Ephesians 1:7–12.

The time when this decree took place was "before the foundation of the world." This time element again rules out any historical contingency in the process. Those whom God has chosen do not become elect in history; they are already elect from before the foundation of the world. This is the very point Paul emphasizes in Romans 9:11–12, when speaking of the priority of Jacob over Esau in God's plan:

> Yet, before the twins were born or had done anything good or bad—in order that God's purpose in election might stand: not by works but by him who calls—she was told, "The older will serve the younger" [Rom. 9:11, 12, NIV].

This same truth is announced in a startling way in Second Timothy by referring to grace given us before the beginning of time:

> who [God] has saved us and called us to a holy life—not because of anything we have done but because of his own purpose and grace. This grace was given us in Christ Jesus before the beginning of time. [2 Tim. 1:9, NIV].

Election becomes manifest in history, having been made before the foundation of the world, by virtue of effectual calling and justification and will reach its proper end in glorification (Rom. 8:30). Therefore, it is not because of anything in us. Spurgeon said, "God must have chosen me before I came into the world. He certainly would not have done so afterward."

The purpose of this decree (not the *cause* of it) was that we might be holy and blameless in his sight (cf. Rom. 8:29). This is accomplished on the one hand by imputation of his righteousness and on the other by the sanctifying work of the Spirit, which will be complete only in the state of glory. God's electing purpose produces spiritual response in the lives of the elect. The pursuit of holiness, or the perseverance of the saints, will always become a mark of the elect. This is no doctrine that cuts the moral nerve but rather places the highest demands on the believer. Paul saw several expressions of the holiness produced by God's election as characteristic of the Thessalonian Christians:

> Brothers loved by God, we know that he has chosen you, because our gospel came to you not simply with words, but also with power, with the Holy Spirit and with deep conviction. You know how we lived among you for your sake. You became imitators of us and of the Lord; in spite of severe suffering, you welcomed the message with the joy given by the Holy Spirit. And so you became a model to all the believers in Macedonia

and Achaia. The Lord's message rang out from you not only in Macedonia and Achaia—your faith in God has become known everywhere. Therefore we do not need to say anything about it, for they themselves report what kind of reception you gave us. They tell how you turned to God from idols to serve the living and true God, and to wait for his Son from heaven, whom he raised from the dead—Jesus, who rescues us from the coming wrath [1 Thess. 1:4–10, NIV].

If it is true that election produces holiness, the characteristics mentioned above would not be exceptional but normal and expected. This is why Paul begins by saying that "we know he has chosen you, *because*. . . ." The concrete evidences that faith has indeed been wrought by the electing purpose of God would fit into the Thessalonian pattern.

1. The preaching is accompanied with deep conviction, probably in the preachers and hearers alike—the former characterized by great earnestness, sincerity, and honesty in presentation, and the latter by a deep conviction of sin and helplessness.

2. The life of the hearers changes so that they emulate the preachers in life and loyalty and seek to live as they learn Christ lived.

3. They come to love the gospel and its power more than all earthly approval, so that they even endure suffering to hear it.

4. Their lives are transformed to the degree that they become models for others.

5. They become active in dispensing the gospel, or as Paul characterized the Philippians, "in the defence and confirmation of the gospel" (Phil. 1:7).

6. They set aside the idols and affections of the past, learn to despise the present world, and place their affections on things above, "to wait for his Son from heaven."

But not only has God destined certain ones to be holy and blameless in his sight, he has destined or elected them to filial privileges. Ephesians 1:5–6 affirms unconditional election by means of a different word—*predestinate*—issuing in a different result, adoption:

Having predestinated us unto the adoption of children by Jesus Christ to himself, according to the good pleasure of his will, To the praise of the glory of his grace, wherein he hath made us accepted in the beloved.

Before analyzing the idea of predestination, focus on the word *adoption*. The word means "a placement as sons." This was not generally part of Jewish practice. The Old Testament references to adoption (Exod. 2:10; Esther 2:7, 15; 1 Kings 11:20) take place in foreign countries.

Paul is most likely borrowing an idea from Roman law, which stated that adoption is taking someone who is *not* a son by nature and marking him *legally* a son. This observes the distinction that adoption into God's family does not result from a natural relationship in which there is obligation on the part of God, but it is clearly and solely an act of free grace. Again, the means through which the divine object is accomplished is Jesus Christ.

The Greek Προόρισας is the word translated "predestinated." From this word, the English word *horizon* is derived. This refers to a visible division between sky and land, the point at which they meet. It means "to mark off." The prefix *pre-* means that we have been marked off beforehand. The object of this aorist verb is "us," specific people who are in Christ. He marked us off beforehand.

Including this usage and the one in verse 11, this verb is used six times in the New Testament, five in Pauline material and once in Acts. The use in Acts comes in the context of a prayer of praise to God. The apostles and the church saw in the opposition of the Jews and their plotting with the Romans a fulfillment of Psalm 2:1–2. Such fulfillment could only happen because the sovereign Lord had decided events should occur in that manner:

> Indeed Herod and Pontius Pilate met together with the Gentiles and the people of Israel in this city to conspire against your holy servant Jesus, whom you anointed. They did what your power and will had decided beforehand should happen [προώρισεν γενέσθαι] [Acts 4:27–28, NIV].

Romans 8:29 pictures God's predestining activity as arising from his foreknowledge (a word to be discussed later). This is then followed by calling, justification, and glorification (v. 30). These last three rest on the foundation of predestination and inevitably occur to all those whom God has predestined to salvation. That predestination always produces holiness of life is seen from the phrase "predestinate to be conformed to the image of his Son."

In 1 Corinthians 2:7 God is pictured as predestining the entire gospel event and message. Again the "date" of this divine activity is "before time began" (NIV). Paul claims that this was destined (προώρισεν) "for our glory," meaning that specific persons, including Paul and the Corinthians, would receive righteousness, holiness, and redemption from God (cf. 1:28–31). God's eternal (πρὸ τῶν αἰώνων) purpose leads to adoption, conformity to the image of Christ, all salvific blessings ("our glory"), and the historic redemptive events.

The verses in Ephesians 1:6, 11–12 introduce the ultimate purpose of God's predestining wisdom: "To the praise of his glorious grace" and "that we . . . might be [exist eternally] for the praise of his glory" (NIV) are phrases that capture the marvelous culmination of all that

God has predestined in working out everything in conformity with his will (cf. v. 11).

Sustaining ideas and activities that highlight and give complete deference to the glory of God are objects toward which each Christian should strive. Personal deportment should reflect God's character. He or she should actively promote thinking that demolishes every argument and pretension that sets itself up against the knowledge of God. The Christian should labor to bring every thought captive to make it obedient to Christ (cf. 1 Cor. 10:3–6).

What brings the greatest glory to God? Nothing tends so significantly toward that end as the true praising of his grace and the proper understanding of the freeness of his gift of salvation. The first step toward proper praise of God's grace is the realization that he is infinitely free in dispensing it and that grace always accomplishes its own ends. However, God has not left the full accomplishment of the praise of his glorious grace to man's perception of its freeness in the present time. Instead, or in addition, he will accomplish this in all the redeemed for their eternal occupation. His grace in salvation, and his sovereign initiative in its accomplishment is the subject of the praise brought forth by the four living creatures, the twenty-four elders, the millions of angels, and every creature in heaven and on earth and under the earth and in the sea, as described in Revelation 5:9–14 (NIV):

> And they sang a new song:
>
> "You are worthy to take the scroll
>   and to open its seals,
> because you were slain,
>   and with your blood you purchased men for God
>   from every tribe and language and people and nation.
> You have made them to be a kingdom and priests to serve our God,
>   and they will reign on the earth."
>
> Then I looked and heard the voice of many angels, numbering thousands upon thousands, and ten thousand times ten thousand. They encircled the throne and the living creatures and the elders. In a loud voice they sang:
>
> "Worthy is the Lamb, who was slain,
> to receive power and wealth and wisdom and strength
> and honor and glory and praise!"
>
> Then I heard every creature in heaven and on earth and under the earth and on the sea, and all that is in them, singing:
>
> "To him who sits on the throne and to the Lamb
> be praise and honor and glory and power,
>   for ever and ever!"

Objections and Rebuttals

Several objections are quite often raised to this doctrine:

"Unconditional election pictures God as unjust." However, this objection is more emotional than biblical or even logical and arises only from the fact that God is merciful and saves some. No one can give the Scripture a fair reading and come away with any other conclusion than that man is a rebellious sinner, deserving of nothing but wrath. The wrath of God is abiding on all the unbelieving world. Ephesians 2 pictures all men as dead in trespasses and sins. They are captive to their own sinful desires, to the age of this world, and to the prince of the power of the air and are by nature children deserving of wrath. Certainly if one desired that God be strictly and solely just, then no person would ever experience salvation. Our sentiments may run against such a conclusion, but no one can deduce from biblical exegesis that man deserves any more than eternal condemnation. In fact, John 3:18 concludes that man is "condemned already."

Therefore, if God elects to save some and makes just provisions for that salvation, he must be considered merciful and loving as well as strictly just in that action. He cannot be considered unjust for condemning those who justly deserve condemnation yet never come to him in repentance nor even desire it. They cannot be considered guiltless when they repent only if omnipotent power causes them to do so. On the one hand, God is strictly just in condemning those who reject him and continue in unbelief, while he shows mercy and compassion on those who are placed by his Spirit in the beloved one. He can be considered unjust only if it can be proved that those he condemns deserve the salvation he unconditionally bestows on his elect. Those who really desire to see how God's justice is related to sin must look to the cross:

> Many hands were raised to wound him
> None would interpose to save;
> But the deepest stroke that pierced him.
> Was the one that Justice gave.

"Election is not unconditional but is based upon foreseen faith in each individual." This objection comes from those who hold a modified view of election whereby God knows beforehand who will and who will not have faith, and he elects them upon that basis. This is the position of Arminianism.

One of the Scriptures used to justify this view is Romans 8:29, which states: "For whom he did foreknow, he also did predestinate to be conformed to the image of his Son. . . ." In addition, the same concept appears in 1 Peter 1:2: "Elect according to the foreknowledge of God the Father. . . ." God looked down the tunnel of time and saw beforehand those who would have faith. The argument affirms that on that basis he predestinated them to salvation.

However, this understanding of the concept of foreknowledge is inadequate at three points:

First, such a concept makes the Scripture guilty of using meaningless language. The predestinating of what one knows is going to happen is a meaningless exercise. It is rather like telling a man who has jumped into the air to come down. He will come down, whether or not one tells him to do so. Your command that he come down, or your prediction that he will, has nothing to do with the actual accomplishment. It might as well not be either commanded or predicted, for such does not alter one thing; nor does it reveal anything substantial about the one who commands or predicts. The concept of predestination, which connotes bringing events to pass, loses any integrity of meaning in this explanation.

Second, since the result of such a scheme is identical with the result of unconditional election, it offers no real alternative in result but only in the means of arriving at the same end. To base God's predestining activity only on his omniscience achieves the same result as unconditional election, but alters the method by removing determining sovereignty from God and giving it to man. It also assumes a basic difference between individuals that causes God's election, thus removing the "freeness" from God's grace and countering the Scriptures that teach there is no difference in men. That the result is the same as with unconditional election can be demonstrated in the following way:

(a) God knew all things that would occur to the created order before he created it.

(b) God created an order, understanding that every event that comes to pass would come to pass.

(c) Therefore, all things happen in accordance with God's will, since he willed into existence an order that would function just as this one functions.

Concerning (b), one cannot argue that God was "taking a chance" without implying that God did not know what was going to happen. If he did not know before creation, he would not know subsequent to creation, and prophesy and fulfillment would be impossible. Therefore, even the understanding of foreknowledge that limits it to cognition of events beforehand must affirm that nothing can happen other than that which God knows will happen.

While accomplishing the same events, however, it rests those events that are supposed to redound unto praise and honor and glory to God in the hands of the creature rather than the Creator. When pushed to a final conclusion, such a scheme can offer no means by which all events will reflect the power and glory of God. Only a *deus ex machina* alien to the plot can rescue the drama.

Third, the word translated "foreknowledge" means more than precognizance. The biblical use of the term means far more than just a preview of events. Thus, the third major problem with the view under discussion is its unbiblical use of the words *foreknowledge* or *foreknow*.

Peter uses the word in 2 Peter 3:17 to speak of mental apprehension of events beforehand. This passage refers to the Christian's knowledge of future judgment and tendencies to apostasy. The Christian knows these things because they are revealed by God. The Scriptures—that is, the writings of Peter and Paul—warn men of these things.

When God is the subject, the word means "to choose" or "love beforehand." Williams translated the passage in Romans 8:29, which uses προεγνω, as "for those on whom he set his heart beforehand." Goodspeed says, "For those whom he had marked out from the first." Rotherham states, "For those for whom he foreapproved." The twentieth-century New Testament translates it as "for those whom God chose from the first."

The noun form is used in 1 Peter 1:2. The King James Bible says, "Elect according to the *foreknowledge* of God the Father." Phillips translates it as "Whom God the Father *knew* and chose." Moffatt translates the words as "Whom God the Father has *predestined* and chosen." The New English Bible says, "chosen of old in the *purpose* of God the Father." The Revised Standard Version states, "chosen and *destined* by God the Father." (Italics were added in these examples.)

Further insight into the meaning of this word is gleaned from its use to affirm God's action in foreknowing Christ. In 1 Peter 1:20 the verb is used in a passive voice, reflecting on the death of Christ for our sins. The King James Version translates it as "Who verily was *foreordained* before the foundation of the world." The Greek word used is προεγνωσμένου. The same word is used actively in Romans 8:29, as described above, and in Romans 11:2. Both passages refer to special plans God has set forth for persons. The noun form of the word is used in 1 Peter 1:2, mentioned above. Certainly one would not conclude from 1 Peter 1:20 that God just knew about Jesus beforehand. The obvious meaning is that he had *determined* beforehand that this should happen.

Peter makes the same use of the word (noun form) in Acts 2:23. He preached to the people in Jerusalem that Jesus was a man approved of God among them and did miracles and wonders and that being "delivered by the determinate counsel and foreknowledge of God, ye have taken, and by wicked hands have crucified and slain." Moffatt translates the phrase in these words as "in the predestined course of God's deliberate purpose." The New English Bible translates it as "by the deliberate will and plan of God." The word καί could be taken as an ascensive conjunction, meaning that the second word is in virtual apposition to the first: "his determinate counsel, yea, even his foreknowledge."

Therefore, the evidence indicates that foreknowledge refers to God's placement of favor on a specific event or person before the event actually occurs or before the person foreknown reaches a particular juncture in history. Because the word *known* denotes an object of pleasure, one may legitimately conclude that God derives pleasure in these events. All possible events in all possible worlds were present to his omniscience, but some particular events in some particular worlds gave him great pleasure—therefore, he brought them all into being (cf. Matt. 11:25–26; Eph. 1:5; Rev. 4:11). God's good pleasure is synonymous with his foreknowledge.

Proceeding on the basis of his pleasure, or having his favor or his heart upon certain persons and events, God then predestines that each shall come to pass in its own time. Predestination, then, is based upon and subservient to foreknowledge. Predestination itself then takes the form of these distinct divine activities: creation, providence, and election.

J. I. Packer has summarized well this biblical truth in an article in *The New Bible Dictionary*.

The New Testament formulates the thought of divine foreordination in another way, by telling us that what motivates and determines God's actions in His world, and among them the fortunes and destiny which He brings upon men, is His own will (nouns, *boulē*, Acts ii:23, iv:28; Eph. i.11; Heb. vi:17; *boulēma*, Rom. ix:19; *thelēma*, Eph. i:5, 9, 11; *Thelesis*, Heb. ii:4; verbs, *boulomai*, Heb. vi:17; Jas. i:18; 2 Pet. iii:9; *thelō*, Rom. ix:18, 22; Col. i:27), or His 'good-pleasure' (noun, *eudokia*, Eph. i:5, 9; Mt. xi:26; verb, *eudokeō*, Lk. xii:32; 1 Cor. i:21; Gal. i:15; Col. i:19), i.e., His own deliberate, prior resolve. This is not, indeed, the only sense in which the New Testament speaks of the will of God. The Bible conceives of God's purpose for men as expressed both by His revealed commands to them and by His ordering of their circumstances. His 'will' in Scripture thus covers both His law and His plan; hence some of the above terms are also used with reference to particular divine demands (e.g., *boulē*, Lk. 7:30; *thelēma*, 1 Thes. 4:3, v. 18). But in the texts referred to above it is God's plan of events that is in view, and it is this that predestination concerns.[1]

"God's predestining purpose eliminates the necessity of the death of Christ." This objection to unconditional election misconceives the nature of predestination as it has appeared in Baptist and Reformed teaching. Not only are persons predestined to salvation, but the means through which they are saved are likewise predestined. Several Baptist writers have stated this clearly. *Cathcart's Baptist Encyclopaedia* states: "Predestination [is] the foreordination of all the elect to heaven, and of all the instrumentalities to secure their conviction and preservation until they reach the skies."[2]

The Second London Confession (1689), Chapter III, paragraph six, treats this in detail:

As God hath appointed the elect unto glory, so he hath by the eternal and most free purpose of his will, foreordained (1 Pet. i. 2; 2 Thess. ii. 13) all the means thereunto, wherefore they who are elected, being fallen in Adam (1 Thess. v. 9, 10), are redeemed by Christ, are effectually (Rom. viii. 30; 2 Thess. ii. 13) called unto faith in Christ, by his Spirit working in due season, are justified, adopted, sanctified, and kept by his power through faith (1 Pet. i. 5) unto salvation; neither are any other redeemed by Christ, or effectually called, justified, adopted, sanctified, and saved, but the elect (John x. 26; xvii. 9; vi. 64) only.[3]

Election is accomplished by means. The fact that God determines he should do something does not diminish the necessity of the means by which he chooses to do it. Since his electing power does not negate his justice, unconditional election does not diminish the need for atonement and redemption. If the elect are unrighteous, their sin must be punished and they must become righteous. Hence it is by means of the death of Christ that God is enabled to forgive the sins of the elect. By imputing their sins to Jesus, atonement for them is made; by imputing his righteousness to them, they stand before him "not guilty."

In the same manner, the preaching of the gospel brings faith to the hearer. Evangelism and missions are means through which God calls

1. "Predestination," *The New Bible Dictionary*, ed. J. D. Douglas (London: Inter-Varsity Press, 1962), p. 1024.
2. *Cathcart's Baptist Encyclopaedia* (1881), s.v. Predestination.
3. William L. Lumpkin, *Baptist Confessions of Faith* (Valley Forge: Judson Press, 1969), p. 255.

his elect. Preaching is a means that God himself has pleasurably fore-known in his infinite wisdom (1 Cor. 1:21). Unconditional election does not diminish the need for either the death of Christ or preaching the gospel. John Bunyan explicitly stated this very point in his Confession of Faith!

> 7. I believe therefore, that election doth not forestal or prevent the means which are of God appointed to bring us to Christ, to grace and glory; but rather putteth a necessity upon the use and effect thereof; because they are chosen to be brought to heaven that way: that is, by the faith of Jesus Christ, which is the end of effectual calling. 'Whereof the rather, brethren, give diligence to make your calling and election sure.' 2 Pet. i. 10. 2 Th. ii. 13. 1 Pe. i. 12.[4]

Unconditional Election Clarifies Other Teachings

The doctrine of unconditional election gives coherence and strength to other clear biblical teachings.

1. Grace as unmerited favor finds full expression and most complete consistency only on the basis of this doctrine. To deny unconditional election on the basis of an apparent "unfairness" assumes that God is under some just obligation to grant all men the same measure of grace. Such an assumption, however, ignores two biblical realities. First, strict justice would result in the condemnation of all men; second, when grace becomes obligatory it loses its free, unmerited character and thus ceases to be grace. Paul has this point in mind when he stresses the distinction between Jacob and Esau in Romans 9:11–12 (NIV): "Yet, before the twins were born or had done anything good or bad—in order that God's purpose in election might stand: not by works but by him who calls—she was told, 'The older will serve the younger.' " If grace is to remain grace, only unconditional election harmonizes with its intentions.

2. The doctrine of unconditional election is used by the apostle Paul in laying aside human pride. When the Corinthians began to flatter themselves and develop a divisive party spirit within the church by glorying in personality traits or intellectual acumen of various teachers, he sought to correct their attitudes by reminding them of God's electing purpose:

4. John Bunyan, *The Whole Works of John Bunyan*, 3 vols., *A Confession of My Faith* (Paternoster Row, London: Blackie & Sons, 1875; reprint ed., Grand Rapids: Baker Book House, 1977). 2:599.

Brothers, think of what you were when you were called. Not many of you were wise by human standards; not many were influential; not many were of noble birth. But God chose the foolish things of the world to shame the wise; God chose the weak things of the world to shame the strong. He chose the lowly things of this world and the despised things—and the things that are not—to nullify the things that are, so that no one may boast before him. It is because of him that you are in Christ Jesus, who has become for us wisdom from God—that is, our righteousness, holiness and redemption. Therefore, as it is written: "Let him who boasts boast in the Lord" [1 Cor. 1:26–31, NIV].

If it is true that one comes into the kingdom in accordance with the strength of mind or philosophical subtlety of the preacher, then it might seem man has something to boast about. But even if he boasts only a little, any is too much. Human pride in native abilities would thus increase rather than diminish. Paul's salvo against such perversion explodes from the gunpowder of unconditional election. No man may boast of anything in himself, because salvation comes only by God's electing some unto himself (ἐξελέξατο ὁ Θεός). Only unconditional election gives consistency to the admonition: "Let him who boasts boast in the Lord."

3. The doctrine of unconditional election destroys the human tendency toward "face-receiving," being a respecter of persons. James confronted that practice in the church at Jerusalem. Many took special care to flatter and curry favor with the rich who attended the Christian gatherings. The poor and powerless who came were merely tolerated. Since fulfilling the royal command of love for neighbors must certainly apply to the rich as well as the poor, it was splendid if deference to the rich arose out of obedience to that command. However, the church members' treatment of the poor indicated that such was not the case. Instead, the people conducted themselves as face-receivers, impressed with the outward appearance, prestige, and power of the rich and condescending in their attitude to the poor.

How does one remedy such a situation? James employs the doctrine of unconditional election as he reminds his readers that their favoritism violates the manifest activity of God. "Has not God chosen those who are poor in the eyes of the world to be rich in faith . . . ?" (James 2:5, NIV). God's redemption comes to those who have nothing outwardly to commend them.

4. The doctrine of unconditional election discourages spurious believers and has the tendency to eliminate them. Many followed Jesus only for the fulfillment of physical and psychological needs. Quite aware of this, Jesus confronted them after the feeding of the five thousand and said, "I tell you the truth, you are looking for me, not because

you saw miraculous signs but because you ate the loaves and had your fill" (John 6:26, NIV). He goes on to explain that they desire only physical bread, but their real need is for spiritual food. None seek it, for, though it is free, the demands are too high. What Jesus was saying was that "only those granted the proper appetite by my Father and drawn by him will truly come to me."

> Then Jesus declared, "I am the bread of life. He who comes to me will never go hungry, and he who believes in me will never be thirsty. But as I told you, you have seen me and still you do not believe. All that the Father gives me will come to me, and whoever comes to me I will never drive away.... Stop grumbling among yourselves," Jesus answered. "No one can come to me unless the Father who sent me draws him, and I will raise him up at the last day" [John 6:35–37, 43–44, NIV].

Jesus continued pressing upon their ears the necessity of absolute identification with him in his incarnation and death (vv. 48–58). His popularity waned quickly, for his teaching was hard. Recognizing their growing reticence about his claims, Jesus again focused on their inability to receive what he said without the effectual drawing of the Father. "This is why I told you that no one can come to me unless the Father has enabled him" (v. 65). At that stabbing truth, "many of his disciples turned back and no longer followed him" (v. 66).

It is noteworthy that Peter, bewildered by all that was happening, nevertheless reflected the attitude of the true believer when confronted with these truths. When Jesus asked the disciples if they, too, would go away, Peter responded, "Lord to whom shall we go? You have the words of eternal life" (v. 68). The truth of unconditional election separates true believers from spurious believers.

Christian Response to the Doctrine

How should the Christian respond to the doctrine of unconditional election?

First, he should avoid indulging his curiosity by plunging into questions that God in his wisdom has not seen fit to answer. One of the soberest warnings against such curiosity comes from the pen of the great Genevan reformer himself. Calvin writes:

> The subject of predestination, which in itself is attended with considerable difficulty, is rendered very perplexed, and hence perilous by human curiosity, which cannot be restrained from wandering into forbidden

paths, and climbing to the clouds, determined if it can that none of the secret things of God shall remain unexplored. . . . First, then, when they inquire into predestination, let them remember that they are penetrating into the recesses of the divine wisdom, where he who rushes forward securely and confidently instead of satisfying his curiosity will enter an inextricable labyrinth. For it is not right that man should with impunity pry into things which the Lord has been pleased to conceal within himself, and scan that sublime eternal wisdom which it is his pleasure that we should not apprehend but adore, that therein also his perfections may appear.

If we give due weight to the consideration, that the word of the Lord is the only way which can conduct us to the investigation of whatever it is lawful for us to hold with regard to him—is the only light which can enable us to discern what we ought to see with regard to him, it will curb and restrain all presumption. For it will show us that the moment we go beyond the bounds of the word we are out of the course, in darkness, and must every now and then stumble, go astray, and fall. Let it, therefore, be our first principle that to desire any other knowledge of predestination than that which is expounded by the word of God, is no less infatuated than to walk where there is no path, or to seek light in darkness. Let us not be ashamed to be ignorant in a matter in which ignorance is learning.[5]

Second, the Christian should joyfully believe and transmit all that is revealed concerning the doctrine of election. Faint indeed is the possibility of overindulgence in this doctrine today. The sin of this age consists of an ignorance of and even indifference to God's revelation of the certainty of his eternal purposes toward those he calls "his people." One should certainly not obligate himself to explain the intricacies and interrelated strands of God's decrees, lest he appear to establish himself as God's counselor. However, faintheartedness in the task of receiving, believing, and teaching all that he has revealed is no less presumptuous nor more admirable than sullish intrusion into the secrets of the Most High. Against, the words of the Genevan are pertinent and clear on this issue:

> 3. There are others who, when they would cure this disease, recommended that the subject of predestination should scarcely if ever be mentioned, and tell us to shun every question concerning it as we would a rock . . . in order to keep the legitimate course in this matter, we must return to the word of God. . . . Everything, therefore, delivered in Scripture on the subject of predestination, we must beware of keeping from

5. John Calvin, *Institutes of the Christian Religion*, 2 vols., trans. by Henry Beveridge (Grand Rapids: Grand Rapids Book Manufacturers, Inc., 1964), 2:203–204.

the faithful lest we seem either maliciously to deprive them of the blessing of God, or to accuse and scoff at the Spirit, as having divulged what ought on any account to be suppressed.

Those, however, who are so cautious and timid, that they would bury all mention of predestination in order that it may not trouble weak minds, with what colour, pray, will they cloak their arrogance, when they indirectly charge God with a want of due consideration, in not having foreseen a danger for which they imagine that they prudently provide? Whoever, therefore, throws obloquy on the doctrine of predestination, openly brings a charge against God, as having inconsiderately allowed something to escape from him which is injurious to the Church.[6]

What parent is not justly displeased when a child refuses to listen to his or her instruction? Much more should God's children heed and place ultimate importance on all that he tells concerning his nature, authority, and eternal purpose. If God's children conduct themselves "as obedient children," they will heed and submit to his gracious revelation.

Furthermore, if it is revealed and should be believed, election must also be taught and preached. No doctrine of God's Word will ever harm his people. Anyone who believes it dangerous or unwise to teach election is accusing God of a lack of compassion and wisdom, for he alone is the preeminent propagator of the doctrine. The proper teaching of this doctrine is no more dangerous than the proper teaching of the deity of Christ. Just as errors must be carefully avoided when formulating one's understanding of God's sovereignty in electing grace, so must devastating errors be avoided when setting the deity of Christ in its proper context with the humanity of Christ and his relationship with the Triune God. If a scalpel is deadly, one should not reject its proper life-preserving function.

Third, the Christian should fall to his knees and worship the God who works all things according to his perfect plan "to the praise of his glory."

"Salvation is of the Lord" (Jon. 2:9).

'Tis not that I did choose thee,
For, Lord, that could not be;
This heart would still refuse thee,
Hadst thou not chosen me.
Thou from the sin that stained me
Hast cleansed and set me free;
Of old thou hast ordained me,
That I should live to thee.

6. Ibid., pp. 204, 205, 206.

'Twas sov'reign mercy called me
And taught my op'ning mind;
The world had else enthralled me,
To heav'nly glories blind.
My heart owns none before thee,
For thy rich grace I thirst;
This knowing, if I love thee,
Thou must have loved me first.
                    Josiah Conder, 1836

11

Depravity and Effectual Calling

The visible and existential manifestation of God's electing grace always produces repentance and faith in the sinner. The investigation of this phenomenon must take into account two realities, the depravity of man and the effectual calling or irresistible grace of the Holy Spirit. As related to the redeemed, these are so vitally linked with each other in biblical soteriology that they can hardly be discussed as separate entities. One is understood only in relationship to the other.

For example, in *Abstract of Systematic Theology*, Boyce closes his section on the "Effects of the Sin of Adam" with the following words:

> Corruption can only be removed by a cleansing of human nature sufficient to root out all taint of sin and to restore a holy disposition and habits. This is the work of the Holy Spirit in the people of Christ. All not thus sanctified by him are left forever corrupt. The Scriptures show such to be man's condition that he cannot cleanse himself. . . .
>
> The following Scriptures distinctly assert this corruption and inability. "Can the Ethiopian change his skin or the leopard his spots? then may ye also do good that are accustomed to do evil." Jer. 13:23. So also Jno. 1:13; 3:3; Rom. 5:6; 7:5, 21; 8:3; 9:16; and Eph. 2:1, 5. Such being the condition of man, it is seen to be impossible for him to be delivered by his own acts, even if he had the will to perform them. But for God's action there would be no deliverance, even if man had the will to deliver himself.[1]

---

1. J. P. Boyce, *Abstract of Systematic Theology* (Philadelphia: American Baptist Publication Society, 1887; reprint ed., North Pompano Beach, FL: Christian Gospel Foundation, n.d.), p. 246.

John L. Dagg also combines these two areas in a section of his *Manual of Theology*:

The Scripture representations of men's inability are exceedingly strong. They are said to be without strength, captives, in bondage, asleep, dead, etc. The act by which they are delivered from their natural state, is called regeneration, quickening or giving life, renewing, resurrection, translation, creation; and it is directly ascribed to the power of God, the power that called light out of darkness, and raised up Christ from the dead.[2]

The Philadelphia Baptist Association demonstrated the same cohesiveness between these doctrines in an answer it gave in 1752 to a query concerning original sin:

That we are originally sinful or partakers of the first sin of human nature, being all included in Adam when he was created, and partakers of that happiness, with which he was indued, as his rightful heir; but he, forgetting that great favor bestowed freely upon him and his posterity, we, as well as himself, are justly shut out of our native happiness, and have lost our right thereunto forever, unless our title be restored by the second Adam, the Lord from heaven, by being effectually called in time. Eph. 2:12, 13; Rom. 5:12 to the end; Ecl. 7:2.[3]

Related Biblical Concepts

Several biblical concepts and analogies lead one to see the truth of the statements above.

The Gift of Grace

One such concept concerns the character of God's grace. We are justified freely by his grace as a gift (Rom. 3:24). The word *freely* (δωρεάν) means "as a gift" and can be translated "without cause." Jesus used this word when he said, "They hated me without cause." If ever anyone lived who did not deserve to be hated, Jesus is that person. He did not sin; he only went about doing good. Nothing in his works or his words could justly call forth hatred. Thus, he was hated

---

2. John L. Dagg, *Manual of Theology* (The Southern Baptist Publication Society, 1857; reprint ed., Harrisonburg, VA: Gano Books, 1982), p. 171.

3. *Minutes of the Philadelphia Baptist Association* from 1707 to 1807 (Philadelphia: American Baptist Publication Society, 1851), pp. 68–69.

"without cause" or "freely" (δωρεάν). We are justified "freely" or "without cause." Nothing in us could call forth the blessing.

This is also the word used in Matthew 10:8, "Heal the sick, cleanse the lepers, raise the dead, cast out devils: freely ye have received, freely give." The Twelve, including Judas Iscariot, were sent on this mission. They had done nothing to deserve the power bestowed on them, and they were to distribute their gifts indiscriminately and freely. Although this passage does not use the word in a salvific sense, it does illustrate the absolutely gratuitous nature of anything bestowed (δωρεάν) "freely."

The gift aspect of justification is highlighted when one realizes that there is no distinction between people. All are equally sinful, so all who are justified must be justified by God's gracious gift. What, then, causes one man who hears the gospel to be justified and another who hears the same gospel not to be justified? If the bestowment of salvation arises from any factor beside the sovereign work of God's effectual grace, then one must conclude that an actual difference exists in the characters or wills of the two respective individuals who responded in different ways to the gospel. The one who received Christ must not have been as hard, rebellious, or captive as the one who rejected.

Those who reject the doctrine of effectual call or irresistible grace must maintain that all men retain the innate capacity to repent and believe when the command of the gospel comes. Accordingly, the lost man needs no special power given him by God before he is able to do so. With this view, the unregenerate do need aid in order to believe, but it comes short of effectuality—and all who hear the gospel receive the same aid.

The next step for the unregenerate would be to believe or not believe, repent or not repent. Those who repent are saved; those who do not are lost (or remain so). If some accuse such a theological position of investing merit in the act of faith because it arises from the human heart apart from the effectual power of God, the reply is simply, "No, faith and repentance are not meritorious; they are merely empty hands which receive the free gift of salvation."

But in reality such a denial does not at all escape the dilemma. If belief arises from the unregenerate heart and distinguishes one man from another while all had the same natural or bestowed capacity, then the exercising of that capacity must be better than not exercising it. If it is better (and arises from a capability of the unregenerate), then the believer has contributed to his own salvation.

If it is not better, then it is either worse or the same. If worse, it should only condemn more severely. If the same, then there is no difference between belief and unbelief, and all unbelievers should be saved as well as believers.

The only escape from this is to acknowledge that faith, like righteousness, is a gift of God and is bestowed gratuitously by him. All sinful humanity is in the same condition; therefore, only distinguishing and effectual grace causes one to differ from another. Neither justification nor faith comes from man's willingness to receive but only from God's sovereign bestowal. Of course, this truth does not mean that the one who is saved is "unwilling" to be saved. The Holy Spirit moves in such a way as to create willingness in the form of repentance and faith. He who is saved is made willing in the day of God's power. None are saved who do not willingly receive "the righteousness that comes from God and is by faith" (Phil. 3:9, NIV). The dead man is made alive, the stony heart becomes flesh, the captive is set free, the slave becomes a son, and the enemy is made into a friend.

> But as many as received him, to them gave he power to become the sons of God, even to them that believe on his name: Which were born, not of blood, nor of the will of the flesh, nor of the will of man, but of God [John 1:12–13].

The emphasis of this passage is not on the order of events (i.e., receiving first, then the giving of authority, and so on) but on the inevitable coexistence of "receiving" and sonship as a gift of God. Notice, the authority to become sons of God was *given* by God.

The truth of this is heightened by the expressions stated negatively—"not of blood, nor of the will of the flesh," nor of "a husband's will" (NIV). These are piled up to be understood in light of Jewish racial pride. John emphasizes the contrary fact that even the noblest human strategies are incapable of bringing about the birth of which he speaks. The positive statement emphasizes the origin as "of God." Human initiative is ruled out; the whole process is divine.

In conformity with the birth figure, the interpreter should understand the word *sons*. This word is not an emphasis on adoption, as in Ephesians 1 and Romans 8, but focuses on community of nature (cf. 2 Peter 1:4). We grow to share his likeness. An expansion of this idea is seen in 1 John 3:1–2. Thus, God's gift produces a receptive heart that actively pursues likeness to Christ. A grace freely given is freely received.

Regeneration

A second concept emphasizing the congruity of the doctrines of total depravity and effectual calling is based on the analogies used to describe the fact of regeneration. One analogy is found in John 3:3–21 and is couched in the sentence "Ye must be born again." Although stated as an absolute, this is not given as a command but as a declaration of necessity. Nicodemus misunderstood the analogy at several points. One misunderstanding came from his inability to go beyond the physical level. Another indicates his inability to dismiss any human involvement in the process. "Can a man enter his mother's womb a second time?" Nicodemus felt bewildered at the analogy because birth is something over which the subject has no control. Jesus used the word δεῖ, an impersonal word variously translated "it is necessary" or "it must be that." It states an essential qualification for some action without reference to the ability of one to achieve the stated requirement. The idea of necessity contained in the word δεῖ is highlighted by its use in John 3:14: "Even as Moses lifted up the serpent in the wilderness, even so *it is necessary* [δεῖ] that the Son of man be lifted up in order that all those who believe in him may have eternal life." Thus, being born "again," or "from above," is an essential qualification for salvation over which man has no control.

How, then, does it occur? Regeneration of sinners is like the birth of a baby, who is actually passive in the process and comes into life as a result of the work of outside forces. The child has nothing to do with being born. Being born again, according to Jesus, is like that. The Holy Spirit, working in a secret and sovereign manner, brings to pass the birth from above: "The wind bloweth where it listeth, and thou hearest the sound thereof, but canst not tell whence it cometh, and whither it goeth: so is every one that is born of the Spirit" (John 3:8).

A second Scripture portrait descriptive of and analogous to regeneration—resurrection—vividly emphasizes divine power and initiative. The sinner is pictured as dead in trespasses and sins. What can a dead person do to revive himself? Nothing. He has no mechanism for responding. He must be acted upon from outside. The case of Lazarus serves well as illustrative of this point. Lazarus had been dead for four days. He had no possibility of saving himself or even calling for help. He was in the grave. Jesus came and, by specifically calling the name of Lazarus and commanding him to come forth, gave life to one who was dead.

God's choice of Israel as his own peculiar people gives a similar picture, striking and vivid in its contrast between Israel's helplessness and God's life-giving sovereignty:

> "... 'This is what the Sovereign LORD says to Jerusalem: Your ancestry and birth were in the land of the Canaanites; your father was an

Amorite and your mother a Hittite. On the day you were born your cord was not cut, nor were you washed with water to make you clean, nor were you rubbed with salt or wrapped in cloth. No one looked on you with pity or had compassion enough to do any of these things for you. Rather, you were thrown out into the open field, for on the day you were born you were despised.

" 'Then I passed by and saw you kicking about in your blood, and as you lay there in your blood I said to you, "Live!" ' " [Ezek. 16:3–6, NIV].

Although this refers to Israel's selection for service as a vehicle for conveying God's law and the Messianic promises, the total biblical witness concerning the bestowment of spiritual life follows upon the same model of gratuitous sovereignty.

Ephesians 2 affirms that God's quickening power comes upon the sinner *while* he is dead. An examination of the context of the passage shows that the prototype of this life-restoring dynamo is the power that exerted itself in the resurrection of Christ, called "the working of his mighty strength, which he exerted in Christ when he raised him from the dead . . ." (Eph. 1:19–20, NIV). The words that pile themselves on each other—"working . . . mighty strength exerted"—give the picture of omnipotence straining to accomplish its design, and this should convince the reader that nothing short of omnipotent power could have done it. This entire excursus forms part of a prayer that the apostle Paul utters on behalf of the saints, that they may know ". . . his incomparably great power for us who believe . . ." (vv. 18–19, NIV). This same power was required to bestow life to the dead sinner. The sign of the restored life, not its cause, is manifested faith. Again, the implication of the analogy—death to life—is that the recipient of salvation is passive in its actual bestowment.

Captivity to Sin

Pictures of captivity form the third analogous setting for discussing the relationship between depravity and effectual call. Ephesians 2; 2 Timothy 2; 2 Corinthians 4; and Romans 6 have key concepts in this area. Ephesians 2 uses the language of "following." The age of this world, the prince of the power of the air, and the cravings of our sinful nature are the ignoble leaders of the unregenerate person.

The position of Satan is reinforced in 2 Timothy 2 and 2 Corinthians 4. In 2 Timothy 2 the objects of Satan's power are those who oppose the Lord's servant. Their intellectual condition is evidence that Satan has taken them captive to do his will. In 2 Corinthians 4 all unbelievers in general are pictured: "And even if our gospel is veiled, it is veiled to those who are perishing. The god of this age has blinded the minds of unbelievers, so that they cannot see the light of the gospel of the glory of Christ, who is the image of God" (vv. 3–4, NIV). Since man is under captivity and blinded by such a powerful foe, his only hope is that God may grant repentance.

Romans 6 pictures the "old man" as a slave to sin. Therefore, in addition to the external activity of Satan in repression of unregenerate man, his own nature ("By nature the children of wrath" [Eph. 2:3]) is captive to a law of sin operative within him. This law of sin manifests itself through use of the members of the body in sinful activity whether it be the tongue, the eyes, the feet, or the sexual organs (cf. Rom. 3:10–18; 1 Cor. 6:12–17; 1 John 2:16).

"Flesh," when used in a moral and spiritual sense in Scripture, denotes an affection in which the primary motivating factor subsists in the enjoyment of created things without gratefulness to God or primary concern for his glory. This affection may manifest itself in apparently harmless activity or in an ever-intensifying practice of vice and immorality. Its presence is unbroken in all persons; its domain quite distinct in the unregenerate as opposed to the regenerate person. The flesh dominates the unsaved but is more and more disarmed, though ever present, in the saved. The term *flesh* is not to be identified with the body parts but almost always exhibits its activities through them. Although the body parts themselves can also be used by the Spirit in the saved person, the flesh (Gal. 5:16–26) is antagonistic to the Spirit. While the saved man is no longer captive to the flesh, but through the Spirit wages a battle against it, the unsaved man is bound by the sin operative within him.

Verses 6, 16, 17, 19, and 20 of Romans 6 all picture man as helplessly captive to an intolerant master, sin. This bondage is only rendered powerless by death to that old life, resurrection ("as men who have been brought from death to life"), newness of life characterized by sanctification, and the end result, eternal life. Galatians says, "Those who belong to Christ Jesus have crucified the sinful nature [flesh] with its passions and desires" (5:24, NIV). The flesh, then, has been dealt the mortal blow and will perish forever when physical death occurs. However, the body, as material, will be resurrected—free from the "flesh" and dominated completely by the resurrection life infused into the believer at the time of regeneration.

Depravity and Free Will

What does this doctrine imply about the concept of free will? A close examination of biblical passages related to man will not lead one to conclude that man has a free will. It will only lead to the conclusion that he is in bondage to several different elements. Man is in bondage to sin, a slave to sin. What he does he does most freely but always in conformity with the flesh, the tyrannical rule of the depraved affections. Both his will and his reason are captive to his flesh (Eph. 2:3).

Since man actively rejects God and becomes futile and senseless in his reasoning, his rational capacities operate from an anti-God bias. This is not to say that people in general are irreligious. In fact, many are "religious" to the point of superstition. But they worship deities of their own making, deities whose nature cannot possibly explain the existence of observable phenomena.

> The wrath of God is being revealed from heaven against all the god-lessness and wickedness of men who suppress the truth by their wicked-ness, since what may be known about God is plain to them, because God has made it plain to them. For since the creation of the world God's invisible qualities—his eternal power and divine nature—have been clearly seen, being understood from what has been made, so that men are without excuse.
>
> For although they knew God, they neither glorified him as God nor gave thanks to him, but their thinking became futile and their foolish hearts were darkened. Although they claimed to be wise, they became fools [Rom. 1:18–22, NIV].

Even the scientific materialist who dismisses the idea of a personal deity has locked himself into an irrational position. He tries to explain present complexity by positing the eternality of matter and hypothesizing some principle by which this matter can become more and more organized and rational, eventuating in rational life forms. He does this in spite of a complete absence of evidence that matter performs that way. Rational power from the outside must be introduced to prompt the organization of matter. Only a God as described in Scripture is sufficient to explain observable phenomena.

The description that Paul gives in Ephesians 4:17–19 aptly describes the world that lives apart from the biblical God:

> So I tell you this, and insist on it in the Lord, that you must no longer live as the Gentiles do, in the futility of their thinking. They are darkened in their understanding and separated from the life of God because of the ignorance that is in them due to the hardening of their hearts. Having lost all sensitivity, they have given themselves over to sensuality so as to indulge in every kind of impurity, with a continual lust for more [NIV].

One can see, therefore, that the Bible represents the unregenerate man as having a rationality that operates in captivity to a hard heart. The Scripture passages that describe man in his volitional life never present him as capable of making an uncaused choice. His choices are always determined by the cravings of his sinful nature or by Satan, who takes the unregenerate man captive at his (Satan's) own will (2 Tim. 2:25–26).

John 3:19–21 gives this picture of the unregenerate person:

> [Jesus said] "This is the verdict: Light has come into the world, but men loved darkness instead of light because their deeds were evil. Everyone who does evil hates the light, and will not come into the light for fear that his deeds will be exposed. But whoever lives by the truth comes into the light, so that it may be seen plainly that what he has done has been done through God" [NIV].

This portrays man's will as determined by his love of darkness. His evil deeds preclude a desire to come to the light. Moreover, he will not even recognize that light has come into the world. Man's will is so dominated by his sin that he willfully ignores something as obvious as light shining in darkness. He must think one of three things: (1) it is not there; (2) it is not significant; or (3) it is not good. So striking is the metaphor of a shaft of light in a dark place that any of the conclusions is ludicrous. Any person with an "unbound" will who stumbles in darkness would conclude, when light comes, that it is there and is significant and is good.

Verse 21 shows that those who come to the light do so because it has been wrought through God. Only divine power can effect this change. Effectual calling is necessitated by man's depravity.

Depravity and Responsibility

If a man is captive in will and reason and is spiritually dead and by nature a child of wrath, how can he be treated as responsible for his sin? This question can be answered by considering how the "nature" of something always determines its use and treatment.

For example, we often argue that people have value solely because they are human beings. This judgment is made quite apart from any evidence that an individual has done deeds or held thoughts worthy of commendation. We merely assume a certain amount of innate worth and respect due to one's nature as human, although the person thus respected has had no more to do with being human than a rock is responsible for being a rock. Therefore, some basic attitudes, judgments, and expectations arise simply out of innate nature, quite apart from any actions of the object in view. Man's "free will" has nothing to do with these expectations. Yet he is responsible for and judged in light of being human, even though he has had absolutely nothing to do with that condition.

Even so, God may regard all men in light of their nature and dispense his actions toward them accordingly. Since all men are by nature children of wrath, it is entirely consistent that the wrath of God abides on us entirely apart from any "free choice" of our own to be a child of wrath. We gained neither the grandeur nor the misery of our condition by our previous choice, but we are subject to the implications of both.

One must never draw the conclusion that moral perversion serves as sufficient excuse for immorality. A kleptomaniac cannot be tolerated in his thievery simply because it is "uncontrollable," a megalomaniac cannot be indulged simply because his ego is "insatiable," and a man who has cheated his way into an unpayable debt cannot be absolved simply because he is an "incurable" swindler. Likewise, none may excuse himself before God by proclaiming, "I was so steadfastly and unalterably opposed to your will that only omnipotent power could change me."

Depravity and Ability

Some will object: "But the 'whosoever will' passages indicate that man can freely choose and is not at the mercy of an arbitrary effectual call from the Spirit." Let us set aside for the moment that the question ironically suggests the root of the matter; the sinner is totally at the mercy of God.

However, can effectual calling and the "whosoever will" implications of many Scripture passages be harmonized? The interpreter of Scripture must be careful not to draw unwarranted inferences from one type of passage and proceed to impose erroneous conclusions upon other biblical doctrines not necessarily related to the passage in question. For example, the Old Testament promises life to one who can keep the law: "He that doeth these things shall live by them." Does fallen man, therefore, have the possibility of completely obeying the law? The clear teaching is that if a man would completely fulfill all the letter and intent of the law, he would have eternal life. While it is true that perfect righteousness is essential for eternal life, it is just as clear in Scripture that the law only serves to aggravate and reveal our sin. Therefore, rather than inferring from the giving of the law that a man has the ability to keep it perfectly, one must conclude that the law's design is to lead him to Christ as the only hope for fulfilling the just demands of the law. Christ's death stands as testimony to the universal incapacity of man to obey the law. Paul argues this very thing in Galatians 2:21: ". . . if righteousness could be gained through the law, Christ died for nothing!" (NIV).

More explicitly, the fact that a commandment says "Thou shalt not covet" does not imply that a man has the ability to be free from covetousness. Rather, it points out the root of all sin and confronts even the most moral of mortals with the stark realization that the righteousness of the law goes beyond human abilities.

In the same way, the New Testament commandments to "repent and believe" do not necessarily imply that man has it within his own power to repent and have faith. Although no natural inability excludes him from repentance and faith, a moral captivity does. The scriptural statement "whosoever believeth in him shall have eternal life" does not imply that man has the power to believe. It only states that those who do believe will have eternal life. Belief is still the result of the effectual call and regenerating power of God. As Jesus taught Nicodemus, "Ye must be born again." This is not an action we perform upon ourselves but one that the sovereign Spirit performs upon those dead in trespasses and sins.

In 1784 John Gano presented a circular letter on effectual calling to the Philadelphia Baptist Association. His final point of exposition is a clear and concise summary of the relation of effectual call to men in a state of total depravity.

Its efficacy. It is effectual to bring the subjects of it to a piercing sense of their guilt and impurity. The mind is deeply convicted, that the fountain is in his very heart or nature, from which all its criminal actions have sprung; and that the lust within disposes us to violate the laws of God in as great a variety of ways as nature is capable of exerting itself, agreeable to Paul's expression, "Sin revived and I died." The soul is affected with a view of its sinfulness and the malignity of sin in its nature, as entirely opposed to the holy law of God; hence arises an abhorrence of sin, as vile and odious, and a sense of its demerit as deserving eternal death. This call produces a consciousness of the absolute impossibility of our contributing in the least degree towards a recovery from this wretched condition, and destroys all confidence of help in the flesh. It is a call to Christ, and gives a view of him in his suitableness and ability as a Saviour; the merit of his obedience and sacrifice, and the treasures of his grace are all brought into view, which creates desires of an interest in him, and resolutions of looking unto and relying wholly upon him for salvation; at the same time cordially acknowledging desert of rejection from him, and yet strengthened to rely entirely upon and surrender all unto the disposal of Christ; setting to our seals that God is true; believing the record he has given of his Son, which is eternal life, and that this life is in his Son. The changes produced are from darkness to light, from bondage to liberty, from alienation and estrangedness to Christ to a state of nearness and fellowship with him and his saints. This call adminsters peace of conscience towards God, and disposes its subjects to peace with mankind so far as is consistent with righteousness.

This is an holy calling, and is effectual to produce the exercise of holiness in the heart, even as the saints are created in Christ Jesus unto good works. God having called us, not to uncleanness, but to holiness, yea, even to glory and virtue, and "to live holily, righteously, and godly in this present evil world;" and to conform us, both as men and as Christians, to the pure dictates of nature and the authority of revelation, in all virtuous actions. To believe what is divinely revealed, and to obey what is divinely enjoined; in which the saints are required to persevere unto "an inheritance incorruptible and undefiled, and that fadeth not away, which is reserved in heaven for them," and unto which this effectual vocation ultimately tends. From all which considerations, we learn what it is to be both good and great, and that the way to advance in durable riches and righteousness; to live on high; live above the vanities and pomp of this trifling world, and to shame those who walk unworthily, is to retain a sense of our heavenly vocation. Thus will the hearts and hands of all God's people, and especially his ministers, be supported and strengthened; thus will the religion of our adorable Redeemer be honored in the world; thus shall we glorify God in life and enjoy his peace in death, and leave behind a finished testimony that our calling was effectual and our profession sincere.[4]

4. Ibid., pp. 202–203.

12

Christ Died for Our Sins, According to the Scriptures

The apostle Paul delighted to flash before his readers some of the brilliance and breathtaking magnitude of God's purpose from eternity past to eternity future. Romans 8:29, 30; Ephesians 1:1–14; 2 Thessalonians 2:11–17; and 2 Timothy 1:9–12 constitute a portion of these dazzling displays of divine activity. Common elements in these passages are several, either expressed or implied: God the Father has set his purpose of grace upon some individuals before the foundation of the world and has elected them to salvation; these individuals will be set apart by the Holy Spirit to a belief of the truth and will be sealed by him with the result that they come at last to glory; the connecting link between the purposeful and specific choosing done by the Father and the equally particularistic sanctifying work of the Spirit consists of the work of the Savior, Jesus the Christ.

As represented in these passages, Christ's work consists of dying as a result of being delivered up by the Father (Rom. 8:32, 34) to become Redeemer (Eph. 1:7) and Savior (2 Tim. 1:9) and Interceder (Rom. 8:34) and Guarantor of an incorruptible eternal life (Rom. 8:30, 34; Eph. 1:10–12; 2 Thess. 2:14; 2 Tim. 1:10).

These passages have no hint of tentativeness or incompleteness about them when describing the results of the work of Christ. According to these Scriptures, Christ accomplished absolutely what his appearance on earth was designed to accomplish. When Paul poses the rhetorical question, "Who is he that condemneth?" his answer—designed to alleviate fully any fears "God's elect" might have (Rom. 8:33)—is, "It is Christ that died." And he continues, ". . . that is risen again, who is even at the right hand of God, who also maketh intercession for us"

297

(v. 34). Christ's heavenly intercession exactly parallels in purpose his death. Both are for God's elect.

The Doctrine Stated

This Pauline understanding of the atonement has been denominated historically as "limited atonement." Other terms such as "definite atonement" or "particular redemption" have been preferred by some, but the content of the reality to which they refer is the same. Christ died for the same people for whom he intercedes; these are the same ones the Father has elected and the Spirit has effectually called.

In short, limited atonement affirms that Jesus Christ in dying bore the sins of his people, enduring all the punishment that was due to them by becoming for them the curse that the law demanded. It pleased the Lord God to set him forth and bruise him for this purpose, for in so doing he gained—by his meritorious death—forgiveness, righteousness, sanctification, and eternal glory for a large and definite number of people, all of whom he knew and to whom he was joined before the foundation of the world. It is for this reason that Christ is called "that great Shepherd of the sheep" in relation to the "blood of the eternal covenant" (Heb. 13:20, NIV).

Difficulties Considered

Some feel that immediate and insuperable difficulties attend such a view despite its apparent congruity with the Scriptures mentioned above. These difficulties arise from two classes of Scripture passages: (1) those passages that employ "world" and "all" when referring to those who should derive benefit from the death of Christ; (2) those passages that appear to teach final perdition for some for whom it is specifically asserted that Christ died.

Interpreting "World" and "All" Passages

The most often mentioned in the first group are 1 John 2:1–2; John 12:32; 1 Timothy 2:4–6; Hebrews 2:9; and Romans 8:32. Rather than attempting complete expositions of these passages, I intend merely to point to keys that eliminate their supposed thrust for general atonement and make them at least harmonious with, if not positively demanding of, the doctrine of limited atonement. As I do this, I bear in mind the warning given by J. H. Hinton that interpreters involved in controversial situations tend to "press one class of passages to an extreme signification, inconsistent with the natural and obvious meaning of others, so that the latter remain rather as difficulties . . . to be evaded than as sources of instruction to be explored."[1] By the same token, however, we must not create difficulties by ignoring the analogy of faith and thus allowing a number of inspired utterances to run into "a mass of inextricable confusion" when they can with utter faithfulness to the text and context be set in harmonious light with others on the same subject.

1 John 2:1–2: The phrase in question is "the whole world" (ὅλου τοῦ κόσμου). John uses the same words (ὁ κόσμος ὅλος) in 5:19, referring to those who are under the control of the wicked one. There it is clear that the phrase does not refer to each and every individual, for the evil one does not touch those who are born of God. In light of this, we conclude that here "the whole world" refers only to all of a certain description, which description must be derived from the context. Thus, "the whole world" may be understood as many people from *all* nations, a concept clearly conveyed in Revelation 5:9 and John 11:51–52, Johannine in content also.

John 12:32: The phrase "draw all men to me" draws attention here. In addition to John's riveting phrase in 11:52—"the children of God that were scattered abroad," (referring to the benefits of Christ's death as going beyond the Jewish nation only)—a consideration from John 12 shows clearly Jesus' intent in this statement. Jesus is responding to information Philip brought him that Greeks were seeking him (12:20–22). This fact gave rise to a discourse upon his death, by which act he becomes Messiah for Greeks as well as Jews—"all men."

1 Timothy 2:4–6: The phrases "all men to be saved" (v. 4) and "ransom for all" (v. 6) pose the reputed problem here. The "therefore" of verse 1 picks up the entire argument of 1 Timothy 1, wherein the law is related to the ungodly (vv. 5–10) and the commission of Paul as apostle to the Gentiles and protector of the purity of the gospel (vv. 11–20). The request for prayers "for all men" (2:1) refers to men in all kinds of authoritative positions, for the specific purpose of maintaining external peace and quiet so that God's people might enjoy opportunity for the proper development of godliness and honesty. Thus, the application of law to civil society by the authorities, for whom Christians should pray, becomes the application of 1:5–10. The "all men" and "all" of 2:4, 6 constitute the fulfillment of Jesus' ministry into the world to save sinners and the justification of Paul's mission

1. J. H. Hinton, *The Theological Works of J. H. Hinton,* 7 vols. (London: Holstin & Wright, 1864–1865), p. 368.

to the Gentiles (2:7). Jesus' death to save sinners is for Gentile as well as Jew; otherwise, Paul has no justification for his ministry. "All," therefore, need not refer to each and every individual who ever lived (many of whom were already suffering the wrath of God) but only to many people from all nations.

Hebrews 2:9 In question is the phrase "taste death for every man," where "every" ("man" is not in the Greek text) has the thrust of assured certainty as well as plurality. "Every" has reference to "many sons" (v. 10), "they who are sanctified" and "brethren" (v. 11), "children which God hath given me" (v. 13), "children" (v. 14), "seed of Abraham" (v. 16), "his brethren" and "the people" (v. 17). Its intent is to give assurance that not a one for whom he has suffered will experience the death of the wicked and, thus, they need not fear it (v. 15). This entire passage is most expressive of the absolute certainty that Christ's death will have its full effect and cannot be mitigated by any circumstance. His suffering shall not suffer loss. It is remarkable also that this work is done not for the seed of Adam (all men without exception) but for the "seed of Abraham" (v. 16), only those who will come to have the faith of Abraham (cf. Rom. 4:22–25).

Romans 8:32: The phrase "for us all" provides the question in this passage. Those to whom the apostle refers ("us all") are the same as the "whom" of verses 29 and 30. The Father delivered Christ up certainly and effectually for all whom he predestined to be conformed to the image of his Son in eternal glory. Additionally, Paul designs by verse 32 to highlight the absolutely gratuitous nature of the salvation enjoyed by the elect: "How shall he not with him also freely give us all things?" Again, assurance and confident trust in the unfettered and benevolent power of God to maintain his people all the way to a sinless glory in eternity dominates the intent of Paul here. True Christians, more and more aware of their indwelling sin and the continual operations of the flesh (7:14–25; 8:17–27) need such a display of omnipotent goodness to encourage and sustain them in their struggle.

Answering the Second "Difficulty"

Two Scripture passages should illustrate the nature of the second class of objections to the doctrine of limited atonement.

2 Peter 2:1: "Denying the Lord that bought them" apparently teaches that some redeemed by the death of the Lord Jesus eventually bring destruction on themselves. The word translated "Lord" could transliterate as "despot." A good translation might be "sovereign master." The church calls upon God as despot in Acts 4:24 when in need of a demonstration of his almighty and irresistible creative power. His roles as creator, revealer, and absolute controller of all events are subsumed under his role as despot in that prayer. In Jude 4, both δεσπότης and κύριος are used together in describing the relation of Christ to the redeemed. While κύριος is not evacuated of the specific meanings bound up in δεσπότης (e.g., Acts 17:24), most of the time it also includes the covenantal character of God's redemptive activity toward his people. For the Christian, therefore, the Lord is κύριος and δεσπότης. In Luke 2:29 Simeon addresses God as δεσπότης in recognition of the power by which he had brought to pass the fulfillment of the prophecies relating to the coming of the Messiah and the promises to him in particular. In Revelation 6:10 the martyrs call upon God as δεσπότης in his capacity as judge and avenger. Our passage, 2 Peter 2:1, uses only the word δεσπότης in referring to the one denied by the false teachers. While κύριος could carry the same meaning, the use of δεσπότης indicates a measured precision in pointing to God as rightful sovereign over all by virtue of sovereign creative power, his might in controlling the affairs of history, and his sureness to take retribution on those who seek to suppress his truth and oppose or ignore his purposes.

Another word demands our attention, ἀγοράζω, translated "bought." When the word is used in reference to the death of Christ as the price of redemption, either by contextual necessity or direct statement, the purchase price is mentioned (Acts 20:28; 1 Cor. 6:20; 7:23; Eph. 1:7; 1 Peter 1:18–19; Rev. 1:5; 5:9). Peter mentions no price of redemption here, and to assume that the blood of Christ is definitely intended begs the question. A clear meaning stands out when given the immediate context of Peter's reference to false prophets among the Israelites in the past, Peter's calling as the apostle to the Jews (Gal. 2:8), and the similarity of the language here to that in Deuteronomy 32:6 (where Moses warned the people of turning from the God who had performed so many mighty deeds to deliver them from slavery). The false teachers deny the same God who delivered them, or bought them, when he brought their forefathers from Egypt. They deny him in the same way their forefathers denied him (cf. Acts 7:51ff.; Matt. 23:29–36; also compare Deut. 31:27–29 and 32:5 with 2 Peter 2:2, 13). Although God performed such great and mighty deeds to buy them from Egypt, form them into a nation, and send the messianic prophecies through them, they still reject him and refuse to receive his revelations with humble obedience. In this manner Peter seeks "to aggravate the ingratitude and impiety of these false teachers among the Jews."[2] No failure in

<hr>

2. John Gill, D.D., *The Cause of God and Truth* (London: W. H. Collingridge, 1855; reprint ed., Grand Rapids: Baker Book House, 1980), p. 61.

effectuality of Christ's redemptive price is in view at all here. Rather, Peter refers to the continual opposition of the Jews who killed the prophets and the Messiah while saying they were the only true followers of God (John 9:28–34).

Hebrews 10:29: The phrase "the blood of the covenant that sanctified him" (NIV) appears to teach that one sanctified by Jesus' blood can finally fall into the hands of the living God to be eternally punished. I merely suggest that the implied subject of "was sanctified" (KJV) is "the Son of God." The blood set Christ apart as the one who fulfilled the eternal covenant, for through that blood (that is, God's acceptance of Christ's sacrifice) Jesus was raised from the dead (Heb. 13:20), and through the resurrection he was declared to be the Son of God—not *made* the Son of God, but marked out and pointed to as the Son of God. Jesus "sanctified" himself for this very purpose in his high priestly prayer (John 17:19). The one who despises this sanctified one deserves extreme punishment.

Two Views of Limited Atonement

Historically, two streams of thought emerge from the writings of those who have defended limited atonement. We must not confuse either with those who purposefully rejected limited atonement. One stream, represented by such Baptists as Fuller in England and Boyce in the United States, affirms both the sufficiency of the atonement in its nature to save all men and the limitation of the atonement to the elect only in its intent. This probably represents a majority view among Calvinists. The second stream, represented by Abraham Booth in England and John L. Dagg in the United States, affirms that it is the nature of the atonement to save all for whom it is sufficient, and therefore its limitation in intent is necessarily a limitation of its sufficiency. (For the remainder of this chapter, I will argue for the second option in understanding limited atonement.)

A View Widely Held

One of the basic claims of the Calvinistic view of the atonement is that the death of Christ is "sufficient to expiate the sins of the whole world." Article three under the second heading of doctrine in the canons of the Synod of Dort states: "The death of the Son of God is the only and most perfect sacrifice and satisfaction for sin; is of infinite worth and value, abundantly sufficient to expiate the sins of the whole world."

In his commentary on First John, Calvin, in harmony with the medieval Fathers, accepts this position. Commenting on 1 John 2:2, Calvin says:

> I pass over the dreams of the fanatics, who make this a reason to extend salvation to all the reprobate and even to Satan himself. Such a monstrous idea is not worth refuting. Those who want to avoid this absurdity have said that Christ suffered sufficiently for the whole world but effectively only for the elect. . . . Although I allow the truth of this, I deny that it fits this passage.[3]

The eminent Presbyterian theologian of the nineteenth century, W. G. T. Shedd, argues in a lengthy section of his *Dogmatic Theology* (Volume II, pp. 464–471) for this same distinction as he says, "Christ's death is sufficient in value to satisfy eternal justice for the sins of all mankind." Later in this same chapter on "vicarious atonement" he states:

> The distinction between the "sufficiency" of the atonement, and its "extent" in the sense of "intent" or effectual application, is an old and well established one. It is concisely expressed in the dictum, that Christ died "sufficienter pro omnibus, sed eficaciter tantum pro electis."[4]

Shedd also quotes a lengthy passage from John Owen's *Universal Redemption* (IV. i), of which one sentence states: "Sufficient we say, then, was the sacrifice of Christ for the redemption of the whole world, and for the expiation of all the sins of all and every man in the world."[5]

Among Baptists, Andrew Fuller, who quotes this section of Owen, espoused this same view of the sufficiency of the death of Christ for the sins of all men. He likewise based this conclusion in the innate worth of one who suffered:

> Calvinists in general have considered the particularity of redemption as consisting not in the degree of Christ's sufferings, (as though he must have suffered more if more had been finally saved,) or in any insufficiency that attended them, but in the sovereign purpose and design of the Father and the Son, whereby they were constituted or appointed the price of redemption, the objects of that redemption ascertained, and the ends to be answered by the whole transaction determined. They suppose

3. John Calvin, *The Gospel According to St. John 11–21 and the First Epistle of John*, trans. T. H. L. Parker (Grand Rapids: Wm. B. Eerdmans Pub. Co., 1959), p. 244.

4. W. G. T. Shedd, *Dogmatic Theology*, 3 vols. (n.p., 1888; reprint ed., Grand Rapids: Zondervan Pub. House, 1971), 2:468.

5. Ibid., p. 468.

the sufferings of Christ, in themselves considered, are of infinite value, sufficient to have saved all the world, and a thousand worlds, if it had pleased God to have constituted them the price of their redemption, and to have made them effectual to that end. . . .
. . . these views of the subject accord with my own.[6]

J. P. Boyce, one nineteenth-century Southern Baptist theologian who thought Andrew Fuller's view of atonement needed amendment, in reality changed nothing and took the same view of the matter. He approvingly quotes A. A. Hodge's *Outlines of Theology*, in which Hodge says, "There is no debate among Christians as to the sufficiency of that satisfaction to accomplish the salvation of all men, however vast the number. This is absolutely limitless."[7] Boyce himself agrees with this sentiment when he says, "Christ did actually die for the salvation of all, so that he might be called the saviour of all; because his work is abundantly sufficient to secure the salvation of all who will put their faith in him."[8] This language has also slipped into Baptist catechisms. For example, Henry C. Fish's *The Baptist Scriptural Catechism* of 1850 contains the following exchange in its section on the atonement of Christ:

> Q. Did the atonement, in its saving design, embrace more than the elect?
> A. The elect only; for whatever he designed he will accomplish, and he saves only "his people from their sins." Matt. i. 21.
> Q. And yet, was it not in its nature of sufficient value for the salvation of all mankind?
> A. It was; and hence God is said to have "sent his Son into the world," "that the world through him might be saved." John iii. 17. Heb. ii. 9. John i. 29. II Cor. v. 14–20. I Tim. ii. 6. I John ii. 2.[9]

Such examples could be multiplied ad infinitum and should be sufficient to demonstrate that such language is characteristic of many proponents of limited atonement and accurately represents a large company of Reformed and Baptist theologians. "The atonement is sufficient for all but efficient only for the elect." The thesis of this chapter

---

6. Andrew Fuller, *The Complete Works of the Rev. Andrew Fuller*, 3 vols. (Philadelphia: American Baptist Publication Society, 1845), 2:488.
7. James Petigru Boyce, *Abstract of Systematic Theology* (Philadelphia: American Baptist Publication Society, 1887; reprint ed., North Pompano Beach, FL: Christian Gospel Foundation, n.d.), p. 338.
8. Ibid., p. 40.
9. Henry C. Fish, *The Baptist Scriptural Catechism*, 2 vols. (New York: Edw. H. Fletcher, 1850), 2:52.

is that such language is ultimately meaningless and misperceives the nature of the atonement. Thus, in the final analysis, it does not distinguish effectual and definite atonement from general atonement.

A View More Consistent

One must understand that those who maintain the above view are certainly in the historic stream of Calvinists who affirm limited atonement. They have no intention of giving ground to general atonement but are true and sincere defenders of the truth that the crucified Savior shall not fail in one iota of his priestly ministry. I feel, however, that both the language and the explanations of this view fall short. In the end, as stated, they fail to differentiate effectual and definite atonement from general atonement.

The defense of this proposal stands on three legs and answers three basic questions. First, it will examine why the language has been adopted; second, it will consider some fundamental errors inherent in the concept; and third, it will put forth a more biblical construction of the doctrine.

1. *Why is the term "sufficient" adopted in the language?*

Fearing that the sinful creature might charge God with injustice unless a sufficient atonement has been made for *all* men, some discussions are permeated with theodical intent. This purpose seems to give rise to Article 6 under the second heading of doctrine of the Synod of Dort.

> And whereas many who are called by the gospel do not repent nor believe in Christ, but perish in unbelief, this is not owing to any defect or insufficiency in the sacrifice offered by Christ upon the cross, but is wholly to be imputed to themselves.

This same concern seems manifest in those who feel that this sufficiency guarantees a bona fide offer of the gospel to all men. Boyce says an interpretation must be adopted that maintains "the sincerity of God's offer of the Gospel to all." Likewise, Andrew Fuller defends the idea of the sufficiency of Christ's death for all as the only ground for the free offer of the gospel. He contrasts this to a view which might assert that Christ's death is sufficient only for the elect. He states: "The one [Fuller's view] while it ascribes the salvation of the believer in every stage of it to mere grace, renders the unbeliever inexcusable; which the other, I conceive, does not."[10]

10. Fuller, *Works*, 2:692.

In essence, J. H. Hinton's view conforms to this pattern, though he states it in more positive terms. "One object," Hinton says, "for which Christ died was to establish a ground of conditional hope." Because of this, "No sinner is any longer shut up to condemnation, but may lay hold on eternal life."[11]

One needs to ask this question: If Christ did not provide sufficient atonement for all men without exception, would we not impute our perishing to ourselves? Would we not still say, "We are without excuse"? Is it only the provision of atonement sufficient for all the sins of all men that renders them without excuse? The apostle Paul never discusses the atonement in terms of rendering men inexcusable. What makes a man inexcusable is his rejection of the knowledge and law of God in nature, on the heart, and in special revelation (Rom. 1:18–20; 3:19–20). Atonement is not designed to render one inexcusable; atonement is designed to save justly some of those who already stand inexcusable and under condemnation. God was certainly under no obligation to provide atonement for even one man, much less all men. The absolute particularity of the atonement needs no more apology than does effectual call or unconditional election. If the theologian must become enamored with demonstrating how God's activity releases him from any likelihood of impugnation, both election and calling would have to be defended in the same way. Can one imagine the statement from Dort amended to reflect such a concern? It would read as follows:

> And whereas many who are called by the gospel do not repent nor believe in Christ, but perish in unbelief; this is not owing to the fact that the Spirit has called them any less effectually or the Father has elected them any less certainly, but is wholly to be imputed to themselves.

Effectual calling as defined in such terms would be meaningless and have no real "effectuality," and unconditional election would undergo the same transformation.

John Leland, a pugnacious Baptist from Virginia and champion of religious liberty during the revolutionary period, has summarized this case very well:

> The principal of universal atonement and limited grace, which is now very popular, gives no relief to but one hitch of the mind. When the mind is burdened with the thought, "Why does God love Jacob more than Esau;" to answer, "a general atonement is made for all alike," may ease

11. Hinton, *Theological Works*, 5:369, 370.

the first thought; but, when we are told that many will gain nothing by the atonement but an aggravated curse, the heart sickens to think that God would be at so much expense to get a pretence to condemn men. In the 8, 9, 10, 11, chapters of Romans, Paul rests the subject logically. He vindicates the sovereignty of God with the hand of a master; but, when he undertook to wade into the goodness and equity of Jehovah, he found the waters swell from the ancles to the knees—to the loins—to the heart; and, rising to the chin, before his mouth was stopped, he cried out, "Oh! the depth is the riches, both of the wisdom and knowledge of God! how unsearchable are his judgments, and his ways past finding out." And there he has left me to grovel still.[12]

A second concern that prompts the language "sufficient . . . but efficient" focuses on the deity of Christ. In discussing the value of Christ's obedience, which he eventually assumes to be coextensive with the sufficiency of the atonement, Shedd says: "But the obedience which the mediator actually rendered to the moral law was not that of a mere man, but of a God-man. It was *theanthropic* obedience, not merely human. As such, it was divine and infinite."[13]

Andrew Fuller mirrors this basic idea when he says:

I know but that there is the same objective fulness and sufficiency in the obedience and sufferings of Christ for the salvation of sinners as there is in the power of the Holy Spirit for their renovation; both are infinite; yet both are applied under the direction of infinite wisdom and uncontrollable sovereignty.[14]

In this particular analogy, Fuller's "proof" is his undoing. None would doubt that Christ by his nature could have provided an atonement sufficient for all men without exception, just as the Holy Spirit could regenerate all men without exception. But in actual fact the Holy Spirit does not regenerate all men, though he is entirely capable of doing so. And even though the Spirit's omnipotent power is called for in the regeneration of any sinner, his bringing one sinner from death to life is not his bringing all sinners from death to life. In addition, one must remember that the death of Christ is a once-for-all historical event—"He died for sins, once for all, the just for the unjust"—and when we speak of atonement, we must speak of what he accomplished during those hours on the cross. The work of the Spirit is fundamentally different in that he continues to work in history and regenerates

12. John Leland, *The Writings of John Leland*, ed. L. E. Greene (n.p., 1833; reprint ed., New York: Arno Press and The New York Times, 1969), p. 626.
13. Shedd, *Theology*, 2:462.
14. Fuller, *Works*, 2:489.

men in every age. Christ's work of atonement is done, but the Holy
Spirit's work does not occur within the framework of an unrepeatable
incarnational event.

Perhaps a more formidable objection by Fuller appears in the conversation he constructs between James and Peter when they discuss
substitution.

> It seems to me as consonant with truth to say that a certain number of
> Christ's acts of obedience become ours as that a certain number of our
> sins become his. In the former case his one undivided obedience, stamped
> as it is with Divinity, affords a ground of justification to any number of
> believers; in the latter his one atonement, stamped also as it is with
> Divinity, is sufficient for the pardon of any number of sins or sinners.[15]

This attempt at *reductio ad absurdum* misconceives the biblical relation of imputation. Justification should not be considered as analogous
to atonement but rather to the imputation of Adam's sin to all his
posterity. We are declared guilty—not because Adam sinned enough
sins to be imputed to all the race that would follow him, but because
he was the head of the race. We are declared righteous—not because
Christ has done enough individual righteous deeds to be scattered
throughout the world of the elect, but because he was the second
Adam. Adam's guilt is imputed to all who follow from Adam and are
included in him. Christ's righteousness is imputed to all who follow
from Christ and are included in him.

Concerning the atonement, although sin is imputed to Christ, Scripture does not allow us to consider his death as an atonement for only
the guilt of Adam to his posterity. As the apostle Peter clearly states:
"He himself bore our sins in his own body on the tree . . ." (1 Peter
2:24, NIV). God's wrath comes not only for what Adam's sin has done
to the race, but for the aggravation the race has added to the original
corruption.

Moreover, it is a *non sequitur* to move from the deity of the sacrifice
to sufficiency for every individual man. Such a conclusion assumes
that deity can perform nothing by measure. Every event of the ministry of Jesus refuses to harmonize with that basic idea. His act of
feeding the five thousand produced just enough food to satisfy those,
plus another day's provisions for the disciples. That action of Jesus
did not multiply all the loaves in the world but just the ones he handled and blessed.

Jesus' raising of Lazarus was designed specifically for Lazarus and

15. Ibid., 2:691.

not for all the dead of that age or any age. He certainly had the power to do that, but he was able to limit himself to just one, if he so chose, by calling him forth. No one could argue that Jesus was unjust in favoring Lazarus and his family, or even that all the dead could have come forth at that time had they so chosen. If someone would argue that these events relate only to material realities rather than the more pervasive moral reality, he needs only to recall Jesus' words to one lame man: "Your sins are forgiven" and, in the same particularity of attention, "Take up your bed and walk." (Another error that accompanies the supposed parallelism between deity and sufficiency will be discussed below.)

2. *What errors are there in the "sufficient" view?*

One error of this view is found in its lack of precise distinction between atonement and either unconditional election or effectual calling—or both. In Shedd's discussion of the extent of the atonement, he differentiates between its passive and active meanings. Passively, he claims, "the extent of the atonement is unlimited." Actively , which denotes the act of extending, it is limited. Shedd elaborates:

> The extent of the atonement, in this sense, means its personal application to individuals by the Holy Spirit. The extent is now the intent. The question, What is the extent of the atonement? now means: To whom is the atonement effectually extended? The inquiry now is not, What is the value of the atonement? but, To whom does God purpose to apply its benefits?[16]

Boyce, from among the Baptists, states "that same death however, secures salvation to the Elect, because by it Christ also obtained for them those gracious influences by which they will be led to comply with the conditions."[17]

Fuller explains it this way:

> It is allowed that the death of Christ has opened a way whereby God can consistently with his justice forgive any sinner whatever who returns to him by Jesus Christ. It is necessary to our salvation that a way and a highway to God should be opened: Christ is such a way, and is as free for any sinner to walk in as any highway whatever from one place to another; but, considering the depravity of human nature, it is equally necessary that some effectual provision should be made for our walking in that way. We conceive that the Lord Jesus Christ made such a provision by his death, thereby procuring the certain bestowment of faith,

16. Shedd, *Theology,* 2:464.
17. Boyce, *Systematic Theology,* p. 340.

as well as all other spiritual blessings which follow upon it. . . . Herein
consists the particularity of redemption.[18]

These statements are tantamount to identifying the doctrine of effectual calling with atonement. This precise position is occupied by J. H. Hinton, who is bold enough to say he believes both in universal and particular atonement. The aspect of particularity, however, does not concern primarily the death of Christ, but, according to Hinton, consists of (1) "an eternal, personal, sovereign election on the part of God of certain individuals"; and (2) the special influence of the Holy Spirit by which "the heart is subdued to the reception of the Gospel."[19] To define the extent of the atonement in terms of personal application by the Holy Spirit is to remove any efficacy from the agony of Christ on the cross and to render his work merely tentative. If he has died for all sufficiently—and the only line of demarcation is the "personal application to individuals by the Holy Spirit" or "the gracious influences by which they will be led to comply with those conditions" or "the effectual provision . . . made for our walking in that way"—I cannot tell how one distinguishes this from the general atonement of the Arminians, who claim that Christ has died for all men, but its benefits accrue only to those who believe. The difference in the two does not lie in atonement, but in the Spirit's work of calling.

A second error is subtle in nature and involves an almost indiscernible shift in the understanding of a sacrificial death. Although Jesus' death is spoken of as passive obedience—and though the concepts of reconciliation and propitiation are defined as activities accomplished in the Father's setting forth God the Son—when the subject of the sufficiency of the death of Christ arises, the emphasis shifts from the Son's passive obedience to what he actively accomplishes by his infinite divine nature. We must avoid this shift and maintain that this was, indeed, a passive obedience in which "the Lord laid on him the iniquity of us all": a passive but obedient receptivity of all the smiting, afflicting, and piercing inflicted by the Father for our sake.

Christ's nature does not increase the intensity or quantity of what was placed upon him but enables him to bear whatever it might have been. An analogy should illustrate but not prove this interpretation: The Virgin Mary doubtless suckled the baby Jesus, Emmanuel, God with us. Does this act of tender affection upon Jesus suffice for the whole world because he was divine? Is that breast-feeding sufficient to sustain all the babies in the world? Obviously not, since Jesus took

18. Fuller, *Works*, 2:489.
19. Hinton, *Theological Works*, 5:374.

only the amount given him by his mother. Likewise, in his propitiatory death, Christ absorbs only as much wrath as the Father inflicts upon him. His deity does not increase the stringency of the punishment but rather gives eternal quality to it and strengthens him to bear its force.

The third misinterpretation of "sufficient" consists of an apparent necessity of separating objectivity from effectuality in order to maintain the concept of sufficiency for the whole world. This view sees the sufficiency of the atonement in Jesus' fulfillment of all the demands of the law for all men. Shedd says:

> Christ's death as related to the claims of the law upon all mankind, cancels those claims wholly. It is an infinite "propitiation for the sins of the whole world. . . ." But the relation of an impenitent person to this atonement, is that of unbelief and rejection of it. Consequently, what the atonement has effected objectively in reference to the attribute of divine justice, is not effected subjectively in the conscience of the individual. There is an infinite satisfaction that naturally and necessarily cancels legal claims, but unbelief derives no benefit from the fact.[20]

Hodge concurs when he avers that the atonement has removed "the legal impediments out of the way of all men."[21] Boyce quotes and agrees with Hodge in affirming that "Christ wrought out a means of reconciliation for all men, which removed every legal obstacle."[22]

One might well ask, "If every legal obstacle to a man's salvation is removed, what hinders his being saved?" Logically, he can no longer be justly condemned for his sins but only for his unbelief. But think further. Is not unbelief a sin for which Christ has suffered the legal penalties? Certainly, for even the elect have been unbelievers for a season. If escape from the dilemma is sought by saying, "Persistent unbelief ranks in a different category," what shall one say of the man who has never had a chance to disbelieve? If all legal obstacles to his salvation are removed and he never hears of Jesus, then certainly no just reason remains why he should be condemned. In addition, if every legal obstacle is removed, why does Scripture persist in teaching otherwise?

> Mortify therefore your members which are upon the earth; fornication, uncleanness, inordinate affection, evil concupiscence, and covetousness

20. Shedd, *Theology*, 2:437.
21. A. A. Hodge, *Outlines of Theology*, 2nd ed., (Carlisle, PA: Banner of Truth Trust, 1972), p. 417.
22. Boyce, *Systematic Theology*, p. 340.

which is idolatry: For which things' sake the wrath of God cometh . . .
[Col. 3:5–6].

After a similar list in Ephesians 5, Paul says "Let no man deceive
you with vain words: for because of these things [διὰ ταῦτα] cometh
the wrath of God upon the children of disobedience" (v. 6, KJV). But if
every legal obstacle has been removed, such could not be the case.
All the words that speak of the atoning death of Christ relate it to
God's righteous wrath: sacrifice, expiation, propitiation, reconciliation. In fact, the work of Christ on the cross *per se* is to be viewed
totally in terms of the vindication of God's law. On the cross he "was
made a *curse* for us" (Gal. 3:13). ". . . God sending his own Son in the
likeness of sinful flesh, and for sin, *condemned* sin in the flesh: That
the *rightousness* of the law might be fulfilled in us, who walk not after
the flesh, but after the Spirit (Rom. 8:4–5). Other graces may accrue
to the believer *because* of that act but not *in* that act. Thus, the removal
of legal obstacles to salvation was the great work of our High Priest.
As Shedd has said, "By the suffering of the sinner's atoning substitute,
the divine wrath at sin is propitiated and *as a consequence* of this
propitiation the punishment due to sin is released."[23]

Shedd should have carried this truth through as consistently as
Abraham Booth (1734–1805) did in *Divine Justice Essential to the Divine Character* (1803). Booth, almost as an aside in his applicatory
section of the sermon, argues the following:

> If, in his perfect obedience and penal death, he acted and suffered as
> the substitute of *all mankind*, they are all redeemed: but if, as the rep-
> resentative of the *elect only*, redemption must be considered as exclu-
> sively theirs. For, to imagine that the death of Christ, as the price of
> deliverance from the curse of the law, redeemed any for whom, as a
> substitute, he did *not suffer*; and to suppose, that any of those for whom
> as a surety, he sustained the penalty of death, are *not redeemed*, seem
> equally indefensible and absurd.
>
> While cheerfully admitting the sufficiency of Immanuel's death to
> have redeemed all mankind, had all the sins of the whole human species
> been equally imputed to him; and had he, as the Universal Represent-
> ative, *sustained that curse of the law* which was due to all mankind; yet
> we cannot perceive any solid reason to conclude, that his propitiatory
> sufferings are sufficient for the expiation of sins which he *did not bear*,
> or for the redemption of sinners whom he *did not represent*, as a sponsor,
> when he expired on the cross. For the substitution of Christ, and the
> imputation of sin to him, are essential to the scriptural doctrine of re-

23. Shedd, *Theology*, 2:391.

demption by our adorable Jesus.—We may, therefore, safely conclude, that our Lord's voluntary substitution, and redemption by his vicarious death, are both of them limited to those, *for whom he was made SIN— for whom he was made a CURSE*—and for whose deliverance from final ruin, *he actually paid the price of his OWN BLOOD.* Consequently, that redemption is particular, and peculiar to the chosen of God.[24]

That Christ was entirely capable in his person and by his death of gaining satisfaction for all the sins of all men admits of no debate, as Booth clearly points out. But that the actual atonement was sufficient in every particular included in the word *atonement* must be doubted.

To say that his death is sufficient for everyone, but not that everyone receives forgiveness, is to say that God accomplishes the greater but not the lesser. He sets in motion a cause—the most powerful and compelling spiritual and moral cause conceivable—that does not consummate in an effect.

As can well be seen, both streams of thought have a healthy and biblical concept of the relation of atonement to law. This understanding, that all legal obstacles to salvation have been removed, is right and cannot be surrendered. It forms the foundation for the view of this chapter. To remove the necessary connection between atonement and satisfaction of the divine law denudes Christ's death of all its moral sublimity and reduces it to an amazing piece of whimsical and romantic extravagance.

Many contemporary Baptist treatments of the atonement seek to interpret Christ's death with little or no reference to God's law, justice, and holy wrath. In fact, many have entirely rejected the specific penal-substitution concept as antiquarian or immoral or both.

Fisher Humphreys plays the part of Abelard against Anselm by rejecting the idea of moral necessity in the atonement and opting for a contemporized setting of moral influence. In preparing the foundation for his rebuilding of a classically inadequate understanding of Christ's death, Humphreys sweeps away the ideas of necessity:

> If we say, "Jesus had to die," we either imply that Jesus' sacrifice made it right for God to forgive whereas it would have been wrong for God to forgive if Jesus had not died, or else we imply that God did not love men enough to forgive them but Jesus' sacrifice purchased God's love for sinners, or both.
>
> Clearly this will not do and that is why it is better to speak of Jesus' sacrifice as constituting divine forgiveness rather than preparing for it.[25]

24. Abraham Booth, *The Works of Abraham Booth*, 3 vols. (London: J. Haddon, 1813), 3:60, 61.

25. Fisher Humphreys, *The Death of Christ* (Nashville, TN: Broadman Press, 1978), p. 117.

In specifically discussing objectivity, Humphreys later allows the concept of necessity to have validity in only two ways. One, Christ's death was "historically inevitable" because of the severe judgment he brought against the religious leaders of Israel. Two, he must be obedient to his own teaching of nonresistance, thus necessarily submitting to the death to which his mission of love to God and man would inevitably take him.

Humphreys clearly rejects any necessity that arises from the moral nature of God: "My conviction is that . . . the idea that the cross of Christ was necessary if God was to save men . . . is a mistaken idea."[26] There are two concerns under which Humphreys seems to labor. First, he considers substitutionary, sacrificial, penal atonement as arising from an undue attachment to "logical necessity." Second, he supposes the biblical writers never tried to explain "how a sacrifice can provide forgiveness."[27]

Concerning the first, that a doctrine is logical and fits beautifully within a system of thought should never in itself be considered a weakness. It is true that if the only concern were for logical coherence, then any number of other systems of thought could be brought forth as self-consistent, unbiblical though they may be. The real concern behind penal substitution is not "logical necessity," but faithfulness to clear biblical teaching—or it could be said, faithfulness to stated Pauline, Petrine, and dominical logic. And their logic, moreover, does not arise from philosophical zeal but from moral passion. Thus, the "logical necessity" of the atonement arises from biblical and moral necessity.

Concerning the second, it simply is not so! The biblical writers focus great intensity upon relating forgiveness to the sacrifice of Christ and in explaining the relationship:

> For all have sinned, and come short of the glory of God [italics added]; Being justified freely by his grace through the redemption that is in Christ Jesus: Whom God hath set forth to be a propitiation through faith in his blood, to declare his righteousness for the remission of sins that are past, through the forbearance of God; To declare, I say, at this time his righteousness: that he might be just, and the justifier of him which believeth in Jesus [Rom. 3:23–26].
>
> So then they which be of faith are blessed with faithful Abraham. For as many as are of the works of the law are under the curse: for it is written, Cursed is every one that continueth not in all things which are written in the book of the law to do them. But that no man is justified by the law in the sight of God, it is evident: for, The just shall live by

26. Ibid., p. 132.
27. Ibid., p. 40.

faith. And the law is not of faith: but, The man that doeth them shall live in them. Christ hath redeemed us from the curse of the law, being made a curse for us: for it is written, Cursed is every one that hangeth on a tree: That the blessing of Abraham might come on the Gentiles through Jesus Christ; that we might receive the promise of the Spirit through faith [Gal. 3:9–14].

Paul thus explains the why and how in terms of the eternal moral nature of God (Rom. 3) as expressed in his law (Gal. 3), and he leaves the reader no liberty to conclude that these are merely time-bound cultural models with which modern man may dispense. Justice and mercy kiss each other on the cross, as the Father himself sets forth the Son as an acceptable and adequate sacrifice. God can now forgive without denying his justice (Exod. 34:6–7; Job 10:14).

Another Southern Baptist who evidences little sympathy for sub-stitutionary and penal ideas in the atonement is James E. Tull. Calling a view of the atonement that rests on the satisfying of God's justice "fallacious" and caricaturing it as representing Christ as inferior to God's justice and disunited in will from the Father, he quotes W. J. Wolf approvingly: "A God who forgives because His justice has been satisfied does not really forgive."[28] Such a position fails to appreciate that forgiveness consists of nonimputation of punishment and is thus inextricably linked to the penal death of the substitute. Tull states his own position in these words: "The character of forgiveness refutes the charge that God cannot give it freely without violating the moral law."[29]

Although the words *love* and *mercy* abound in these contemporary attempts at explaining the atonement, they become meaningless. It has yet to be shown how an indulgence in the moral non-sense of the cross (for that is what it must be if there exists no direct connection with the law and justice of God) demonstrates God's love and mercy. If forgiveness could come apart from the cross (and surely it must if the cross in no way affects God's justice in dealing with sinful man), the love of the Father for the Son certainly comes into question. In addition, the attempt to explain God's love to man in terms of the cross falls empty when God's just wrath evacuates the premises.

Therefore, while confidently affirming the substitutionary and legal-penal aspects of atonement, one must also realize that applying this concept to all men without exception relegates the atonement to a

28. James E. Tull, *The Atoning Gospel* (Macon, GA: Mercer University Press, 1982), p. 57.
29. Ibid., p. 66.

nonefficacious state. This approaches the mistake of those who believe in general atonement and even contains elements of nonsubstitution.

3. *What biblical truths must be present in a doctrine of the atonement?* In discussing a fully biblical view of the atonement, several features must be carried through consistently. Each of these features has its place in historic, Reformed, and Baptist theology but, more often than not, has not been handled consistently and allowed to rule its proper domain.

The first two features relate to sin, which must be seen in two aspects: nature and degree of heinousness. First, in its nature, all sin is the same. Whether it is merely eating a piece of forbidden fruit or maliciously cursing the God of creation, the offense is eternal in nature and is deserving of eternal punishment. This is the point James makes when he says:

> If you really keep the royal law found in Scripture, "Love your neighbor as yourself," you are doing right. But if you show favoritism, you sin and are convicted by the law as lawbreakers. For whoever keeps the whole law and yet stumbles at just one point is guilty of breaking all of it. For he who said, "Do not commit adultery," also said, "Do not murder." If you do not commit adultery but do commit murder, you have become a lawbreaker [James 2:8–11, NIV].

In the same way, greed is likened to idolatry, for it values material objects above placing one's affections on heavenly things. All violations are deserving of eternal punishment in that they are against an eternal God. Breaking the principle of obedience at any point calls for a punishment that is eternal in nature.

The second feature to be handled in a doctrine of atonement concerns the degrees of heinousness of sin. Virtually all theologians, Catholic and Protestant alike, recognize the validity of this distinction. J. H. Thornwell, the Presbyterian theologian of the nineteenth century who was preaching when the Baptist J. P. Boyce was converted, expounds this thesis as eruditely as any theologian. Thornwell discusses the Ten Commandments in terms of degree; he sees them as moving from the most heinous to the least heinous.

> The arrangement of the Decalogue turns upon the intrinsic importance of the various spheres to which the precept or prohibition pertains. First come God and the whole department of Divine worship; then comes the family, the very keystone of the arch which sustains society; then come the interests of man in the order of their magnitude—first, the protection of life, next the purity of families, then the rights of property, and finally the security of character. Here, therefore, is an obvious ground of dis-

tinction in the object-matter of the law. It is intrinsically a greater evil to insult God than to reproach our neighbours, because God is greater than our neighbours. It is a greater sin to be contemptuous to a parent than wanting in respect to others, because the parental is the most solemn and sacred of all social ties. It is a greater crime to rob a fellow-man of his life than to defraud him of his property, because life is more than meat or raiment. It is a greater crime to defile a man's wife than to circulate a lie to his injury, because the purity of families can never be restored when once lost, but an idle lie may be refuted or lived down.[30]

Baptist catechisms set forth the same hierarchy of heinousness. John Bunyan's *Instruction for the Ignorant* contains the following exchanges.

(54) Who are likely to be most punished there, men or children?

The punishment in hell comes not upon sinners according to age, but sin; so that whether they be men or children, the greater sin, the greater punishment; "For there is no respect of persons with God." Ro. ii. 11.

(55) How do you distinguish between great sins and little ones?

By their nature, and by the circumstances that attend them.

(56) What do you mean by their nature?

I mean when they are very gross in themselves. 2 Ch. xxxiii. 2. Eze. xvi. 42.

(57) What kind of sins are the greatest?

Adultery, fornication, murder, theft, swearing, lying, covetousness, witchcraft, sedition, heresies, or any the like. 1 Co. vi. 9, 10. Ep. v. 3–6. Col. iii. 5, 6. Ga. v. 19–21. Re. xxi. 8.

(58) What do you mean by circumstances that attend sin?

I mean light, knowledge, the preaching of the Word, godly acquaintance, timely caution, &c.

(59) Will these make an alteration in the sin?

These things attending sinners, will make little sins great, yea greater than greater sins that are committed in grossest ignorance.

(65) How will godly acquaintance greaten my sin?

When you sin against their counsels, warnings, or persuasions to the contrary; also when their lives and conversations are a reproof to you, and yet against all you will sin. Thus sinned Ishmael, Esau, Eli's sons, Absalom and Judas, they had good company, good counsels, and a good life set before them by their godly acquaintance, but they sinned against all, and their judgment was the greater. Ishmael was cast away, Ge. xxi. 10. Esau hated, Ge. iv. 30. Eli's sons died suddenly, Mal. i. 2. 1 Sa.

---

30. J. H. Thornwell, *The Collected Writings of James Henley Thornwell*, 4 vols. (Edinburgh: The Banner of Truth Trust, 1974), 1:429, 430.

ii. 25, 34; iv. 11. Absalom and Judas were both strangely hanged. 2 Sa. xviii. Mat. xxvii.[31]

In summarizing his argument and representing what he felt to be the consensus of theological opinion, Thornwell related the *nature* of sin to the *degree* of sinfulness in the following way: "With one voice they protested that all sin, in its own nature and apart from the provisions of grace was deadly, and yet that all sins were not equally heinous. Death was due to the least, but death had its degrees, and in the adjustment of these to the degrees of guilt the justice of God was realized."[32]

Jesus' warning to Bethsaida and Chorazin that the punishment of Sodom and Gomorrah will be more tolerable than theirs expresses pungent testimony to this same truth. Even so does the writer to the Hebrews warn his readers, "For if the message spoken by angels was binding, and every violation and disobedience received its just punishment, how shall we escape if we ignore such a great salvation?" (Heb. 2:2–3, NIV). And again he shows the severe gradation of guilt involved in the difference of opportunity: "Anyone who rejected the law of Moses died without mercy on the testimony of two or three witnesses. How much more severely do you think a man deserves to be punished who has trampled the Son of God under foot . . . ?" (Heb. 10:28–29, NIV). Thus, one should readily see that though all sin deserves eternal punishment, some are worthy of more intense punishment or a greater display of wrath. Because of this truth, Hodge's statement that "what would save one would save another" is only partially true. Yes, in its eternal nature; no, in its intensity of punishment. To accept Hodge as accurate at this point would be to say that Bethsaida and Chorazin need not suffer any more than Sodom and Gomorrah.

The third and final feature in a doctrine of atonement highlights the truth that God's justice is exact. The Westminster Confession and the Second London Confession state that Christ, by his sacrifice, "hath fully satisfied the justice of God," and that he has provided justification for the elect so that in their justification "both the exact justice and the rich grace of God might be glorified." Paul affirms this in Romans 3:25–26 by relating the justice of God to the propitiatory death of Christ:

---

31. John Bunyan, *The Miscellaneous Works of John Bunyan*, Vol. VIII, gen. ed., Roger Sharroch, *Instructions for the Ignorant*, ed. Richard L. Greaves (Oxford: At the Clarendon Press, 1979), p. 15.

32. Thornwell, *Collected Writings*, 1:427.

God presented him as a sacrifice of atonement, through faith in his blood. He did this to demonstrate his justice, because in his forbearance he had left the sins committed beforehand unpunished—he did it to demonstrate his justice at the present time, so as to be just and the one who justifies the man who has faith in Jesus [NIV].

The only sense in which the demands of justice have been relaxed consists of God's permitting a vicar to suffer for the criminal. However, the wrath inflicted is the same as if the criminals themselves were being punished. The suffering does not involve remorse of conscience, for Christ is not actually a sinner, and those pains are not in the strictest sense inflicted. However, the inflicted punishment is neither less nor more than what strict justice demands. As Shedd himself says clearly:

> Christ's sufferings were of a different nature or quality from those of a lost man. But there was no difference in quantity or value. A less degree of suffering was not exchanged for a greater degree. The sufferings of the mediator were equal in amount and worth to those whose place he took.[33]

Andrew Fuller, as quoted in the chapter devoted to him, gives implicit support to this position when he says, "If God required less than the real demerit of sin for an atonement, then there could be no satisfaction made to divine justice by such an atonement." Indeed, Fuller argues that an atonement by a substitute requires that the same end be answered, "as if the guilty party had actually suffered."[34] Because of this suffering, forgiveness—that is, the "non-imputation of punishment"—can come to the sinner; yea, if we affirm the meritorious nature of the substitution of Christ, it *must* come to the sinner for whom Christ has died.

Conclusion

The proper combination of these elements should encourage Calvinistic Baptists (and Calvinists of all sorts) to reexamine the traditional formula of "sufficient but efficient" and perhaps question its aptness as an accurate description of effectual or limited atonement— for, in actuality, such a phrase does not distinguish this view from the view of general atonement. Much less should one affirm that the intent

33. Shedd, *Theology*, 2:455.
34. Fuller, *Works*, 2:694, 695, 410.

of Christ's death was the same for all men and that he has died indeed for all men without exception. When the necessary benefits of Christ's death do not actually terminate on all men, one should see the impossibility of such a view.

A proper biblical understanding of the atonement must be built upon the following elements:

1. The creature's sin must be punished eternally and in differing degrees of intensity.

2. Forgiveness of sin means that some other way has been found to inflict an eternal punishment of the necessary intensity.

3. A substitute must meet those qualifications: that is, by his nature give eternal value to the sufferings and in his person be able to absorb the just intensity of wrath.

4. The just nature of God does not permit him to inflict more wrath on the substitute than actually becomes effectual for forgiveness of the criminal. Nor does the love of God for the Son permit such an overkill. With these four elements in place, it is proper to speak of a quantitative, as well as a qualitative, element in the atonement.

This doctrine is well adapted to strengthen two great evangelical realities: first, complete submission of the sinner to the Lordship of Christ; second, the joyful assurance of a reconciled God. The first of these is enunciated beautifully by John L. Dagg as he concludes his argument for a limited and quantitative atonement:

> Some have maintained that, if the atonement of Christ is not general, no sinner can be under obligation to believe in Christ, until he is assured that he is one of the elect. This implies that no sinner is bound to believe what God says, unless he knows that God designs to save him. God declares that there is no salvation, except through Christ; and every sinner is bound to believe this truth. If it were revealed from heaven, that but one sinner, of all our fallen race, shall be saved by Christ, the obligation to believe that there is no salvation out of Christ, would remain the same. Every sinner, to whom the revelation would be made, would be bound to look to Christ as his only possible hope, and commit himself to that sovereign mercy by which some one of the justly condemned race would be saved. The abundant mercy of our God will not be confined to the salvation of a single sinner; but it will bring many sons to glory through the sufferings of Jesus, the Captain of our salvation. Yet every sinner, who trusts in Christ for salvation, is bound to commit himself, unreservedly, to the sovereign mercy of God. If he requires some previous assurance that he is in the number of the elect, he does not surrender himself to God, as a guilty sinner ought. The gospel brings every sinner prostrate at the feet of the Great Sovereign, hoping for mercy at his will, and in his way: and the gospel is perverted when any terms short of this are offered to the offender. With this universal call to

absolute and unconditional surrender to God's sovereignty, the doctrine of particular redemption exactly harmonizes.[35]

The great Baptist preacher C. H. Spurgeon brings the pastoral and kerygmatic concerns of assurance to bear upon the marvelous truth of a just and infallible atonement in a sermon entitled "Christ's Determination to Save His People":

> First, I say it was necessary to make the atonement complete. I do not think that if our Saviour had drunk this myrrhed cup the atonement would not have been valid. It strikes me that if he had drunk this wine mingled with myrrh he would not have suffered to the extent that was absolutely necessary. We believe that Christ did on the cross suffer just enough and not one particle more than was necessary for the redemption of his people. If then this wine cup had taken away a part of his sufferings the ransom price would not have been fully complete. It would not have been fully paid. And if it had been taken away so much as a grain the atonement would not have been sufficiently satisfactory. If a man's ransom is to be paid it must be all paid. For though but a single farthing be left unpaid a man is not fully redeemed and he is not yet totally free. If then this drinking of the wine cup had taken out the smallest amount from that fearful price of agony which our Saviour paid the atonement would have been insufficient to a degree, however small, would have been enough to have caused perpetual despair, yea enough to have shut the gates of heaven against all believers. The utmost farthing must be paid. Inexorable justice never did omit so much as a fraction of its claim nor would it in this case have exonerated in any measure. Christ must pay all. The wine cup would have prevented his doing that. Therefore, he would suffer and go the whole length of suffering. He would not stop but would go through it all.[36]

Thus, the concept of definite, quantitative atonement is uniquely capable of bringing sinners to a truly penitent state in absolute submission to a holy God, and, finally, to give them assurance of his mercy toward them. Praise be to God for his unspeakable gift.

---

35. John L. Dagg, *Manual of Theology* (n.p., The Southern Baptist Publication Society, 1857; reprint ed., Harrisonburg, VA: Gano Books, 1982), pp. 330, 331.

36. C. H. Spurgeon, *A Treasury of Spurgeon on the Life and Work of Our Lord*, 6 vols. (Grand Rapids: Baker Book House, 1979), vol. 4, *The Passion and Death of Our Lord*, p. 467.

13

Perseverance of the Saints

The doctrine of perseverance of the saints partakes naturally from the influence of the other Doctrines of Grace. While often perverted into a very shallow, unbiblical, easy-believism way of thinking, this doctrine teaches us the true nature of saving grace, when properly presented in all its parts. Through the window that perseverance provides into the grace of God, one sees whether a person's repentance and faith have been prompted by the fright of the moment or by the sovereign effectual working of the Spirit. This window also casts a beam of light on the deceitfulness of the human heart and—conversely but consequently—reflects the beautiful colors of the power of God's grace.

Essential Elements

A thorough understanding of perseverance depends upon gaining a sufficient grasp of three areas: first, God's activity in preserving the believer; second, the believer's activity in persevering; third, the reality of the believer's continued sinfulness or "perfectionlessness."

Preservation: God's Activity

The idea of the eternality of salvation may be inferred from many passages in Scripture. Exceedingly familiar are the words of John 3:16: "For God so loved the world, that he gave his only begotten Son, that whosoever believeth in him should not perish, but have everlasting life." Indeed, the timeworn argument wears its strength well. If a person's belief finds Christ as its true object and thus gains life, the character of which is everlasting, it would be a strange contradiction to retain the specter of condemnation in such a condition. Something eternal destroyed in a while? How absurd. The very concept of everlasting life, premised upon the death of Christ and received by faith, carries enough weight in itself to develop a doctrine of the perseverance of true believers.

Other passages and Scripture terminology imply the final perseverance of the saints. John 5:24 so combines the sequence of hearing, believing, possession of eternal life, avoidance of condemnation, and passing from death to life that no other conclusion than that of final perseverance can be drawn. This hearing-and-believing issues in the final verdict of "no condemnation." This hearing consists not of mere sound registering in the physical faculties but of an understanding that results in hearty consent and assent. Belief in "him that sent" Jesus involves a crediting of the testimony of the Father to the person and work of Christ. Since such a hearer is presently having eternal life and therefore will not pass under the future condemning judgment, he stands in the condition of having passed from all that spiritual death involves to an irreversible condition of spiritual life, which will finally culminate in the enjoyment of all that eternal life means.

Paul also enjoys these ideas of "no condemnation" and resurrection from death to life. Romans 8:1 has as its goal the building of assurance in the life of the true believer. For those who are in Christ Jesus, "No condemnation." If that verdict could ever be changed, little real assurance could be given. Ephesians 2 pictures the saved person as the object of the movement of resurrection and ascension power. The reader may infer from this that a regenerate person might be lost again if Christ's resurrection and ascension might be reversed.

Not only is the doctrine inferred from Scripture, but the other elements of the Doctrines of Grace imply this as a necessary corollary. Insisting that the doctrine of perseverance is a part of the "Faith once delivered to the saints," for which we are to contend earnestly, A. W. Pink writes:

> In it is displayed, respectively, the honor and glory of the Father, of the Son and of the Holy Spirit, and therefore they who repudiate this truth cast a most horrible aspersion upon the character of the triune Jehovah. The final perseverance of the saints is one of the grand and distinctive blessings proclaimed by the Gospel, being an integral part of salvation itself, and therefore any outcry against this doctrine is an attack upon the very foundations of the believer's comfort and assurance.[1]

1. A. W. Pink, "The Importance of This Doctrine," from *Sword and Trowel*, Vol. IV, No. 10.

T. T. Eaton credits the doctrine of election with such a necessary outcome when he says, "If the doctrine of election be true, then the final perseverance of the saints follows as a necessary corollary."[2] Eaton supports this confidence from the scriptural foundation of 1 Peter 1:1, 2 and 2 Thessalonians 2:13.

P. H. Mell followed the same procedure but greatly expands the theological bedrock which undergirds the necessity of perseverance:

> Those whom God hath accepted in Christ, effectually called and sanctified by His Spirit cannot finally fall from grace. Calvinists argue this from the perfections of God, from the immutability of His decrees; from the covenant of redemption between the Divine Persons of the Trinity; from the covenant of grace which God has made with His people; from the atonement of Christ by which He paid the full price for the redemption of His people; from Christ's intercession; from the inhabitation of the Spirit; and from the distinct and explicit declarations of the scriptures.[3]

R. B. C. Howell, second president of the Southern Baptist Convention, followed the same course in his book *The Way of Salvation*.

> Now if in Christ Jesus you were from the beginning chosen, to salvation, and to secure it you have been actually called, and endowed with faith, and sanctification; if through him you have been pardoned, and the claims of the law against you fully satisfied; if you are recognised, and proclaimed heirs with Christ of the heavenly inheritance; if you already have everlasting life; and have his glorious promise—"Because I live ye shall live also;" what can we conclude but that your connection with Christ secures effectually, your final and complete salvation?[4]

Spurgeon argued in much the same way when he preached on this subject at the Metropolitan Tabernacle:

> You, dear friends, have most of you received as a matter of faith the doctrines of grace, and therefore to you the doctrine of final perseverance cannot require any proving, because it follows from all the other doctrines. We believe that God has an elect people whom He has chosen unto eternal life, and that truth necessarily involves the perseverance in

2. T. T. Eaton, in *Baptist Doctrines*, ed. Rev. Charles A. Jenkens (St. Louis, 1884), p. 517.

3. Patrick Hues Mell, *Predestination and the Saints' Perseverance, Stated and Defended* (Charleston: Southern Baptist Publication Society, 1851; reprint ed. The Wicket Gate, n.d.), p. 67.

4. R. B. C. Howell, *The Way of Salvation* (Charleston: Southern Baptist Publication Society, 1857), pp. 232–233.

grace. We believe in special redemption, and this secures the salvation and consequent perseverance of the redeemed. We believe in effectual calling, which is bound up with justification, a justification which ensures glorification. The doctrines of grace are like a chain—if you believe in one of them you must believe the next, for each one involves the rest; therefore I say that you who accept any of the doctrines of grace must receive this also, as involved in them. But I am about to try to prove this to those who do not receive the doctrines of grace; I would not argue in a circle, and prove one thing which you doubt by another thing which you doubt, but "to the law and to the testimony," to the actual words of Scripture we shall refer the matter.[5]

W. T. Conner's view falls well within the parameters defined by the foregoing Baptist witnesses. Election includes all the elements of providence necessary to produce perseverance:

The salvation of a man elected to salvation is from all eternity certain in the mind and purpose of God, yet it is conditioned upon faith; and it is conditioned upon a faith that perseveres and conquers. A man may be elected to salvation and yet his salvation conditioned upon the fact that somebody shall preach to him the gospel. One might ask: "Suppose God should elect a man to salvation and then the proper conditions not arise." One might as well suppose any other absurdity. That assumption assumes that a set of conditions might arise that God did not know about and had not provided for. Such is the assumption that a regenerated man should not persevere in faith.[6]

But the doctrine of perseverance does not come to us merely by inference. Although deduction is certainly not an illegitimate enterprise in theological thinking, the security of belief need not trust in that one lock only. Preservation finds unmistakable allies in the direct and unequivocal testimony of many Scripture passages. For example, in John 6 Jesus sets forth the nature of salvation as a divine enterprise from start to finish:

Then Jesus declared, "I am the bread of life. He who comes to me will never go hungry, and he who believes in me will never be thirsty. But, as I told you, you have seen me and still do not believe. All that the Father gives me will come to me, and whoever comes to me I will never drive away. For I have come down from heaven not to do my will but

5. C. H. Spurgeon, "The Final Perseverance of the Saints," from *Sword & Trowel*, Vol. IV, No. 10, p. 5.
6. Walter T. Conner, *The Gospel of Redemption* (Nashville: Broadman Press, 1945), p. 256.

to do the will of him who sent me. And this is the will of him who sent me, that I shall lose none of all that he has given me, but raise them up at the last day. For my Father's will is that everyone who looks to the Son and believes in him shall have eternal life and I will raise him up at the last day." [John 6:35–40, NIV]

In one magnificent opening of divine purpose, Jesus moves from eternity past to eternity future, showing why some are pliable and some are hard, why some come and some remain afar. "All that the Father gives me"—the covenant of redemption made with the Son from before the foundation of the world—pinpoints the particular persons on whom the blessings fall. They will come so that hunger and thirst are quenched forever. In addition, he will raise up at the last day those who are the objects of this special grace. All of those who have already been given by the Father will be drawn by the Father and will be raised up by the Son. The preservation of the believer inheres necessarily in the eternal work of God. It is the natural outflow of unconditional election, definite atonement, and effectual calling. Paul's thought in Romans 8 is the same. In an unbroken and unbreakable chain designed to focus attention on God's trustworthiness, Paul says:

> For whom he did foreknow, he also did predestinate to be conformed to the image of his Son, that he might be the firstborn among many brethren. Moreover, whom he did predestinate, them he also called: and whom he called, them he also justified: and whom he justified, them he also glorified [Rom. 8:29–30].

Every major verb in the passage is in the aorist tense, emphasizing the past and punctiliar, facticity of each action. The action moves again from eternity past to eternity future, and each verb arises in the sentence as if already accomplished. When was this accomplished? In the covenant of redemption, when God set forth the counsel of his own will as it regarded the eternal destiny of his creature, man. Yet Dale Moody suggests that this chain might be broken at any point by the noncooperation of man:

> It is not predetermined that foreknowledge will always be followed by predestination, calling, justification and glorification as were the words at the end of Romans 8. That is the normal sequence but the sequence can be broken at any point by turning again to slavery. . . . Calvinism stubbornly and mistakenly held to an unbroken sequence. It was an iron chain. . . . God indeed had a program, but it is not programmed without a place for human freedom either before faith or after faith.[7]

7. Dale Moody, The Word of Truth (Grand Rapids: Eerdmans, 1981), pp. 343–344.

Moody handles his view of freedom of the will in a thoroughly consistent manner throughout his systematic theology. Just as the man who has only general revelation can follow conscience and be saved, so can the man who hears the gospel exhibit faith in Christ by virtue of powers resident within him as an unregenerate, natural man. In like manner, according to Moody, the regenerate man does not lose this freedom and may decide at any point in his Christian pilgrimage to forsake saving faith.

The first objection to Moody's proposal is that it arises from nowhere in the text. There is not a scintilla of a suggestion in the text that man's will may thwart God's purposes. Moody's suggestion that this chain of events occurs only in the presence of faith would never be rejected by the historic Baptist Calvinists. It admits of no controversy that faith is essential and he who does not have it is not saved. The question then becomes what kind of faith saves, and how does one person have it as opposed to another. Does human faith effectuate election and so forth, or does God's power and purpose in election effectuate faith? B. H. Carroll's comment on 1 Peter gives the biblical answer and the general consensus of the first three hundred years of Baptist thought on the subject: ". . . election was not based upon any foreseen goodness in man or any foreseen repentance or faith in man, but . . . repentance and faith proceed from election, and not election from them."[8]

Thus, saving faith arises from the creative power of the divine spirit, and the test of its existence rests in the continual pursuit of a spiritual lifestyle (Rom. 8:1–17; Eph. 4:17–32). That some who begin the journey leave the road before the final destination does not at all prove that the saved man may lose his salvation; that phenomenon does demonstrate that saving faith prompted by God's Spirit manifests an enduring qualitative difference from the spurious faith prompted by the temporary carnal excitement of the unregenerate man.

A second objection to Moody's suggestion, in addition to its unwarranted imposition from outside the text, is that it contradicts the express purpose of Paul in Romans 8. The fear often manifested by one whose sins have been written plainly before him, and who rightly recognizes the subtlety of his heart, is that his own weakness and ignorance might cause him to fall. Such a one knows his inability to meet the holiness of the law (Rom. 7:14–25); but Paul assures him that the first requirement of the law has been fulfilled on his behalf by Christ (Rom. 8:1–4). Still he might be overcome by the flesh, for

8. B. H. Carroll, *An Interpretation of the English Bible*, ed. J. B. Cranfill (New York: Revell, 1913–1917), 1 Peter 1:1, 2.

he knows it is still present; but Paul assures him that the powerful presence of the Holy Spirit will cause him to mortify the flesh, to celebrate joyfully God as Father, and to share in the sufferings of Christ (vv. 5–17). The saved man senses that the glory of his salvation is not manifest as it should be, that the complete liberty of redemption fails to find sufficient expression, and that his adoption is not fully recognized; but Paul assures him that such an incomplete state is as it presently should be, and he should patiently await its completion in God's time (vv. 18–25). The saved man senses his own ignorance in his prayer life and perhaps fears that, because of this ignorance, he may miss God's will; but Paul assures him of the effectual intercession of the Spirit so that God works all things in their connections for good. Further, he reminds such a sensitive believer (and all believers should be) that these events occur, even as his calling, in accordance with God's purpose (vv. 26–28). Thereupon follows the "iron chain" of verses 29 and 30.

How incongruous and defeating of purpose would it be for Paul to intend that the reader understand he could somehow fail at any point and remove himself from God's favor! Obviously it is understood that this certainty is only for those who are "in Christ Jesus," but for such believers no hint of a possible fall should invade their confidence. John 10:25–30 contains the same direct emphasis:

> Jesus answered, "I did tell you, but you do not believe. The miracles I do in my Father's name speak for me, but you do not believe because you are not my sheep. My sheep listen to my voice; I know them, and they follow me. I give them eternal life, and they shall never perish; no one can snatch them out of my hand. My Father, who has given them to me, is greater than all; no one can snatch them out of my Father's hand. I and the Father are one" [NIV].

Here the doctrine of final preservation of the saints is tied not only to effectual call but also to particular atonement. Jesus had said earlier: ". . . I know my sheep and my sheep know me . . . I lay down my life for the sheep" (vv. 15–16, NIV). Therefore, the will, power, and moral nature of God determine the final end of those given to the Son. Father and Son are one in their determination to save and in their essential abilities to do so. God is not only willing to save but is able, or has the power; indeed, none is able to withstand or thwart his purpose, for he is omnipotent. This power of God extends not only to threatening forces outside the sheep but to the subduing of the rebellious heart, which otherwise would remain dead in its hardness (Eph. 2:1–3; 4:17–19).

In 1 Corinthians 1:8 Paul reinforces this truth by affirming: "He will keep you strong to the end, so that you will be blameless on the day of our Lord Jesus Christ" (NIV). Likewise, that this same preservative power is operative on the heart and will of the objects of grace is echoed in Philippians 1:6: ". . . he who began a good work in you will carry it on to completion until the day of Christ Jesus" (NIV).

The strong material of Philippians 2:12–13 constitutes a bridge between the concepts of preservation and perseverance:

> Therefore, my dear friends, as you have always obeyed—not only in my presence, but now much more in my absence—continue to work out your salvation with fear and trembling, for it is God who works in you to will and to act according to his good purpose [NIV].

In this Scripture, the doctrine of perseverance involves the perfect confluence of divine sovereignty in preserving us and human initiative, work, and energy in pursuing holiness. When the doctrine of the perseverance of the saints is transformed into "once saved, always saved," one needs to take great pains in defining "saved." In this aphorism, "saved" quite often equals human performance of a certain prayer formula, a certain kind of emotional experience, or a certain type of mentality at one time about the Lord Jesus Christ. Faith is reduced to "inviting Jesus into your heart," and repentance becomes an admission of sinfulness. The realities of the changed mind that now delights in God's law, the repentant spirit that mourns its sinfulness, and the hungering, thirsting, and panting after God and his righteousness tends to be shifted into the province of follow-up, rather than established in its rightful place as the essence of the gospel message.

According to the passage at hand (Phil. 2:12–13), those upon whom God's good pleasure is operative will work in accordance with (κα⁻ τεργάζεσθε) their own salvation (the salvation that has already come to them and is their present possession by God's grace). God preserves all of those he has chosen as his own, but he preserves them not only from eternal ruin and the consequences of sin. He fulfills the angels' prophetic announcement, "He shall save his people from their sins."

Perseverance: The Believer's Activity

One striking truth about the biblical doctrine of salvation is that perseverance is of its essence; it is not a mere by-product or lagniappe but an inseparable element of the one reality. Within this doctrine, three further truths melt together to give full biblical strength to its exposition: first, perseverance is inevitable; second, struggle characterizes its manifestations; third, the deceitfulness of the human heart is laid bare by the continued application of the principle of perseverance.

THE INEVITABILITY OF PERSEVERANCE

The apostle Peter captured the first truth in these words: "His divine power has given us everything we need for life and godliness through our knowledge of him who called us by his own glory and goodness" (2 Peter 1:3, NIV).

Not only does life come by "his divine power" but godliness also. If we affirm that God's power grants life to the believer, we cannot evacuate such life of godliness, the presence of which is the only evidence of life and thus of the presence of divine power. Godliness does not come in a climactic second experience, nor as a result of a second "more meaningful" decision, but is the natural outgrowth and increasingly dominating concern of the truly saved person. Why is this true? God's power has granted it!

Paul's letter to Titus is zealous of the same truth: "For the grace of God that brings salvation has appeared to all men. It teaches us to say "No" to ungodliness and worldy passions, and to live self-controlled, upright and godly lives in this present age" (Titus 2:11–12, NIV).

What grace teaches us to say "No" to ungodliness? The grace that brings salvation. What grace teaches us to live self-controlled, upright, and godly lives? The grace that brings salvation!

Both the power and grace of God operate to produce salvation— but only a salvation that includes godliness. Where no godliness is in process, one can only conclude that neither the power nor grace of God has worked effectually.

Inevitability of perseverance is assumed in Ephesians 4:20–24, and its companion passage, Colossians 3:5–10. Godliness is argued in these passages from the standpoint that the purpose of salvation is the eventual restoration of the *imago dei* in man.

Common elements in the passages are several: the old man is replaced by the new man; knowledge contributes to the transformation; the result points toward likeness to God, reflective of his holiness. The new man in both passages arises from the creative act of God (Eph. 4:24; cf. Col. 3:10).

In essence, the Christian life progresses from one act of taking off the practices and attitudes characteristic of the unregenerate life to other and more thorough disrobings throughout life. The command in Ephesians 4 to put off the old man (also a grammatical possibility in Colossians 3:9) does not contradict Paul's affirmation in Romans 6:6 that the old man was crucified. The old man, any man in his unregenerate condition, is dominated by the flesh and is no partaker of the Spirit. When the Spirit regenerates and indwells a person, the flesh begins to undergo a gradual process of being subdued. Thus dies the old man, and his deeds are gradually replaced with those of the new man—after true righteousness and holiness in accordance with proper knowledge. It is inevitable that what is alive and growing will overcome what is dead.

As that occurs, the proper relationship between one's affections, will, and mind is restored. The renewing of the mind gradually and inevitably transforms the rest of the life unto the image of the Creator, the very purpose for which God initiated salvation.

The indwelling of the Spirit, according to Romans 8, makes perseverance inevitable. Only two options exist for any person—to be carnally minded or to be spiritually minded. The first results in death—eternal death—and is the condition of every man outside of Christ. The second results in life and peace and is the condition of every man in Christ, for "if any man have not the Spirit of Christ, he is none of his" (Rom. 8:9). Every Christian is in the Spirit, spiritually minded, and, as a result, mortifies the deeds of the body. Paul could not conceive of a Christian who did not progressively pursue the way of the Spirit.

THE ONGOING STRUGGLE

A second undeniable aspect of one's perseverance encompasses the reality of struggle. The idea of struggle is almost swallowed up by the emphasis many place on the victorious Christian life. Anyone who experiences struggle and striving from day to day and is aware of an ongoing internal conflict finds little but ridicule from the many who deny that such inheres within even the most mature Christian experiences.

Paul affirms the necessity of vigorous struggle in 1 Corinthians 9:27 when he confesses: "But I keep under my body, and bring it into subjection: lest that by any means, when I have preached to others, I myself should be a castaway." In order that he not play the part of a mere proclaimer of events yet have no place in the game, Paul trained to enter into the conflict that he, too, might gain the crown. There may perhaps exist a multitude of gospel proclaimers who never train for combat and thus meet disapproval when they stand before the Judge. John L. Dagg clearly understood the force of this Pauline manifesto:

> The explanation which has been given of this passage, removes all appearance of inconsistency between it and the doctrine of the saints' final perseverance; yet it admits that Paul was stimulated to activity and

perseverance in the Christian conflict, by the belief that his obtaining of the crown depended on his perseverance and success in the struggle. They who understand the doctrine of perseverance to imply that God's people will obtain the crown without the struggle, totally mistake the matter. The doctrine is, that God's people will persevere in the struggle; and to suppose that they will obtain the crown without doing so, is to contradict the doctrine. It is a wretched and fatal perversion of the doctrine, if men conclude that, having been once converted, they will be saved, whatever may be their course of life. God's word plainly declares, that "he who soweth to the flesh shall of the flesh reap corruption:" and every man who does not keep under his body and bring it into subjection, and who does not endure to the end, in this spiritual conflict, will assuredly fail to receive the crown. Without this, no conversion which he may have undergone, and not even a call to apostleship, will secure the approbation of the final Judge.[9]

The refusal to admit that the struggle is normal as well as necessary belittles the Bible's description of fleshly lusts as "warring against the soul" (1 Peter 2:11). The refusal to engage in the struggle marks one as disapproved or reprobate.

Paul's discussion of the struggle in Romans 7 must be understood as that of a Christian. He wants to do good; a lost man loves evil. He delights in God's law; the lost man is hostile to God and does not submit to God's law. Then why does he describe himself as a slave to sin and a prisoner to the law of sin? Certainly, some would contend, such a condition cannot be true of a Christian. The careful reader must see that, though the law of sin is present "in my members," it is only "with the flesh" that Paul says he serves the law of sin (Rom. 7:23, 25). The flesh, that principle of seeking pleasure from the created order without primary allegiance to the glory of God and obedience to God, is no friend to the Spirit nor to the process of sanctification. It should not be startling that Paul claims that "with the flesh" he serves the law of sin. Romans 8 continues to represent the flesh, a principle or affection that dominates the "old man," as the enemy of life in the Spirit. So it is with Galatians 5. Rather than deny the captivity of the *flesh* to the law of sin (even Romans 8:1–4 reaffirms this while affirming that the person as a whole is free from the law of sin and death), the Christian must realize that it is exactly because of this reality that he is called on to mortify the flesh. Thereby continues the truth that struggle is exactly the condition of a Christian. The slavery to sin is not absolute but is in the context of the Christian's desire to follow

9. John L. Dagg, D.D., *Manual of Theology* (The Southern Baptist Publication Society, 1857; reprint ed., Harrisonburg, VA: Gano Books, 1982), p. 144.

God's law. His status as prisoner is true in the context of his effort to attain the proper freedom for which Christ has freed him. In light, therefore, of the new love for God's law, the desire for holiness and freedom in Christ that is set before the saved person, Paul describes a constant state of struggle the redeemed one has in seeking to consummate these growing desires. Because of this, the Christian's constant confession must be: "I do not consider myself yet to have taken hold of it. But one thing I do: Forgetting what is behind and straining toward what is ahead, I press on toward the goal to win the prize for which God has called me heavenward in Christ Jesus" (Phil. 3:13–14, NIV).

The promise of struggle also permeates Paul's remarks concerning the flesh versus the Spirit in Galatians 5:16–26. The reality of the warfare described leads Paul to a conclusion: "You do not do what you want" (v. 17, NIV). This is a strangely comforting statement. On the one hand, its message clearly precludes the Christian's complete satisfaction in any spiritual activity. His perception of God's holiness and the demands of proper spiritual worship always outstrip his performance. The Christian desires more than he can accomplish, so that the presence of the flesh truly means "you do not do what you want." On the other hand, the flesh can never win an unchallenged battle. Since any movement the Christian makes toward gratification of the flesh finds immediate resistance from the Spirit, sin never produces joy. Again, "ye cannot do the things that ye would." Further, the passage clearly teaches that since the Christian, by the Spirit, will continually wage warfare against the flesh, in truth he lives by the Spirit (v. 25).

The Human Heart's Deceitfulness

The third reality to be affirmed in light of the doctrine of perseverance is the deceitfulness of the human heart. The final conclusion that true faith exists may not be drawn from any apparent sincerity, fervency, or emotion at the initiation of a supposed Christian life. Although the first moments of repentance and faith may have all the marks of genuineness, they may fail to produce a continued harvest of righteousness. Therefore, a true biblical understanding of saving faith must always include the element of longevity—for the faith that ends never really partook of the nature of true saving faith. This element of perseverance, then, allows for the deceitfulness and perversity of the human heart. Even as Paul told the Corinthians when he heard of their divisions, "No doubt there have to be differences among you to show which of you have God's approval" (1 Cor. 11:19, NIV), so the process of time brings enough pressure to bear on professors of the faith to show which have God's approval.

The refiner's fire blazes in three forms as it burns out the dross and refines the gold. Moral tests cause many a failure in the demonstration of true faith. The pressure of persecution—mental, physical, social, or economic—eliminates others as candidates for persevering faith. Doctrinal unfaithfulness proves the spurious nature of many other professions of faith. Slight divergences or temporary lapses in these areas do not necessarily prove that one's faith is false (though they might), but continued and undaunted pursuit of unacceptable positions in any of these categories reveals a heart of unbelief.

Moral Failure. The sorry spectacle that invaded the glorious life of David and brought sorrow till the end of his days demonstrates that isolated moral failure does not necessarily point to a false faith. Continued pursuit of the way of the flesh, however, is a sure sign that one's profession is vain. "If we claim to have fellowship with him yet walk in the darkness, we lie and do not live by the truth," says the beloved apostle John (1 John 1:6, NIV). He develops this thought further when he asserts, "No one who is born of God will continue to sin, because God's seed remains in him; he cannot go on sinning, because he has been born of God. . . . Anyone who does not do what is right is not a child of God. . . ." (1 John 3:9–10, NIV). Such clear and powerful proclamations should clear away any doubt that a lifestyle of pursued disobedience to the moral demands of God is absolutely incongruous with a faith born of the Spirit. John's onslaught against moral laxity continues intermittently until the end of his First Epistle, when he introduces his parting paragraph with the reminder, "We know that anyone born of God does not continue to sin; the one who was born of God keeps him safe, and the evil one does not touch him" (5:18, NIV).

Paul's concordance with John on this issue is no less clear. After describing the deeds of the flesh in Galatians 5, Paul concludes that "those who live like this will not inherit the kingdom of God" (v. 21, NIV). In Romans he warns: "For if ye live after the flesh, ye shall die . . ." (8:13). In Ephesians, after a detailed exhortation concerning the character of a Christian's moral life, Paul reminds his readers: "For of this you can be sure: No immoral, impure or greedy person—such a man is an idolater—has any inheritance in the kingdom of Christ and of God. Let no one deceive you with empty words, for because of such things God's wrath comes on those who are disobedient" (Eph. 5:5–6, NIV).

E. C. Dargan handily summarizes the Pauline development of the relation between faith and works.

In the sixth chapter of Romans Paul indignantly repels the idea that the believer may continue in sin, and declares on the contrary that he who is united with Christ by a living faith is really dead to sin, and as one who is alive from the dead, should offer himself unto God for the exclusive work of righteousness. Moreover, he declares that such union with Christ as the believer has in faith is really a new creation, a new life, a new motive and help to righteousness. (Cf. 2 Cor. 5:14; Gal. 6:15; Col. 3:3–11; Titus 2:11–14, and many others.) In all his epistles he enjoins a noble morality and a warm-hearted benevolence as the outcome of the faith which unites us with the pure and loving Jesus. "If any man have not the spirit of Christ, he is none of his", is the emphatic saying of Rom. 8:9. It is as certain as anything can be that in teaching justification by faith Paul does not mean an empty thing called faith which leaves the heart destitute of holiness, the life barren of good deeds.[10]

James firmly established the same point throughout his Epistle. He discusses how true faith exhibits itself in a variety of situations and in relation to a number of sinful human tendencies. In 2:14–26 his point becomes uncomfortably and irrefutably displayed by a threefold demonstration. First, true faith reacts lovingly and correctively to physical needs of a "brother or sister," while false faith indulges only in religious platitudes. Second, false faith, characterized only by intellectual comprehension, differs in no essential from the "faith" of demons. Third, the Old Testament examples of true faith lived by virtue of an inseparable connection between faith and faithfulness. "As the body without the spirit is dead, so faith without deeds is dead" (2:26, NIV).

Persecution and Trial. The restoration of Peter and perhaps the recovery of John Mark demonstrate that a temporary lapse under the pressure of a situation by no means shuts the door against the possibility of true faith. The history of the church uncovers many a faltering and faint soul who eventually seals his faith with his blood. The opportunities have been abundant and will continue to be so, in one form or another. "The testing of your faith develops perseverance," says James (1:3, NIV). "Ah, yes," adds Peter: "All kinds of trials have come so that the genuineness of your faith may be demonstrated (and genuineness in faith is more desirable than refined gold) and may result in praise glory, and honor when Jesus Christ is revealed" (1 Peter 1:6–7, paraphrased). Paul speaks in unanimity with James and Peter as he reflects on his own experience: "That is why I am suffering as I am. . . . Endure hardship with us like a good soldier of Christ Jesus.

10. E. C. Dargan, D.D., *The Doctrines of our Faith* (Nashville: Sunday School Board of the Southern Baptist Convention, 1905), pp. 161–162.

. . . I am suffering even to the point of being chained like a criminal.
. . . I endure everything for the sake of the elect . . ." (2 Tim. 1:12; 2:3,
9–10, NIV).

Paul, in Romans 8, lists the willingness to suffer as one objective
element of the witness of the Spirit. We are heirs of God "if indeed we
share in his sufferings in order that we may also share in his glory"
(v. 17, NIV). Moreover, Paul considered suffering an opportunity granted
by the grace of God just as surely as saving faith had been granted:
"For it has been granted to you on behalf of Christ not only to believe
on him, but also to suffer for him, since you are going through the
same struggle you saw I had, and now hear that I still have" (Phil.
1:29–30, NIV). The thought centers on the fact that Spirit-wrought faith
inevitably leads to suffering, for it cannot compromise with the world.
Thus, opportunity for suffering becomes the gracious evidence of the
reality of faith as well as the means of purifying it.

In the parable of the sower (Matt. 13:3–23), the second seed sown
resulted in apparent success. But in the end, the "stony ground hearer"
(as the Puritans generally referred to this type) fell away. And what
caused the fatal lapse? "When trouble or persecution comes because
of the word, he quickly falls away." So it was with By-Ends in *The
Pilgrim's Progress*. He gives a clear exposition of his view of religion in
the following speech:

> Why, they, after their headstrong manner, conclude that it is duty to
> rush on their journey all weathers; and I am for waiting for wind and
> tide. They are for hazarding all for God at a clap; and I am for taking
> all advantages to secure my life and estate. They are for holding their
> notions, though all other men are against them; but I am for religion in
> what, and so far as the times, and my safety, will bear it. They are for
> religion when in rags and contempt; but I am for him when he walks in
> his golden slippers, in the sunshine, and with applause.[11]

This attitude in reality characterizes all who would fall from the truth
in time of persecution.

Persecution and the possibility of faltering under its load appear to
be part of the background of the admonitions in the Book of Hebrews.
The passage in Hebrews 10:26–39 specifically mentions this exposure
to "insult and persecution," the imprisonment of many, and the con-
fiscation of the property of others. While the writer appeared confident
that his readers were not among those who would shrink back and be

11. John Bunyan, *The Whole Works of John Bunyan*, 3 vols., *The Pilgrim's Progress*
(Paternoster Row, London: Blackie & Sons, 1875; reprint ed., Grand Rapids: Baker
Book House, 1977), 3:134.

destroyed, he nevertheless warned them that a faith that could not overcome persecution was not saving faith at all. To succumb to Jewish intimidation was to reject the uniqueness of the content of the Christian faith. First, the atoning work of Christ must be cast aside. Jesus was set apart, sanctified as the only Savior and fulfillment of the sacrificial system by his death. No sacrifice for sins remains if any is sought outside him (vv. 26, 29). Second, the Spirit realizes the work of Christ in the life of the believer. If his gracious activity finds no place in our apprehensions and loyalties, we can look to nothing but the reality of facing the living God with all our unholiness still upon us. Therefore, persecution tests the genuineness of one's understanding and mental acceptance of divine things, as well as his steadfast faithfulness to them.

The Epistle to the Hebrews assures its readers that Christ has died effectually to secure salvation for his people (Heb. 2:9–18; 6:16–20; 7:20–28; 9:11–15, 27–28; 10:14). God's own faithfulness sets itself toward the identical goal (Heb. 6:13–18). He will not fail. Hebrews 11 demonstrates that faithfulness unto death characterizes the people of God. Therefore, if one seeks to avoid persecution by denying the faith, he demonstrates only that he partakes not of the faith of Christ, and he gains only a delayed terror, and that under the wrath of almighty God.

Doctrinal Failure. That Apollos could be instructed in the way of Christ more perfectly and that Peter considered some Pauline utterances hard to understand indicate that some degrees of doctrinal ignorance and variation are tolerable within Christian parameters. Those truly converted, however, will be reclaimed from error when properly instructed. Those who persist in doctrinal error give evidence that they do not have true faith.

Paul indicated that some members of the Galatian churches perched on a dangerous theological precipice. When he says, "You have fallen away from grace" (Gal. 5:4, NIV), he is speaking of their theological understanding. A false teacher had so influenced them that he caused them to cease "obeying the truth" (v. 7). If they are not recovered from this error, which sets aside unmerited grace for human performance of the law, they would obligate themselves to gain salvation by absolute obedience to the whole law. Thus, their falling away from the teaching of grace would become proof that they never received the righteousness of Christ; for he who knows that he must have the righteousness of Christ credited to his account can never flatter himself with his own righteousness.

John approaches the doctrine of the incarnation with the same seriousness. Any who deny that Jesus is the Christ come in the flesh are not of God (1 John 2:22, 4:2–3). Perhaps such people were aligned with the church for a season. That does not matter. Visible identification with the church is no proof of true faith. John is convinced that those who "went out from us," that is from the church's teaching as well as its fellowship, demonstrate that they never possessed true saving faith (1 John 2:18–20).

Those, however, who are truly saved will recognize and believe the truth about God incarnate. The effectual working of the Spirit has taught them the truth experientially. Their minds, therefore, receive propositionally what the Spirit approves to them experientially. Only those who receive and abide in that doctrinal truth have eternal life (1 John 2:20–25).

Timothy's congregation reeled under the blow of some false but influential teachers. Paul gave serious instruction to Timothy in light of those serious realities:

> Avoid godless chatter, because those who indulge in it will become more and more ungodly. Their teaching will spread like gangrene. Among them are Hymenaeus and Philetus, who have wandered away from the truth. They say that the resurrection has already taken place, and they destroy the faith of some. Nevertheless, God's solid foundation stands firm, sealed with this inscription "The Lord knows those who are his," and, "Everyone who confesses the name of the Lord must turn away from wickedness" [2 Tim. 2:16–19, NIV].

Their denial of the resurrection destroyed the faith of some. But what kind of faith could be destroyed? That of those who really belong to the Lord? Not at all. The *temporary* faith of spurious believers is destroyed. God's elect will certainly maintain true faith, for the Lord knows those who are his. They are the ones who flee (doctrinal) wickedness.

Persevering in the (doctrinal) faith serves as the backdrop for several of the warnings in Hebrews. True believers will not lapse back into the observance of Jewish ritual and sacrifice clearly fulfilled by Jesus. He is faithful in maintaining God's house, which house is composed of all who hold on to courage and hope (3:6). Those who hold their confidence till the end are the ones who have come to share in Christ (3:14). Continued and clear demonstration of the truth of the gospel is of no value to one who does not mix hearing it with faith (4:2).

Such clear presentation is doubly troublesome when combined with undeniable accompaniments of spiritual power and temporary manifestations of repentance, followed by a final and knowledgeable departure from the truth of the gospel (Heb. 6:4–6). For such a one, the verdict is "impossible to renew unto repentance." Unbelief combined with ignorance will damn a man in eternity, but leaves him open to the grace of God in this life. Unbelief with knowledge shuts one off from the possibility of repentance in this life. Such was the danger of the Pharisees who attributed to Beelzebub the miracles of Jesus done in the Spirit's power. Many who stoned Stephen doubtless raged against him as, in their understanding, a blasphemer against the law; others just as surely raged against God as they in truth "resisted the Spirit."

Thus, Hebrews 6:4–6 intensifies the total biblical picture of the nature of true repentance. The next two verses clarify that it runs well—not for only a time but to the end—and produces proper fruit. Some ground produces only a pestiferous crop though blessed with rain and proper light; other ground produces the good crop. True repentance and faith always produce the latter.

One can see the necessity of affirming that perseverance is the essence of saving faith. The deceitfulness of the human heart and the subtlety of sin demand it. True faith is that which perseveres and progresses under trial, in true holiness.

No Perfection

In addition to preservation and perseverance, the doctrine of perseverance of the saints assumes that those being made holy never achieve sinlessness. The sharp razor-edge of truth must be walked carefully at this point.

ABSOLUTE VERSUS RELATIVE DEFINITIONS

While affirming the continual and inevitable pursuit of holiness that characterizes the Christian, one must also affirm that the holiness, righteousness, and perfection attained by the Christian in the power of the Spirit are relative, not absolute.

The Bible employs the word *righteousness* in both an absolute and a relative sense. Philippians 3:9—"the righteousness that comes from God"—speaks of absolute righteousness. The same is true in 2 Corinthians 5:21, Romans 4:4, 5, 22–25. The "righteousness" of Matthew 5:20 and 6:1 is a relative righteousness. The righteousness of true believers conforms to the guidelines of internal holiness rather than mere external performance such as the Pharisees pursued. Such is the "true righteousness" spoken of by Paul in Ephesians 4:24. It involves an understanding of the righteous demands of God's law, coupled with a persevering pursuit to be "like God" in true righteousness and holiness. Those who pursue such righteousness find fulfillment when Christ appears (1 John 3:1–3).

The apostle John identifies those who do what is right as righteous, just as Christ is righteous (1 John 3:7). The double entendre holds the interpretive key. Those who see the true righteousness of Christ and truly have it credited to them will make it not only the object of their trust but the pattern of their practice.

"Perfect" also has this double connotation. For example, Matthew 5:48 and Philippians 3:12 employ it in an absolute sense as a standard by which the Christian judges his life. As an absolute, perfection constitutes the goal of God's grace in his elect in that "he which hath begun a good work in you will perform it until the day of Jesus Christ (Phil. 1:6). Departed saints, though not yet recipients of the resurrected body, are called "just men made perfect" (Heb. 12:23).

"Perfect" in a relative sense, can also refer to various stages of Christian progress. Enlarged understanding of divine truth and consistent exhibition of Christian character are described by the word *perfect*. In this sense the apostle Paul includes himself among the "perfect" (Phil. 3:15), although he had just confessed that he did not consider himself perfect (Phil. 3:12). Job, though called "a perfect man," confessed truly: "If I justify myself, mine own mouth shall condemn me: if I say, I am perfect, it shall also prove me perverse" (Job 9:20).

Therefore, while affirming the necessity of holiness and warning against any excuse for indulging in sin, the Christian must avoid teaching "perfectionism." This error has risen intermittently in the history of the church, and in the present generation again threatens to dismember the gospel. Those involved do not regard it as a classical error but likely see themselves as the harbingers of pious, godly ideas that can lead only to greater honoring of God. Such a phenomenon demonstrates that some of the contemporary generation exhibits a poverty of understanding of classical Protestant theology and the errors it has confronted and refuted.

The Errors of Contemporary Perfectionism

In the history of the church, perfectionism has appeared in many forms. From the Montanists through the Pentecostal-type exaggeration of Wesleyan perfectionism, several errors manage to repeat themselves. This last quarter of the twentieth century, however, supplies its own vocabulary and *sitz im leben*, to recast the old coin.

David Needham, in his book *Birthright*,[12] and Peter Lord, in his

12. David C. Needham, *Birthright* (Portland, Multnomah Press, 1979).

sermon "Turkeys and Eagles,"[13] provide contemporary examples of the dominant expressions of this recurring error. The book and the sermon employ highly popularized and sometimes offensive language and develop their positive content largely in opposition to popular caricatures and straw men. Although their style increases audience appeal, it does little to enhance theological understanding. Often the real issues involved are obscured. Because of its currency, this expression of perfectionism will provide the springboard for a brief analysis of the critical problems raised by the issue of perfectionism. The errors are of two sorts: (1) those directly stated, and (2) those that certainly follow.

Errors Directly Stated. The first error lies in the definition of sin and owes its content to contemporary existentialism and old-time Pelagianism. Needham describes sin variously as "a strange abiding emptiness . . . a shallowness, a vague loneliness." In essence, he says:

> Sin is more pointedly the expression of man's struggle with the meaning of his existence while missing life from God. It is all the varieties of ways man deals with and expresses his alienation from his Creator as he encounters the inescapable issue of meaning.[14]

Needham later expresses the nonnegotiable character of his understanding of this point when he reminds the reader to bear in mind "the relationship between sin and the problem of meaning because the rest of the book builds on this fundamental concept."

Needham denies that any principle of indwelling sin, evil in its nature, remains in the Christian. He prefers to speak of a principle, "not evil in itself," of the "incessant demand for meaning." As he summarizes sin in the Christian, he defines it as "the avoidable failure of the individual to fulfill the purpose for which he exists."[15]

Although a lengthy treatise could be consumed in discussing the errors involved in such a view, three brief but suggestive statements must suffice. One, that sin primarily consists of moral rebellion against the holy law of God virtually escapes consideration. This view substitutes a man-centered "quest for meaning" for the God-centered obligations of moral law. Man is only an uninformed and misguided "Alfie" to be pitied, rather than a wicked rebel deserving condemnation. Two, that sin exists only in knowledgeable volitional activity is the heart of Pelagianism. The will, rather than the essential affections, are the seat

13. Peter Lord, "Turkeys and Eagles," *Fulness,* ed. Ras Robinson (Fort Worth: Nov–Dec 1981), pp. 8–11.
14. Needham, *Birthright,* p. 25.
15. Ibid., p. 124.

of sin in this view. Three, the implicit perfectionism of this position is subject to all the criticisms brought against it throughout the history of the church (see Warfield's *Perfectionism*). *The Baptist Mission Magazine of Massachusetts* published this simple but perceptive poem:

> Perfection! Tis a mark divine,
> In all God's works we see it shine
> From man's best deeds excluded;
> And who to claim it does presume
> Incurs perversion in its room
> And shows himself deluded.[16]

A second fundamental error is the identification of "flesh" with strictly material realities. The activities of the flesh, according to Needham, are merely habits practiced due to years of programming the brain in a certain way. He describes flesh as "bones and muscles, glands and senses" and, in addition, "the vast, unbelievably intricate, electronic chemical complex which is culturally, genetically, diabolically (at times), geographically, and pathologically-influenced mortality."[17] The flesh extends its influence into the Christian's life by "constantly receiving independent 'meaning possibilities' from its vast, computerized brain reservoir."[18]

Serious misunderstandings plague such a view. Although "flesh" sometimes refers to "body" in Scripture, when viewed as a principle of sin in opposition to the Spirit, it refers to a moral and spiritual reality (Gal. 5:13–21; Rom. 8:5–14). Its relationship to the body rests only in its present manifestation through the pre-resurrection body. The fact that "flesh" does not equate to body should be demonstrated clearly by Romans 6, which admonishes the Christian to submit the parts of his body to God as instruments of righteousness. But if the body is "flesh" that lusts against the Spirit, it cannot be an instrument of righteousness. After the resurrection, though the child of God will still have the flesh of the body, he will no longer experience the presence of the "flesh" that operates in opposition to the Spirit. In short, flesh is an affection that focuses on enjoyment of the creature without primary reverence for and worship of the Creator. In the unregenerate man, this affection dominates all his activities; in the regenerate, the flesh is ever-present as a hindering force but is more and more mortified and subjugated: "If you are living according to the flesh you are on the verge of dying, but if, by the Spirit, you are consistently putting

---

16. *The Baptist Mission Magazine of Massachusetts*, Vol. IV, No. 5.
17. Needham, *Birthright*, p. 79.
18. Ibid., p. 82.

to death the practices characteristic of the flesh, you shall live" (Rom. 8:13, paraphrased).

The third error, and perhaps the most devastating, consists of an unfortunate misunderstanding of "righteousness." Although Needham's work is confusing because of his mingling of theological categories, if one works through the morass of misperceptions, he will basically find a rejection of the doctrine of justification by faith and an approximation of the Roman Catholic doctrine of justifying righteousness.

Needham's failure to appreciate the doctrine of imputed righteousness involves him in further errors. The biblical distinction between regeneration and justification falls by the wayside. In addition, this theological oversight produces a sad misrepresentation of the two parts of justification (pardon for sins and imputation of righteousness). He writes:

> Contrary to much popular teaching [whose?], regeneration is more than having something taken away (sins forgiven) or having something added to you (a new nature with the assistance of the Holy Spirit). . . . This miracle is more than a "judicial" act of God. It is an act so REAL that it is right to say that a Christian's essential nature is righteous rather than sinful.[19]

Peter Lord, a Baptist pastor, popularized this concept. Although motivated by earnestness, his communicative style so ridicules imputed righteousness that it borders on blasphemy:

> Do you know what the gift of righteousness is? Righteousness is not a gown with which I cover my dirty, filthy self. That is the picture of righteousness I heard most of my life. People told me that God says, "You are a dirty, rotten wretch. I'm going to put a gown around you so when I look down from Heaven, I won't see your dirty, rotten, wretched self." The Bible says I am as righteous as Jesus. Was Jesus a dirty, rotten, wretched thing with a gown wrapped around him? No, he was righteous on the inside.[20]

Perhaps one should read Zechariah 3:3–5 before considering the clothing illustration contemptible.

Several problems with the above view of righteousness deserve expansion but must be satisfied with a brief statement. First, regeneration is not judicial at all, but should be identified with a change of

19. Ibid., pp. 25–30.
20. Lord, "Turkeys and Eagles," p. 11.

affection and a renewed mind. Scripture employs such ideas as quickening, birth from above, the new birth, and creation to communicate this truth (Eph. 2:1–4; John 3; 1 Peter 1; Eph. 2:10). Next, justification should be seen as pardon for sin and imputation of righteousness, both of which gifts come from the passive and active obedience of Christ. Finally, "actual" righteousness, or righteousness on the inside, never becomes final in this life but is progressive and gradual and must never be made the basis on which we stand before God. Therefore, any view that substitutes internal, personal righteousness for external, imputed righteousness dooms the believer by robbing him of the forensic declaration of "no condemnation."

There is a striking congruity between the view of justification espoused by the Council of Trent and that endorsed by Needham and Lord. Such similarity in itself should give pause to those who view this phenomenon with uncritical approval. Compare Needham's definition above with the Roman Catholic definition set forth at Trent:

> This disposition, or preparation, is followed by Justification itself, which is not remission of sins merely, but also the sanctification and renewal of the inward man, through the voluntary reception of the grace, and of the gifts, whereby man of unjust becomes just, and of an enemy a friend, that so he may be an heir according to hope of life everlasting.[21]

The fourth directly stated error is the affirmation of sinless perfection. Although Needham says that "absolute perfection" is a "tragic distortion" early in his book, the logic of his own position eventually forces him to admit that it is the logical outcome. In a footnote he states, "Not only is sin avoidable, but righteousness is assumed to be the norm for every believer's behavior. . . . Therefore, in some sense sinless perfection must be seen as a theoretical possibility."[22] Again, Peter Lord gives sermonic expression to this idea:

> "How many sins did you commit yesterday, and how many acts of righteousness did you do yesterday?" Let me tell you my record. Sins—0; righteous acts, I think around 300. That's right—around 300. The first act of righteousness I did yesterday was take a bath. Do you know something? Everything a Christian does, except the sins he chooses to do, is an act of righteousness. Let me say that to you again. Everything a Christian does, except when he sins, is an act of righteousness. For years I lived under the bondage of sin all the time—thinking that everything

21. Philip Schaff, *Creeds of Christendom*, 3 vols. (Grand Rapids: Baker Book House), 2:94.
22. Needham, *Birthright*, p. 135.

I liked was illegal, immoral, or fattening. If you did more sins than righteousness yesterday, or any day, you are in danger.[23]

The "new perfectionism" appears to have arisen from a truncated Darbyite anthropology. Affirming two natures in the regenerate man, the Plymouth Brethren, following J. N. Darby, contended that the old nature retains all its distinctiveness, affections, and tendencies; the new nature takes residence alongside it and remains uncontaminated by the old nature with which it is in ceaseless conflict. Proponents of the "new perfectionism" simply erase the concept of the old nature and define the Christian totally in terms of a Darbyite new nature. Therefore, sin, when it does recur, is an accident to be overcome simply by remembering and confessing who we are in our new nature.

The rejection of the two-nature theory is proper, for that theory was always a perversion of biblical sanctification. To substitute only one-half of it, however, is a worse perversion. A proper understanding of sanctification must grasp the biblical teaching that human nature is unchanging in its makeup; mind, affections, and will are present in both unregenerate and regenerate man. The fall produced a condition in which the affections dominate and therefore render a man captive to every suggestion of self-seeking instigated by the world and the devil. The regenerate man is freed from that absolute dominance of the self-seeking affections (flesh) and is made new in the attitude of his mind. The mind, in turn, which receives and understands the biblical revelation more and more (but never perfectly in this life), rules and properly aligns the affections and, thus, the will. Therefore, while a man may do what could be considered right externally, it is never "actually" righteous, for it proceeds from a nature in which the crea-ture-centeredness of the affections is not absolutely mortified though consistently dying (Rom. 8:1–15; 12:1–2; Eph. 4:17–24. Gal. 5:13–16).

Errors That Certainly Follow. In addition to the four hurtful errors mentioned above, the position under discussion rests upon several erroneous presuppositions that—if carried forth logically—result in several destructive implications.

First, this view eliminates the necessity of Christ's continued intercession. Only as one continues as a sinner does he need Christ to intercede. All sin, however slight, deserves eternal death, and only Christ's interceding for his elect on the basis of the atonement keeps one preserved from hell. If one has done 300 acts of righteousness and no sins, he can dispense with Christ's intercession that day.

Second, this denies the biblical teaching that sanctification is con-

---

23. Lord, "Turkeys and Eagles," p. 10.

tinuous as well as inevitable in this life (1 Thess. 5:23–24; Phil. 3:12–16) and, instead, plots it as a jagged line with long periods of completion punctuated by accidental falls.

Third, it reduces justification to one-half of its biblical self. Only forgiveness at the beginning, and thereafter intermittently, is necessary. Imputed righteousness falls away as unnecessary in light of the "actual righteousness" the Christian achieves. "Not having a righteousness of my own" (Phil. 3:9) could not fall from the lips of one who affirmed such actual righteousness.

Fourth, it assumes that actions may have integrity apart from their source and remain untarnished by a coexisting area of holiness in the one doing the action. This particular concept of isolated holiness is a hangover from Darbyite dualism and is certainly not an enemy to Gnostic anthropology. In actuality, however, the nature of an act is determined by the full character of the person who does it. Neither holiness nor sin can be abstracted from the subject. A cup of cold water given in the name of Jesus by one who is regenerate is better than exorcism of demons by one who is not known by the Lord (Matt. 7:21–23; 10:40–42). Paul's painful appraisal of himself in Romans 7:14–25 does not attempt to abstract sin as an entity apart from his "nature" as a regenerate person. Rather, he recognizes its operation through the flesh, as defined above, as an ever-present hindering factor in the amazing complex of factors present in the redeemed person. His mind agrees that the law is good (v. 16), recognizes the complete vacuity of virtue in the flesh (v. 18), delights in God's law (v. 22), is at war with the flesh (v. 23), and is itself a slave to God's law (v. 25). His mental comprehension of the good and excellent always goes beyond his ability to perform it, as he is in process of being molded according to the image of Christ. Till then, he finds himself pursuing godliness in his whole nature but never counting himself to have attained it (Phil. 3:12–14).

Fifth, this view confuses heaven with a world still held in bondage. That the Christian should become neither hopelessly frustrated with the incompleteness of his present experience of holiness nor overzealous in his estimation of his attainments is the teaching of the entire eighth chapter of Romans. The bondage of the created order is analogous to the incompleted state of redemption of the children of God. But justification (vv. 1–4), sanctification (vv. 5–17), the promises of glorification, including the struggles demonstrating that God has designed us for it (vv. 18–28), and the summation of all of this in the eternal purpose of God (vv. 29–39) tell the redeemed that an eternity waits in which he will experience complete freedom in service and unhindered enjoyment of the forever-blessed Triune God.

Sixth, the view has no coherent explanation for the necessity of suffering to develop Christian character (Rom. 5:1–4) and demonstrate true perseverance. Hebrews 12 clearly sets forth hardship as the chastening of God to produce invigorated struggle against sin so that a crop of holiness and righteousness eventuates. Such struggle is unnecessary if a man's new nature already possesses "actual righteousness" and commits sin only by accident.

Seventh, this view teaches that sin is so easily recognizable that one will know every sin he commits. Peter Lord asks rhetorically, "Do you think I could have the Holy Ghost living inside me, and sin, and Him not blow the whistle on me? This is turkey theology designed to keep you in the dark woods."[24]

Such a statement embraces a form of the error of immediate inspirationism and greatly underestimates the deceitfulness of the human heart. The Holy Spirit does not give immediate revelation of new laws but continually enlightens the mind to understand the full implications of the laws that are written. Both Psalm 19:12–13 and 1 Corinthians 4:1–5 indicate that we all have a depth of sinfulness of which we are unaware. Sinfulness, however, does not decrease in proportion to our lack of sensitivity to it. Rather, our unawareness demonstrates the desperate deceitfulness of our hearts and the criminal dullness of our minds, which should wrench from our lips the constant confession William Carey had engraved on his tombstone: "A wretched poor and helpless worm, on thy kind arms I fall."

Conclusion

The historic Baptist, or Calvinistic, view of perseverance produces the highest of human endeavors, evoking the noblest thoughts and works from man while ascribing all praise to God and glorying alone in his free grace, eternal purpose, and almighty power.

The Arminian view, while ostensibly seeking to prompt the believer to noble efforts, leaves him without hope, insults the grace, power, and purpose of God, and allows man to share in glory that belongs to God alone. Arminianism also underestimates the power and tragedy of sin and opens wide the door to errors of opposite tendency—an unsanctified salvation on the one hand and perfectionism on the other.

May God in his grace deliver his church from such theological tragedy.

24. Ibid., p. 9.

PART THREE

Practical
Exhortations

14

The Doctrine of Assurance
Grace Manifest in Godly Confidence

Godly assurance of salvation rests upon the Doctrines of Grace. The certainty of unconditional election bequeaths great security to the one who truly discerns the movement of God's grace in his life; the rigorous demands of the doctrine of perseverance eliminate false hopes built on an inadequate foundation; the intensely convicting doctrine of total depravity destroys all rest based on personal merit; the power of the doctrine of effectual call prompts earnest efforts to walk in the Spirit; and the completeness of the doctrine of particular redemption holds out the certainty of a reconciled God to one who truly credits the faithful saying, "Christ Jesus came into the world to save sinners."

Perhaps the most succinct yet sensitive treatment of the doctrine of assurance was constructed by the divines of the Westminster Assembly in chapter 18 of the confession they produced. Following their lead virtually word for word, seventeenth-century English Baptists and eighteenth-century American Baptists approved the same view by adopting the Second London Confession and Philadelphia Confession respectively. Although full exposition of the doctrine of assurance is distilled into one chapter, its important place—indeed, its pervasive and strategic connections—appears eloquently if only subtly in virtually all the soteriological chapters.

In *effectual calling* (Chapter X of the Second London Confession), a man is "enabled to answer this call, and to embrace the Grace offered and conveyed in it" (X.2). In *justification*, though God continues to forgive sin, justified persons may fall under God's fatherly displeasure; however, through humbling themselves, confessing sin, begging par-

351

don, and renewing faith and repentance, the "light of his Countenance [may be] restored unto them" (XI.5). In *adoption*, those who are justified "are enabled to cry 'Abba Father' " (XII). In *sanctification*, the lusts of the body of sin are more and more weakened so that the saints grow in grace, "perfecting holiness in the fear of God, pressing after an heavenly life" (XIII.3). Although *saving faith*, "whereby the elect are enabled to believe to the saving of their souls" may be weak or strong, it is different in kind from the faith of temporary believers, and it may grow up in many to the "attainment of a full assurance through Christ, who is both the Author and Finisher of our Faith" (XIV.1, 3). *Good works*, actions done in obedience to God's commandments, not only evidence a true and living faith, demonstrate the believer's thankfulness, and edify the brethren, they also strengthen the assurance of the believer (XVI.2). Even the section elucidating the decrees of God reflects on the concept of assurance: "The doctrine of this high mystery of predestination, is to be handled with special prudence, and care; that men attending the will of God revealed in his word, and yielding obedience thereunto, may from the certainty of their effectual vocation, be assured of their eternal election" (III.7).

Although the doctrine of assurance is present in piecemeal fashion throughout the Second London Confession, one welcomes its clear and systematic presentation in chapter XVIII, which treats four major aspects of assurance in its four paragraphs. If they were titled according to subject matter, the paragraphs might well bear the following headings: (1) The Reality of Assurance, (2) The Foundations of Assurance, (3) The Duty to Seek Assurance, and (4) The Temporary Loss of Assurance.

The Reality of Assurance

1. Although temporary believers, and other unregenerate men, may vainly deceive themselves with false hopes, and carnal presumptions, of being in the favour of God, and in a state of salvation, which hope of theirs shall perish; yet such as truly believe in the Lord Jesus, and love him in sincerity, endeavouring to walk in all good Conscience before him, may in this life be certainly assured that they are in the state of Grace; and may rejoice in the hope of the glory of God which [page] hope shall never make them ashamed.[1]

This section begins by warning against the deceitfulness of some kinds of assurance. These "false hopes, and carnal presumptions, of

1. William L. Lumpkin, *Baptist Confessions of Faith* (Valley Forge: Judson Press, 1969), p. 274.

being in the favour of God" are doomed to perish. Temporary believers may gain this false assurance and feel they are in a state of salvation. However, based on Job 8:13–14 and Matthew 7:22–23, this assurance is no stronger than a spider's web and will be crushed by the words "Depart from me, ye that work iniquity." When Joshua Jones expounded this article in 1792 in a circular letter for the Philadelphia Baptist Association, he was aware that his use of such language as "false hope and counterfeit assurance" could be unsettling. He contended, however, that such an unsettling should lead to a healthy and edifying examination:

> But by thus observing, we do not mean to discourage you, dear brethren, from appropriating to yourselves the riches of divine grace, and an assurance of an eternal weight of glory. But there is such a similarity between a sincere Christian and a nominal one, as there is between wheat and tares in the blade, which teaches us that a close inspection ought to be exercised by everyone of us, whether we have in possession a vital principle of true religion.[2]

Despite the false assurance that many have, those who "truly believe in the Lord Jesus, and love him in sincerity," and seek to live godly before him "may in this life be certainly assured that they are in the state of Grace." The quest for true assurance and the inability of many to find it burdened Spurgeon and at times became subject matter for his sermons:

> Many sincerely-seeking souls are in great trouble because they have not yet attained to an assurance of their interest in Christ Jesus: they dare not take any comfort from their faith because they suppose that it has not attained to a sufficient strength. They have believed in the Lord Jesus, and they have his promise that they shall be saved, but they are not content with this—they want to get assurance, and then they suppose they shall have a better evidence of their salvation than the bare word of the Saviour. Such persons are under a great mistake; but as that mistake is a very painful one, and exercises the most injurious influence upon them, we will spend this morning in trying, as God shall help us to clear up their difficulty, and to let them see that if they believe in the Lord Jesus Christ, even though they should not have attained to the precious grace of full assurance of faith, yet nevertheless they are saved, and being justified by faith, may rightfully enjoy peace with God through Jesus Christ our Lord. Their mistake seems to me to be this—they look for ripe fruit upon a tree in spring, and because that season yields nothing but blossoms, they conclude the tree to be barren. They go to the

2. *Minutes of the Philadelphia Baptist Association from 1707 to 1807* (Philadelphia: American Baptist Publication Society, 1851), pp. 288–289.

head of a river—they find it a little rippling brook, and because it will not float a "Great Eastern," they conclude that it will never reach the sea, and that in fact it is not a true part of the river at all.[3]

Even as Spurgeon sought to apply a balm to the saved-but-uncertain, the Confession of Faith, drawing legitimate conclusions from Scripture, points to the same truth. This truth was distilled from 1 John and Romans 5. "We know that we know him. . . . we know that we have passed from death unto life. . . . we know that we are of the truth. . . . we know that he abideth in us. . . . that ye may know that ye have eternal life" (1 John 2:3, 3:14, 19, 24; 5:13). The cumulative effect of these phrases is the demonstration that assurance is possible for the true believer. The citation of Romans 5:2, 5 indicates that the framers of the confession interpreted "hope" in that passage in a subjective sense, identifying it with true Christian assurance. Such assurance, or hope, will not be disappointed.

The Foundations of Assurance

2. This certainty is not a bare conjectural and probable persuasion, grounded upon a fallible hope; but an infallible assurance of faith, founded on the Blood and Righteousness of Christ, revealed in the Gospel and also upon the inward evidence of those graces of the Spirit unto which promises are made, and on the testimony of the Spirit of adoption, witnessing with our Spirits that we are the children of God; and as a fruit thereof keeping the heart both humble and holy.[4]

Paragraph two of the confession lays to rest any suspicion that Christian hope or assurance, though subjective in the believer, glimmers and dances but eventually fades and falls with no place to rest. Neither "bare conjectural" nor even "probable" persuasion are adequate terms to describe the assurance of the Christian; only the words *infallible assurance of faith* carried sufficient weight for accurate characterization.

External Evidence of Assurance

By "infallible assurance of faith" (a side note refers to Hebrews 6:11, 19), the confession does not mean that assurance never wavers. Rather,

3. *Spurgeon's Expository Encyclopaedia*, Sermons by Charles H. Spurgeon, 15 vols. (n.p., n.d.; reprint ed., Grand Rapids: Baker Book House, 1977), 1:269.
4. Lumpkin, *Baptist Confessions*, p. 274.

it draws attention to the fact that a concrete object of assurance external to the believer himself bolsters the doctrine. Assurance is not a conjured, psychological peace of mind for its own sake but a humble confidence resulting from an actual peace with God.

The immortal dreamer, John Bunyan, sheds light on this same reality and couches his understanding of the doctrine in a conversation between his Pilgrim and a young lady named Prudence. While discussing the continuance and perplexing nature of indwelling sin, Prudence asks Christian a question, and he responds:

> Pru. Can you remember by what means you find your annoyances, at times, as if they were vanquished?
>
> Chris. Yes; when I think what I saw at the cross, that will do it; and when I look upon my broidered coat, that will do it; also when I look into the roll that I carry in my bosom, that will do it; and when my thoughts wax warm about whither I am going, that will do it.[5]

The cross, of course, as in the experience of all Christians, loosed the burden of sin from Christian's back, whence it tumbled into the sepulchre.

Pilgrim does refer primarily to his inner sense of forgiveness as much as he does the historical reality of the atonement. As Christian stood at the cross after seeing his burden loosed, he stood a while to look and wonder. As he began to leave he sang of the forgiveness and ended the song with a couplet: "Blest Cross! Blest Sepulchre! Blest rather be/The Man that was there put to death for me!"[6]

His focus was on the objective reality of the cross. Issuing from this reality came his persuasion that the way of the cross was to be preferred above all the treasures of Egypt. Thus none could render it odious to him, and its power dispelled despair and made him quicken his steps in the journey to the Celestial City. There, indeed, he would "see him alive that did hang dead on the cross."[7]

The "broidered coat" represents the imputed righteousness of Christ. This was given him when one of the shining ones stripped Christian of his rags and covered his nakedness with the new clothes. Reliance on any other kind of righteousness gave only false hope, as far as Bunyan was concerned. Ignorance incarnated the false hope of many who maintain erroneous perceptions of the nature of justification:

5. John Bunyan, *The Whole Works of John Bunyan*, 3 vols., *The Pilgrim's Progress* (Paternoster Row, London: Blackie and Sons, 1875; reprint ed., Grand Rapids: Baker Book House, 1977), p. 108.

6. Ibid., p. 103.

7. Ibid., p. 108.

I believe that Christ died for sinners; and that I shall be justified before God from the curse, through his gracious acceptance of my obedience to His law. Or thus: Christ makes my duties that are religious acceptable to His Father, by virtue of His merits, and so shall I be justified.[8]

This will never do for Bunyan's Pilgrim. Not only is it such a "fantastical faith," but a false faith, "because it taketh justification from the personal righteousness of Christ"[9] and seeks justification for one's works rather than one's person. It is thus a deceitful faith and "will leave thee under wrath in the day of God Almighty."[10]

The righteousness of Christ alone imputed to sinners grants undefiled assurance.

The meaning of the roll, or scroll, is somewhat ambiguous, but it appears to be the witness of the Spirit, using the objective evidence of a changed life to grant assurance of salvation and greater striving for holiness. This scroll was given to Christian at the same time he was marked with the seal of the Holy Spirit. He was admonished to look on it as he ran, and to give it in at the Celestial Gate. Christian told Formalist and Hypocrisy that the scroll was "to comfort me by reading as I go in the way."[11] Indeed, he was to give it at the Celestial Gate "in token of my going in after it."[12] An afternoon of sleep caused Christian to lose the scroll temporarily. He returned hurriedly to the place it was lost in order to retrieve it. With great joy he found it again, "for this roll was the assurance of his life and acceptance at the desired haven."[13] Later, when recounting his tale to the porter at the Palace Beautiful, Christian tells that in his sleep he "lost his evidence."[14] Thus, the roll (scroll) appears to be the objective evidence of the new birth, such as the ever-increasing virtues described in 2 Peter 1:5-9, and the sealing of the Spirit.

In addition to his contemplating the cross, the broidered coat, and the roll, Christian receives great joy when he thinks about his destiny, for he knows that he will see the Lord there:

Why there I hope to see Him alive that did hang dead on the cross; and there I hope to be rid of all those things that to this day are in me and annoyance to me. There, they say, there is no death; and there I shall

8. Ibid., p. 158.
9. Ibid.
10. Ibid.
11. Ibid., p. 104.
12. Ibid.
13. Ibid., p. 106.
14. Ibid.

dwell with such company as I like best. For, to tell you the truth, I love Him because I was by Him eased of my burden; and I am weary of my inward sickness. I would fain be where I shall die no more, and with the company that shall continually cry, "Holy, holy, holy!"[15]

The joy of assurance, according to *The Pilgrim's Progress*, arises from the contemplation of forgiveness, justification, the changed life, and a new and all-consuming affection for God and his glory.

Very similar ideas form the strength of the "infallible assurance." The word *infallible* does not exaggerate the certainty, for the first element of the foundation is "the Blood and Righteousness of Christ, revealed in the Gospel" (cf. Heb. 6:17–18). As in Bunyan, the subjective element of hope finds rest like an anchor upon the sure and steadfast rock of the historical person and work of Jesus.

The scriptural passage cited in support of this affirmation may appear somewhat perplexing. Whereas Hebrews 6:11, 19 naturally supports the possibility of assurance, Hebrews 6:17–18 makes no immediate reference to "the Blood and Righteousness of Christ":

Wherein God, willing more abundantly to shew unto the heirs of promise the immutability of his counsel, confirmed it by an oath: That by two immutable things, in which it was impossible for God to lie, we might have a strong consolation, who have fled for refuge to lay hold upon the hope set before us.

Evidently the framers of the confession considered the two unchangeable things as a reference to Christ's immutable righteousness and his once-for-all death. While on the surface this appears strained and without support from the context, on closer examination the reader might conclude that the confession is precisely right. Or, if his spiritual insight gains sufficient excitement, he might even attribute profundity to the confessional reference.

Hebrews 6:20 makes it clear that the hope that is an anchor to the soul hooks upon Christ's Melchisedec priesthood. After an intervention of sixteen verses that explain the necessity of such a priesthood, Hebrews 7:17 begins to apply all this to the Christ. How he became such and what benefits derive from it constitute the remainder of the chapter. The surety of hope is based directly on the oath of God (7:19–20; cf. 6:17). Through the oath, Jesus was made eternal priest, after the order of Melchisedec, who saves forever those who draw near to God through him (7:21–25). In his priesthood Jesus is (1) "holy, innocent, undefiled," and (2) he offered up sacrifices for the sins of the people

15. Ibid., p. 108.

"once for all when He offered up Himself" (7:26, 27, NASB). Thus, the unchangeableness of God's purpose is given historical certainty by two things—"the Blood and Righteousness of Christ, revealed in the Gospel"—that we may have strong encouragement.

While Christ's sinlessness and sacrificial death (his active and passive obedience) relate primarily to justification, the importance of the confession's utilization of these concepts for assurance must not be diminished. Other elements in assurance fluctuate in the Christian's experience (cf. paragraph four, to be discussed below), but the righteousness and death of Christ appeared in history—unrepeatable and ineradicable. Thus, when all else may falter, the true believer may still cling to the unchangeable "Blood and Righteousness of Christ."

Evidence in the Believer

The second element in the foundation of assurance is the necessity for objective evidence in the believer's behavior and attitudes. Similar in part to Bunyan's "roll" and based upon 2 Peter 1:4–11, the confession encourages the believer in recognizing "the inward evidence of those graces of the Spirit unto which promises are made." True biblical assurance cannot come for one who is not increasing in faith, virtue, knowledge, perseverance, godliness, brotherly kindness, and Christian love. The presence and augmentation of these qualities render one useful and fruitful in the true knowledge of the Lord Jesus Christ.

In 2 Peter 1:10 the apostle speaks of making certain of one's calling and election. Peter does not teach that human righteousness produces divine election. Rather, pursuing a course of holiness (in conjunction with the hearty acceptance of saving truth) provides evidence that one is indeed elect and not merely self-deceived. Paul affirms essentially the same understanding of election and its evidences in 1 Thessalonians 1:4–7.

Robert Hall, pastor of Broadmead Chapel in Bristol, England, confronted errors relating to this very point in an article he wrote confuting antinomianism:

> He who flatters himself with the hope of salvation, without perceiving in himself a specific difference of character from "the world that lieth in wickedness," either founds his persuasion absolutely on nothing, or on an immediate revelation, on a preternatural discovery of a matter of fact, on which the Scriptures are totally silent. This absurd notion of unconditional promises, by severing the assurance of salvation from all the fruits of the Spirit, from every trace and feature of a renovated nature and a regenerate state, opens the widest possible door to licentiousness.

As far as it is sustained by the least shadow of reasoning, it may be traced to the practice of confounding the secret purposes of the Supreme Being with his revealed promises. That in the breast of the Deity an eternal purpose has been formed respecting the salvation of a certain portion of the human race, is a doctrine, which, it appears to me, is clearly revealed. But this secret purpose is so far from being incompatible with the necessary conditions of salvation, that they form a part of it; their existence is an inseparable link in the execution of the divine decree; for the same wisdom which has appointed the end, has also infallibly determined the means by which it shall be accomplished; and as the personal direction of the decree remains a secret, until it is developed in the event, it cannot possibly, considered in itself, lay a foundation for confidence. That a certain number of the human race are ordained to eternal life, may be inferred with much probability from many passages of Scripture; but if any person infers from these general premises, that he is of that number, he advances a proposition without the slightest color of evidence. An assurance of salvation can consequently, in no instance, be deduced from the doctrine of absolute decrees, until they manifest themselves in their actual effects, that is, in that renewal of the heart which the Bible affirms to be essential to future felicity.[16]

The Witness of the Spirit of Adoption

The third element mixed into the foundation for assurance (arising from Romans 8:15–16 as its scriptural basis) is, as the confession states, "the testimony of the Spirit of adoption, witnessing with our Spirits that we are the children of God." While biblical translators vary in their understanding of the nature of this witness (whether internal and subjective, or external and objective; cf. Phillips and New English Bible respectively), the confession apparently treats it in a subjective sense. Thus, the witness of the "Spirit of adoption" complements the first two elements, which are more objective in nature, and becomes the essence of assurance.

One should not consider the witness of the Spirit as a special revelation from God apart from the clear teachings of Scripture or discernible changes in the character and affection of the person. Such special revelations are clearly excluded in paragraph three, cited below. Rather, through the Spirit one learns to trust completely in Christ's sufficiency and his power to cleanse from sin and bestow his righteousness.

Nor should disengagement of man's rational faculties be assumed

16. The Rev. Robert Hall, A.M., *Works*, 2 vols. (New York: G. & C. & H. Carvill, 1830), 2:327–328.

in such a witness of the Spirit, for the Scripture quite clearly affirms that this witness is "along with our spirits." One's own rational faculties, his ability to reflect, observe, and draw conclusions, must enter the process, albeit under the sanctifying power of the Holy Spirit. This thought finds a parallel in Paul's formula for sanctification: ". . . continue to work out your salvation with fear and trembling, for it is God who works in you to will and to act according to his good purpose" (Phil. 2:12–13, NIV).

The context of Romans 8:15–16 closely aligns inner assurance with at least three gauges to measure the true nature of the supposed Christian's faith. Through the Spirit the Christian mortifies the deeds of the flesh, comes to a point of humble revelry in God as Father, and determines to live in obedience, even to the point of suffering. These evidences of Romans 8, combined with the spiritual bestowal of the great and precious promises of 2 Peter 1:3–4, place inner assurance and external evidence in a Chalcedonian relationship—they cohere inconfusedly, unchangeably, inseparably, and indivisibly.

True assurance keeps the heart both humble and holy. No cocksure arrogance can coexist with an apprehension of the grace of God. If such an attitude does arise, one lacks the full biblical basis of assurance. Arguing from 1 John 3:1–3, the framers of the confession understood that purification of the heart caps the whole doctrine of assurance. The Spirit bears witness to genuine salvation where there is a right relation to the historical person and work of Christ and where there are holy evidences in the believer's life. But from the Spirit's witness to the believer's heart (tantamount to assurance itself) must flow an attitude of gratefulness and a desire to glorify God.

The Duty to Seek Assurance

> 3. This infallible assurance doth not so belong to the essence of faith, but that a true Believer, may wait long and conflict with many difficulties before he be partaker of it; yet being enabled by the Spirit to know the things [page] which are freely given him of God, he may without extraordinary revelation in the right use of means attain thereunto: and therefore it is the duty of every one, to give all diligence to make their Calling and Election sure, that thereby his heart may be enlarged in peace and joy in the Holy Spirit, in love and thankfulness to God, and in strength and cheerfulness in the duties of obedience, the proper fruits of this assurance; so far is it from inclining men to looseness.[17]

17. Lumpkin, *Baptist Confessions*, pp. 274, 275.

This section makes three points: (1) a true believer may lack assurance; (2) everyone is under obligation to seek assurance through the proper use of means; (3) the doctrine of assurance encourages holiness rather than looseness.

The Believer's Struggle for Assurance

Because this "infallible assurance doth not [necessarily] belong to the essence of faith," a true believer "may wait long and conflict with many difficulties" before he partakes of it.

A popular caricature of the necessity for assurance of salvation states: "If you can have it and not know it, you can lose it and not miss it." Such a statement indicates a confusion between salvation and assurance, oversimplifies the comprehensive set of factors that contributes to assurance, and betrays a shallow view of the deceitfulness of the human heart. The true believer may at times feel he is "counted with them that go down into the pit" and may ask the mournful question, "LORD, why castest thou off my soul? why hidest thou thy face from me?" (Ps. 88:4, 14).

While Spurgeon ministered at Waterbeach, he had many opportunities to observe and counsel people struggling with assurance. One notable case concerned a godly woman whom Spurgeon called Mrs. Much-afraid. Spurgeon tells the story:

> I feel quite sure she has been many years in Heaven, but she was always fearing that she should never enter the gates of glory. She was very regular in her attendance at the house of God, and was a wonderfully good listener. She used to drink in the gospel; but, nevertheless, she was always doubting, and fearing, and trembling about her own spiritual condition. She had been a believer in Christ, I should think, for fifty years, yet she had always remained in that timid, fearful, anxious state. She was a kind old soul, ever ready to help her neighbors, or to speak a word to the unconverted; she seemed to me to have enough grace for two people, yet, in her own opinion, she had not half enough grace for one.
>
> One day, when I was talking with her, she told me that she had not any hope at all; she had no faith; she believed that she was a hypocrite. I said, "Then don't come to the chapel any more; we don't want hypocrites there. Why do you come?" She answered, "I come because I can't stay away. I love the people of God; I love the house of God; and I love to worship God." "Well," I said, "you are an odd sort of hypocrite; you are a queer kind of unconverted woman." "Ah," she sighed, "you may say what you please, but I have not any hope of being saved." So I said to her, "Well, next Sunday, I will let you go into the pulpit, that you may tell the people that Jesus Christ is a liar, and that you cannot trust Him." "Oh!" she cried, "I would be torn in pieces before I would say such a

thing as that. Why, He cannot lie! Every word He says is true." "Then," I asked, "Why do you not believe it?" She replied, "I do believe it; but, somehow, I do not believe it for myself; I am afraid whether it is for me." "Have you not any hope at all?" I asked. "No," she answered; so I pulled out my purse, and I said to her, "Now, I have got £5 here, it is all the money I have, but I will give you that £5 for your hope if you will sell it." She looked at me, wondering what I meant. "Why!" she exclaimed, "I would not sell it for a thousand worlds." She had just told me that she had not any hope of salvation, yet she would not sell it for a thousand worlds![18]

Similarly does Bunyan describe Mr. Little Faith, who had been assaulted by three thieves, Faint-heart, Mistrust, and Guilt, and made the entire journey to the Celestial City with no spending money. Although they could not rob him of his jewels, he was never able to derive proper advantage from them that he might finish his course with joy. Not only do Miss Much-Afraid and Mr. Little-Faith walk haltingly and insecurely, but Christian himself at the moment of death feared he would not feel the bottom of the river and would perish before he reached the other side.

The Believer's Obligation to Seek Assurance

Although assurance may elude the justified person temporarily, it is his duty to seek it. The confession assures its reader that assurance may be grasped through the proper use of means "without extraordinary revelation." The writers did not intend to eliminate or minimize the witness of the Spirit of adoption in the process of gaining assurance, but desired to focus on the necessity of the doctrinal, ethical, and spiritual evidences as the vehicle of the secret working of the Spirit. This position demonstrates a consistent application of the principle enunciated in the confession's paragraph six of chapter I, entitled "Of the Holy Scriptures."

> The whole Councel of God concerning all things necessary for his own Glory, Man's Salvation, Faith and Life, is either expressly set down or necessarily contained in the *Holy Scripture*; unto which nothing at any time is to be added, whether by Revelation of the Spirit, or traditions of men.
>
> Nevertheless we acknowledge the inward illumination of the Spirit of God, to be necessary for the saving understanding of such things as are revealed in the Word....[19]

---

18. C. H. Spurgeon, *Autobiography*, 2 vols., revised ed. (Carlisle, PA: The Banner of Truth Trust, 1962), Vol. 1: *The Early Years* 1834–1859, p. 202.

19. Lumpkin, *Baptist Confessions*, p. 250.

Because assurance is attainable only in this biblical way, God is glorified when a person seeks it. The gaining of assurance brings glory to God by affecting the believer in three ways: (1) his heart is enlarged "in peace and joy in the Holy Spirit," (2) he manifests "love and thankfulness to God"; and (3) he is fortified with "strength and cheerfulness in the duties of obedience, the proper fruits of this assurance."

The Philadelphia Baptist Association listed three advantages of assurance to those who possess it during their pilgrimage here on earth:

(1) It enables them to submit, with cheerfulness, to adverse dispensations, upon the account that they are enabled to believe that their heavenly Father does everything for good to them that love him.
(2) Full assurance of hope enables them to believe whatever God is pleased to reveal concerning himself, because that there is now a greater nearness to God than heretofore, and the more knowledge the believer has of God, the more acquaintance he has with himself, whereby he is made to behold his own impotence and ignorance; for until such time as the believer attains to some degree of assurance, carnal reason will retard his progress in the exercise of faith, particularly in some points that are beyond his rational comprehension.
(3) The grace of assurance will be of the greatest use in our last conflict with death, knowing that Christ has taken away the sting of death, and that death itself will be destroyed; so that the assured Christian is made to rejoice, that he has no cause to fear that any ill consequence will attend his exit out of time into eternity. . . .[20]

The Encouragement of Holiness

The doctrine of assurance, perceived in this way, encourages holy living. Its caricature pictures a cocksure manner, flippancy toward sin, and slight if any desire for holiness. Such an attitude may be encouraged by some teachings that ostensibly aim at giving assurance, but not by the Doctrines of Grace. Donald Lake verifies this contention when he rejects what he understands as a Puritan concept of assurance and affirms a view of assurance that calls for a much less personal examination:

From the psychological perspective, we can understand the inherent insecurity of the Puritans whose theology combined a high view of predestination with an almost morbid sense of introspection. The Puritan diaries reveal a constant searching for signs of confirmation that they were numbered among the elect. When we understand the truly uni-

20. *Minutes*, pp. 288–289.

versal significance of the atonement, such introspection becomes unnecessary.[21]

The doctrine of assurance taught in the Second London Confession would never endorse such detachment from striving to ascertain one's calling and thus one's election. Rather than "inclining men to looseness," godly and biblical introspection for the sake of assurance develops a tested character, a desire for holiness, and a love for "righteousness, and peace, and joy in the Holy Ghost" (Rom. 14:17). For when one knows the grace of God, it truly teaches him "that, denying ungodliness and worldly lusts," his life should be characterized by sobriety, godliness, and righteousness in the present world and that he should look for "that blessed hope, and [even] the glorious appearing of the great God and our Saviour Jesus Christ" (Titus 2:12–13; cf. 1 John 3:1–3).

The Temporary Loss of Assurance

4. True believers may have the assurance of their salvation divers ways shaken, diminished, and intermitted; as by negligence in preserving of it, by falling into some special sin which woundeth the conscience and grieveth the Spirit; by some sudden or vehement temptation, by God's withdrawing the light of his countenance, and suffering even such as fear him to walk in darkness and to have no light, yet are they never destitute of the seed of God and life of faith, that love of Christ and the brethren, that sincerity of heart and conscience of duty out of which, by the operation of the Spirit, this assurance may in due time be revived, and by the which, in the meantime, they are preserved from utter despair.[22]

True believers may have their assurance "shaken, diminished, and intermitted." The paragraph lists four factors that might contribute to such a phenomenon and closes with an affirmation that, in such times, true saving faith continues to produce fruit.

Assurance may be diminished when one neglects to preserve it. The confession lists Song of Solomon 5:3, 6 in support of this point. It might well have added 1 John 3:18–22. Like all Christian graces, assurance must be exercised and cultivated. Loving in deed and truth

21. Clark H. Pinnock, ed. *Grace Unlimited* (Minneapolis: Bethany Fellowship, Inc., 1975), p. 44.
22. Lumpkin, *Baptist Confessions*, p. 275.

permits us to assure our hearts before God, and confidence before him comes when our hearts condemn us not.

Special sin in the believer's life may also cause the flight of assurance. Such sin wounds the conscience and grieves the Holy Spirit. David's turmoil and tragic life following his sin with Bathsheba leaps out as the supreme biblical example of this. Psalm 51 presents the spiritual struggle and earnest quest for God's favor that resulted from David's repentance.

Sometimes a "sudden or vehement temptation" causes the waning of assurance. Psalm 77 appears to reflect this kind of disposition. The writer cries (vv. 7–9):

> Will the Lord cast off for ever? and will he be favourable no more? Is his mercy clean gone for ever: doth his promise fail for evermore? Hath God forgotten to be gracious? hath he in anger shut up his tender mercies? Selah.

At other times assurance may fail simply because God withdraws "the light of his countenance" and allows "even such as fear him to walk in darkness and to have no light." Even after the unshakable confidence painted in the words "I shall never be moved," the believer may experience a day in which he says that "thou didst hide thy face, and I was troubled" (Ps. 30:6–7). Such times come that we might seek the Lord more earnestly and humbly acknowledge our dependence upon the manifestation of his presence.

Again, the inimitable Spurgeon has adorned this element of the doctrine of assurance with his unparalleled verbal pictures. After discussing the mysterious congruity between the witness of the Holy Spirit and the witness of our spirits that we are children of God, Spurgeon continues:

> And so to conclude, this is desirable to the highest degree, for it is the earnest of the inheritance. It is a part of heaven on earth to get an assurance wrought by the Spirit. It is not a pledge merely, for a pledge is given back when you get the thing itself, but it is an earnest; it is one cluster from the vines of Eshcol—one shekel of the eternal wage-money of the free-grace reward—what if I say it is a stray note from the harps of angels!—it is a drop of the spray from the fountains of life; it is one ingot of gold from the pavement of heaven; it is one ray of heavenly light from the eternal Sun of Righteousness. O Christian, if you have ever known assurance, you will pant till you have it again. You can never, after seeing the sunlight, put up with the candle-light of your doubts and fears in the dungeon of despondency. But if assurance be gone, do still hang on Jesus.

When your eye of faith is dim,
Still hold on Jesus, sink or swim;
Still at his footstool bow the knee,
And Israel's God thy peace shall be.[23]

As Spurgeon indicated, in harmony with the confession, even in these periods of apparent abandonment, the believer is "never destitute of the seed of God and life of faith, that love of Christ and the brethren" and other Spirit-wrought graces by which he may in due time be blessed with renewed assurance. The distinction between saving faith and assurance must be maintained. Saving faith continues in pursuit of holiness even in the absence of assurance and preserves a man from utter despair even while he prays, "Help thou mine unbelief."

Perhaps Francis Wayland, speaking in the last week of his earthly life, summarized the doctrine of assurance in as succinct a manner as possible, giving expression to the calm confidence for which all should pray:

I feel that my race is nearly run. I have, indeed, tried to do my duty. I cannot accuse myself of having neglected any known obligation. Yet all this avails nothing. I place no dependence on anything but the righteousness and death of Jesus Christ. I have never enjoyed the raptures of faith vouchsafed to many Christians. I do not undervalue these feelings, but it has not pleased God to bestow them upon me. I have, however, a confident hope that I am accepted in the Beloved.[24]

23. *Spurgeon's Expository Encyclopaedia*, 1:279–280.
24. Francis Wayland and H. L. Wayland, *A Memoir of the Life and Labors of Francis Wayland*, D.D., LL.D., 2 vols. (New York: Sheldon and Co., 1867), 2:360.

15

Liberty of Conscience
Grace Trusted to Produce
and Preserve the Saints

The *Abstract of Principles*, written by Basil Manly, Jr., and adopted as the confessional statement of Southern Seminary in Kentucky, contains the following article on "Liberty of Conscience."

> God alone is Lord of the conscience; and He hath left it free from the doctrines and commandments of men, which are in any thing contrary to His word, or not contained in it. Civil Magistrates being ordained of God, subjection in all lawful things commanded by them ought to be yielded by us in the Lord, not only for wrath, but also for conscience sake.[1]

This principle as a positive doctrine affirms the priority of the Word of God over the words of men; it leaves man free from the latter and free to be conquered by the former. Additionally, it affirms the necessity of God's immediate action upon the conscience of man if man is to do what is right in matters pertaining to God and avoid what is false and heretical. Further, the authority of civil magistrates in matters related specifically to the order, peace, and prosperity of civil society is clearly supported by this principle.

Because liberty of conscience speaks specifically to the relationship of all men, regenerate and unregenerate, within civil society, the concept resists being molded to serve as an instrument for condoning and

---

1. Basil Manly, Jr., *Abstract of Principles* in James P. Boyce, *Abstract of Systematic Theology* (Philadelphia: American Baptist Publication Society, 1887; reprint ed., North Pompano Beach, FL: Christian Gospel Foundation, n.d.), Appendix B.

protecting infidelity within the church. Instead, its tendency should be to protect the purity of the church, since those who disagree with the theology of one communion are free to go to a communion with which they more nearly agree, and this without any threat or interference from civil authorities or even the incurrence of any civil disability. That some have used this doctrine as a cloak for their unfaithful dealing with God's people tragically perverts its historical use. Not only do such show themselves unfaithful, but they add to their spiritual ills the moral affliction of ungratefulness and the academic woe of historical incompetence. An investigation of the theological underpinnings of this historic Baptist principle should aid in one's understanding of its specific applications.

Early Struggles for Liberty of Conscience

Unconditional election and other doctrines finding root in the sovereignty of God also find practical expression in liberty of conscience. It is not merely coincidental that Calvinists were among those who suffered longest and fought hardest for religious liberty. The English Particular Baptists, such as Benjamin Keach, and Americans, such as Roger Williams, John Clarke, Obadiah Holmes, Isaac Backus, and John Leland, all sought expressions of worship unencumbered by civil coercion. That observation should not be taken as a denigration or even an underestimation of the value of General (Arminian) Baptist contributions to the struggle for liberty of conscience. The writings of Thomas Helwys, John Smyth, John Murton, and Leonard Busher pioneered this liberty in the English-speaking world. Smyth, toward the end of his life (1612) wrote: "The magistrate is not by virtue of his office to meddle with religion, or matters of conscience, to force or compel men to this or that form of religion, or doctrine." Helwys, who died in prison in 1616, wrote in his famous *Mistery of Iniquity*: "Our lord the king is but an earthly king, and he has no authority as a king but in earthly causes. . . . for men's religion to God is betwixt God and themselves." John Murton's *A Most Humble Supplication* (1620) provided Roger Williams both the occasion and many of the arguments that sustained him in his polemical confrontation with John Cotton over liberty of conscience. Leonard Busher's *A Plea for Liberty of Conscience* (1614) contains the following passage:

> But . . . the scriptures do teach, that the one true religion is gotten by a new birth, even by the word and Spirit of God, and therewith also it is only maintained and defended.
> Therefore, may it please your majesty and parliament to understand

that, by fire and sword to constrain princes and peoples to receive that one true religion of the gospel, is wholly against the mind and merciful law of Christ, dangerous both to king and state, a means to decrease the kingdom of Christ, and a means to increase the kingdom of antichrist. . . .

And no king nor bishop can, or is able to command faith; that it is the gift of God, who worketh in us both the will and deed of his own good pleasure.[2]

Both the courage and the arguments of these men, all Arminian, greatly aided both England and America in achieving liberty of conscience. The ammunition they used, however, fit much better in the Calvinist cannon than in the Arminian popgun. Their general appeal to the sole prerogative of God over soul matters, Busher's specific emphasis on the centrality of regeneration by the Word and Spirit, as well as his strong reminder of the gracious character of faith, proceed with much more theological and logical consistency on a Calvinistic foundation than on a non-Calvinistic one. I contend, therefore, that though others contributed, the sword that cut the nerve of religious repression was, in the final analysis, a Calvinistic sword.

One could legitimately point out that the repressors were also Calvinists. This is partially true, for one should also remember that the most vigorous and intemperate of the seventeenth-century oppressors was William Laud, a strong Arminian. Also, Roman Catholics of all ages who repressed any kind of dissent and laid claim to absolute civil and religious power would loathe to be classed as Calvinists. Reformation Calvinism failed to produce religious liberty or separation of church and state in the Netherlands or in Geneva. It did, however, lead to a defining of the separate roles of church and state in both of those Reformation centers and prompted even greater precision in these definitions for Massachusetts Bay. While John Cotton and his sympathizers tried to maintain the "magistrate" in his lofty position as protector of the true faith, the logic of their Calvinistic Puritanism was hacking away at branches that were simply incapable of supporting true worship of God.

The same logic that made Calvinistic Anglicans become Puritans, or Puritans become Separatists, also made Separatists become Baptists, who desired that worship of the Holy Sovereign of the Universe be true and uncoerced. This theological persuasion drove Baptists to suffer, write, and fight for concrete assurances that they could worship God in accordance with the Scripture.

2. Leonard Busher, "Religion's Peace: A Plea for Liberty of Conscience," in *Tracts on Liberty of Conscience and Persecution, 1614–1661*, ed., Edward B. Underhill (London: J. Haddon, 1846), pp. 9–81.

Many different streams of thought converged to inject the concepts of separation of church and state, liberty of conscience, and freedom of religion into the United States. While others joined Baptists in this struggle, the approach and concept contributed by the Baptists was unique. In reality, some contemporary and ostensibly Baptistic expressions of religious toleration differ from that espoused by Baptists on the basis of Reformed theology. The "natural rights" philosophy of Jefferson and the agnosticism of Niebuhr will serve to highlight the uniqueness of the Baptist view.

Jeffersonian Rationalism

Randall Thompson, in a musical delight entitled *Testament of Freedom*, has set to music some of the writings of Thomas Jefferson. The text of the opening number says: "The God who gave us life, gave us liberty at the same time. Though the hand of force may destroy them, it cannot disjoin them." This, in capsule form, is Jefferson's view of natural rights.

Although sometimes popularly conceived as a deist, Jefferson escapes that category by his regular appeal to "Providence" in the documents of the American Revolution. His rationalism did lead him into Unitarianism in his last days, although he had occasionally worshiped in an Anglican church in Virginia. Jefferson felt a strong attachment to the teachings of Jesus, but he could accept neither his deity nor the supernatural phenomena surrounding his life. In an effort to salvage what he thought was credible and useful, he edited his own version of the gospel and published the results in a book entitled *The Life and Morals of Jesus of Nazareth*.

Jefferson's contributions to the American system were many. He was one of the first advocates of public education. He proposed the decimal system for American coinage to supplant the cumbersome system of pounds, shillings, and pence. On his tombstone are listed the three accomplishments by which he wished to be remembered: "Here was buried Thomas Jefferson, author of the Declaration of American Independence, of the statute of Virginia for religious freedom, and father of the University of Virginia."

The last accomplishment of the three has etched in stone one of Jefferson's most famous sayings, "I have sworn upon the altar of God, eternal hostility against every form of tyranny over the mind of man." Jefferson was as consistent as he was insistent in applying this premise: that the final court of appeals in any matter was the unencumbered mind of man.

The implication of this premise for religious liberty was beneficent, and the documents of history demonstrate the effectiveness of the united efforts of Baptists and Jefferson in this battle. However, significant differences in foundations are obvious. That Jefferson's intent and motivating force differed from that of the Baptists is evident in the following extract from a letter he wrote as President of the United States to the famous Unitarian Dr. Joseph Priestly in 1801:

> It is with heartfelt satisfaction that, in the first moments of my public action, I can hail you with welcome to our land, tender to you the homage of its respect and esteem, (and) cover you under the protection of those laws which were made for the wise and good like you.[3]

Jefferson's fundamental difference from the Baptists was clarified further in a note he wrote to his nephew:

> Your reason is now mature enough to examine religion. Shake off all the fears and servile prejudices under which weak minds are servilely crouched. Fix reason firmly in the seat and call to her tribunal every fact, every opinion. Question with boldness even the existence of God, because if there be one he must more approve of the homage of reason than that of blindfolded fear. You will naturally examine first the religion of our country. Read the Bible. Then as you would, read Livy or Tacitus. Your own reason is the only oracle given you by heaven and you are answerable not for the rightness but for the uprightness of the decision.[4]

Upon this proceeded his advocacy of the natural rights of man. We see this phrase, "natural rights," used twice in his statute for religious liberty in Virginia:

> Be it therefore enacted by the general assembly that no man should be compelled to frequent or support any religious worship, place or ministry whatsoever, nor shall he be enforced, restrained, molested, or burdened in his mind or goods, nor shall otherwise suffer on account of his religious opinions or belief. But that all men shall be free to profess and by argument to maintain their opinions in matters of religion and that the same shall in no wise diminish, enlarge or affect their civil capacities. And though we well know this assembly elected by the people for the ordinary purposes of legislation only have no power to restrain the acts of succeeding assemblies, constituted with the powers equal to our own, and that therefore to declare this act irrevocable, would be of no effect

3. *The Life and Selected Writings of Thomas Jefferson*, edited and with an introduction by Adrienne Koch & William Peden (New York: The Modern Library by Random House, 1944), p. 562.
4. Ibid., p. 431.

in law, yet we are free to declare and do declare that the rights hereby asserted are of the natural rights of mankind and that if any as shall be hereafter passed to repeat the present or to narrow its operation, such act will be an infringement of natural rights.[5]

Great confidence in man's reason and an assertion of his natural rights formed the basis for Jefferson's contribution to religious liberty.

Niebuhr's Humble Agnosticism

Another expression of religious liberty is expressed by Reinhold Niebuhr in *The Nature and Destiny of Man*. Although most could not express it as felicitously as Niebuhr, the basic agnostic sentiment is highly characteristic of today's generation. Niebuhr says:

> Truth as it is contained in the Christian revelation includes the recognition that it is neither possible for man to know the truth fully nor to avoid the error of pretending that he does. It is recognized that grace always remains in partial contradiction to nature and is not merely its fulfillment.[6]

One can discern something of the self-defeating nature of agnosticism in this statement. Niebuhr implies that a claim to sure and certain knowledge of truth is the same as claiming to know truth in its fullness. But, according to Niebuhr, since we do not know with fullness, we cannot know with certainty. The only thing that is sure is that we must be uncertain. One might ask, "But how can we be sure of that?" Niebuhr seeks to escape this dilemma by endorsing Tillich's identification of this knowledge with a simple absolute judgment about the relation of the conditioned to the unconditioned. Niebuhr explains this as spiritual realization of human finiteness. That he identifies sure truth with full truth is demonstrated in his discussion of toleration:

> The test of how well this paradox of the gospel is comprehended and how genuinely it is entered in human experience in the attitude of Christians toward those who differ from themselves in convictions would seem vital to each. The test, in other words, is to be found in the issue of toleration. To meet the test, it is necessary not merely to maintain a tolerant attitude toward those who hold beliefs other than our own. The

5. Ibid., p. 313.
6. Reinhold Niebuhr, *The Nature and Destiny of Man* (New York: C. Scribner's Sons, 1941–43), p. 217.

test is twofold and includes both the ability to hold vital convictions which lead to action and also the capacity to preserve the spirit of forgiveness towards those who offend us by holding to convictions which seem untrue to us.[7]

Niebuhr is not unaware that he premises religious liberty upon an agnostic basis. As he begins to conclude his argument, he makes a painfully honest admission: "Nevertheless, complete skepticism is always a possible consequence of the spirit of toleration, for no toleration is possible without a measure of provisional skepticism about the truth we hold."[8]

Critique of "Natural Rights" and "Provisional Skepticism." Both the natural-rights rationalism and the provisional-skepticism motifs end at least partially happily in that they seek to protect religious liberty. However, one problem that the Baptist and other biblical Christians encounter with this arises from the nonscriptural framework of both opinions. Even though the desire for an unencumbered mind expressing its natural rights leads to asserting the same freedoms that Baptists treasure, it proceeds upon a false foundation. The kind of mind it assumes for man simply does not exist as far as Scripture is concerned. Rather than operating in an unencumbered manner, when the mind of fallen man asserts what it claims as natural rights, the only result is man's rebellion against God. Paul deals with this succinctly in Romans, chapters 1, 2, and 3. The argument of those chapters is summarized well in Ephesians 4:17–19:

> This I say therefore, and affirm together with the Lord, that you walk no longer just as the Gentiles also walk, in the futility of their mind, being darkened in their understanding, excluded from the life of God, because of the ignorance that is in them, because of the hardness of their heart; and they, having become callous, have given themselves over to sensuality, for the practice of every kind of impurity with greediness [NASB].

Natural freedom in the biblical context always bears the fruit of rebellion against God and eventual moral perverseness. Therefore, Baptists should not assert freedom of religion on the assumption that unregenerate man desires truth and has a mind capable of an objective evaluation of the evidence. The "natural rights" of man will never lead him to truth.

"Provisional skepticism" is equally untenable for Baptists and other

7. Ibid., p. 219.
8. Ibid.

biblical Christians. Skepticism is at least as unbiblical as a natural-rights philosophy. Jesus indicated no skepticism concerning who he was. He did not doubt that he was "the way, the truth, and the life" and that "no man cometh unto the Father," except by him (John 14:6). Apostolic confidence in the clarity of the gospel and its application makes "provisional skepticism" a stranger in a foreign land. The biblical writers believed that they did possess certain truth, fully worthy of complete confidence. In 2 John the beloved apostle affirms several things about truth: (1) it can be known; (2) it is unchanging (eternal); (3) it is identified with Christ's teaching or apostolic teaching about Christ, or both; (4) knowing God is dependent upon abiding in that truth; (5) the Christian must not have fellowship with those who do not abide in the truth:

> The elder to the chosen lady and her children, whom I love in truth; and not only I, but also all who know the truth, for the sake of the truth which abides in us and will be with us forever. . . . Anyone who goes too far and does not abide in the teaching of Christ, does not have God; the one who abides in the teaching, he has both the Father and the Son. If anyone comes to you and does not bring this teaching, do not receive him into your house, and do not give him a greeting; for the one who gives him a greeting participates in his evil deeds [2 John 1:9–11, NASB].

The apostle Paul was so certain that the gospel he preached originated from divine revelation that all who differed from him were declared anathema, enemies of the cross of Christ with a destiny of destruction (see Gal. 1; Phil. 3).

If anyone seeks to hold skepticism as a basis for religious liberty, then one must conclude that religious liberty is not an absolute. Theoretically—with uncertainty of truth as the "reason" for toleration—if uncertainty were to vanish and someone *did* come to possess the truth and lose the possibility of skepticism, it would follow that he could legitimately enforce his views upon others and force them to worship as he worships. The context of religious liberty as a moral absolute would be lost, and the Christian could not claim that there is a distinctively Christian view of religious liberty. Therefore, skepticism, or benign agnosticism, cannot be the Christian basis for religious liberty.

A Historic Christian Position

Both rationalism, or natural rights, and agnosticism are unbiblical. They are also untrue to Baptist history. In the Baptist struggle for liberty of conscience, the issue was treated as an absolute concept demanded by the nature of the gospel. Although the Anabaptists and General Baptists developed a rich doctrine of religious liberty based upon the doctrines of the incarnation and the necessity for an un-coerced response to the gospel, strong arguments also came out of Calvinistic Baptist writings.

The proper correlation between the intolerance that the certainty of the gospel demands and the tolerance that the grace and faith of the gospel demand is demonstrated well in the writings of John Le-land.[9] Both the necessity for belief and the necessity for toleration are seen in the following "Thoughts" of Leland:

The strange and unmeaning creeds that have been formed on the Trinity, with the punishments that have been inflicted on those who could not believe them, have astonished the mere reasoner—sickened the grave philosopher, and saddened the pious saint. But, on the other hand, when the doctrine is denied, or despised, with a view to destroy the dignity and glory of Christ, it merits the indignation and pity of all the humble followers of the Lamb.

Perhaps an objector may say, "these observations are applicable to Massachusetts, where the people generally believe in the Holy One of Israel, and in the divinity of the Christian Scheme." That the people of this state generally believe in the Holy One of Israel, may pass for truth, but that they generally believe in the divinity of the Christian scheme is not so true. As a religionist, I wish both articles were believed through this state, and throughout the world; yet, as a statesman, let me ask, why do they not learn to imitate their God, and regarding the scheme of his government, in which they professedly believe, reason thus with themselves: "God bears with wicked men, and so must we: God does not force all to believe alike, nor should we attempt it: Jesus never forced any man to pay him for preaching, and we must imitate him. The New Testament never calls in the aid of the magistrate to carry folks to prison, or take away their cows, or other property, to pay men for preaching, or build temples, and therefore, we will not. The apostles never taught the churches, which they planted, to be incorporated bodies politic, to make use of the civil law to regulate their concerns, nor will we. The New Testament nowhere says, that towns, parishes, precincts, etc., shall have a teacher of morality, piety and religion, three months in six, or pay a fine of sixty dollars, and, therefore, we will have no such laws. The New Testament churches were formed by the laws of Jesus, and the acts of the apostles only, and so it shall be among us." These observations show,

9. John Leland, *The Writings of John Leland*, ed. L. E. Greene (n.p., 1833; reprint ed., New York: Arno Press and The New York Times, 1969), p. 534.

that men wish to avail themselves of the advantages of religion, without regarding the laws thereof.[10]

Isaac Backus also saw clearly the distinction between freedom of religion in the civil state and the necessity for strict discipline and conformity within an individual church. In his pamphlet "Government and Liberty Described," which he based on Galatians 5:1, Backus contends that true Christian liberty and purity of the gospel are possible only in a state that allows liberty of conscience to its constituents:

> Those laws are contrary to Christian liberty, exclude Christ from being the only lawgiver and head of his church, and are a branch of public faith as they tax people where they are not represented. . . .[11] How can liberty of conscience be rightly enjoyed till this iniquity (taxation of dissenters in Massachusetts) is removed? . . . (Holy Scripture) says, "in vain do they worship me, teaching for doctrines the commandments of men. . . . The Lord hath ordained that they who preach the Gospel should live of the Gospel. Let him that is taught in the word communicate unto him that teacheth in all good things. Be not deceived, God is not mocked." And Christ solemnly forbids the giving of any countenance or support to teachers who bring not his doctrine, of which each rational soul has an equal right to judge for himself.[12]

Implied in the above and explicitly stated in other places, is Backus's view that doctrinal purity demands liberty of conscience. If the church is to be pure, then it must be free to disicipline itself under the authority of Scripture, and individuals must be free to unite with the religion they believe to be true. In *An Appeal to the People of Massachusetts State* (1780), Backus remonstrated against an attempt to impose taxes for the support of ministers:

> Now you are to note that Christ himself came on purpose to make divisions upon earth; therefore it is not all divisions but only such as are contrary to his doctrine in that HE IS HEAD OVER ALL THINGS TO THE CHURCH, and that she is *complete in him.* . . . And those are to be marked as deceivers who do not thus hold THE HEAD . . . another article in his doctrine is that no man can *see his kingdom* nor have the right to any *power* therein without *regeneration.* . . . And the first man that offered *money* as a means of obtaining power therein is marked with an eternal

10. Ibid., p. 249.
11. *Isaac Backus on Church, State, and Calvinism,* ed. William G. McLoughlin (Cambridge, MA: The Belknap Press of Harvard University Press, 1968), pp. 332, 333.
12. Ibid., pp. 356–358.

brand of infamy. . . . A third article is that the whole of our duty is included in love to GOD and love to our neighbor. . . . A fourth is that the civil magistrate's power is limited to the last of these and that his sword is to punish none but such as *work ill to their neighbors*. . . . A fifth is that those who receive instruction and benefit from Christ's ministers are required freely to communicate, according to this ability, to their temporal support as they will answer it to him in the great day. . . . A sixth is that none should hear nor give countenance to any teachers who bring not Christ's doctrine but pervert his Gospel, as they would avoid partaking in their guilt. . . . These are plain points of law. The facts and evidence that you are called to judge upon are as follow. [The article proposed for insertion in the Bill of Rights for Massachusetts] asserts a right in the people of this State to make and execute laws about the worship of God, directly contrary to the truth which assures us that we have but one lawgiver in such affairs, Isaiah xxxiii, 22; James iv, 12.[13]

Furthermore, the truth of Christianity means that its doctrines are true, and these doctrines militate against government-enforced religion. In a speech before the Massachusetts House of Representatives in 1811 Leland had this to say:

> Mr. Chairman, if Christianity is false, it cannot be the duty of government to support imposture; but if it be true, the following extracts are true: "The natural man receiveth not the things of God, neither can he know them; the world by wisdom knew not God; none of the princes of this world, know the genius of Christ's kingdom." If, sir, Christianity is true, these sayings are true; and if these sayings are true, natural men, as such, with all the proficiency of science, cannot understand the religion of Christ; and if they cannot understand the subject, they must be very unfit to legislate about it.[14]

This same concern for purity of worship and knowledge of God animated Isaac Backus in his fight for religious liberty in Massachusetts:

> In civil states the power of the whole collective body is vested in a few hands that they may with better advantage defend themselves against injuries from abroad and correct abuses at home, for which end a few have a right to judge for the whole society. But in religion each one has an equal right to judge for himself, for we must all *appear* before the judgment seat of Christ, that *every one* may receive the things *done in his body* according to that *he hath done* (not what any earthly representative hath done for him), 2 Cor. v, 10. And we freely confess that we

13. Isaac Backus, *An Appeal to the People of the Massachusetts State, Against Arbitrary Power* (Boston: Benjamin Edes and Sons, 1780) 8 pp.
14. Leland, *Writings*, pp. 356–357.

can find no more warrant from divine truth for any people on earth to constitute any men their representatives to make laws, to impose religious taxes than they have to appoint Peter or the Virgin Mary to represent them before the throne above. We are therefore brought to a stop about paying so much regard to such laws as to give in annual certificates to the other denomination (i.e., the Congregational, or Standing Churches) as we have formerly done.

The scheme we oppose evidently tends to destroy the purity and life of religion, for the inspired apostle assures us that the church is subject to him in everything as a true wife to her husband.[15]

In addition, government-enforced religion bases worship on the fear of man rather than on the fear of God. True worship of God, according to Backus, arises from a proper fear and respect of his power and his sovereign rights over all his created order:

And on the other hand, how do many people behave as if they were more afraid of the collector's warrant and of an earthly prison than of him who sends his ministers to preach his Gospel and says, *He that receiveth whomsoever I send, receiveth me*, but declares that it shall be more tolerable in the day of judgment *for Sodom* than for those who *receive them not?* Yea, as if they were more afraid of an earthly power than of our great King and Judge who can *this night* require the soul of him that layeth up *treasure for himself and is not rich towards God*, and will sentence all either to Heaven or Hell according as they have treated him well or ill in his ministers and members.[16]

In their arguments for religious liberty, Backus and Leland sometimes appealed to Jefferson and/or Locke. However, this is normally done simply to demonstrate that a highly respected thinker approaching the question on different premises agreed with the conclusion of liberty of conscience.

While John Leland was an enthusiastic supporter of Thomas Jefferson and sometimes used his vocabulary, Leland's concept of liberty of conscience and "inalienable rights" were derived from his Calvinistic theology and not Jefferson's rationalism. In 1801, during the presidency of Jefferson, Leland presented a fast-day sermon entitled "A Blow at the Root," in which he defined liberty of conscience as "the inalienable right that each individual has, of worshipping his God according to the dictates of his conscience, without being prohibited, directed, or controlled therein by human law, either in time, place, or

15. *Backus on Church, State*, pp. 332–333.
16. Ibid., pp. 334–335.

manner."[17] It is clear in Leland's discussion that these "inalienable rights" are not rationalistic but derive from Christian theology. The inalienable rights spoken of are "not subject to legal control," but each individual must be "fully persuaded in his own mind" the nature of what "God has appointed in his word." No legislature, "uninspired by the Holy Ghost, has any right to appoint fixed sabbaths."[18] Leland was persuaded that the "same spirit that influences men to love God, and their neighbors, also influences them to give willingly to those who preach the word, and for other necessary uses."[19]

In fact, according to Leland, the spiritual nature of Christianity defies any eternal legal enactment of its essence. Laws can only effect the most human and unnecessary elements of the faith and leave the root of the matter untouched. Therefore, any attempt of civil government to enforce a code on religion is as ludicrous as it is abominable. Leland elaborates:

> How often have I wished, that when rulers undertake to make laws about religion, they would complete the code—not only make provision for building meetinghouses, paying preachers, and forcing people to hear them, but also to enjoin on the hearers, repentance, faith, self-denial, love to God and love to man—that every one who did not repent of his sin, should pay five pounds—that all those who did not believe, should pay ten pounds—that every soul who did not deny himself, and take up his cross daily, should pay fifteen pounds—that if a man did not love God with all his heart, he should be imprisoned a year—and that if a man did not love his neighbor as himself, he should be confined for life.
>
> That all these duties are taught in the New Testament is certain; if, therefore, the laws of man are to enjoin moral duties, these important ones should not be neglected but, on only hearing of them, our minds are struck with the absurdity of reducing them to civil legislation and jurisprudence, and had not the poison of anti-christ infected the minds of men, they would be equally struck with the idea of making human laws about any religious article.
>
> It follows then, that the money necessary in the Christian cause, is to be raised by moral obedience.
>
> The gods of Egypt could not speak for themselves, and therefore Pharaoh spoke for them, and made a law to assign the priests a portion, by which means they saved their lands in the seven years of famine. Baal was asleep and could not provide for his prophets, and therefore Jezebel fed them at her table; but Jehovah, being a living God, made a law for the maintenance of the priests in the Mosaic economy, but he never

17. Leland, *Writings*, p. 231.
18. Ibid., p. 248.
19. Ibid.

empowered magistrates to execute that law. It was a *divine* and not a *human* law, and when the people neglected it, they had to answer to God and not to man. And when two of those priests grew lordly and said, "thou shalt give us not, and if not we will take it by force," their sin was great, and they were both slain in one day. Even so has the Lord ordained in the New Testament, that those who preach the gospel should live of it. God has ordained it, but has not ordained that rulers should enforce it. Whenever, therefore, money is given for religious purposes, it is given in obedience to the law of God, and not in obedience to the laws of men: I mean when it is *rightly* given.[20]

In the same way, Backus sometimes approves of John Locke's thought, but only where he can expand it upon the basis of biblical authority and merge it with his thoroughgoing Calvinism.[21] For example, in his draft for a Bill of Rights for the Massachusetts Constitution, he uses the terms *unalienable* and *natural* in speaking about rights. However, this is sublimated to the necessity of voluntary obedience to God and not to the inherent goodness or rationality of man.

> All men are born equally free and independent, and have certain natural, inherent and unalienable rights, among which are the enjoying and defending life and liberty, acquiring, possessing, and protecting property, and pursuing and obtaining happiness and safety.
> As God is the only worthy object of all religious worship, and nothing can be true religion but a voluntary obedience unto his revealed will, of which each rational soul has an equal right to judge for itself, every person has an unalienable right to act in all religious affairs according to the full persuasion of his own mind, where others are not injured thereby.[22]

Backus's primary mentor in theological methods leading to religious liberty was Roger Williams. He first mentions reading the works of Williams on February 2, 1773, and quotes him in opposition to John Cotton in a tract Backus wrote that year entitled "An Appeal to the Public for Religious Liberty." After quoting Williams, Backus remarked, "How weighty are these arguments against confounding church and state together?"

Backus would especially enjoy the arguments of Williams, for Williams reasoned from a foundation of Calvinistic theology. The doctrines of unconditional election, total depravity, bondage of the will, perseverance of the saints, and the absolute holiness of God dominated

20. Ibid., p. 247.
21. *Backus on Church, State*, pp. 39, 43, 297.
22. Ibid., p. 487.

Williams's writings on liberty of conscience. For example, the doctrine of total depravity necessitates freedom of conscience. When John Cotton objected that people would be infected by allowing heresy in the land, Williams replied:

> I answer secondly, dead men cannot be infected. The civil state the world being in a natural state in sin whatever be the state religion under which persons are forced, it is impossible it should be infected. Indeed, the living, the believing, the church and spiritual state, that and that only, is capable of infection.[23]

In a later section he applies this same doctrine to prove the futility of forced worship:

> Accordingly, an unbelieving soul, being dead in sin, although he be changed from one worship to another, like a dead man shifted into several changes of apparel cannot please God. And consequently, whatever such an unbelieving and unregenerate person acts in worship of religion, it is sin.[24]

The doctrines of the perseverance of the saints, unconditional election, and reprobation contribute to this statement by Williams:

> So here, whatever be the soul infection breathed out from the lying lips of a plague sick Pharisee, yet . . . not one elect or chosen of God shall perish. God's sheep are safe in his eternal hand and counsel and he that knows his material knows also his mystical stars their numbers and calls them everyone by name. None falls into the ditch on the blind Pharisees' back but such as were ordained to that condemnation, both guide and followers.[25]

Bondage of the will and the holiness of God are essential to a proper concept of religious liberty. In the conversation between Peace and Truth in the *Bloudy Tenet* . . . Williams puts these words in the mouth of Peace:

> Me thinks I discern a three-fold guilt upon such civil powers as imposed upon and enforce the conscience. Either to depart from that worship which is persuaded of, or to exercise any worship which it has not faith

23. Roger Williams, *The Complete Writings of Roger Williams*, 7 vols. (New York: Russell & Russell, 1963), vol. 3, *Bloudy Tenet of Persecution for Cause of Conscience*, pp. 125–126.
24. Ibid., pp. 137–139.
25. Ibid., pp. 208–209.

in. First, of an appearance of that Arminian popish doctrine of free-will as if it lay in their own power and ability to believe upon the magistrate's command. Since it is confessed that what is submitted to by any without faith is sin be it never so true and holy. Second, since God only opens the heart and works the will, it seems to be a high presumption to suppose that together with a command restraining from or constraining to worship, that God is also to be forced or commanded to give faith to open the heart and to incline the will. And third, a guilt of a hypocrisy of their subjects and people enforcing them to act and practice in matters of religion and worship against the doubts and checks of their consciences. Causing, their bodies to worship when their souls are far off, to draw near with their lips, their hearts being far off.[26]

A biblical example of liberty of conscience proceeding from divine election and total depravity can be found in John 10:22–39. In their efforts to trap Jesus, the Jews ask him if he was the Messiah. Jesus indicated that they should be convinced of that by both his words and his works. They showed their depravity by trying to kill him or have him arrested, even while he was giving them irrefutable evidence of his messiahship. How ridiculous it would have been for the Roman emperor to seek to enforce a feigned worship upon such recalcitrant minds.

In this same passage Jesus also said, "But ye believe not, because ye are not of my sheep. . . . My sheep hear my voice . . ." (vv. 26–27). Had Jesus desired their eternal worship and following, he would have wrought internal submission in their lives. Again, to use government to enforce a show of worship unprompted by the electing power of God would be totally out of harmony with this passage, with the entire New Testament, and with the truths of God's sovereign election and man's total depravity and deadness in sin.

The only consistent basis on which to affirm liberty of conscience is the bedrock of unconditional election. The wheat and tares will stay in the world together until separated by God's angels. The tares must not be forced into the church, the pillar and bulwark of the truth. Only in this way will the prerogatives and worship of God be properly safeguarded.

26. Ibid., pp. 255–259.

16

World Missions and Bold Evangelism

The Power of Grace Exhibited

The Bible is a book of evangelism. No, not a "how to" handbook, but in its message and purpose one cannot escape the evangelistic passion of God's Word. This is so because the Bible is a gospel book from beginning to end. How does God, consistent with his glory and righteousness, demonstrate his love in the redemption of his fallen creature, man? That is the theme of Scripture. And because the Bible is a gospel book, it is indeed a book of evangelism; that is, in itself the Bible is a public display of the evangel. This brings on an important question: What is evangelism?

Evangelism Defined

In arriving at any useful definition, we are not necessarily limited to the exercise of deducing specific descriptions from general premises. Such deductions have to be made at times and are helpful and instructive when carried through carefully. The investigation of some facets of the evangelistic enterprise must be carried on that way, and Christians should not be afraid of careful and tough thinking in such an important area. However, specific help in this matter comes from the pages of the New Testament. While a much larger study would include critical investigation of masses of scriptural evidence, the outlines of this definition will be derived from three specific descriptions of "evangelists" in the New Testament.

In Ephesians 4:11 Paul lists "evangelists" as one of God's gifts to the church. The intended ultimate effect of these gifts is that "we all attain to the unity of the faith" (v. 13, NASB). The steps to attain the goal include equipping God's people to do works of service for the purpose of building up the body of Christ (v. 12). Approximation of the goal becomes evident when the people manifest doctrinal discernment and a healthy unwillingness to be moved into beliefs or practices that compromise their knowledge of the Son of God (vv. 13–16).

Philip is called an evangelist (Acts 21:8). Selected as one of the seven helpers mentioned in Acts 6:5, he went into Samaria when Saul's persecution brought about a dispersion of the church from Jerusalem. Acts 8 describes his work in Samaria, where he proclaimed Christ and was granted apostolic powers in healing and performing wonders. As Philip preached the gospel about the kingdom of God "and the name of Jesus Christ," the men and women who believed were baptized. Philip was soon led to a desert where he confronted an official in the court of Candace, queen of the Ethiopians. The official, evidently returning from worship in Jerusalem, was reading Isaiah 53. Philip came near his chariot and, as the conversation led to it, "preached unto him Jesus." The official, a eunuch, was baptized. Philip, snatched away by the spirit of God, found himself at Azotus. He preached the gospel there and to all the cities as he walked up the coast to Caesarea (Acts 8:40). It is no wonder that Acts 21:8 describes him as "the evangelist."

Paul admonishes Timothy, his "own son in the faith" (1 Tim. 1:2), that in fulfilling his ministry, he must do the work of an evangelist (2 Tim. 4:5). Paul had delineated certain duties incumbent upon the title: preach the Word and be ready for such in season and out of season; reprove, rebuke, exhort with both patience and instruction. The inculcation of sound doctrine was to be the goal of such endeavors (vv. 2–4), for its faithful maintenance becomes a mark of those who are truly saved. Diminution of any aspect of the person and work of Christ is unacceptable in the task of evangelism. Separate doctrines do not present themselves autonomously for our acceptance or rejection, but cohere in the person of the Son sent by God. In 2 Timothy 2, Paul reminds Timothy that he writes from experience as well as revelation in these matters. Paul characterizes his ministry—in light of this glorious purpose and these sobering facts (that some go astray from the truth and upset the faith of others, but the Lord knows who are his own [vv. 16–19])—as enduring all things for the sake of the elect (v. 10).

What, then, can we discover about biblical evangelism from these passages?

1. Evangelism's message content is the gospel, summarized in a

person, Jesus Christ, and its individual truths cannot exist apart from this person.

2. Evangelism is the constant engagement of those called to it.

3. Evangelism's most common expression is in public preaching, but it includes personal encounter.

4. Evangelism is constantly on guard to protect the purity of its message and cannot tolerate compromise in content or endure flippancy or flattering craftiness in methodology (2 Cor. 4:1–7).

5. Evangelism's corporate result is public identification with Christ by baptism and submission to the loving discipline of a church, so that unity in the faith is reached.

On this basis of those five points, I will attempt a definition of evangelism:

> Evangelism is the constant and uncompromising proclamation of the gospel and refutation of that which detracts from it, with views to the glory of God, the clear display to all of God's righteousness and mercy, and the salvation and incorporation of the elect, employing preaching as the primary means, with the ancillary use of other means consistent with biblical example, and avoiding all means that diminish the necessary offense of the gospel.

Some may now be exclaiming, "What does the doctrinal content of this book have to do with evangelism? Evangelism becomes an absolute absurdity in the presence of the doctrine of unconditional election." It is true that some types of Calvinists have not bothered themselves very much with evangelism and have been resistant to the duty of exhorting men to faith in Christ. The position of this book, however, is diametrically opposed to the errors of hyper-Calvinism. Therefore, after showing briefly the strategic differences between Calvinism and hyper-Calvinism, this chapter will attempt to demonstrate two truths. First, the Doctrines of Grace are consistent with and supportive of evangelism and missions. Second, since evangelism and missions gather their purest and most consistent support *only* from the Doctrines of Grace, evangelistic methodology should harmonize with that theological framework.

Calvinism Is Not Hyper-Calvinism

Within the last two decades, at least two highly detailed studies of hyper-Calvinism have emerged: Peter Toon's *The Emergence of Hyper-Calvinism in English Nonconformity 1689–1765,* and Curt Daniel's unpublished doctoral dissertation for the University of Edinburgh (1983), "Hyper-Calvinism and John Gill." Toon gives the following descriptive definition of hyper-calvinism:

> It was a system of theology, or a system of the doctrines of God, man and grace, which was framed to exalt the honour and glory of God and did so at the expense of minimising the moral and spiritual responsibility of sinners to God. It placed excessive emphasis on the immanent acts of God. . . . In practice, this meant that "Christ and Him crucified", the central message of the apostles, was obscured. It also made no distinction between the secret and the revealed will of God, and tried to deduce the duty of men from what it taught concerning the secret, eternal decrees of God. This led to the notion that grace must only be offered to those for whom it was intended. . . . So Hyper-Calvinism led its adherents to hold that evangelism was not necessary.[1]

Curt Daniel, in his dissertation of over 900 pages, defined the phenomenon as:

> . . . that school of Supralapsarian 'Five Point' Calvinism which so stresses the sovereignty of God by overemphasizing the secret over the revealed will and eternity over time, that it minimizes the responsibility of Man, notably with respect to the denial of the word 'offer' in relation to the preaching of the Gospel of a finished and limited atonement, thus undermining the universal duty of sinners to believe savingly with the assurance that the Lord Jesus Christ died for them. . . .[2]

Daniel then goes further and reduces his definition to one factor: "it is the rejection of the word 'offer' in connection with evangelism for supposedly Calvinistic reasons . . . the only real tangible thing which differentiates the Hyper from the High Calvinists is the word 'offer.'[3]

R. T. Kendall (D.Phil.Oxon.), pastor of Westminster Chapel, defines hyper-Calvinism in the appendix of his book *Stand Up and Be Counted*.

> Hyper-Calvinism. This is a spirit that militates against evangelism and the free offer of the gospel. It has its roots in high Calvinism but goes beyond it. Many high Calvinists would still hold to the free offer of the gospel—that you should offer the gospel to everyone even though Christ

1. Peter Toon, *The Emergence of Hyper Calvinism in English Nonconformity 1689-1765* (London: The Olive Tree, 1967), pp. 144, 145.
2. Curt Daniel, "Hyper-Calvinism and John Gill" (Unpublished Ph.D. dissertation, University of Edinburgh, 1983), p. 767.
3. Ibid., p. 767.

did not die for everyone. Hyper-Calvinism holds that one must not say "Christ died for you" lest one should not be telling the truth. The most that the hyper-Calvinist feels that he can do is to say "Christ died for sinners" and leave the rest to the Holy Spirit. Hyper-Calvinism does not essentially differ from high Calvinism except in actual practice, which is why I define hyper-Calvinism as a spirit.[4]

It is unfortunate that each of these definitions focuses attention on "Five-Point Calvinism" as somehow the same in essence with hyper-Calvinism, with special reference to the doctrine of limited atonement. It is mystifying to me that Kendall could reduce the distinction merely to one of "spirit" and overlook any distinction in essence. Each of the definitions is helpful, however, for in the combination we have elements which must be considered in plunging to the core of hyper-Calvinism.

The two elements within these definitions most pertinent for understanding hyper-Calvinism are the word *offer* and the statements concerning the responsibility of man. The first I will discuss negatively, since too strenuous a focus on the word *offer* leads to a distortion of some larger issues. Within the second, the responsibility of man, I believe we find the sum and substance of hyper-Calvinism.

The Use of the Term "Offer"

Curt Daniel reduces his fine research too severely in defining hyper-Calvinism solely on the basis of its use of a word. The heated controversy and vilification of reputation surrounding this issue for the past two and a half centuries has had more foundation than the use of, or refusal to use, the word *offer*.

Several good reasons exist why the word itself would not prolong the controversy. I perceive that something more substantial is at issue. First, "offer" is not normally used in Scripture to describe how God gives his gifts to men. Offerings are made to God: Abraham offered Isaac; priests offer sacrifices to God; Christ offered himself once for all. Paul considered that in his martyrdom he would be "offered" (Phil. 2:17; 2 Tim. 4:6). Paul speaks once of offering the gospel (1 Cor. 9:18, NASB). His use of the word points to his unbounded preaching ministry in contrast to one that might limit its sphere to those who actually give monetary support to the preacher. Normally the word *offer* has too dormant a connotation to incorporate the vivid and active images

---

4. R. T. Kendall, *Stand Up and Be Counted* (London: Hodder and Stoughton, 1984), p. 120. Compare his statement also on p. 63, where he links hyper-Calvinism specifically with the doctrine of limited atonement.

picturing the effectuality of gospel preaching: the blind see, the dead live, the sleepers awaken, the sinners' resistance is aggravated, and a sweet-smelling savor rises to the nostrils of God. In apostolic examples of preaching, we see little of what might be called "offer" and much of what is called "command." Men are commanded to lay down arms and surrender to God, who demonstrates his sovereign holiness in all his actions—creation, providence, and redemption—and promises of forgiveness encourage those who truly comply. The unabridged version of the gospel simply cannot be contained within the normal connotations of the word *offer*.

A great historical misfortune agitates the misunderstandings at this point. Joseph Hussey's remarkable defense of hyper-Calvinism (1707) had within its title the words "No Offers of His Grace." This tends to focus the controversy on that phrase and justify neglect of the root problem. Offers may be rejected or engaged in, depending on the content of the offer; but at bottom the question is this: How much responsibility does a man have to God, and on what ground is that responsibility established?

Before we look at that question, the "offers" problem must first be set in precise focus. There is one sense in which the idea of making an offer is inaccurate, and there is another sense in which it is acceptable. The issue must not be allowed to become narrowly verbal but must maintain a conceptual framework. So let us continue our reasons why the mere use of or refusal to use the word *offer* should not be a point of controversy.

Second, grace cannot be "offered." Grace is purely within the sovereign prerogatives of God, and those who argue for the validity of offering grace place themselves in the position which they claim is so presumptuous in the hyper-Calvinist. To offer grace is to determine human responsibility from a supposed knowledge of the divine intentions toward all men in particular. Those who argue for general atonement on this basis pursue the same erroneous line of thought. Neither the evangelist nor the sinner need have guarantees that grace accompanies their interaction for the responsibility of either to be established. It is enough that both know that God commands all men everywhere to repent and has highlighted the absolute seriousness of the matter in the entire Christ event culminating in the resurrection from the dead. Grace is the sovereign bestowment of salvific blessings; its appearance among men is purely a matter of sovereign discrimination. Such an understanding is nothing less than historic evangelical Calvinism. An "offer" of grace, therefore, presupposes a redefinition of the word *grace*.

Third, Christ offers himself in his entirety to all who want him as

such: "Come unto me, all ye that labour and are heavy laden . . ."
(Matt. 11:28). He offers no individual blessings apart from receiving
him and the reproach the world has for him. He does not offer forgiveness without repentance, nor celestial glory without the straight
and narrow road to it, nor wisdom without long hours in the school
of Christ, nor the wearing of a crown without the bearing of a cross,
nor the enjoyment of God without the denial of self, nor redemption
from the penalty of sin without deliverance from its power, enjoyment,
and eventually its presence. All who seek to have any blessing Christ
gives, apart from Christ himself and all he brings, have not received
him as he offers himself. In this sense Paul offered the gospel. In this
sense the minister of the gospel must offer Christ—"He that hath the
Son hath life; and he that hath not the Son of God hath not life"
(1 John 5:12)—the Son in his entirety for life in its entirety. On this
basis the evangelist says, "Come to Jesus," for in this sense Jesus said,
"Come unto me." One who scruples at the word *offer* in this matter
should not be maligned.

The Moral Responsibility of Man

At this point hyper-Calvinism should be defined. Toon says that the
system in question exalted the honor and glory of God "at the expense
of minimising the moral and spiritual responsibility of sinners to God."[5]
That is the crux of the issue. Man's responsibility may be neither established nor diminished by grace but exists apart from it. Article 26
of the Gospel Standard Articles is a good example of the denial of
human responsibility on the basis of the necessity of grace:

> We deny duty faith and duty repentance—these terms signifying that it
> is every man's duty spiritually and savingly to repent and believe. . . .
> We deny also that there is any capability in man by nature to any spir-
> itual good whatever. So that we reject the doctrine that men in a state
> of nature should be exhorted to believe in or turn to God.

The stream of thought is obvious. A man may not be exhorted to do
anything he is spiritually incapable of doing. The end of such a line
of reasoning, if carried through rigorously, is disastrous indeed.

The strategic question at this point is: 'Whence this lack of ability?'
Here we discover the actuating premise of hyper-Calvinism. According
to the true hyper-Calvinist, this lack of ability "to any spiritual good
whatever" does not arise from the fall. It is, rather, an ability with

5. Toon, *Emergence of Hyper Calvinism*, p. 144.

which man was never endowed, and it contemplates activities that in his unfallen state were both not required and not necessary. Lewis Wayman, an independent minister who died in 1764 after pastoring the same church for forty-six years (Kimbolton, England), took an active part in the "modern question" controversy of the mid-eighteenth century. In his book, *A Further Enquiry After the Truth*, he contends that saving faith "was not in the power of man, in his best estate before the fall." That idea carries great significance for the sinner today. Why?

> What Adam had we all had in him; and what Adam lost we all lost in him, and are debtors to God on both accounts; but Adam had not the faith of God's elect before the fall, and did not lose it for his posterity; therefore, they are not debtors to God for it while in unregeneracy.[6]

Wayman was simply following the Congregational minister Joseph Hussey (d. 1726) in arguing against the duty of unregenerate man to believe. Hussey had also argued strenuously against "offers of grace" and had connected this as a natural concomitant to the issue of duty-faith: "But invitations to any Supernatural acts, such as the exercise and putting forth of Saving Faith into the Person of Christ, have no footing in the Sacred Oracles."[7] This connection between "offers" and "duty faith" has no warrant, however, for the issues move within two different spheres. One concerns God's secret counsels, while the other concerns the necessity of man's submission to the Creator in all things. The first cannot extinguish the second. Hussey's use of the phrase "invitations to . . . Saving Faith" shows his subtlety in the use of language, representing as an invitation what should be set forth as an imperative.

John Brine, an eighteenth-century Baptist (1703–1765), developed Wayman's thought further. Brine taught that every duty incumbent on man in his unfallen state he also had power to perform; the duty extends to all men in the fallen state "notwithstanding their present want of ability." Therefore, it is not lack of present ability that releases a man from duty. The issue of salvation, however, is in a different category; for "with respect to special faith in Christ, it seems to me," says Brine, "that the powers of man in his perfected state were not fitted and disposed to that act."[8] Saving faith lay not within the powers of man in his unfallen state, because there was no necessity for

6. Lewis Wayman, *A Further Enquiry after Truth* (London: printed and sold by J. & J. Marshall, 1738), p. 51.

7. Joseph Hussey, *God's Operations of Grace: but No Offers of His Grace* (London: printed by D. Bridge, 1707) p. 372.

8. John Brine, *A Refutation of Arminian Principles* (London: n.p., 1743), p. 5.

such. Since, therefore, it was no part of his powers in the unfallen state, it could not now be required of him in the fallen state. On this basis, duty-faith and duty-repentance are denied. This is the essence of hyper-Calvinism.

Where Calvinism Stands: Calvinists, on the other hand, consider repentance and faith as means by which the commandment to love God and neighbor eventually finds fulfillment. In repentance and faith, the sinner finds justification, perseverance in sanctification, and eventually glorification, whereby he shall enjoy God forever and love him in an unhindered fashion. That duty to love God and neighbor existed before the fall, and man enjoyed the strength to pursue it. Since it is still obligatory, the means, through which it eventually becomes a reality are obligatory. The fact that God bestows repentance and faith on some diminishes not one scintilla its obligatory character. That is the position of the author of this book and Evangelical Calvinists in general.

The Congruity of the Doctrines with Evangelism

Objections to the Doctrines of Grace out of an ostensible concern for evangelism often arise from earnest hearts. Such objections, however, betray at least three serious problems. First, the objection reveals a basic creature-centered approach to life. Second, such reaction highlights several areas of undeveloped and inconsistent thought in relating doctrine to practice. Third, the objection betrays an inadequate concept of the rationale for human action.

Creature-Centeredness

The first issue relates to creature-centeredness, the common malady of all of fallen mankind. One must not fall into the trap of determining to do only those things over which he has final control or which have as their ultimate motivation the pleasures of man. A refusal to participate in missions, or a suspicion that missions is ultimately unprofitable—based on the discovery that only God has absolute, predetermined control of the results—betrays a deep-seated case of what Augustine called concupiscence. This term refers to a desire to enjoy one's self or one's neighbor without primary reference to God and his glory. A concupiscent attitude toward the exalted enterprise of missions gives vibrations of irony and self-contradiction, but it is nevertheless a real phenomenon if a confrontation with God's absolute sovereignty diminishes one's sense of obligation and resolute purpose to preach the gospel. Such an attitude elevates the second greatest commandment over the first and should call forth two antidotes: (1) repentance for subduing God's glory to man's interest; and (2) a prayer of humble petition that God might grant us grace to be God-centered in our evangelism.

Relation of Doctrine to Practice

Second, to conclude from God's sovereignty that evangelism is "vain" reveals an inconsistency in the way one relates doctrine to practice. That both of these realities, doctrine and practice, are necessary parts of the Christian life is virtually axiomatic. It is impossible even to conceive of human existence apart from thought and action. In the same way, the Christian life is based on belief of the truth that results in godly deportment. Commandment, exhortation, and admonition never stand alone but are always based upon theological truth.

These two ideas are combined in a striking manner in 2 Timothy 3:16: "All scripture is given by inspiration of God, and is profitable for doctrine, for reproof, for correction, for instruction in righteousness." This passage mentions two areas in which the God-breathed Scripture is profitable—what one thinks and what one does. Being profitable for doctrine and reproof, as the King James Version says it, refers respectively to positive and negative teaching. Scripture provides the truths that build the world view of the believer and prepare him to reject, reprove, and expose erroneous teaching. The phrase referring to "correction and instruction in righteousness" signifies a rebuke to one's manner of life and a positive instruction in right living. The inspired Word gives guidance in both these areas.

The believer is not given theological teachings in bare abstract and then left to draw his own conclusions about practices. Nor is he given a list of activities to perform apart from the theoretical basis for those activities. Given the sinful condition of man, even the regenerate would draw ambiguous and improper conclusions without specific instruction in righteousness or doctrine, as the case may be. Therefore, both what to believe and what to do as a result of that belief are part of the revelation of God.

Under the heading of "doctrine," one may learn many things about the character and prerogative of God that are designed to make the believer's worship purer and the Divine Being more exalted in the eyes of all who behold him. These truths in no way diminish, but only augment, the Christian's obligation to be obedient to "the instruction in righteousness" given in Scripture. Anything one may learn about God's majesty, faithfulness, truthfulness, providence, wrath, and so on, is certainly not designed to make his children less eager to do his specific revealed will.

For example, the Second London Confession interprets John 13:18 and 2 Timothy 2:19 to mean that the number of the elect "is so certain and definite, that it cannot be either increased or diminished." If a person consented to this interpretation of the biblical language and thereby embraced the doctrine of unconditional election as from "before the foundation of the world" (Eph. 1:4), should this make the worshiper less zealous for the gospel? Absolutely not! In fact, the doctrine should prompt the believer to call all men to bow and worship before this awesome God. If it does inhibit his zeal, perhaps the zeal he inhibited formerly had been misdirected. The method of evangelism may be altered severely, but its *reality* should not be eclipsed, and its *purity* should be heightened.

Table 2 should illustrate the point that God's prerogative is independent of man's obligation.

Does the fact that God is creator and owner make it right that his children violate the commandment "Thou shalt not steal"? Nor does God's sovereignty over life and death mean that a murderer cannot be held accountable for his crime. God's ultimate control of satanic ac-

TABLE 2   **Bible as Authority**

Doctrine	Practice
1. God is creator and owner of all things. *Daniel 4:34–35; Revelation 4:11; Romans 11:35–36.*	1. Thou shalt not steal another man's property. *Exodus 20:15.*
2. The Lord giveth, the Lord taketh away. He brings death and sickness to whom and how he pleases. *Job 1:21; 2:10; 2 Samuel 17:14; Numbers 12:9–10; Acts 5:1–10.*	2. Thou shalt not kill. *Exodus 20:13; Matthew 5:21–24.*
3. Satan works only where and to the extent that God permits him. *Job 1; Luke 22:31.*	3. Resist the devil. Stand against the fiery darts of the evil one. *James 4:7; Ephesians 6:11.*
4. God works all things for good to those who love God and are the called. *Romans 8:28; 1 Peter 2:20–21; 4:19.*	4. Weep with those who weep, etc. *Romans 12:13–15.*
5. He chose us in him before the foundation of the world. Whom he foreknew he also predestined to be conformed to the image of his Son. *Ephesians 1:3–14; Romans 8:28–30.*	5. Come unto me all ye that labor and are heavy laden: Go ye therefore and make disciples of all nations. *Matthew 11:28–30; Matthew 28:19–20.*

tivity to his own purposes does not eliminate the necessity of our waging spiritual warfare against the wiles of the evil fiend. That God works "all things after the counsel of his own will" (Eph. 1:11) and purposes all things for good to those who are the called (Rom. 8:28) surely brings comfort to the believer, but it does not make suffering only imaginary or invalidate the Christian responsibility for weeping with those who weep. John Leadley Dagg affirmed this by saying, "The purpose of God determines his own action; but his revealed word is the rule of ours."[9]

In the same way, God's prerogative to choose, out of his own purpose, some to salvation does not erase the Christian's call to biblical witnessing. The Particular Baptist Foreign Mission Society rediscovered this truth in 1792. In an address to "their fellow Christians at large," they expressed this concept succinctly:

> Without the divine blessing we readily believe nothing to purpose can be effected. But is this an excuse for inactivity and sloth? Are we not encouraged by innumerable promises of the divine word? . . . Let then every Christian who loves the gospel, and to whom the soules of men are dear, come forward in this noble cause.[10]

Truth in the doctrinal area does not eliminate truth in the practical. Nor do God's commandments to us (the practical area) indicate that he Himself will not perform what he commands. "For it is God who works in you to will and to act according to his good purpose" (Phil. 2:13, NIV).

Rationale for Human Action

The truth that God's prerogative does not determine man's obligation leads naturally to the answer for the third problem in establishing the congruity of the Doctrines of Grace with evangelism: What is the rationale for human action?

One should easily see that both doctrine and practice are derived from the same source of authority. Therefore, the careful interpreter, while not rejecting the practical implications of theology, does not allow either to be tyrant over the other. The doctrine of divine election should not suffer emasculation by virtue of the existence of the Great Commission; nor should the Great Commission be ignored by virtue

9. John L. Dagg, *Manual of Theology* (n.p., The Southern Baptist Publication Society, 1857; reprint ed., Harrisonburg, VA: Gano Books, 1982), p. 316.
10. *Baptist Periodical Accounts* (1800), 1:12–13.

of the doctrine of election. The same source of authority teaches both, so the Christian is obligated to believe the one and do the other. This is the only adequate and defensible rationale for human behavior—the sovereign God, who cannot lie, commands certain actions of his people, and they should not be deterred from fulfilling those commands.

Although the commandment to preach the gospel is, in itself, sufficient rationale for Christian involvement in missions, Scripture has not left the church without further explanation of what is at stake in such endeavor. The necessity for witness is implied from at least three other biblical ideas—the glory of God, the Christian's call to suffer for the elect, and the call to suffer for the defense and confirmation of the gospel.

FOR THE GLORY OF GOD

The irresistible logic, as well as the explicit teaching of the Bible, is that man's highest calling is to glorify God. Jesus gives consistent testimony to this reality in his own ministry. According to John 11:38–42, the resurrection of Lazarus was to be a demonstration of the glory of God. Other purposes, however real, must be subsumed beneath the primary end. According to John 12:28, the main concern of Jesus in approaching the agony of death centered on the glory of the Father. True, the salvation of sinners constituted a goal, but it was a sub-final goal. The display of the glory of God in the harmonization of love and justice stands peerless as the preeminent purpose of the cross.

In 1 Corinthians Paul uses this principle to give the Christians in Corinth guidance concerning their decisions in eating food and drink previously used in pagan worship. "So whether you eat or drink or whatever you do, do it all for the glory of God" (10:31, NIV). The same purpose governs the Pauline benediction of Ephesians 1:3–14. The purpose of God the Father in electing a people before the foundation of the world and predestining them to be adopted as sons through Christ, according to the purpose of his will, is that his glorious grace might be praised (v. 6). The purpose of God the Son in dying to redeem the elect and reveal the mystery of God's will is that he who works all things after the counsel of his own will might purchase for himself a people who will live "to the praise of his glory" (v. 12). The purpose of God the Spirit in bringing to completion the salvation of all the elect by sealing them and becoming their earnest until they acquire possession of their inheritance is that praises from God's creatures might redound in eternity "unto the praise of his glory" (v. 14).

The Westminster Catechism in its first section of questions asks, "What is the chief end of man?" The respondent is instructed to say,

"The chief end of man is to glorify God and enjoy him forever." James Petigru Boyce wrote a catechism of Bible doctrine for children. The third question under the section on God asks, "For what purpose did he create all things?" The answer: "That he might show forth his glory." If man's highest call and guiding ethical rationale is glorification of God, and God's own activities are pointed to that purpose, then to miss that ideal would be the essence of sinfulness. The biblical statement of this is found in Romans 3, when Paul summarizes the sinfulness of man by the succinct analysis, "For all have sinned, and come short of the glory of God" (v. 23). The eschatological dimension of Scripture also points to this as perhaps the most conspicuous element of the final consummation. Revelation 21 describes the wife of the Lamb as coming down from heaven and "having the glory of God" (v. 11). This bride, the New Jerusalem, the dwelling place of those whose names are written in the Lamb's Book of Life, has no need of sun or moon, for the glory of God illumines it (Rev. 21:23). Whatever else these words imply, they at least mean that this present evil age will issue into an eternity that is characterized by an unbroken vision and inextinguishable presence of the glory of God.

The Triune God works to his own glory; the purpose of man is to live to God's glory; the essence of sin is that one falls short of God's glory; and the age of the ages will be an unbroken revelation of that glory. Therefore, the whole purpose of the created order, the events of history, and the individual activities of man is that the Sovereign of the Universe be glorified.

This insight was captured very well by John Calvin in his letter to Jacopo Sadoleto in 1538. Calvin asserted:

> . . . it is not very sound theology to confine a man's thoughts so much to himself, and not to set before him, as the prime motive of his existence, zeal to illustrate the glory of God. . . . He has taught that this zeal ought to exceed all thought and care for our own good and advantage, and since natural equity also teaches that God does not receive what is His own, unless He is preferred to all things, it certainly is the part of a Christian man to ascend higher than merely to seek and secure the salvation of his own soul.[11]

Not only is this the biblical approach and the historical position of Protestant evangelicalism, it is the most rational concept of the nature of the universe. If there is to be ultimate meaning and unity to all

11. John Calvin, "Calvin's Reply to Sadoleto," *A Reformation Debate*, ed. John C. Olin (n.p., Harper and Row, n.d., reprint ed., Grand Rapids: Baker Book House, 1976), p. 58.

things, and not eternal division and chaos, then all events and beings must be directed toward the same purpose. If all things are not to be forever penultimate in achievement, then this one purpose must be the highest and best of all purposes. The only purpose that answers this requirement is that the God of the Bible—the personal and infinite Being who is the embodiment of all beauty and excellence and the greatest and best of beings—be glorified and uplifted in everything. If the purpose of the universe falls short of this, then the highest and noblest aspirations of man are doomed to frustration. This does not imply that man naturally desires that God be glorified. Nothing could be further from the truth. But man does desire that the "best thing" happen, even if he views that "best thing" through self-centered eyes. The truth that God will be glorified changes the content of that basic human aspiration, but it does not alter the reality of its existence. Therefore, if there is to be final order and ultimate fulfillment, the consummation of history must consist of the glorification of God. The biblical picture of this reality is vivid and impressive:

> Wherefore God also hath highly exalted him, and given him a name which is above every name: That at the name of Jesus every knee should bow, of things in heaven, and things in earth, and things under the earth; And that every tongue should confess that Jesus Christ is Lord, to the glory of God the Father [Phil. 2:9–11].

Given the purpose of creation and the glories of the gospel, how could any be reticent about the necessity of the task of preaching the gospel to every creature? Francis Wayland, preaching before the Boston Baptist Foreign Mission Society in 1823, lay before his hearers "The Moral Dignity of the Missionary Enterprise" and drove home this very point:

> Having paid this our honest tribute to the dignity of man, we must pause, and shed a tear over somewhat which reminds us of any thing other than his dignity. Whilst the general assertion is true, that he is awake to all that is sublime in nature, and much that is sublime in morals, there is reason to believe that there is a single class of objects, whose contemplation thrills all heaven with rapture, at which he can gaze unmelted and unmoved. The pen of inspiration has recorded, that the cross of Christ, whose mysteries the angels desire to look into, was to the tasteful and erudite Greek, foolishness. And we fear that cases very analogous to this may be witnessed at the present day. But why, my hearers, should it be so? Why should so vast a dissimilarity of moral taste exist between seraphs who bow before the throne, and men who dwell upon the footstool? Why is it that the man, whose soul swells with

ecstasy whilst viewing the innumerable suns of midnight, feels no emotion of sublimity when thinking of their Creator? Why is it that an enterprise of patriotism presents itself to his imagination beaming with celestial beauty, whilst the enterprise of redeeming love is without form or comeliness? Why should the noblest undertaking of mercy, if it only combines among its essential elements the distinctive principles of the gospel, become at once stale, flat, and unprofitable? When there is joy in heaven over one sinner that repenteth, why is it that the enterprise of proclaiming peace on earth, and good will to man, fraught, as it would seem, with more than angelic benignity, should to many of our fellow men appear worthy of nothing better than neglect or obloquy?

The reason for all this we shall not on this occasion pretend to assign. We have only time to express our regret that such should be the fact. Confining ourselves therefore to the bearing which this moral bias has upon the missionary cause, it is with pain we are obliged to believe, that there is a large and most respectable portion of our fellow citizens, for many of whom we entertain every sentiment of personal esteem, and to whose opinions on most other subjects we bow with unfeigned deference, who look with perfect apathy upon the present system of exertions for evangelizing the heathen; and we have been greatly misinformed, if there be not another, though a very different class, who consider these exertions a subject for ridicule.

Later in this same message, Wayland described the arduous task of the missionary enterprise and rallied his hearers to the work by reminding them that such an undertaking called for "the noblest energies of man." Wisdom, perseverance, self-denial, courage, and faith "which enables a poor feeble tenant of the dust to take strong hold upon the perfections of Jehovah" were all urged by Wayland as indispensable characteristics of the missionary. Wayland highlights the two motivations absolutely essential in missionary and evangelistic work as (1) the mere favor of God, and (2) the salvation of the heathen.

This undertaking calls for self denial of the highest and holiest character. He who engages in it must, at the very outset, dismiss every wish to stipulate for any thing but the mere favor of God. His first act is a voluntary exile from all that a refined education loves; and every other act must be in unison with this. The salvation of the heathen is the object for which he sacrifices, every thing that the heart clings to on earth. For this object he would live; for this he would die; nay, he would live any where, and die any how, if so be he might rescue one soul from everlasting woe.

For the Sake of the Elect

Wayland's passion focuses attention on a second rationale for witness, the suffering of all things for the sake of the elect. The doctrine of election, rather than deterring evangelism, should encourage faithful and biblical exercise of it. Such has been the opinion of Baptists of the past. P. H. Mell, eminent Southern Baptist of the nineteenth century, speaks of the encouragement of the doctrine in these terms:

> 2d. It tends to make those engaged in the service of God labor with more diligence. While nothing is more paralyzing than the apprehension that with all our exertions, we shall fail of the attainment of our object: so, nothing is more stimulating than the assurance that success will crown our well-directed efforts. Now, if predestination be true, we know that God has purposes concerning us, and that all those purposes will be infallibly secured. And whenever, in a right spirit, and in a proper way, we attempt any thing that is in accordance with His revealed will, we are assured that our labor will not be in vain in the Lord. Are we laboring for God's glory by seeking to obey Him in heart and in life? We know that He wills the sanctification of His people, and therefore, we run not as uncertainly, we fight not as those that beat the air. Are we laboring as God's ministers for the salvation of sinners, and for the edification of His people? We have the strongest assurance in God's purpose, and God's promises, that our sincere exertions will not be unavailing. Though all our unaided efforts will be ineffectual to destroy the enmity in the heart of a single sinner, yet we know that the Lord has a purpose to accomplish in the preaching of the Gospel, and that He has declared His word shall not return unto Him void, but shall accomplish the thing whereto He sent it. Having, therefore, the conviction that He has called us into the ministry, though set down in the midst the valley that is full of bones—many and very dry—we can, by the Divine command, prophecy unhesitatingly, and look with confidence, to see "bone come to his bone," and perhaps an exceeding great army standing up upon their feet, having in their nostrils the breath of spiritual life. (Ez. 37:10)[12]

J. B. Tidwell saw similar advantages and outlined his understanding of the powerful nature of the doctrine of election. In his *Christian Teachings*, he asks the question, "What are the values of the doctrine?" and answers:

> (a) Encourages evangelistic effort—giving assurance that some are certain to be saved, Acts 18:10.
> (b) Encourages the penitent sinner by showing him that some will be saved. Hence he has a chance. . . .
> (c) Teaches the Christian worker that he is wholly dependent upon God's power for success.

12. P. H. Mell, *Predestination and the Saints' Perseverance, Stated and Defended* (Charleston: Southern Baptist Publication Society, 1851; reprint ed., The Wicket Gate, n.d.), p. 49.

(d) Enables Christian workers and missionaries to endure suffering "for the elect's sakes," 2 Tim. 2:10.[13]

In spite of such historical encouragement, many still object to the Doctrines of Grace, insisting that missionary endeavors become meaningless by such a system. Such an objector certainly cannot have thought deeply about the implications for either his attitude or the gospel.

I would charitably suggest that these objections do not arise from a disdain for the doctrine that grace is indeed unmerited favor, but rather flow from the love of souls and zeal for evangelism. One wonders what response would be forthcoming from contemporary Christians if given the commission of Isaiah. When God's sovereign majesty swept him into service and enjoined upon him a preaching ministry, the message he was given was quite discouraging: "And he said, Go, and tell this people, Hear ye indeed, but understand not; and see ye indeed, but perceive not" (Isa. 6:9). Isaiah then asked, "How long?" He was told, "Until everything is utterly ruined except one glimmer of hope that exists because of the life that remains in the stump of a felled tree."

The present-day response to such a commission might well be: "I would not dare serve such a monster of a God"—or "This prospect of desolation certainly cannot be true. For why would Jehovah bother to send me forth if he has already decided what shall happen?" Yet Isaiah, who saw a vision of the glory of God, proceeded into his desolate ministry.

But the promise today rings a far different tune: "I endure all things for the sake of the elect that they too may obtain salvation"—"God is not slack concerning his promise"—"Our Lord's patience means salvation." The doctrine of election is the promise of success for the power of the gospel.

This was the promise that prompted the entire modern missions movement. Has the contemporary Baptist world lost sight of its origin? Do the names of Carey, Fuller, Pearce, and Ryland no longer mean missions for the glory of the sovereign God?

One motivating factor for Carey and his associates draws life from the humiliation of Christ. If Christ could "stoop so low as to visit our benighted, wretched, sinful world" and be moved with compassion upon the "most undeserving and guilty, the most sinful and depraved" in order to recover an apostate race from deserved ruin, in what better

---

13. Josiah Blake Tidwell, *Christian Teachings* (Grand Rapids: Wm. B. Eerdmans Pub. Co., 1942), p. 54.

way could we demonstrate that we are partakers of his grace "than by earnest endeavor to imitate his example . . . by labouring to promote the salvation of the most ignorant and helpless of mankind?"[14]

Certainly this example must speak volumes to the believer who understands the nature of Christ's ministry. He came into the world with the knowledge that he would be rejected and that most would turn away from following him. No doubt, only those who were given him by the Father would come. Jesus declared:

> "All that the Father gives me will come to me, and whoever comes to me I will never drive away. For I have come down from heaven not to do my own will but to do the will of him who sent me. And this is the will of him who sent me, that I shall lose none of all that he has given me. . . . No one can come to me unless the Father who sent me draws him, and I will raise him up at the last day. [John 6:37–39, 44, NIV].

Later, in Jerusalem, at the Feast of Dedication, Jesus confronted the Jews with the reality of their condition when he said, ". . . you do not believe because you are not my sheep. My sheep listen to my voice; I know them, and they follow me" (John 10:26–27, NIV).

Could any Christian possibly imagine Jesus saying to the Father, "If there are only certain ones that you have given me, then I will not go"? The fact of particular election did not diminish either his obedience to the Father or the necessity of his death to redeem those whom he would call. The words Paul spoke of himself could well be applied to Jesus: "I endure all things for the sake of the elect, that they may obtain salvation, and with it eternal glory" (cf. 2 Tim. 2:10).

Thus, election serves as a great impetus to missions, for we emulate Christ in suffering for the elect. God himself has placed his love on them, and as long as his coming is delayed, there are yet more elect to be saved. Obtaining the object of our endeavors is sure. Energy could not be expended for a more noble company of creatures—the elect of God.

For the Defense and Confirmation of the Gospel

In light of its view of the glory of God and its emphasis on enduring all things for the sake of the elect, not only is election consistent with evangelistic and mission concerns, but the concern such a position demonstrates for the defense and confirmation of the gospel enforces true evangelism upon it.

Paul rejoiced in the maturity of the Philippian church because of

---

14. *Accounts of the Baptist Mission Society*, Vol. 1.

their "participation in the gospel" (by their monetary support of his ministry) and in their partaking of the grace of "the defense and confirmation of the gospel" (Phil. 1:5, 7, NASB). Part of his consolation during his imprisonment as he wrote the Philippian letter came from his conviction that he was "appointed for the defense of the gospel" (v. 16, NASB). Moreover, the attitudes of preachers concerned him little when compared with the matchless content of the gospel: ". . . whether in pretense or in truth, Christ is proclaimed; and in this I rejoice . . ." (v. 18, NASB).

Paul did not view it as his calling to make the gospel palatable, but to make it plain. In 2 Corinthians 4, Paul expressed his concern clearly:

> . . . we faint not; But have renounced the hidden things of dishonesty, not walking in craftiness, nor handling the word of God deceitfully; but by manifestation of the truth commending ourselves to every man's conscience in the sight of God. But if our gospel be hid, it is hid to them that are lost: In whom the god of this world hath blinded the minds of them which believe not, lest the light of the glorious gospel of Christ, who is the image of God, should shine unto them [2 Cor. 4:1–4].

The clear presentation of the gospel in a persuasive way (5:11) clearly consumed Paul's energies. Its outlines were so clear, its truth so inviolable, its glory so matchless, and its power so effectual that his ministry was defined largely, if not exclusively, in terms of straightforward, plain presentation of the gospel (cf. 1 Cor. 15:1–11).

The Christian sees the gospel as the power of God and desires its open proclamation, for in it the righteousness of God is revealed. This display of God's righteousness will be a "savour of death unto death" for some and a "savour of life unto life" for others (2 Cor. 2:16). Either way, its proclamation is a positive good and should be one of the greatest desires of all Christians.

God's Sovereignty—the Only Consistent Basis for Evangelism

The preceding several pages have sought to demonstrate that no contradiction exists between the Doctrines of Grace and true evangelism. The next section will candidly affirm that true evangelism can proceed exclusively on the basis of these doctrines, if theological consistency is maintained.

Arminianism Destructive of True Evangelism

Rejection of the distinguishing doctrines of Calvinism eventually disintegrates the gospel and makes Christ's death vain. A discussion of the implications of the doctrines of general atonement and free will should illustrate that conclusion, if not demonstrate its accuracy.

GENERAL ATONEMENT

Given the thesis that Christ died for all the sins of all men, certain results must follow. Unless one also denies substitutionary atonement, he must thereby conclude that no one can legitimately be brought under the condemnation of the law. Christ's death fulfills the demands the law maintains over those who have disobeyed it. Death, or eternal wrath, justly falls upon the one who falls short of the law's demands. God the Father set forth Christ as a curse to redeem those who were under the curse of the law. If Christ has done this for all men equally, they must no longer be under the curse of the law, else Christ died nonobjectively and ineffectually.

If the affirmations above are presumed true—and they must be for those who affirm general atonement—one can be condemned only for denying Christ. The sin of unbelief (so the argument often goes) becomes the only condemning sin. Other conclusions, however, must naturally follow. If one never hears of Christ, he never denies him. Moreover, he can never be justly condemned, for God certainly would not hold one responsible for rejecting what he had never heard. The ultimate extension of this position then affirms that many, (if not most or all) who never hear the gospel are saved.

Two examples of such conclusions demonstrate fully that the present description is not merely a construction of the proverbial straw man. The seventeenth-century General (Arminian) Baptist, Thomas Grantham, encloses this universalistic tendency in his catechism, *St. Paul's Catechism.* The following exchanges occur:

S. But can Man please God, under any of these manifestations of himself, without an Assistant?

F. No, he cannot, therefore God provided an Assistant, the Lamb slain from the Foundation of the World, to take away the Sin of the World, John 1:29. Rev. 13:8, whom he placed as a Mediator between himself and Man, I Tim. 2:3, 4, 5, 6.

S. But how shall any Man have benefit by this Lamb of God, or this Mediator, who have not the means to know him by his Name, nor his Offices?

F. Many who never had the means to know the Mediator particularly and definitely, must yet have Salvation by him, or else none of the Infant-race, dying such, could be saved.

2. All that know the Lord to be such a God as does exercise loving-Kindness, Judgment, and Righteousness in the Earth, do know this Me-

diator virtually, and believing on the Lord as such, do know him savingly, Jer. 9:24. Psal. 86:5.[15]

A contemporary Arminian treatment of the atonement strongly maintains a similar position. Donald Lake in the book *Grace Unlimited* spends much energy seeking to refute particular redemption. Then, opting for universalistic reconciliation, he discusses its implication for missions and draws a revealing conclusion:

> A valid offer of grace has been made to mankind, but its application is limited by man's response rather than God's arbitrary selection. God knows who would, under ideal circumstances, believe the gospel, and on the basis of his foreknowledge, applies that gospel even if the person never hears the gospel during his lifetime.[16]

It should be clear that these positions severely alter the ends of evangelism and eliminate its uniqueness. According to this view, no longer is the preaching of the gospel essential to the salvation of men. Ponder the situation and ask, "Is general atonement the friend of the gospel, and can it sustain true evangelism?"

FREE WILL

The doctrine of free will manifests the same tendencies but exhibits its weaknesses in slightly different form. A summary of the logic that naturally follows the assumption of free will would proceed in the following way:

1. A man is entirely able to obey the gospel commands, repent and believe.

2. If so, why could one not also obey the law written on the heart?

3. But if one can obey the law written on the heart, it is theoretically possible he could obey the law written on tablets of stone.

4. If one can obey the law, either on the heart or stone, he can be saved apart from the gospel.

It really admits of no debate that free will is a cardinal tenet of most non-Calvinistic systems. Most of them clearly insist on its necessity. This insistence transforms grace from its character as free unmerited favor into the inalienable right of all men if the duties of religion are legitimately to be required. Grace becomes the ground of

15. Thomas Grantham, "St. Paul's Catechism" in *Baptist Catechisms*, ed. Tom J. Nettles (Tom J. Nettles, 1983), p. 73.

16. Clark H. Pinnock, ed., *Grace Unlimited* (Minneapolis: Bethany Fellowship, Inc., 1975), p. 43.

duty. Thomas Grantham's *St. Paul's Catechism* demonstrates the truth of this characterization:

> S. Was Adam left in a capacity to do this [love and serve Almighty God] after the Fall?
> F. By the free Grace of God, he and all his Posterity are left or put into a capacity to obey God, so as he will accept them, when and in what he requires their Obedience, else they could not sin by not obeying him, Rom. 2. 1, 2, 14, 15, 16.
> S. Surely, if God Almighty do indeed require the Duties of Religion of all Men, then there is undoubtedly a possibility of Salvation for all Men.[17]

Dale Moody, Baptist author of *The Word of Truth*, shows similar ideas to Grantham's. His optimistic evaluation of man's ability to respond properly to general revelation equals a strong doctrine of free will. According to Moody, man may gain salvation without ever hearing of Jesus or the gospel that exalts his person and work. All one must do is react admirably to the revelation of God in nature. According to Moody, many do come to a true knowledge of God in this way:

> A last-ditch stand against a personal revelation of God outside the covenant with Abraham is usually made by using John 14:6: "No one comes to the Father but by me." However, this must be understood in the light of the pre-existence of the Son of God. Abraham was indeed saved by believing the promise. . . .
> Could not the pre-existent one make himself known to people before Abraham and to those today who never heard of Abraham, much less Jesus? The post-existent Jesus can make himself known also to those who do not know about the historical Jesus. . . .
> Those who perish, according to the Gospel of John, are those who are confronted by the Light of the world shining through Jesus and who reject this light, not those who have only the starlight of general revelation. . . .
> Guilt before God is gauged by the light people have, and those who follow the light they have will surely be accepted by God. A high view of the pre-existent and post-existent Son of God avoids the problems of a low missionary theology that confines all the revelation of the Son of God to the days of his flesh.[18].

According to such a view, one must conclude with Paul that "Christ died in vain," or at least unnecessarily. In addition, the argument Paul

17. Thomas Grantham, *St. Paul's Catechism* (London, 1687), p. 8.
18. Dale Moody, *The Word of Truth* (Grand Rapids: Wm. B. Eerdmans Pub., Co., 1981), pp. 61, 62.

pursues in Romans 1 and 2 to demonstrate the absolute essentiality of the power of the gospel to bring salvation is strangely controverted into an argument that men may be saved without the gospel. For example, Moody states:

> In the New Testament the witness to a general revelation of God in creation and conscience outside the covenant and prior to Christ is implied in many places, but the *locus classicus* is Romans 1:18–4:25. A general revelation of God is possible in creation at any time, in any place, and to any person. . . .
> It is possible to say that this general revelation of God has only a negative function that leaves man without excuse. . . . But what kind of God is he who gives man enough knowledge to damn him but not enough to save him? . . .
> The witness of conscience, when followed, may lead to acquittal at the final judgment.[19]

Again one must ask the questions, "Is the gospel honored in such presentations? Can true evangelism proceed on such a basis?"

Calvinism Protects True Evangelism

Why is Calvinism the only system that can maintain true evangelism without surrendering theological, biblical, and philosophical consistency? Two reasons suffice for an answer. One, the glory of God is the goal of Calvinism, and the system refuses to surrender any truth that heightens awe and reverence for his holiness. Two, for the Calvinist, the message of the gospel is the only method of evangelism.

THE GLORY OF GOD

The splendorous and multifaceted display of God's perfection seen in the gospel events must never be put under a cloak. If one desires to show forth God's glory in its fullest, he can do no better than meditate upon and give full public exhibition to the events and theological meaning of the cross. This clearly was the ministry of Paul to the Galatians: "You foolish Galatians! Who has bewitched you? Before your very eyes Jesus Christ was clearly portrayed as crucified" (Gal. 3:1–2, NIV). Paul then proceeds with vivid explication of Christ's penal, substitutionary atonement and the uniqueness of the historic gospel as the way of salvation. Only that message preached by Paul to the Galatians brings honor to God.

The great Baptist missionary Adoniram Judson compromised not

19. Ibid., pp. 58, 59.

one iota on this point. After the church in Burma was established, Judson devised a liturgy and a creed for the public worship of the believers. These documents express the doctrines Judsón taught as he evangelized, bringing the Burmans from worship of false gods to worship of the living and true God. The following articles from both the liturgy and the creed demonstrate his concerns:

> 5. The God who, free from all darkness and depravity, is perfectly holy and good, all whose deeds are righteous; who feels tenderly compassionate towards all creatures, and desires to make them happy; who, in order to display his perfections and promote the happiness of intelligent beings, has created this system, the heaven and earth, and all things; and who, being the Creator of all, is the sovereign Lord of all, with right to do his own pleasure in all things, we worship. . . .
>
> 7. The God who pitied the sinful race of man, and sent his only, beloved Son into the world, to save from sin and hell; who also sends the Holy Spirit to enable those to become disciples who were chosen before the world was, and given to the Son, we worship.
>
> Art. III According to the Scriptures, man, at the beginning, was made upright and holy; but listening to the devil, he transgressed the divine commands, and fell from his good estate; in consequence of which, the original pair, with all their posterity, contracted a depraved, sinful nature, and became deserving of hell.
>
> Art. IV. God, originally knowing that mankind would fall and be ruined, did, of his mercy, select some of the race, and give them to his Son, to save from sin and hell.
>
> Art. V. The Son of God, according to his engagement to save the elect, was, in the fulness of time, conceived by the power of God, in the womb of the virgin Mary, in the country of Judea and land of Israel, and thus uniting the divine and human natures, he was born as man; and being the Saviour Messiah, (Jesus Christ,) he perfectly obeyed the law of God, and then laid down his life for man, in the severest agonies of crucifixion, by which he made an atonement for all who are willing to believe.[20]

The clearest image of God's holiness, the most awesome display of his wrath, the most sublime measure of his righteousness, the fullest commendation of his love, and the most spotless exhibition of the inviolability of his truthfulness shadowed Calvary's hill when the impeccable Lamb of God died, the just for the unjust, that he might bring us to God. All who believe that pressing toward the glory of God should claim man's noblest energies—and this is the stated aim of Calvinists—will never compromise or amend the gospel as deposited in

20. Francis Wayland, *A Memoir of the Life and Labors of the Rev. Adoniram Judson, D.D.* (Boston: Phillips, Sampson & Co., London: Nisbet & Co., 1853), pp. 468, 469.

Scripture. For this reason, Calvinism is the only system of theology that will maintain a pure presentation of the gospel and thus perpetuate true evangelism.

This truth is admitted candidly by many of the most ardent enemies of coherent Calvinism. For example, Dale Moody admits this and contrasts it to his own view:

> Calvinism has tended toward an exclusive view that sees no value in other world religions, but Catholicism has seldom closed the door of possibility that a personal encounter with God may take place outside the special revelation of the Scriptures and Church tradition. . . .
> The exclusive Calvinistic view has been presented in great detail by Hendrik Kraemer, the first Director of the Ecumenical Institute of the World Council of Churches. . . . His view excludes all valid revelations of God and genuine encounters with God other than with the Word of God made flesh in the concrete historical revelation of Jesus Christ.[21]

Kraemer later slightly altered his view to the point that he feels salvation is possible for those who live apart from the biblical revelation. Moody was delighted. He now rejoices that Kraemer "has gotten out of the straight-jacket of early Barthianism."[22] Moody again contrasts his inclusivism against the exclusivism of Calvinism: "The missionary theology of Catholicism may be contrasted with that of Calvinism. This inclusive view, finally and painfully presented by Kraemer, is not far from the official pronouncements of Vatican Council II.

> Those also can attain to everlasting salvation who through no fault of their own do not know the Gospel of Christ or His Church, yet sincerely seek God and, moved by grace strive by their deeds to do His will as it is known to them through the dictates of conscience. Nor does divine Providence deny the help necessary for salvation to those who, without blame on their part, have not yet arrived at an explicit knowledge of God, but strive to live a good life, thanks to His grace.

Things like this were being said by W. O. Carver of Southern Baptist Theological Seminary at the beginning of the twentieth century."[23]

Thus fades the glory of God as seen in the cross of Christ, and one must conclude that he may be seen just as brightly in the funeral pyre of the Hindu. The serious Christian who has confronted his own sin in

21. Moody, *Truth*, p. 65.
22. Ibid., p. 66.
23. Ibid.

the cross of Christ must ask, "Can any system that sees salvation outside the gospel truly bring glory to God and perpetuate biblical evangelism?" According to Moody, only Calvinism maintains the doctrines that jealously guard the uniqueness of the Christian faith.

Centrality of the Message

The second factor within Calvinism that protects true evangelism is its conviction that the message is the method.

Historically, substitutes for the gospel have been numerous. Roman Catholicism replaces the immediacy of God's grace through the gospel with mediate dependence of grace upon the administration of the form and matter of the sacraments. The Reformers, beginning with Wycliffe, rejected such concepts of mediation and argued for the dominion of grace directly conquering the sinner's heart when the gospel is preached.

This immediacy advocated by the Reformers is abundantly confirmed in the Bible. The converts at Pentecost, the inhabitants of Samaria, and the pious searchers in the house of Cornelius heard the Word of God and were converted (Acts 2; cf. 4:4; 8:12; 10:42–45). Paul consistently points to the content of the gospel as the divine power that issues in salvation (Rom. 1:15–17; 10:12–15; 1 Cor. 1:17–31; 4:15; 9:16–23; 2 Cor. 4:1–6).

The effectual work of the Holy Spirit issuing in salvation becomes manifest on the basis of the proclaimed gospel—and nothing else. Various stimuli may prompt a thousand different motivations to draw forth responses, but only one message places sinners at the mercy of God, induces them to worship God in the Spirit, gives them no confidence in the flesh, and lifts them to glory only in Christ Jesus (Phil. 3:3). No other message can save, though other messages may evoke human confidence and activity.

The message of conditional election does not produce proper worship, for it rests God's activity upon man's response and thus magnifies the flesh. The message of free will cannot properly answer the question "What made you to differ from another?" for the answer ultimately must be that "I made myself to differ." The message of general atonement cannot say, "If we died with him, we shall also live with him," for the conclusion is tentative and depends finally on man and not the completed work of Christ. The message of apostasy cannot say, "Faithful is he that calleth you, who also will do it" (1 Thess. 5:24), for his doing it depends in the final analysis on the human will. Although some may be saved in the midst of such preaching, through the truth that often clings to the misperceptions, evangelism in its truest form will always point the sinner only to the cross of Christ, the grace of

God, and the exceeding greatness of the power of the Spirit. Anyone who points the sinner inward to make him dependent finally on his own will departs from the gospel at that point.

Therefore, all methods that focus on human abilities or the desires of natural man betray the gospel. Such methods cannot be justified as biblical evangelism. Falling into this error are many contemporary quick-gospel presentations and most uses of the public invitation or altar call.

Quick-Gospel Methods: Evangelism procedures that focus on a full and meaningful life or a "wonderful plan for living" have built-in dangers.

First, they minimize ideas that Jesus maximized: the forsaking of self-interest, the bearing of the cross, the suffering of shame for the cause of righteousness, and walking a path that is straight and narrow. Salvation in such approaches is prescribed as the answer to loneliness and lack of meaning. It becomes secondary and optional that one is changed from a life of rebellion against God, granted forgiveness of sin, and introduced into newness of life characterized by mortification of the flesh. Many times such concepts are embarrassing, for they tend to defeat the goal of getting a decision.

Second, such procedures pander to the material desires of unregenerate men, rather than confront them with the ungodliness and destructiveness of their own pursuits. "Joy inexpressible" or a "fulfilled life" seldom or never bring pictures to the unregenerate mind of endless adoration before the glory and excellence of the Creator. Instead, joy and fulfillment often imply merely freedom from harassment and daily demands, financial and psychological security, and indulgence of the demands of the flesh. The message sent is that—if Jesus can provide this on the simple conditions of admitting one's failure to find fulfillment and requesting that Jesus enter one's heart—why not try it? Although one may have to admit being a sinner, the power to decide whether to pursue a rich and meaningful life or continue a frustrated and unfulfilled existence remains. The admission of sinfulness simply becomes a part of the formula to receive the abundant life. Many an unregenerate person has been assured of eternal salvation through such evangelistic pandering. Again, the desire for a decision, based on the assumption of partial depravity and free will, results in a forsaking of the gospel.

This criticism does not arise from a detached, unconcerned analyzer whose hobby is to subject every phenomenon to the investigation of pure theory. For several years the above method constituted the passion of the writer's Christian work. Nor does sour grapes prompt this basically negative evaluation; for, judged by the design and content of the method employed, "success" more often crowned the efforts than failure. Nor were the weaknesses and misconceptions referred to above purposefully pursued. Sadly, they inhere within the system, for such methods are designed to be as inoffensive and attractive to the unregenerate as possible. This is most unfortunate and dangerous for the potential convert, for he may never be led to see that danger in which he abides because of God's righteous wrath. Consequently, he will never see how utterly detestable are his sin and rebellion. With that result one must not conclude that such an approach is only inadequate; instead, even its "success" defeats the true goals of evangelism.

Criticism of some methods of personal confrontation in no way implies rejection of all. The use of tracts, carefully written so as not to compromise the gospel, the distribution of Bibles and books, and the giving of printed copies of the Gospel of John may all lead to fruitful and edifying gospel confrontations. Open-air preaching offers a good opportunity for tract distribution accompanied by proclamation of the full counsel of God. Many contacts prompted by the power of the gospel may arise in this setting. Earnest application of energy and intellect to the necessity for personal confrontation can lead to a number of viable ways of setting forth the full force of the gospel message to lost men. This should be pursued with vigor and with the determination that the methods and instruments used will not eclipse the offense of the gospel.

The Invitation System: Another method of evangelism designed to promote decisions and quite often substituted for the message of the gospel is the invitation system. When this chapter speaks of "invitation," the reader should be attentive to the distinction between the biblical invitation and post-sermonic altar calls. The two should not be considered identical. The former is necessary to New Testament preaching; the latter, as many use it, is an unfortunate perversion of the gospel.

One should never speak against invitations, for they arise out of the necessities of New Testament faith. The gospel message itself consists of an invitation to all sinners to find forgiveness, to all the weary to find rest, and to all heavy-laden to find relief. Those who want to learn from Christ are urged to come to him. Thus, the whole message either implies or consists of invitation—yea, even beyond invitation unto command. The reality of this, however, should not be confused with public altar calls, or what this section will call the invitation system.

The invitation system prompts many pastors to focus on smooth methodology rather than faithful gospelizing. Unobtrusive transitions from sermon to invitation, mood, warmth, and music usurp the place of the gospel. Although characterized as evangelistic, such approaches do not deserve the distinction of the name.

Many feel that instruction in the most effective use of the invitation system is at least as important as discerning the true nature of the gospel. Such instruction follows:

> You can't hatch eggs in a refrigerator! The successful invitation will have positive results only when extended in a warm, spiritual, bright, living atmosphere—an atmosphere which is created long before the invitation begins. . . .
> Preaching for evangelistic results need not necessarily include evangelistic preaching. *The message is not as important as the atmosphere* [italics in original article]. . . .
> In the actual extending of the invitation, I try first to use a stirring illustration or challenge as far before twelve o'clock as possible. The later the invitation is given, the less the results will be. Normally, the shorter sermon will be more conducive to better results. It is of significant importance to attempt to go as smoothly into the invitation as possible. Ideally, the congregation should not be aware when the transition is made.[24]

Some insist that not only is the invitation the most important part of the service; it is the part in which God is most active and about which one should pray the most. Many times pre-service prayer meetings include such appeals as "Lord, when we come to that most important part of the service, the invitation, work in special power." One noted Baptist pastor has affirmed, "This is the part of the service, above all other parts, in which the Holy Spirit is in absolute control."[25]

Although such inadequacies abound, some pastors who use the public-invitation system carefully seek to avoid using its subtleties as a substitute for the gospel. True evangelism may then possibly occur, even under the burden of such a practice. Its presence, however, tends strongly toward compromise of pure evangelism. An example of an attempt to introduce theological integrity into the use of the method is seen in R. T. Kendall, in his book *Stand Up and Be Counted*. Aspects of his discussion will be alluded to at various points below.[26]

On the other hand, rejection of the present-day invitation system

---

24. *Proclaim* (Jan., Feb., Mar., 1977), p. 40.

25. Ibid., p. 41.

26. At the close of his chapter on abuses, Kendall says, "This is why I have endeavoured to build my case on Scripture and why I have sought to put forward a practice that honours Christ, safeguards theological integrity, allows people to respond to what they have heard and, should God be willing (blessed thought), allow Him to work in the hearts of people in an extraordinary manner" (*Stand Up*, p. 92).

does not always mean that a church is dead, liberal, or unevangelistic. Although that may assuredly be the case at times, such situations quite often reflect genuine, deep, and wise concern for biblical evangelism and demonstrate true trust in the power of the gospel. Many of those who refuse to engage in public altar calls feel that the weaknesses and misconceptions endemic to them override and destroy any possible advantages they might have. And numerous weaknesses there are.

First, although occasionally someone will defend the invitational system from the standpoint of the psychological release it immediately provides, this psychological factor in reality compromises the gospel in at least two ways:

The invitation system tends to redefine repentance and faith. These two evangelical graces are metamorphosed into decisions a person makes by external activity. In extreme cases one can easily see that the mentality of creating decisions greatly overshadows the gospel. Many statements of appeal demonstrate this: "If you need to come for any reason, come. . . . If God tugs at your heartstrings, then come. . . . You're not so bad, you're good and fine, just come and ask Jesus into your heart." Such appeals have so little to do with biblical repentance and faith that one can conclude it is a different gospel.

The sacramental tendency of this practice could not have more graphic illustration than that provided by R. T. Kendall in an anecdote he tells in his book. He relates a story about a meeting Arthur Blessit held in a posh English home. At the end of his presentation he had people stand to be "identified with the Lord Jesus Christ." He had them pray aloud. Some who did not respond felt ashamed later. One of these told another guest, "I have sinned greatly tonight. I didn't stand. But I did pray the prayer and towards the end I did say it out loud. Do you think that will do?" Graham, the other guest and a friend of the evangelist, assured him that God had accepted him.[27]

In relating this anecdote, I do not intend to call into question either the zeal or the motives of the evangelist. More, including this author, should emulate his compassion and zeal for wide dissemination of the message of Jesus Christ. I only intend to point out that the person not initially responding had an obvious sacramental understanding of the physical activity called for in the "invitation." Since he prayed the last part of the prayer "out loud," he wanted to know if that would do. It appears that he was only encouraged in this misunderstanding rather than instructed as to the true nature of evangelical repentance and faith.

More subtly, however, many preachers who mourn the worldly con-

27. Kendall, *Stand Up*, pp. 101, 102.

ditions of the church ironically, if not iconically, perpetuate the error. Extended jeremiads bewailing the existence of many who have "made decisions but are not born again" issue immediately into an extended decisionistic appeal. Spurious faith and false repentance are the most likely results of such a maneuver; thus, the error lamented becomes the error extended.

The psychology of the invitation system encourages pharasaism. With this attitude, movement down an aisle to stand before a congregation equals doing God's will. Doing something to be seen of fellow religionists replaces the worship God actually requires—pursuit of God in closet prayer (Matt. 6:6) and adorning the gospel with a lifestyle of godliness. Kendall considers the public pledge as a demonstration of courage, especially in countries under anti-Christian totalitarian regimes. Given the situation of freedom in the West, he surmises, "It seems to me to be a very small thing to ask people to do."[28] Doubtless the action is courageous in the U.S.S.R. and a "very small thing" to do in England, but the public pledge, as Kendall calls it, can hardly be identified with what God wants people to do. No one would call into question the necessity for courage; nor is public identification with Christ and the people of God argued against. Those who have reservations about equating immediate post-sermonic calls for a physical response (initiated by a planned appeal for such) with following the will of God desire strong biblical rationale before they can approve it. Baptism, incorporation into a believing group, regular worship and fellowship with other believers, and day-by-day pursuit of holiness and acts of Christian love—all these have the character of confessing Christ before men and are specifically commanded, as well as notably exemplified, in Scripture. Where is either mandate or example of the engineered call to "come to the front" stated as an act of obedience to God's call to repentance? When walking down an aisle is tantamount to following Christ and professing him before men, the biblical idea of godliness has vanished. The system that relies on the altar call encourages these perversions.

In addition to compromising the gospel, a second major problem with this practice arises from its historical pedigree. Rarely (if ever) used before the late eighteenth century, its absence did not seem to militate against seasons of great gospel flourishing in the history of the church. In a dissertation written at Southwestern Seminary in Fort Worth, Texas, Oscar Thompson concludes that the issuance of a public invitation at the close of the service is an American invention.

28. Ibid., p. 99.

Such a reality in itself should eliminate efforts to defend it as a necessary part of New Testament evangelism.

Thompson locates traces of public response at the end of a service as early as 1745 under the preaching of Eleazar Wheelock. Joseph Tracy, with help from the records of Thomas Prince, Jr., records the event:

> In the afternoon, Wheelock preached a "close, searching, experimental, awful and awakening" sermon on hypocrisy and self-deception. After a short intermission, he preached again. This was to be his last sermon in the place. As "he was delivering his discourse very plesantly and moderately," the depth and strength of feeling increased, till "some began to cry out, both above and below, in awful distress and anguish of soul, upon which he raised his voice, that he might be heard above their outcries; but the distress and outcry spreading and increasing, his voice was at length so drowned that he could not be heard. Wherefore, not being able to finish his sermon, with great apparent serenity and calmness of soul,—he called to the distressed, and desired them to gather themselves together in the body of the seats below. This he did, that he might the more conveniently converse with them, counsel, direct, exhort them, &c."[29]

One should notice that the response came spontaneously, and the suggestion to come forward was prompted only by the impossibility of continuing without some such remedy. Tracy severely criticized Wheelock's action, contended it should never have been done, and laid the blame for the increase in spurious believers and decline of revival at the feet of this growing practice. Wheelock's hearers were in no condition properly to reflect on the character of their disturbance of mind and should have been sent home "to engage in solitary, serious thought, in reading the Bible and in prayer."[30]

Perhaps Tracy's reaction is a case of hindsight superiority. Wheelock had to react quickly and with proper concern for the distress of the people. In any case his action has few, if any, parallels with today's invitation system of evangelism.[31]

29. Joseph Tracy, *The Great Awakening* (Edinburgh: The Banner of Truth Trust, 1976), p. 167.

30. Ibid., p. 168.

31. Kendall sees in this event the auspicious beginning of the modern invitation. It was "born in authentic revival" (*Stand Up*, pp. 47, 48). He then traces it through the First Great Awakening, Second Great Awakening, Finney, Moody, and enlists even Spurgeon as its advocate. Billy Sunday "did more to cheapen the practice of going out to the front than any well-known figure of the twentieth century." A reference to Billy Graham closes his historical discussion pp. 46–59). Dr. Kendall recognizes the use of the mourner's bench in revival time also, but concludes, "But to keep up the mour-

Although some eighteenth-century Separate Baptists appear to have closed their preaching with calls to prayer or some other public response, the practice cannot have been widespread. The following interesting anecdote concerning Jeremiah Vardeman from the pen of John Mason Peck is instructive in this respect:

> The next Sabbath he was at meeting again, where a crowd of people had gathered. He was expected to speak . . . [and] with deep emotion and the tears gushing from his eyes, he gave an exhortation, . . . and entreated his young associates to forsake the sinful amusements into which he had led them, and follow Christ. To his great surprise, young and old pressed forward to offer him their hands, and with audible voices exclaimed,—"Oh, Mr. Vardeman, pray for me"; and one said,—"Do pray for me, Mr. Vardeman, for I'm a heap bigger sinner than you ever was." . . .
>
> These social meetings were continued on each successive Sabbath, and two or three times during the week, with similar effects; though, before they closed, he gave an invitation to all who felt conscious of their sinfulness and need of the power and grace of Christ, and who desired the prayers of God's people, to come forward and give him their hands, and he would offer special prayer to God in their behalf. This practice became very common, especially in seasons of revival, with most religious denominations through this Valley. . . . *I have not been able to trace the practice beyond the social meeting described*, of the people spontaneously moving forward and entreating the speaker to pray for them [italics mine].
>
> Connected as it was with his first effort to exhort sinners to forsake their sins and flee to Christ, he always observed the practice, when he saw those signs of seriousness and anxiety which he was to quick to discern. He was opposed to all artifice and all preternatural excitements and contrivances to work on the passions of the people, and cautiously guarded his congregation from mistaking willingness on their part to have the prayers of Christians for submission to the terms of the Gospel.[32]

James E. Welch supplements this information concerning Vardeman with his own analysis of Vardeman's techniques:

ner's bench because it was born in revival is like trying to imitate shaking, jerking, quaking, wailing and other hysterical manifestations which were not uncommon in those times of revival" (p. 84). He does not conclude the same about "going out to the front." He says, "So in summary, although the practice of going out to the front was born in revival, it does not follow that the practice itself is valid only in revival times. . . . Making the public pledge available shows that the minister is motivated by a spirit of expectancy even in non-revival times" (p. 85).

32. William B. Sprague, *Religion in America, Annals of the American Pulpit* (New York: Robert Carter & Brothers, 1865; reprint ed., New York: Arno Press & The New York Times, 1969), Vol. VI: Baptist, pp. 422, 423.

When he perceived that his preaching had interested the feelings of the unconverted, he was in the habit of proposing to pray with them. All that he would do was to make them the offer, that if they came forward for prayer, they might regard it as a privilege. He never urged them forward, nor, as in modern times, did he go through the congregation, persuading persons to occupy the "anxious seats," and by such means induce those under the influence of excited feelings, to make a profession of religion, and thus introduce into the church those whose zeal prompts them to "run well for a time," but passes away "like the morning cloud and early dew."[33]

Several significant details should capture one's attention in the incidents related. First, John Mason Peck knew of no instance of public calling for overt acts prior to this one in 1799. Because he traveled and preached constantly on the frontier, his judgment should be granted a high degree of authority. Second, it arose, as in the case of Wheelock, out of spontaneous response. Third, the coming was never confused with identification with Christ. Fourth, if conversion resulted, recognition of it normally came days, weeks, or even months after the original response. Fifth, the practice was still rare enough that it was remarkable in Vardeman. Sixth, James Welch, highly prominent in the American Baptist Home Mission Society and one of its founding lights, was wary of the dangers of decisions prompted by the urgings of preachers in post-sermonic calls to go forward.

The Kehukee Association in North Carolina experienced revival in the early part of the nineteenth century. According to Lemuel Burkitt, the invitation for prayer occupied a pivotal place in the success of the days:

Giving the people an invitation to come up to be prayed for, was also blessed.

The ministers usually, at the close of preaching, would tell the congregation, that if there were any persons who felt themselves lost and condemned, under the guilt and burden of their sins, that if they would come near the stage, and kneel down, they would pray for them. Shame at first kept many back, but as the work increased, numbers, apparently under strong conviction, would come and fall down before the Lord at the feet of the ministers, and crave an interest in their prayers. Sometimes twenty or thirty at a time. And at some Union Meetings, two or three hundred would come, and try to come as near as they could. This very much engaged the ministers; and many confessed that the Lord heard the prayers of his ministers, and they had reason to hope their souls were relieved from the burden of their sins, through the blood of

33. Ibid., p. 427.

Christ. It had a powerful effect on the spectators to see their wives, their husbands, children, neighbors, &c., so solicitous for the salvation of their souls; and was sometimes a means of their conviction. Many ladies of quality, at times were so powerfully wrought on, as to come and kneel down in the dust in their silks to be prayed for. The act of *coming to be prayed for* in this manner had a good effect on the persons who came, in that they knew the eyes of the congregation were on them, and if they did fall off afterwards it would be a disgrace to them, and cause others to deride them; this, therefore, was a spur to push them forward.[34]

The force of the last sentence should demonstrate that unworthy concepts often cling to the most worthy objects. To use the invitation for exerting social pressure compromises the simplicity that is in Christ and builds unworthy motives for upright living. In fact, such pressures never do more than produce apparent uprightness; by nature they are opposed to true godliness.

Elements of priestcraft are frighteningly real in the practice as recorded. It is surprising that Burkitt, instead of showing alarm or even caution, celebrates the activities of the people coming "as near as they could" to "the feet of the minister." Yet, relief of souls from the burdens of their sins closely adhered (in the minds of the petitioners) to the act and to the prayers of the ministers, and this seems not a hair's breadth from the Romish doctrine of penance. No wonder that some who have seen the worst features of this system employed have dubbed it "Protestant absolution."

When, in the 1830s, Charles Finney began using the "anxious seat" and enquiry room as a regular part of his meeting, he bolstered his practice with the theology that revival is a work of man. In *Finney's Systematic Theology* he affirms the necessary freedom of the human will:

> 1. The moral government of God everywhere assumes and implies the liberty of the human will, and the natural ability of men to obey God. Every command, every threatening, every expostulation and denunciation in the Bible implies and assumes this. Nor does the Bible do violence to the human intelligence in this assumption; for,—
> 2. The human mind necessarily assumes the freedom of the human will as a first truth.
> . . . In all our judgments respecting our own moral character and that of others, we always and necessarily assume the liberty of the human will, or natural ability to obey God.[35]

34. Elders Lemuel Burkitt and Jesse Read, *A Concise History of the Kehukee Baptist Association*, revised and improved by Henry L. Burkitt (Philadelphia: Lippincott, Grambo & Co., 1850), pp. 149-151.

35. Charles G. Finney, *Finney's Systematic Theology*, edited and abridged by J. H. Fairchild (Minneapolis: Bethany Fellowship Inc., 1976), pp. 261, 262.

This assertion of free will led Finney into a high estimate of the contribution one may make to his own regeneration. After discussing the biblical relationship between the words *regeneration* and *conversion*, Finney concludes:

> Regeneration then is a radical change of the ultimate intention, and, of course, of the end or object of life. We have seen, that the choice of an end is efficient in producing executive volitions, or the use of means to obtain its end. A selfish ultimate choice is, therefore, a wicked heart, out of which flows every evil; and a benevolent ultimate choice is a good heart, out of which flows every good and commendable deed.
>
> Regeneration, to have the characteristics ascribed to it in the Bible, must consist in a change in the attitude of the will, or a change in its ultimate choice, intention, or preference.[36]

In short, Finney saw regeneration as an act of man's will, when supplied with enough truth. Although God is active in the clarification of truth, each man possesses sufficient natural and moral abilities to convert, or regenerate, himself upon hearing this truth. "Regeneration is nothing else than the will being duly influenced by truth."[37]

36. Ibid., p. 223.
37. Ibid., p. 225. R. T. Kendall seeks to move himself away from this error to maintain a Calvinistic view of regeneration (*Stand Up*, pp. 75, 76). He openly affirms his Calvinistic persuasion (pp. 15, 71), and, because he is aware of the tendency to abuse, makes a laudable effort to remove any sacramental overtones from his explanation of the "public pledge" (pp. 76, 78). In fact, his chapter "The Purpose of the Public Pledge" says the essential purpose of it is "confessing openly what is already true." He subordinates the instrumental purpose, that of actually prompting a conversion experience, to that essential purpose of open testimony to a previously existing conversion. On the other hand, he seems much more moved by pragmatism than theological truth in many places and chides those who seek to maintain unity between Calvinistic theology and evangelistic methodology (pp. 16, 22, 25, 54). In addition, though ostensibly subordinating the instrumental purpose, it squeezes back into the limelight by Kendall's tying the effectuality of the Holy Spirit's work to the use of the public pledge. For example: "Many times people will feel a great surge of warmth towards the message they have just heard but lose it partly because there was no opportunity to 'strike while the iron is hot.' It is sometimes countered by Calvinists, 'But if it is really the Holy Spirit dealing with them, that feeling will not go away.' I wonder. I also wonder if we have a right to 'play God' like that and judge just how deeply the Spirit may be at work" (p. 25). Kendall has no hesitancy in judging when the Spirit is at work in power (pp. 80, 81). Another quote related to instrumentality of the public pledge: "The very practice of the public pledge often releases the Spirit to work more deeply. Why? Because it is so easy to quench the Holy Spirit. When the Spirit is at work in the message but no opportunity for an open, public response is given, the Spirit will often be quenched by the sheer uninterest that usually comes after a person has gone back to the daily routine of life" (p. 82). I can't see how failure to offer the opportunity for the public pledge inhibits a born-again person from being public in his allegiance to Christ. And Kendall doesn't indicate how this understanding of "quenching the Spirit" coordinates with his belief in effectual calling.

The view of salvation formerly espoused in pulpits of New England by Edwards, Whitefield, and Tennent and blessed of God for revival of saints and conversion of sinners was viewed as simply incredible by Finney:

> What! call on him, on pain of eternal death, to believe; to embrace the gospel; to love God with all his heart, and at the same time represent him as entirely helpless, and constitutionally the enemy of God and of the gospel, and as being under the necessity of waiting for God to regenerate his nature, before it is possible for him to do otherwise than to hate God with all his heart![38]

Arising from this confidence in man's abilities came Finney's revival methods. Anything that could jolt the sinner and convince him to change his life was viewed as legitimate. Novelty for the sake of novelty could be justified on the supposition that it arrested the attention of the unregenerate.

Asahel Nettleton, an older contemporary of Finney's and an effective revival preacher, viewed Finney's methods "As exceedingly calamitous to the cause of revivals."[39] Such proceedings produced an abundance of "stony-ground hearers," according to Bennett Tyler.[40] Ironically, Finney's methods were much sounder and designed for more prolonged investigation than are many modern techniques in the invitation system.

Nevertheless, the invitation system has come to dominate not only modern revivalism but the very life and worship of many denominations, especially Southern Baptists.

Although isolated instances can be found of Spurgeon's use of an immediate call for physical response,[41] when he reflected on the implications of institutionalizing the practice, his conscience was stirred against the system's tendency to sacramentalism:

> ... Let me say, very softly and whisperingly, that there are little things among ourselves which must be carefully looked after, or we shall have a leaven of ritualism and priesthood working measures of meal. In our revival services, it might be well to vary our procedure. Sometimes shut up that enquiry room. I have my fears about that institution if it be used in permanence, and as an inevitable part of services. It may be a very

38. Ibid., p. 226.
39. Bennett Tyler, *The Life and Labours of Asahel Nettleton*, (n.p., 1854; reprint ed., Edinburgh: The Banner of Truth Trust, 1975), p. 335.
40. Ibid., p. 340.
41. Kendall, *Stand Up*, pp. 56, 57.

wise thing to invite persons who are under concern of soul, to come apart from the rest of the congregation and have conversation with godly people; but if you should ever see that a notion is fashioning itself that there is something to be got in the private room which is not to be had at once in the assembly, or that God is more at the penitent form than elsewhere, aim a blow at that notion at once. We must not come back by a rapid march to the old way of altars and confessionals, and have a Romish trumpery restored in a coarser form. If we make men think that conversation with ourselves or with our helpers is essential to their faith in Christ, we are taking the direct line for priestcraft. In the Gospel, the sinner and the Savior are come together, with none between.[42]

Three observations conclude this brief historical portion of the argument. One, the invitation system is a purely American phenomenon that arose gradually and almost accidentally. It cannot be viewed as an essential of evangelistic orthodoxy. Two, in the early stages of its development, response at the time of invitation was not viewed as equivalent to response to Christ in repentance and faith. In fact, the preachers sought to discourage such identification. Three, the regular use of the invitation system came as a result of shifting theology. The emphasis on free will and man-centered revival heightened the use of extended altar calls. Having already discovered how the doctrine of free will ultimately destroys the uniqueness of the gospel message as a way of salvation, one should be extremely cautious of employing any method built upon that theology.

Not only do the psychological tendencies and the historical evidences reflect negatively on the invitation system, the biblical material makes it fare no better. Acts 2:40, "and with many other words did he testify and exhort, saying, Save yourselves from this untoward generation," is often viewed as supportive of the invitation system. Yet so few parallels exist between Peter's situation and the contemporary pastor's situation that the enlistment of this passage as scriptural warrant for the modern practice becomes a prime example of the development of an argument after the fact. Pentecost stands as a unique event in the history of redemption, and the exhortations with "many other words" came after the cry from those "pricked in their heart" (v. 37). Furthermore, the content of the exhortation mentions nothing about coming forward but much about repentance and separation from a condemned generation; the public and physical act of identification with Jesus Christ is baptism. If the equivalent of the modern invitation system is present in Peter's words or actions, the biblical writer hides it under a veil.

42. Charles H. Spurgeon, "An All-Round Ministry," in *Good News*, Vol. 13, No. 5, April 15, 1981 (North Pompano Beach, FL: North Pompano Baptist Church).

R. T. Kendall points to Genesis 14:22–23 as the root of what he prefers to call the "public pledge." He argues convincingly for the necessity of public commitment to Jesus Christ, just as Abraham raised his hand and pledged publicly his allegiance to Jehovah as his only provider. But Kendall argues for what no one argues against in his call for an open nonsecretive identification with Christ. It is a *non-sequitur* to move from that into a defense of public altar calls, especially when he defends it as a temporary replacement of baptism.[43] This, of course, amounts to an admission that baptism is, in the New Testament, the formal public profession of faith. That the Bible ever warrants a temporary replacement of it will be difficult to establish.

In the actions of Jesus, the Bible does provide us with a clear view of the nature of invitations to come to Christ. A careful analysis of Jesus' actions towards men reveals three types of invitations: (1) those designed to encourage the penitent with assurance that he can surely be saved, for those whom God has elected he will surely bring and sustain; (2) those designed to draw radical attention to the urgency of the eternal as overriding all temporal concerns; (3) those designed to discourage those who come to Jesus for any less reason than a discernment of their sin and acknowledgement of his worthiness and ability to save.

Two major passages, Matthew 11:20–30 and John 6:31–40, 43–47, 65–69, vividly illustrate the first type of invitation. Matthew 11:20–24 magnifies the awesomeness of human responsibility in light of the great advantages offered. Sodom and Tyre and Sidon would have been converted had greater divine actions been done in them. These actions were not forthcoming, however, and the condemnation still remains great and just. Greater works by a greater person were performed in Bethsaida, Chorazin, and Capernaum; yet they were not converted. They rejected the Savior, and their condemnation will be proportionate.

Why do such realities exist? When God leaves men to their own powers, they always resist his call. If he does not move irresistibly, it is tantamount to God's hiding things from "the wise and learned." If any understand and come to Christ, it is only because he has revealed himself effectually as to babes, persons weak and helpless without him and dependent on his activity toward them.

The principle is thus established. Only God's sovereign activity endows anyone with divine saving knowledge: "All things have been committed to me by my Father. No one knows the Son except the Father, and no one knows the Father except the Son and those to whom the Son chooses to reveal him" (Matt. 11:27, NIV). On this prin-

43. Kendall, *Stand Up*, pp. 15, 45, 53, 96, 97, 123.

ciple, therefore, great encouragement comes to the one who discerns the infinite worth of Jesus and desires to come to him. The one who feels his own weakness and unworthiness and desires to find mercy and knowledge from Christ may justly be assured that he is the object of God's good pleasure: "Come to me, all you who are weary and burdened, and I will give you rest. Take my yoke upon you and learn from me, for I am gentle and humble in heart, and you will find rest for your souls" (vv. 28–29, NIV).

Similar dynamics control the situation described in John 6. When Jesus finally summed up his followers' reaction to him by stating, "This is why I told you that no one can come to me unless the Father has enabled him" (v. 65, NIV), many so-called disciples turned away and followed him no more. Rather than run after those leaving, Jesus turned to those staying and asked, "Will you go away, too?" Peter answered in the spirit of one who truly seeks Christ by responding, "Lord, to whom shall we go? You have the words of eternal life" (v. 68, NIV).

Neither of these biblical examples justifies public altar calls at the end of a service; instead, they discourage them. Luke 14:15–23 fits the same pattern. The consistent preaching of the Word of God will draw and keep those who sincerely want to learn of Christ and who realize he has the words of eternal life. The others must be allowed to go away. The one is easily distinguished from the other over the long term, but the public altar call tends to eliminate the opportunity for such discernment.

The second class of biblical invitations draws radical attention to the urgency of the eternal. Here we find such passages as Matthew 5:27–30; 7:13; 18:6–9; Luke 13:22–30. Other Scriptures fall into this group, but these suffice to demonstrate the point. Each passage contains exhortation to do something radical in order to gain heaven. If sin could be isolated to the hand and eliminated by cutting off the hand, then cut it off, Jesus admonished. Compared with the terrors of hell, no amount of pain, however severe, is worth fearing. Such solemn reflection, demanding such energetic and extended commitments, does not come in a flash. Instead, the realization normally comes with great deliberation and only after experiencing a gradually intensifying conviction that goes unabated. A public altar call is not of the character to enhance significantly these growing concepts, and the lack of one will certainly do nothing to diminish their intensity.

The third group of biblical invitations comes to those seeking Jesus with wrong motivation. These are actually designed to discourage the false disciple. Matthew 16:24–26 bridges the gap between the second and third categories. Jesus' demand to take up your cross and "follow me" is silhouetted against the background of gaining the world but losing one's soul. Many, however, fail to see the great disparity between eternity and time and thus live under the tyranny of the temporal. Matthew 8:18–22; 19:16–26, and Luke 9:57–62 picture some apparently eager to follow Christ or to find eternal life. Jesus dissuades all of them by describing the harsh realities his true disciples must face. In the case of the rich young ruler, Jesus' subsequent commentary, "With men this is impossible; but with God all things are possible" (Matt. 19:26) demonstrates that only those enabled by the omnipotent and effectual calling of God will be willing to pursue persistently the demands of the cross. The public altar call hardly ever engages in this sort of biblical discouragement. Moreover, the realities pictured in these passages preclude the possibility of registering accurately such a commitment in the moments following the sermon.

The invitation of Revelation 22:17 stands as the call for all who will enter through the gates into the city where stands the tree of life (v. 14) and where flows the pure river of life (v. 1). All who enter into that blessed place will join the call of the Spirit into one rousing chorus of joyful release and praise: "Come, drink of the water of life freely."

Conclusion

The Doctrines of Grace are consistent with and supportive of evangelism and missions. Not only is this so, but the Doctrines of Grace are the only system that necessitates the preaching of the gospel for salvation without forsaking philosophical, theological, and biblical consistency. If one says, "But you beg the question. You assume your system to be the gospel; therefore, only those who agree with that system preach it," I answer that all that is maintained as a presupposition is the following: The cross is necessary for salvation; the gospel is unique and exclusive as a means of bringing men to God. Based on those two assumptions, I have sought to demonstrate that only the Doctrines of Grace conform consistently to the necessities of the situation.

The Doctrines of Grace demand pure, unadulterated spiritual worship—and in fact produce such in true believers. Some methods, such as some modern witnessing techniques and the invitation system, tend definitely toward a compromise, if not a denial, of the gospel.

Conclusion

In the course of this book we have sought to answer this question: What place does Calvinism have in Baptist life? Historical, dogmatic, and practical areas have received the energies of our investigation. Before these answers are summarized, perhaps we should explore why the question has even been asked.

No doubt some will feel peeved at not only my answers but my question and methods. They may believe the entire enterprise is irrelevant. They may argue, "Certainly no benefit comes from resurrecting antiquated ideological systems when the complexities of the present have far outstripped the usefulness of those systems. It is far better to adopt contemporary modes and categories of thought in which to perpetuate whatever is experientially beneficial from the past. In that way, the faith is not embarrassed by its being identified with what finally proves untenable." The lack of systematic coherence and doctrinal absolutes provides a handy way out of any conflict with modern thought. The absolutizing of human experience, of which there is always plenty, offers a supposed nonfalsifiable explanation of metaphysical reality. See how easy it is to rescue the faith from any attack upon it!

In the form of Process Theology, modern theological thinking has finally reached its logical antithesis to the God of Calvinism and the Bible. The god of Process Theology is hardly identifiable as a person, has no power to control history, has only a relative understanding of justice, and knows little more than man does about what is right and wrong in the terribly complex problems that confront us today. Process Theology views history as moving and fluctuating and undulating with no ultimate goal or purpose and, in the process, "god" is being formed. It is, therefore, essentially atheistic.

425

That is the only resting place for theology, once the sovereign God of the Bible has been compromised in any way. The Christian faith is devastated beyond recognition in this system, and any hope of justice and purpose in human affairs is crushed sadistically. The biblical hope of the beatific vision becomes completely excluded from consideration, for nothing beatific can be seen in such a god. Again, once the God of the Bible, as clearly set forth in the Reformed faith, is sidestepped, there remains only nihilistic despair.

It is for that reason the question has been asked—What place *does* Calvinism have in Baptist life? It is the belief of the author and the demonstration of history that true theism must present a God of absolute sovereignty. Only within this sphere can any human responsibility and justice be maintained. Once God's sovereignty is diminished for the supposed sake of human freedom, we take a path that will ultimately shatter all meaning and justice and leave us not only with no god but with no humanity. When this happens, there is also no gospel, no true Christian mission, no holiness to pursue, no standard to which we are to be conformed.

Now back to the answer—which has three parts: historical, theological, and practical. First, I have affirmed historically, and I hope demonstrated, that Calvinism was the dominant theology in the most enduring areas of Baptist life for the first 275 years of modern Baptist history. Its energy generated the establishment of churches, the missionary enterprise, and the agencies and institutions of Baptist life. This fact raises several interesting possibilities. First, we could decide that our forefathers were right. Therefore, their answer to the question, "How is a man made right with God?" is right, and their contemporary heirs must do everything within the realm of godliness to continue on that foundation. Or, second, if we decide that our forefathers were wrong, we must repent of our past, expose their errors, overtly reject on an institutional as well as individual basis the theological moorings established at first, and reconstitute on some other basis. (It might be noted that the current scene of theological anarchy would severely test any effort of that nature.) Or, third, we could conclude that no such thing as truth and error exists in theological categories.

The third option cannot be right, for then all further discussion, writing, and investigation would be useless. On its own foundations, it becomes impossible to affirm that even the statement itself is true. It can only be affirmed as "true" on the basis of the first option; but the first option categorically rejects the viability of the third. So the third option is self-defeating.

Option two must be rejected as well, for it leads inexorably, historically, and logically to option three.

Option one must be right. The lesson of history then is one that screams to us, "REPENT!" We must turn from our wicked ways and recapture our vision of the glory of God before the cherubim whisk it off to another place.

The second part of our answer has been theological and expositional. These doctrines are the soteriological portion of a system that in its whole and in its parts is comprehensive, coherent, cogent, and clear. Their scope is comprehensive since these doctrines give credible answers about God, man, sin, righteousness, heaven, hell, time, eternity, the natural, the supernatural, good, evil, justice, and mercy. These doctrines are coherent in that they stick together; they do not alienate themselves from one another, but rather mutually serve to explain and clarify each other. They are also cogent in that their harmony with other data is observable and remarkable. The most important aspect of this observation is that these doctrines harmonize with Scripture because they arise from Scripture. No other reason exists for the construction of such a view of the world than that the Bible itself clearly displays it. It may be called Calvinism for convenience, Augustinianism for patristic pedigree, or Jansenism to highlight its persistence in appearing under the most unlikely circumstances, but at bottom it is pure dominical and apostolic teaching.

Finally, this system of theology has such clarity that it has universal appeal. The basic premises of the Doctrines of Grace are so simple, strong, and clear that many unschooled saints who have embraced the reality of which they speak have become undeniably effective exponents of the doctrines. But they are also a sun without a sphere and an ocean without a shore. He who gazes into these doctrines can gaze for eternity and never reach the end of their grandeur and brightness; and he who plunges in can swim forever and never exhaust the routes and currents that might be taken.

Because of these theological and expositional qualities, Calvinism has been unparalleled in producing hope, character, and self-sacrifice at every level of society. The theological answer, therefore, should be: Calvinism should still occupy the place of universal adherence in Baptist life. To reject it is not theological progress, but decline; not theological wisdom, but folly; not theological erudition, but fragmentation.

We have sought the third part of the answer from three practical categories. How do these doctrines affect one's understanding of God's intentions toward the individual? How do they affect the coexistence of the body of the regenerate with the body of the unregenerate? How do they affect the activity of the regenerate toward the unregenerate? Thus, chapters on assurance of salvation, liberty of conscience, and evangelism close the discussion. The answer that is given affirms that the Doctrines of Grace produce a more defensible, coherent, and biblical construction of each of these practical areas. Therefore, if we are to maintain a proper foundation for personal counseling in spiritual matters, the Doctrines of Grace must inform all of our dealings. If we are to maintain a pure church in a free society, we must understand and propagate the nature of God's purposes with his fallen race. And if our evangelism is to be uncompromising in its adherence to the gospel, we cannot forfeit that view of salvation as presented to us in those doctrines fondly embraced by the Baptist forefathers.

To him who is able to keep you from falling and to present you before his glorious presence without fault and with great joy—to the only God our Savior be glory, majesty, power and authority, through Jesus Christ our Lord, before all ages, now and forevermore! Amen [Jude 24–25, NIV].

Index of Subjects

429

Index of Persons

Index of Scripture References

437